## 10<sup>th</sup> Anniversary Edition

# Nuts And Bolts Guide
# To Rigging

### One Hundred and Fifty Steps
### to Help You Get the Most
### From the Rigging of
### Your Rowing Equipment

D1073054

## Mike Davenport

### Illustrated by Peter Martin

**Foreword by Joe Murtaugh**

**The Nuts and Bolts Guide to Rigging**
**10th Anniversary Edition**
**One Hundred and Fifty Steps to Help You Get the Most from the Rigging of Your Rowing Equipment**

Library of Congress Catalog Card Number: 92-91056
ISBN: 978-0-9639300-9-5

**Produced and distributed by SportWork, Inc.**
Main Street • P.O. Box 192 • Church Hill, MD • 21623
(410) 556-6030 (Phone/Fax)
mike@helpingcoaches.com

Printed in the United States of America

All illustrations by Peter Martin, unless otherwise noted.

Once again, for Tracy . . .

For never once saying I shouldn't . . .
or couldn't.


And for Brook and Ben . . .

Thanks for the company.

# TABLE OF CONTENTS

# JOBS INDEX

## CHAPTER 21   RIGGING FOR SCULLING

# FOREWORD

I was well into my second year of coaching at Virginia when our team bought a new eight. I "rigged" it. By this, I mean I removed the complete riggers from their boxes, slapped them on the shell opposite the appropriate seat, and told my crew to launch.

Our first race was the next weekend. They rowed the new boat and won a gutsy race with a closely matched opponent. As it happens, Princeton University was racing a different crew at the same venue. Frank Bozarth, Princeton's ace rigger for many years, examined the new boat, which our crew had placed in slings after their race. Looking at the riggers, Frank screwed up his face and asked me what spread I was using. To this, I replied, "Heh, heh."

The ridiculously heavy gearing, which Frank's perceptive eye picked up immediately, could be best described as being well out of any acceptable range for a collegiate women's eight. All of a sudden, it made sense why the crew had struggled to achieve their normal race cadence since moving into the new shell.

This episode also taught me a lesson that I've tried to remember for the nearly twenty years that have passed since that day. Spirited, talented athletes can often find ways to overcome significant coaching ineptitude. In this case, my crew was able to succeed in spite of a hideously uncomfortable rig. Rigging is important, but it is often not a critically important part of our sport.

While this story effectively illustrates my lack of rigging knowledge at the outset of my career, it might seem like an odd way to introduce Mike Davenport's latest contribution to rigging literature, his 10th anniversary edition of *The Nuts and Bolts Guide to Rigging*. But *Nuts and Bolts* is the first book on the topic I've read that presents rigging as a practical rather than as a scientific endeavor.

Mike, a fine coach himself, doesn't demean our profession by suggesting that rigging is a Sorcerer's Stone. It won't make up for bad coaching. Mike takes the topic of rigging and boat care seriously, but not TOO seriously. His book is comprehensive but accessible. It's art before engineering, a stroll along the lake chatting with friends rather than a session in the stacks hammering out problem sets. Charts and equations are balanced with cartoons and anecdotes. Mike has a light touch with the material. I find this book succeeds in encouraging the reader to learn more about the basics and the fine points of rigging without making him feel an idiot for not having known more in the first place.

Don't get me wrong. Like most folks who know how to fix stuff and who care about equipment and tools, Mike can be evangelical in his advocacy of boat care. Let's face it: he recommends that we clean the tracks in EVERY BOAT, EVERY DAY. Still, it's tough to fault him for being thorough. And for those of us who get strung tighter than piano wire during our racing seasons and use rigging to release our tension, Mike includes a helpful section on saws and hammers—my favorite rigging tools.

Effective coaching and teaching begin with passion and commitment. Mike brings both to his coaching education efforts as well as to his athletes every day on the water at Washington College. I still don't know that much about rigging. Fortunately, I now work at a place where I am surrounded by people who do.

Much of what I have gleaned recently has been from *Nuts and Bolts*. The subtitle of this edition is *150 Steps to Help You Get the Most from the Rigging of Your Rowing Equipment*. They are steps well worth taking in the interest of your crew's safety, comfort, and speed.

Joe Murtaugh
October 3, 2002
Princeton, NJ

*Women's Coach, University of Virginia, 1984–1986;*
*Lightweight Coach, Princeton University, 1988–present;*
*Lightweight Eight Coach, U.S. National Team,*
*World Champions, 1999, 2000*

# INTRODUCTION

W ay back when, in 1992, I wrote and published the first edition of this book. It was a wild time for me. I had never written a book before, let alone self-published one. Whenever I told anyone about what I was doing and that the topic of the book was rigging, I would get these really incredibly strange looks, and comments such as:

> "Rigging? Rigging? Really?
> Why the heck would you want to write a book about rigging?"

I was sure that failure was on its way.

I can remember the exact day when the book came out and the very first comment I received about it. I was standing at one of the vendors' booths at USRowing's Annual Convention in Pittsburgh. The book had been on sale since the day before. A fellow came up to me and it was pretty obvious that he had bought a copy of the book since he was waving it very excitedly around in front of him. He said,

> "Pardon me. Did you happen to write this book on rigging?"

I panicked. I remember thinking,

> "Oh no. I'm sure that this guy wants his money back—and I don't have a penny in my pockets. Geez, I hope he doesn't take a swing at me. . . ."

Luckily, before I could open my mouth and say something stupid, he stopped me.

"Look, I just want to tell you that this book, why . . . this book is good. And I read it all last night. And . . . and . . . thanks."

And then he was gone. And I exhaled—like I have never exhaled before.

Then it started.

The *it* I am referring to encompassed the questions, comments, and inquiries about rigging. They started small, one at a time. A dribble here, drabble there—then the floodgates opened. Questions came from everywhere. People wanted to know why this happens, what works best here, how to do that. Letters came, calls came, faxes arrived. It was pretty wild.

Ten years later, they still come. And I feel good about that. Why?

You see, I wrote the first edition of the book way back when because I felt that there was a need for a simple, basic information source on rigging. In my coaching, I kept seeing way too many rowers and coaches get bent out of shape about rigging. Needlessly. So I was motivated to write the book. Since then, all the comments/questions/inquires have shown me that the need was really there.

And ten years later, the need is still here—even more so. That is why I've written this new edition, with tons more information.

What I find very interesting today is that over the past ten years rigging has gotten simpler—in some ways that is. We've got the Internet, which makes information transfer so much easier, and a great new rigger design—the Euro-style rigger, which is very easy to work with.

Yet, at the same time, things have gotten much more difficult in the world of rigging. That difficulty is due to the overwhelming load of information, the slew of equipment choices, and the ever-increasing adjustability of the equipment. Additionally, many coaches and rowers have moved away from the basic guiding principles of rigging and are trying to make things just too darn fancy.

I notice that time and time again at the rigging clinics I run. Folks focus on the fancy stuff, like the rigging numbers from the latest national team boats or how a new innovation will make their team faster (and of course they want it right now!) and ignore many of the basic principles of rigging. Unfortunately, their rigging and rowing are paying a price for forgetting the basics.

What are the basic principles? Well, this book is full of them, but here are what I consider the three most important ones:

- ➤ Keep it simple
- ➤ Make changes gradually
- ➤ Rigging is not as critical in the big picture of boat speed as most people think it is

If you shut this book right now and read not one more word, but take away those three simple principles, I will consider my job more than well done. And your rigging and rowing will be much better off. However, there is more—a lot more—in the pages that follow.

So how about this . . . let's get down to the basics.

Look around and find yourself a comfortable seat. Get a nice cup of your favorite beverage. And let me be your guide to the wonderful world of rigging.

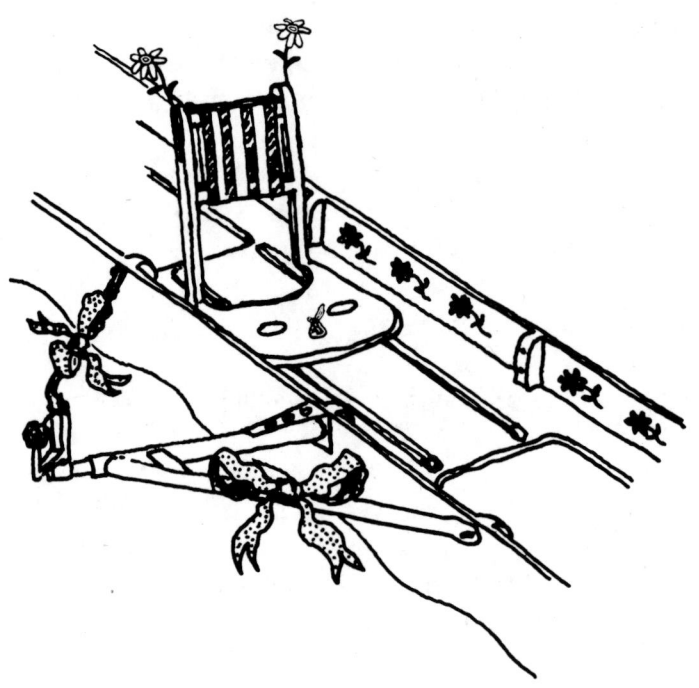

MARTHA STEWART RIGS A ROWING SHELL

# SECTION ONE
# RIGGING CONCEPTS

**Chapter One: Using This Book**

**Chapter Two: Karma of Rigging**

**Chapter Three: Karma of Tools**

**Chapter Four: The Equipment**

**Chapter Five: Safety**

**Chapter Six: Your Rigging Environment**

# Chapter One: Using This Book

Go to your local bookstore and look for a book on rigging. Not much of a selection, is there? But notice all the books on every other subject known to man. Why the difference?

For a multitude of reasons, there is a lot of secrecy, confusion, and mystery surrounding rigging. Starting here, I hope to take away some of the mystique about rigging and rowing equipment, and to help you get comfortable with it. As usual, the best place to start is at the beginning, so . . .

## 1.1 Definitions

There are a few words we need to discuss before we get going. In this book the word ***Rigger***, when it begins with a capital ***R***, is used to describe the person who adjusts rowing equipment. On the other hand the word ***rigger***, with a small ***r***, describes that funky metal thing hanging off of the shell or lying on the boathouse floor. Officially, it's called an ***outrigger***, but this has been shortened to *rigger* in crew-speak. ***Rigging***, regardless of whether the *r* is capitalized or not refers to the adjustments done to a rigger and to other rowing equipment, and, of course, that should be done with *rigor*.

The word ***work*** with a small ***w*** means what you'd think: effort or activity directed to the accomplishment of something. I know for some of you work is a four-letter word, but don't let it scare you off. When ***Work*** is written with a capital ***W*** it describes the place where energy is being transferred from one system to another. For example, when we talk about a rigger and its oarlock, they could be called "the Work" because it is where one system, the rower, is transferring energy, the rowers' power, to another system, the oar. Got it?

In each chapter I've included some important ideas that I want to call your attention to. They will look like this:

> How confusing can things be? Several items in rowing are actually called by more than one name. For example, the end of an oar is known as the "spoon" or "blade," and vertical braces in a boat can be called "ribs" or "knees." Don't worry about which name is proper; use the one that works best for you.

The sport of rowing itself can be divided into two distinct fields: sculling and sweeping. The difference is simple. Scullers use two oars, one in each hand. Sweepers use one oar, with two hands on it.

Now there is an old saying, "Twice the oars, half the rower," or is it, "Twice the oars, twice the rower"? I can never get that right.

Either way you look at it, sculling and sweep rowing are actually quite closely related—especially as far as rigging is concerned—and many of the subjects I will cover can be applied equally to either activity. There is a chapter towards the back of the book specific to the unique details of sculling.

## 1.2 Metric vs. U.S. Customary System

In rigging you will have to deal with two different measuring systems: the **Metric System** and the **U.S. Customary System** (sometimes mistakenly called the **British Imperial System**). I will discuss them in full detail in Chapter Three, but I wanted to let you know before then that most of the measurements in this book will be metric. I mention this because many folks have difficulty with the Metric System. Not to worry, especially if you're not comfortable wit the Metric System.

I remember when I first began rigging, I used both systems. I measured everything in metric except for the height of the oarlock and oar length, which I measured in inches. Now I use metric for all of my measurements, and my life has been simplified. In the rigging charts in Chapter Fifteen, all of the dimensions are in the Metric System. I strongly support the

Metric System and I think it should be used everywhere. If you don't share my views, that's fine, just realize you're going to run head first into the Metric System sooner or later. You really should give metric a chance; it's a handy little system. I've included a few tips in Chapter Sixteen on how to convert metric to U.S. By the way, there are only a very few countries in the world that use the U.S. Customary System, besides the U.S. Know one of them? (Libya!)

---

To learn more about the Metric System visit the site for the U.S. Metric Association, Inc: <http://lamar.colostate.edu/~hillger/>. Or to learn about converting metric to US system visit <http://www.wihatools.com/conversion.tm>

---

## 1.3 Layout

This book has been arranged to be used as a reference book. Basically the chapters are arranged in the order in which you should rig. As you go through each chapter you will see that they are dependent on the chapter before them—a cumulative effect. But at the same time, if you have a problem with one specific area, you will be able to turn directly to that section for help. If you have a problem and don't know where to turn, flip to the index in the back; I've tried to make it as thorough as possible.

There is a very wide range of rigging knowledge out there. Beginning Riggers have different needs from experienced folk. In an effort to make things easier for everyone, I have divided up some parts of the chapters into different levels of knowledge. They are fairly easy to identify.

The beginning of each chapter gives information about a specific topic. At the end of each chapter are **JOB**s. The JOBs are tasks, broken down into steps, that you may need to do to your equipment. Each JOB describes a problem, recommends tools to use, suggests other items you might need, and outlines the task, step by step. The JOBs are based on many years of experience and suggestions of experts and lay-people in the field. A complete list of all the JOBs is in front of the book. In an attempt to make the JOBs as accurate as possible, I've had several friends test them (at least they were friends when we started). But a word of caution here:

Everything in this book, including all information, has been checked for accuracy. The JOBs, tips, and information are not guaranteed, nor are they necessarily the recommendations of the builders of the equipment. They are only suggestions. There is a possibility that they may not work. Use them at your own risk to body, life, equipment, and happiness. This is especially true of the jokes.

With that out of the way, let's get back to our regularly scheduled reading.

## 1.4 Types of Rowing Equipment

In the first edition of this book, I went into specific detail on how to adjust each boat. I have not gone into as much detail in this edition, and there are three reasons for that.

First, over the years, I've received feedback from many readers that having all that information in the book made it overwhelming. The readers who cared about Pocock didn't want to be bothered with the info about Vespolis.

Second, to put all that detail into this edition would make this book unwieldy. In all honesty, it would be nearly impossible to include all of the specifics on each type of boat, rigger, and oar that are now being made and to do them justice. The size of this book would be so big you'd probably need an assistant coach just to carry it.

Third, with the advent of the Web, I can now offer more specific and up-to-date information on my Web site. In fact. I offer downloads for working with many of the different types of pieces of equipment there. To check it out, go to my Web site at <http://www.MaxRigging.com> or turn to Appendix Two for a listing of the documents you can find there.

If you are one of those people who has a different make of boat or different type of equipment (especially sculling), and after searching this book and after trying my Web site you cannot find information, then there are two things for you to try. First, it's quite possible that the JOBs I detail in this book may work on your equipment. Most rowing equipment is similar. But I must repeat myself here and say: ***Do so at your own risk and be careful so that you don't hurt yourself or the equipment.***

Second, connect directly with the manufacturer for advice. Even though you'll probably be in a big-time hurry, slow down and take a few minutes to get the information—usually you'll find it to be time well spent.

Many of the equipment makers are getting much more service oriented these days and they can be helpful. You will find a list of their names, addresses (postal, e-mail, Web) and phone numbers in the *Suppliers* section in the back of this book. All the information contained here is as up-to-date as possible, but things are changing quickly with new manufacturers and designs quickly popping up.

Speaking of Web site addresses, throughout the book I've placed URLs where appropriate. They will look like this:

> Learn more about this book and other
> resources for rigging and rowing at:
> <http://www.MaxRigging.com>

Rest assured, as I mentioned, I've tried to make sure that all the links are correct and current, but no guarantees; things are changing quickly on the Web. If you find one that does not work, please let me know.

## 1.5 Read It

I like shortcuts, you like shortcuts, everyone likes shortcuts, but there are few shortcuts to becoming a competent Rigger. Don't try shortcuts with the procedures in this book. You should have no trouble with the JOBs as long as you read and follow all the steps. A lot of errors are made because people skip steps. Read the JOBs and follow them the way they are written.

There are several JOBs that over the course of a season you may repeat a hundred or so times (i.e., height adjustment). Once you become confident and knowledgeable in what is going on, go for the shortcuts. If you find a good one please, let me know, so I can tell others and also to make my life easier.

A suggestion: use index tabs to mark each chapter in this book. Then, when you are in the middle of a job, you can flip to a chapter and not get your pages greasy. I use Post-It brand Tape Flags. They are inexpensive, flexible, you can write on them; and if they get grimy you can take them off and replace them.

## JOB 1.1: HOW TO COMPLETE A JOB.

**Problem:** You are here to learn how to do a JOB.

**Needed:** A few minutes to read this section.

As I explained, each chapter contains JOBs. A complete list of all JOBs ahead is in the front of the book. Before you undertake any JOB, I suggest you read the pertinent chapter so you have as much info as possible. This will make things go more smoothly and it will also ensure that you are there for the right reason. After that, gather the tools and other items that I recommend.

Once you have the equipment and knowledge, you're ready to begin a JOB. Allow yourself extra time, about twice as much as you think it will take. Read the JOB all the way through once. Then go back to the beginning and start the task, going step by step. As I've said before: **don't skip STEPS!** Sometimes it is easier to have a friend read the procedures to you. It will help keep your pages cleaner and it sure is nice to have a friend there to keep any sagging spirits from getting too low. When you have done the task, check your work, put away your tools, clean up, and head on to other things.

# Chapter Two: The Karma of Rigging

O ver the years of hanging out at boathouses and race courses, I've run into a lot of folks who get stressed about rigging. In fact, I've been doing a continual survey at many of my rigging clinics and what I've found is that about 50% of the rowers and coaches expressed that rigging produced a moderate to high level of anxiety for them. In other words, a lot of people get torqued out over rigging.

Why?

Well, one reason is that I think that a lot of folks don't understand how important—or unimportant—rigging is. To get a good handle on rigging, you need to know where it fits into the **Big Picture**. The better you understand the Big Picture, the better of a Rigger you are going to be.

## 2.1 The Big Picture

Do you know what it takes to make a boat (**shell**) go fast? I'm serious. Think about it for a minute.

Do you truly know what it takes to make a shell go fast? Grab a pencil and piece of paper and see if you can list five items.

Once you've got your list done, prioritize your items in the order in which you think they impact boat speed.

I know, some of you could care less about boat speed; you just want to rig your equipment so you can go out and have fun on the water. That's fine and dandy, but follow along—it might help you later on down the road.

Now take a look at your list. If rigging was one of the top items on your list, you and I need to have a little chat. You see, rigging isn't that important. In fact, in the world of competitive rowing, rigging is down there at the bottom of the list of the critical things which make a shell go fast. Let me explain.

To generate boat speed, there are five critical things you need, and I call them the **Five Basic Elements**. Here they are in order of importance:

## FIVE BASIC ELEMENTS OF BOAT SPEED

1. Athletes

2. Training

3. Technique

4. Equipment

5. Rigging

The athletes, or rowers, are the most important element in getting a shell to go fast. They impact performance more than anything else. You need to have horsepower if you want your boat to move, and if you have slow rowers you'll have a slow shell. The training of these rowers (conditioning) is more important than the rowers' technique, and their technique is more critical than what type of equipment is being rowed. All of these things—athletes, training, technique, and equipment—are more important to the performance than rigging.

I remember losing one of my first races as a coach by a couple of feet. I was really bummed out. I was trying to figure out why we had lost and finally convinced myself it was due to some dumb rigging mistake on my part. After the race, the winning coach stopped by to chat and brought the team captain along. They congratulated us on a good race. I felt better about our race when I found out that their rowers were about thirty pounds heavier than ours, they had two national team candidates in the boat, they had been practicing three weeks longer than us, and they had an out-of-the-crate new boat to row in. My rigging was fine; we were beaten by a stronger and faster crew in better equipment. Catch what I am getting at?

This is the **Big Picture**. It's the horses that make the chariot go fast, not necessarily how the chariot is rigged!

And why are some people so resistant to that little but very important point? Time and time again, when I do rigging clinics, which I've done all across the country, I stumble upon people who just don't believe me when I tell them this. They seem more willing to believe that a one-centimeter difference in the spread of a rigger has a greater impact on boat speed than a major difference in the strength and/or rowing ability of a rower. Please, if you are one of these folks, put down the book, take a few deep breaths and try to get those evil thoughts out of your mind right now.

> A little clarification here: When I talk about the impact rigging has, I'm talking about differences in fine-tuning the adjustments <u>within acceptable standards</u>. I'm not talking about mistakes like riggers being put on upside down or wheels being left off seats. In those cases, bad rigging is a huge handicap.

All right, if rigging is low on the list, then why do people get so torqued out over it?

I've got it pinned down to three reasons. First, some folks feel adjusting the rigging is "the solution" to all their problems. If their boat is slow, they assume it must be the rigging. If the rowers' technique is bad, they assume it must be the rigging. If they aren't winning, they assume it must be the rigging, and their tools can change this. According to the Big Picture, you and I know that they've missed the point.

Second, there is a lot of mystery surrounding rigging and at the same time not a whole lot of information to reduce that mystery. Most folks like a good mystery, but they get frustrated when they are not given enough information to solve it. Sometimes folks simply don't have enough info to rig right.

And third, rigging is one of the few things in rowing that you may need to change quickly. Let's say you have been coaching a team in preparation for a big race. You've had the same group of athletes for the past few weeks, they have been training in the same boat, and they have been rowing with the same technique. When you get to race day, none of these things (athletes, equipment, technique) are likely to change. But on a moment's notice you might need to change your rigging, and this can cause terror—sheer terror—in some folks.

For example, there you are, standing on shore, looking at the race course and suddenly a head wind blows up. Uh, oh . . . this means you might need to change the rigging, possibly the inboard (**collar**) on the oars. You change them and five minutes later the wind switches to a tail wind—should you change the inboards back?

And what about the rowers? You are sharing boats and your women's team is rowing in a men's boat. The water is getting rough. Are you sure you have the boat rigged right for them? And then the lightweights. Oh, no . . . (gulp) lightweights. They've just left their seats at home because they were so worried about their weights. Sounds like more rigging work.

And then there are the novices. Oh, good God, not novice rowers . . . not *now*. They left their riggers in the parking lot and a truck ran over two of them. Now what are you supposed to do?

All of these things have happened to me at one time or another. How are you supposed to handle situations like these and be that cool, calm individual that everyone looks up to? It will help you keep your composure if you remember where rigging fits into the Big Picture.

## 2.2 Mindset of a Rigger

I hope you now have a better understanding of the importance of rigging. Let's move one step further and look at some of the finer points of rigging. Specifically the *What?, Who?, Where?, When?, Why? and How?* of rigging.

**What is rigging?** You may think rigging is just adjusting the riggers on a shell. That's like saying teaching is just writing on a blackboard or that plumbing is unstopping a clogged toilet. There's more to rigging than making adjustments—a lot more.

For instance, you'll have to figure the best type of equipment for your team to row, especially considering their size and the conditions they row in. You'll have to use your brain to figure out what numbers to use when you make the adjustments, when and where to make the adjustments, and how to do them. You'll need to get your hands on tools and to be concerned about the safety of the equipment that is rowed. And when all this is done, you'll need to check your work to see if you did a good job. Aaah, things get complicated.

**Who should rig?** In high school and collegiate programs the task of rigging usually falls upon one of the coaches, or on a designated Rigger or Boatman. This situation is best because athletes tend not to have the knowledge, experience, or objectivity to rig correctly; although I've seen one or two rowers who were wizards at rigging.

Once you get outside a well-organized program, it's not so clear-cut who does the rigging. It's best that the same people always do the rigging to insure consistency—that is, if they can do a good job. In club programs, work schedules can cause big problems, and it is often very hard to get rigging, especially good rigging, done. I suggest you take responsibility for your own rigging, or appoint a **rigging coordinator**—someone who will be in charge of getting the rigging done. But whoever ends up doing your rigging, they need to have three things:

1. A dose of common sense

2. A willingness to learn

3. A solid work ethic

**Why should you rig?** Two main benefits come to mind. Speed is one. Squeezing the most speed out of your equipment is a tough job, especially when you are trying to get a group of athletes of different sizes, strengths, and abilities to function together. A properly rigged boat will be faster than a badly rigged boat if everything else is equal.

Comfort is the other benefit. The rigging has to be comfortable for the rower. If it's not, injuries might happen.

Oh yeah, another benefit from rigging—safety. Making sure the equipment you use is safe and dependable for the rowers is a major benefit of rigging. Equipment takes a lot of abuse and it breaks. You don't want it to happen during a practice or race, causing someone to get hurt. That would be very un-cool.

> Three Benefits of Rigging:
> 1. Speed
> 2. Comfort
> 3. Safety

And there are other benefits besides these three. We'll discuss those later in the book.

**How should you rig?** Pardon me while I go off on a small tangent for a moment. In the first edition of this book I wrote that one thing I noticed in the rowing world was that there was a serious lack of written material on rigging, especially coming from the manufacturers. When you bought a shell you hardly got anything to help you with the rigging. People would spend a lot of money, sometimes more than on a new car, and basically the only thing they got was a hardy "Good Luck!"

Well, I'm happy to say, things have changed.

For example, Vespoli USA, <http://www.vespoli.com> has an *Owners Manual* that you can download right from their Web site. Concept II, <http://www.concept2.com>, has a great site full of information. And there are also other examples.

Yup, some manufacturers have really gotten on the customer service bandwagon. The Web is really helping a lot. Hopefully, things will keep improving.

Okay, so now back to the question at hand: how should you rig? Basically there are two ways: the right way and the wrong way. The right way works and the wrong way doesn't. Pretty simple.

Well, what is the right way? I consider the methods in this book and those on my Web site the right way, but I'll let you in on a little confession: many of those methods are not actually my own.

Over the past several years I've been fortunate enough to hang around and be taught by some pretty smart Riggers and coaches. How did I repay them? I stole their techniques—although I prefer to think of it as inheriting them. But that's okay, most of them inherited their methods from someone else.

Now I'm passing them on to you. So as you read this book and get more comfortable with rigging, you can decide for yourself right from wrong. Just keep in mind that the major determinant is that the "right way" to rig is the way that works best for you. That's the bottom line on how to rig.

**Where should you rig?** Usually the most convenient place to rig is inside the boathouse. Usually, but not always. I've seen some pretty crowded boathouses where leaving a shell in slings for more than five minutes causes major hassles. So you have to find the place that suits you best, preferably a clean and safe area.

Some of the things you should look for in a rigging area are: good lighting; protection from the environment—for both your sake and the shell's; and being out of the way so you can work with a minimum of distractions, hassles, and aggravations.

Sometimes you'll find yourself doing rigging in some pretty weird spots. I've had to rig standing in water up to my chest, in a barn, in a tent, in a parking lot with the shell on stacks of life jackets, in a hotel ballroom, in a parking garage, in the hold of a ferry boat, and on the top deck of a freighter in the Caribbean, just to mention a few. Make do with wherever you find yourself. Just use common sense and be safe—no need to get hurt in pursuit of boat speed. See Chapters Five and Six for suggestions on creating a safe rigging environment.

> If you must put your boat in slings outside, be cautious of the wind—even a slight breeze can knock the boat over and then you've got major repair work in addition to your rigging.

**When should you rig?** There are basically six times when you should rig a shell.

1. **Purchasing-rigging** is planning and buying the equipment you'll be using for practices and racing.

2. **Practice-rigging** is preparing and adjusting your equipment for practices. This includes rigging to help correct technique problems and also those instances when you might have to adjust or repair riggers or equipment on the water.

3. **Race-rigging** is more involved because you are dealing with traveling, race-day preparations, and those nervous butterflies that make everything seem like a major undertaking. Specifically, race-rigging involves the fine tuning adjustments you make to squeeze the last ounce of speed from your team.

4. **Peace-of-mind-rigging** is simply adjusting your riggers because you think or feel something may be off.

5. **Maintenance-rigging** is a routine you perform to help your equipment survive longer. For more info on maintenance, see the Special Report *Six Steps to Get the Most from Your Rowing Equipment* on my Web site.

6. **Individual-rigging** is setting up the equipment for an individual. This differs from practice-rigging in that it is more specific to finding the proper rigging a specific person.

This may sound like a lot of rigging. Now I'm certainly not suggesting you walk around all the time with a handful of wrenches. Just the opposite: **rig only when you have to!** After you make an adjustment correctly you shouldn't have to readjust it for quite a while. Exactly how long depends on usage, abuse, and other variables. Always look and listen to your equipment and the athletes. They will usually give you a good indication when things are wrong and it's time to rig. My motto is to be an "energy-conserving Rigger," which my mom used to call "being lazy."

Plan your rigging well and you'll find you can save yourself a lot of time and hassles downstream.

## 2.3 Who Are You?

Before we go any further into the specifics of rigging, it's important for you to have an idea of exactly what type of Rigger you are. This will be helpful because some of the **JOB**s in this book are geared towards different levels of knowledge.

Remember Socrates, the old Greek gent with the flip-flops and robes? Quite a smart guy, he was. Well, Mr. Socrates had a way to classify how much a person knew about a subject. What he did was divide a person's knowledge into four different Dimensions. The First Dimension consisted of no knowledge and the Fourth Dimension was absolute knowledge. To show what he meant, let's take peanut butter as an example.

If you know nothing about peanut butter, nothing at all (doesn't sound normal does it?), then Socrates would say you were in the First Dimension of knowledge. If you happen to know a little bit about peanut butter, like what shelf it's on in the store, then you are in the Second Dimension. If you know even more about peanut butter—like how to make a mayonnaise, peanut butter, and banana sandwich—Socrates would put you into the Third Dimension. And say you know everything there is to know about peanut butter, absolutely everything, then you make the Fourth Dimension of knowledge.

With me? Okay, go get something to eat, I'll wait.

---

Time for another definition. The word "dimension" with a capital "D" refers to the level of your rigging knowledge. When used with a small "d," dimension will be referring to numbers used for rigging measurements.

---

All of this is important because you need to have an honest assessment of where you stand in the world of rigging. We need to determine what Dimension of rigging you are in, and we need to do it before you go any farther. I'm going to give you a little quiz now. There are twenty questions. Check your ego at the door, take your time, and be honest with yourself. If it turns out you fit into the First Dimension, be calm—there's help, and hope, ahead.

Answers are at the end of this chapter.

No peeking.

I'm serious.

## QUIZ

### Please mark your best response to the following questions.

1) How often should you clean the tracks on a rowing shell?

    a. Monthly
    b. Weekly
    c. Daily
    d. Whenever the coxswain yells at you

2) How often should you check the rigging of a rowing shell?

    a. Daily
    b. Weekly
    c. Monthly
    d. Annually

3) What is a dependable source of rigging numbers?

    a. A fellow coach
    b. A book on rigging
    c. A good-looking writer, like the one doing this book
    d. All of the above

4) Using improper rigging numbers can lead to:

    a. Slower hull speed
    b. Athlete injuries
    c. Broken equipment
    d. All of the above

5) A sound reason to purchase a new set of oars is:

    a. Speed
    b. Price
    c. Cool names like *Vortex*
    d. Replacing an older set

6) A well-maintained shell should last:

    a. One race
    b. One racing season
    c. One year
    d. Upwards of one-million strokes

7) In a pinch, what size metric wrench will best fit on a 7/16 inch nut?

    a. 10 mm
    b. 13 mm
    c. 11 mm
    d. 12 mm

8) Why should you wax the hull of a rowing shell?

    a. For speed
    b. For protection
    c. To decrease pollution
    d. To decrease wind resistance when transporting

9) Which of the following should you use to polish the hull of a rowing shell?

    a. Rubbing compound
    b. Wet sandpaper
    c. A belt sander
    d. A Glocksteir rotary degrubber

10) When you have a piece of broken equipment, how soon should you repair it?

    a. The following season
    b. As soon as the coxswain starts yelling at you
    c. As soon as feasibly possible
    d. As soon as you run out of replacement parts

11) The most dependable source of information about repairs to rowing equipment would be:

    a. The manufacturer
    b. Bob the Builder
    c. A local welding shop
    d. The magazine *Independent Rowing News*

12) One of the best steps you can take to maintain the moving parts in a rowing shell is:

    a. Keep them clean
    b. Keep them lubricated
    c. Keep them away from a rower with a hammer
    d. Keep them below 120° C

13) In a shell where two unlike metals touch, you might find:

    a. Weakness
    b. Corrosion
    c. Pitting
    d. All of the above

14) Most rowing shells that are damaged are damaged when they:

    a. Are being transported
    b. Are being rowed
    c. Fall off of racks
    d. Are worked on by a rower with a hammer

15) Whenever transporting a rowing shell, you should do which of the following?

    a. All of the below
    b. Place two straps on the front part of the shell
    c. Check the boat at least every one hundred miles
    d. Place flag(s) on the boat

16) How many wraps of electrical tape around an oarlock equals 1/2 degree of stern pitch?

    a. 1 to 2
    b. 12 to 14
    c. 3 to 4
    d. 8 to 9

17) With slower hull speed you should _____ the *work through* measurement?

    a. decrease
    b. increase
    c. rotate
    d. remove

18) Your oar has 2 degrees positive pitch. The oarlock has 3 degrees stern pitch and 1 degree outward pitch. What would you guess to be the stern pitch of the oarlock and oar at the mid-drive?

    a. 8 degrees
    b. 5 degrees
    c. 7 degrees
    d. 3 degrees

19) Your oar has 1 degree positive pitch. The oarlock has 4 degrees stern pitch and 1 degree outward pitch. What would you guess to be the total pitch of the oarlock and oar at the <u>catch</u>?

    a.   5 degrees
    b.   4 degrees
    c.   6 degrees
    d.   3 degrees

20) At a position in a shell, the boat is 58 cm wide from gunwale to gunwale. At the same spot, the center of the oarlock pin is 56 cm from the closest gunwale. What is the spread of this rigger?

    a.   82 cm
    b.   83 cm
    c.   84 cm
    d.   85 cm

## 2.4 So Whaddaya Know?

Now take your answers and compare them with mine that are located at the end of this chapter. Add up your score. Don't get focused on "right" versus "wrong," and don't get tied up with your score—there's already enough of that in today's world.

Instead, we are trying to figure how comfortable you are with rigging—that's it. So, I'm going to suggest this—if it took you five minutes to figure out the correct answer to Question 18 then count it wrong because you had to work so hard for it.

It's good that you got the right answer, but to be a true member of a specific Dimension, to really belong there, you need to feel comfortable with the level of knowledge in that Dimension. Having to struggle is a sure sign that you are not comfortable.

Take your score and compare it with Table 2.1, and you'll get an idea of what Dimension you are in. And the question will soon arise in your mind (especially if you are one of those competitive types that rowing always seems to attract), "How do I get better?"

Regardless of what Dimension you are in, rest assured that you will improve quickly—quite quickly. There are several things that you can do to catalyze your improvement.

One, for example, is reading this book. That should put you into a different Dimension. Another is to find a rigging friend, someone who can help you rig, and you, in turn, can help him or her rig. Best bet: find someone who knows more than you. Then you become smarter and they have someone who can pick up the washer that fell on the floor that rolled into the spider web in the corner that no one else is going to dare to pick up.

Yet another suggestion is to rig when you have some real peace and quiet: a setting where you can experiment, make mistakes, and jump up and down and do your little anger-dance when you're frustrated is a much better learning environment than when 35 rowers and their parents are staring at you, or when race officials are tapping their feet waiting for your boat.

### Table 2.1: What Dimension Are You?

| Number of Answers Correct | You Are in The: |
| --- | --- |
| 1–4 | First Dimension |
| 5–9 | Second Dimension |
| 10–16 | Third Dimension |
| 17–20 | Fourth Dimension |

One of the quickest ways to increase your knowledge and advance to another Dimension is to watch someone else rig a boat. Watch what they do right and learn it, watch what they do wrong and avoid it.

## **<u>Answers to Quiz</u>**

1. c: daily

2. a: daily

3. c: all of the above

4. d: all of the above

5. d: replacing an older set (although *Vortex* is a cool name).

6. d: upwards of one-million strokes

7. c: 11 mm

8. b: for protection

9. a: rubbing compound

10. c: as soon as you can

11. a: the makers of the equipment

12. a: keep them clean

13. d: all of the above

14. a: in transport is where most get damaged

15. a: all of the below

16. c: depending on the tape, around 3 to 4 wraps should do

17. a: decrease

18. b: 5 degrees

19. a: 6 degrees

20. d: 85 cm

# Chapter Three: The Karma of Tools

Stick your arm out in front of your face. Take a look at the funny thing dangling off the end of it. Yeah, I'm talking about your hand.

Take a good look.

What you're staring at is one of the most amazing pieces of bio-machinery around. What a wonderful thing a hand is. You can scratch your nose, surf the Internet, play the piano, and do about a million things with it, including rigging rowing stuff.

But for all its greatness, the hand has limitations. Its skin is soft and can easily be cut, the grip isn't all that powerful, and the knuckles can easily be bruised or smashed. The hand is a great thing but it can, and has been, improved upon. Those improvements are called **tools**.

We and our ape-like friends came up with tools a long time ago because there were a bunch of things that we couldn't do with our bare hands. To-day, tools help us get JOBs done quickly and easily while giving us spare time to go to the local tavern for refreshments. But for all their good, tools have some limitations.

For example, some folks think that as soon as they pick up a tool, they automatically inherit some mystical mechanical knowledge and they know everything. Other folks think that if they use a tool they will be destined to wear overalls dripping with grease, to drink cheap beer, and to work under cars all night.

Unfortunately, tools have this "I may be dumb, but I can lift heavy things" stigma attached to them that they cannot seem to shake. If you don't believe me, check out how many ladies or gents in three-piece suits are browsing around the hardware aisles in your local department store. Needless to say, this reputation is baloney and certainly not helpful to the cause of getting people involved in rigging.

Tools are just an extension of your hand, nothing more.

Personally, I think tools are cool. Look at some of the folks who have made it into the big time using tools: Alexander Graham Bell, the Rolling Stones, Thomas Edison, Bill Gates, and of course Pete "If I Had a Hammer" Seger. One positively cool thing about tools is they don't discriminate. A person of any age, sex, or race can get a tool to perform equally well, or equally badly.

Well, enough of the philosophy, back to the subject at hand.

Before you try to pick up a single tool you'll need a plan, a good plan—reason being that the world of tools is a zoo, especially for the uninitiated. There are long tools, short tools, fat tools, big tools, and little tools. There are measuring tools, hitting tools, holding tools, turning tools, cutting tools, and scraping tools. Nowadays if you have a JOB to do, there is a specific tool for it. It is pretty easy to get lost and confused out there without a plan. So if I may, I'm going to offer this fairly straightforward plan for you:

> Identify the JOB you need to do.

> Pinpoint the type of tool(s) you need.

> If you don't have the tool(s), go get it/them.

> Learn how to use it/them.

A simple plan, but it works. However, before you go zipping off to the store, we should do a little background work, and there are a couple of things we need to mull over. Open up the memory bank and prepare to download.

## 3.1 The Nitty Gritty

**The nuts and bolts of it.** Nuts, bolts, and all the other assorted little goodies, such as washers and screws, are not tools, they are called **fasteners**. Eighty percent of the time you use your tools it will be to adjust one of these fasteners. If you plan on doing a good JOB rigging you need to know what these fasteners are and the differences between them. If you look at a rigger carefully you will notice it is chock full of **nuts and bolts**. Time for a quiz:

- ❑ Do you know the difference between a nut, a bolt, a washer, and a screw?

- ❑ Do you know how to tell if something is made of stainless steel or not?

- ❑ Do you know what a *nylon-locknut* or a *stop-nut* is?

If you know the answers to these questions, then pat yourself on the back, skip this next part, and we will catch up to you in a moment.

The principle behind nuts and bolts is simple: you take a long, round, skinny piece of metal (the bolt), and put threads on the outside of it. Then take a short, fat piece of metal (the nut), poke a hole in it and put threads on the inside of it.

If the manufacturer measured things correctly, the long, skinny piece should fit into the short, fat piece in such a way that the threads will work together and pull the nut up the bolt. This action, called "threading," is what nuts and bolts are all about.

FIGURE 3.1

HERE IS SOMETHING THAT MAY HELP YOU REMEMBER THE DIFFERENCE BETWEEN A NUT AND A BOLT

In shells you might end up adjusting certain nuts and bolts a thousand times or more. Threading squeezes things together between the nut and the head of the bolt so they won't come apart until you want them to. Sometimes, you squeeze together two pieces of metal, and other times, as in the case of **rigger bolts**, it's the metal of the rigger and the material of the **gunwale** that are pressed together. (Rigger bolts are the bolts that attach the rigger to the shell.) To see what I mean, take a quick break and look at a few of the nuts and bolts on your shell.

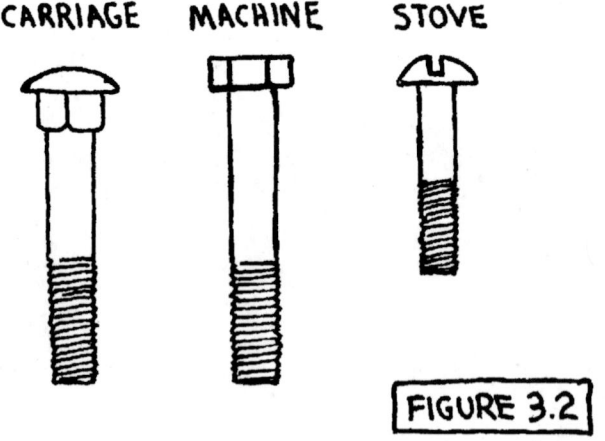

CARRIAGE    MACHINE    STOVE

FIGURE 3.2

The world is full of hundreds of different kinds of nuts and bolts, but in rigging you need be acquainted with only a few. The most common type of bolts you will encounter are **carriage**, **machine**, and **stove** (see figure

3.2). Most rigger bolts on the older shells are carriage bolts. Their heads are designed to anchor themselves securely into one of the materials being squeezed.

Machine bolts are designed to be turned at both ends by wrenches and are now replacing carriage bolts in many shells. Stove bolts are not very common on shells but you may see some on older riggers, or on some shell foot stretchers.

There is also a large variety of nuts, such as **wing**, **hex**, **square,** and **nylock** (**stop**) nuts. Wing nuts are designed to be used where the desired amount of tightness can be obtained by the fingers. You usually find wing nuts used on the foot stretchers. Hex and square nuts are the most commonly used nuts and you'll find them throughout your rowing equipment. Stop, or nylock nuts, are used when it is important that the nut should not come loose. There is a small ring of plastic built into this nut that is compressed against the bolt's threads when the bolt is tightened, providing a holding tension. Stop nuts are used on the riggers where the vibrations could loosen normal nuts.

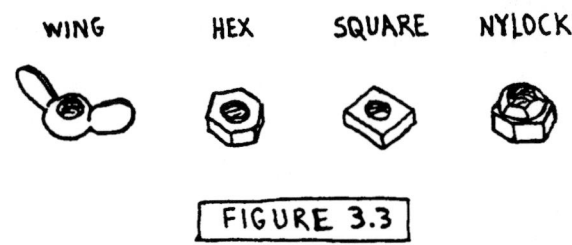

WING     HEX     SQUARE     NYLOCK

FIGURE 3.3

Recycling is great, so do yourself a favor and don't get rid of any old fasteners unless they are damaged. Keep a collection of your old nuts, bolts, and washers—especially rigger bolts (carriage bolts). Sort them, throw them into an old can (coffee cans work great) and label them. In the long run you'll save money and time. I call these things M.C.I.H.'s (Might Come in Handy).

And usually they do.

If nuts and bolts were the only things you had to be concerned about, rigging would be sooooo much easier, but this is not the case. So here are a couple of little things you need to be aware of.

**Washers**. Washers are flat discs with holes drilled in their centers. They basically have two functions. One is to act as a shield to protect the material being fastened from the nut and the head of the bolt. The other function is to keep motion and vibration from loosening the nut and bolt. In your travels around the boathouse you'll encounter two varieties: **flat** and **lock**.

Flat washers are designed for the first function, protection—they back up bolt heads and nuts and prevent damage to the Work surfaces. Their counterpart, lock washers, are used when the nuts and bolts are subject to vibration or rotational movement which may cause the fasteners to loosen.

When compressed, lock washers exert a slight force away from the bolt head causing tension between the nut and bolt threads, preventing slippage. As you can see in figure 3.4, the ends of lock washers are angled and they dig into both the nut and the Work—this will reduce slippage but may damage the material compressed. If you're worried about something coming loose, use stop nuts instead of lock washers.

FLAT          LOCK

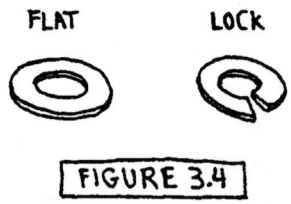

FIGURE 3.4

**Screws.** The basic principle behind screws is slightly different from that of nuts and bolts. Screws, like bolts, are long threaded pieces of metal. But screws, unlike bolts, are tapered at one end. This taper allows them to *bite* into a hole. Whereas a nut and bolt *push* two pieces together, a screw will *pull* two pieces together as in figure 3.5.

Most screws, unlike nuts and bolts, are not meant to be adjusted—you drive them in and leave them. Screws are driven by screwdrivers, which fit into indentations in the screw's head (see figure 3.6). These indentations come in two basic designs: **Philips** and **Standard**. An easy way to tell them apart is to look at the end of the screwdriver: The Philips looks like a plus (+) sign (and both begin with "P") and the Standard looks like a minus (-) sign. Because both styles are widely used, you should own both types of drivers, and in a variety of sizes.

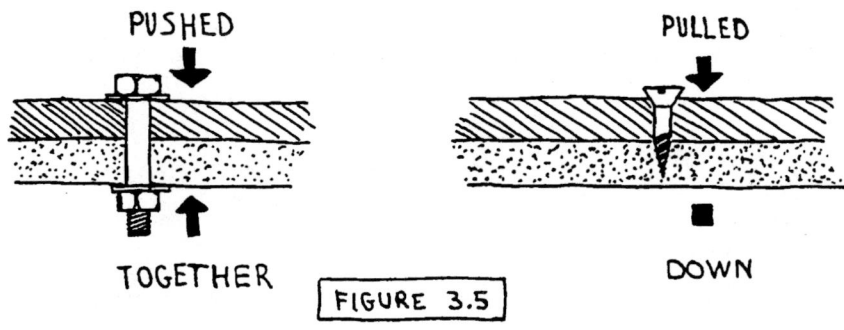

FIGURE 3.5

As mentioned, screws do a lot of work in your shell—they hold together many parts. There aren't many screws used in the newer synthetic shells; however, you'll find a lot in the older boats with wooden parts. As far as rigging is concerned, you're only going to have a few screws to contend with, like those that secure the **rigger plates** on the gunwales of some boats, or those screws attaching bow balls. Make sure any screws you use are made of noncorrosive metals, such as stainless steel, which we will discuss in a moment.

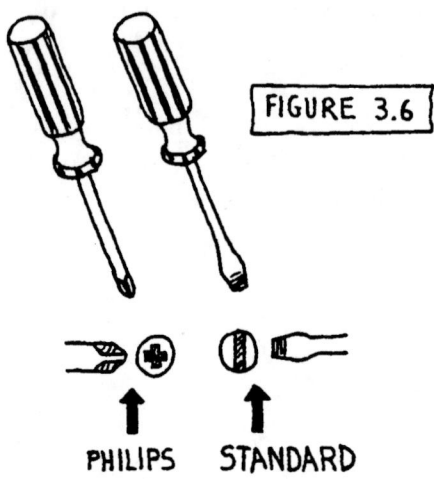

When using screws, make sure you select a properly sized screwdriver. Avoid using substitutes like dimes, fingernails, or knife blades. This will prevent destroying the screw head, damaging the Work, and a lot of cussing.

**Adjusting.** All of the fasteners in your shell are designed to be adjusted easily. By using your tools you should be able to tighten or loosen nuts, bolts, and screws with no hassles. That, of course, is the theory—reality is definitely different. So be prepared because more often than not you're going to run into difficulties.

The most common problem with fasteners is people. They tend to forget which way to turn them, and that causes problems. One way will tighten, the other will loosen, and major hassles can occur when you tighten when you meant to loosen. In most shells the threads are right handed, which means you turn the nut, bolt, or screw clockwise to tighten and counter-clockwise to loosen. This little ditty helps me out in times of trouble:

If you have other problems, such as a fastener that is frozen and definitely won't turn no matter how much you plead with it, or one that has stripped threads, turn to JOB 16.3 for input. Never give up hope; it's possible your equipment and cheerful attitude may be saved.

**Rust never sleeps.** Somewhere in your life you've probably bumped into corrosion, or **rust,** as it's more commonly called. It may have been on your sled, your car, or your yacht. You need to worry about rust, although you shouldn't lose any sleep over it. Rust is a brownish substance which forms on the surface of iron and steel. It is formed by oxidation, the mixing of oxygen from the air with iron. Two things that speed this reaction are heat and water, both of which you find around rowing. Those folks who kept their cars in warm garages during the winter may have been toasty when they got into their cars, but they weren't doing their automobile any favors.

Most parts of rowing equipment that could rust have been replaced by either **stainless steel,** brass, nylon, or plastic. Almost all of the metal fasteners used in rowing shells today are made of stainless steel, because it resists corrosion, is very tough, is widely available, and is cheaper and tougher than many other materials typical used that are noncorrosive. There are three ways to distinguish if something is made of stainless.

First, most stainless is nonmagnetic, so it will not be attracted to a magnet, and this is a fairly good reason to keep a small magnet in your boathouse. Second, you can tell a stainless bolt by the markings on its

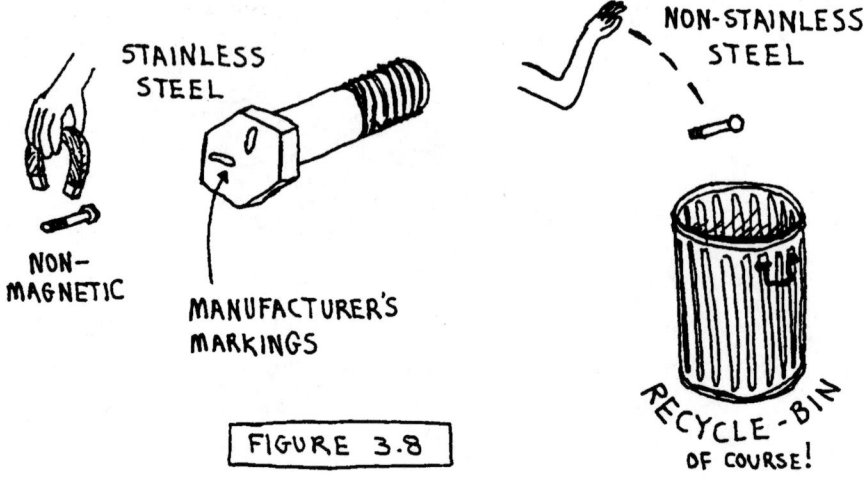

FIGURE 3.8

head. There are usually two lines angling away from each other, like in figure 3.8, which are the manufacturer's markings indicating a stainless steel product. Third, given time a metal fastener not made of stainless will corrode, look awful, and probably make life very tough for you when you try to use it. I prefer using the first two ways myself.

**Buying.** Sooner or later you are going to lose a fastener or wear one out and you're going to need to go to the store to get a replacement. When you buy replacement parts, make sure you get the right ones. Take an old one with you to compare. I call this *counter-intelligence*. All the little beasties we have just discussed will come in a mind-blowing variety of different lengths, diameters, material, and thread sizes, so don't expect to waltz into the shop and get satisfaction using only your memory.

To learn more bout screwdrivers, fasteners, etc. check out some of the interesting Web sites such as <http://www.aaronsgeneralstore.com> or do a search on your favorite search engine.

## 3.2 Metric System VS. U.S. Customary System

Ever have one of those days when you just throw your hands up in frustration because this world of ours is so confusing? Well, there may be a few more of these days ahead of you now that you are into rigging.

Here's why: Americans know how to measure things, and do it very well, I might add. And the French know how to measure things equally well, as do the British, and the Chinese. But what all these smart people don't know is how to measure things the same way. Catch this . . .

In America we use a system of measurement called the **U.S. Customary System**. This system uses such units as the inch and foot which have been derived from the length of human body parts. In the rest of the world they use the **Metric System**, or actually a modification of it, called the **International System**. This system is based on the meter, which is derived from the Earth—a meter is defined as one ten-millionth of an Earth quadrant. Interesting, huh?

Basically, the Metric System is used worldwide, except for a few countries, notably ours. There have been many, many efforts since the 1800s to bring the Metric System full force into the U.S., but it has never truly caught on. Could it be because of our fixation with body parts instead of quadrants?

How does all this effect you in your realm of rigging? Two ways—and this is where it gets confusing. First off, the type of tools you use will depend on what type of system the maker of your shell used. If the manufacturer used the Metric System, then all of the fasteners (nuts, bolts, etc.) will be metric. This means only metric tools will fit them. If the maker used the U.S. system then only U.S. system tools will fit. Of the more common manufacturers of shells we will discuss, most use U.S. Customary System, except for Empacher. Kaschper, made in Ontario, Canada, has been nice enough to put U.S. system nuts and bolts on his boats.

Secondly (as if tool selection wasn't enough of a hassle), you're going to find almost all of the measurements used for rigging are given in metrics. If you're like most high school, college, or club programs in the U.S., most of your equipment will be U.S.-made. So, this means you will be using metric dimensions on equipment with U.S. system fasteners. Did I mention this could be confusing?

So how do you cope with these two systems? First, determine what system your shell(s) use. Unless you have Empachers, or another foreign make of equipment, you'll probably be using the U.S. system. Then buy tools according to your needs.

Before you buy any metric tools, check the conversion chart for *Switch Hitters* (JOB 16.4) to save a few bucks. Then, become acquainted with the Metric System because life will be easier if you use it for your measurements. To help make conversion easier, make sure your tape measure has both U.S. and metric measurements on it. Whatever happens, don't let the different systems blow your cool. Get comfortable with both systems, smile when it gets confusing, and hope for the day when we all use the same system.

My first experience with the Metric System was, well, not exactly charming . . . many years ago we were lucky enough, or so I thought at the time, to get one of the first Carbocraft eights (a predecessor of Vespoli) in the U.S. When it arrived on a Saturday afternoon everyone was excited—that is until we discovered we couldn't rig it because none of our tools fit. Someone mumbled something about the Metric System (which I found out was not a way to meet people named "Rick") and I was sent on a journey to get metric tools. I felt like I was searching for the Holy Grail—metric wrenches aren't something you find easily on a weekend in a small Florida town.

After five hours of searching and hunting I found a few wrenches (I bought them used from an auto repair shop) and proudly reported back—to find the boat had already been rigged using adjustable wrenches and a few U.S. tools.

---

Check out these sites for more information on the Metric System:
    <http://www.encyclopedia.com/articlesnew/04129.html>
    <http://www.unc.edu/~rowlett/units/custom.html>

---

## 3.3 The Tools

Now that we've done some background work, let's get down to the specifics of tools. You aren't going to need a lot of them; just a few simple ones will let you do most of the rigging tasks. Down the road, when you get fancier with your rigging, you'll want to add some special tools, but to start off, your needs are going to be fairly simple. As a matter of fact, you might even have some of them around the house or in the trunk of your car.

Let's discuss the types of tools you'll be using for rigging, their specific purposes, and correct use.

**Homo sapiens tool.** Of all the tools you are going to use, this is the most important. Your brain, eyes, and hands working together as a team are going to make things happen when you rig. I realize for some of you this may be a terrifying concept—but have no fear. Absorb as much knowledge as possible, open your eyes, practice with your hands, and together we can make it work. Following these four simple principles may help:

---

### PRINCIPLES OF TOOLS

1. As a *Homo sapien* (if you're not one you shouldn't be reading this) you don't have everything you need to rig. You need help—you need tools. And to do a competent and safe JOB you need the right tools.

2. On the flip side, tools can't rig a boat by themselves, they need something—they need you.

3. Without a good relationship between principle #1 and principle #2, you're going to waste time, be inefficient and probably destroy something—like yourself or that valuable chunk of material called a rowing shell.

4. And lastly, tools have a memory. If you mistreat them, sooner or later the relationship will break down and they will get back at you.

---

## 3.4 Turning Tools

Every time a rigger is adjusted, nuts and bolts will be loosened and tightened. There may also be a screw or two that needs to be turned. In the lifetime of a shell, these nuts, bolts, and screws may be turned hundreds if not thousands of times. This is why quality is extremely important with turning tools. If the tools you have are schlock then you are going to start destroying these nuts, bolts, and screws, and in turn your life as a Rigger is going to be a drag. Following are some of the common turning tools you will need to use.

**Wrenches** are your most important turning tool. They are used to exert a twisting force. This twisting force is called **torque**. There are hundreds of different types of wrenches in the world but we need only be concerned with a few.

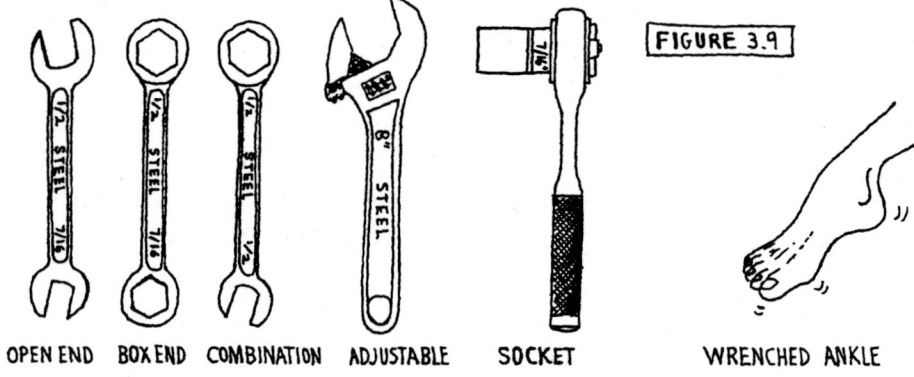

| OPEN END | BOX END | COMBINATION | ADJUSTABLE | SOCKET | WRENCHED ANKLE |

FIGURE 3.9

One of the first wrenches to add to your tool stock is the adjustable wrench, which is also known as a **crescent wrench.**

Adjustables are extremely handy because they don't care whether a nut is metric or U.S. system or whether it's small or big—they fit all sizes. They are easy to use, the key being to adjust the wrench so it fits snugly on the nut or bolt. You do this by adjusting the lower jaw by rotating the thumbscrew on the shaft of the wrench, like this:

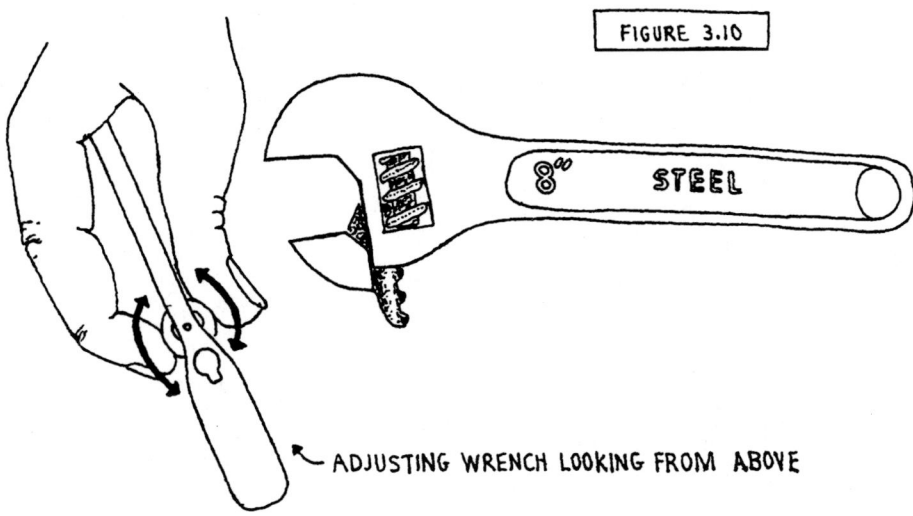

FIGURE 3.10

8" STEEL

— ADJUSTING WRENCH LOOKING FROM ABOVE

Although they are handy-dandy, adjustable wrenches do have a major disadvantage. They have a tendency to slip off the Work if they are not snugly tightened around the nut or bolt, or if the wrench is old and worn. Because of this, only use adjustables if you cannot find the proper wrench!

If an adjustable wrench does slip off, it can damage the corners of the thing you are trying to turn. This is called **rounding** and will quickly destroy your rigger hardware. Worse yet, if the wrench does slip, your hand, which is mightily pushing on the wrench handle could end up flying and you'll probably end up doing a number on your knuckles. That's exactly how they got the nickname "knuckle-busters." The way to save a couple of bashed joints and to minimize rounding damage to nuts and bolts is to always <u>pull</u> an adjustable wrench towards you and don't <u>push</u> it away.

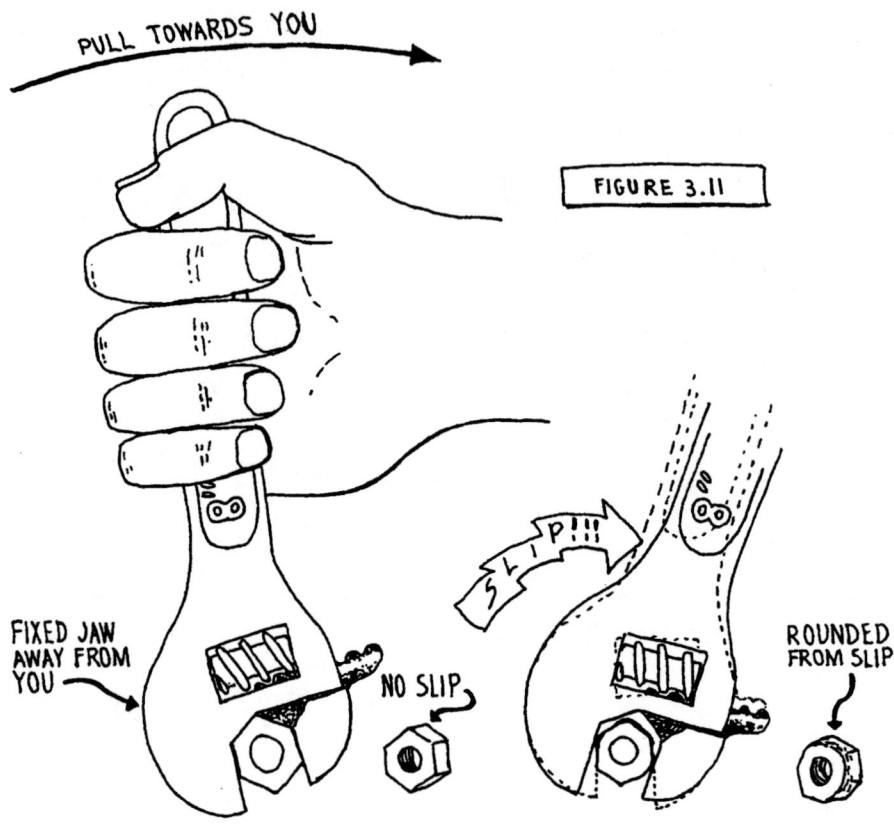

PULL TOWARDS YOU

FIGURE 3.11

FIXED JAW AWAY FROM YOU

NO SLIP

SLIP!!!

ROUNDED FROM SLIP

If, because of limited space or an awkward angle, you must push the wrench away from you, do so with an open grip, with the wrench handle in your palm.

If the Work is fairly tight I suggest you forget about using an adjustable, and instead use an **open-end** or **box-end** wrench. Open-end wrenches are nonadjustable wrenches with openings in one or both ends. The ends will fit specific size Work. A box-end is similar to an open-end wrench except the jaws are closed. A box-end is much safer to use than an adjustable or open-end because it completely surrounds the nut or bolt head and this reduces the chance of rounding and knuckle-busting.

When looking for box-end wrenches you will notice they may have different patterns inside the head. Go for the one with a six-point pattern instead of the twelve-point pattern. The six-point one will give a better fit.

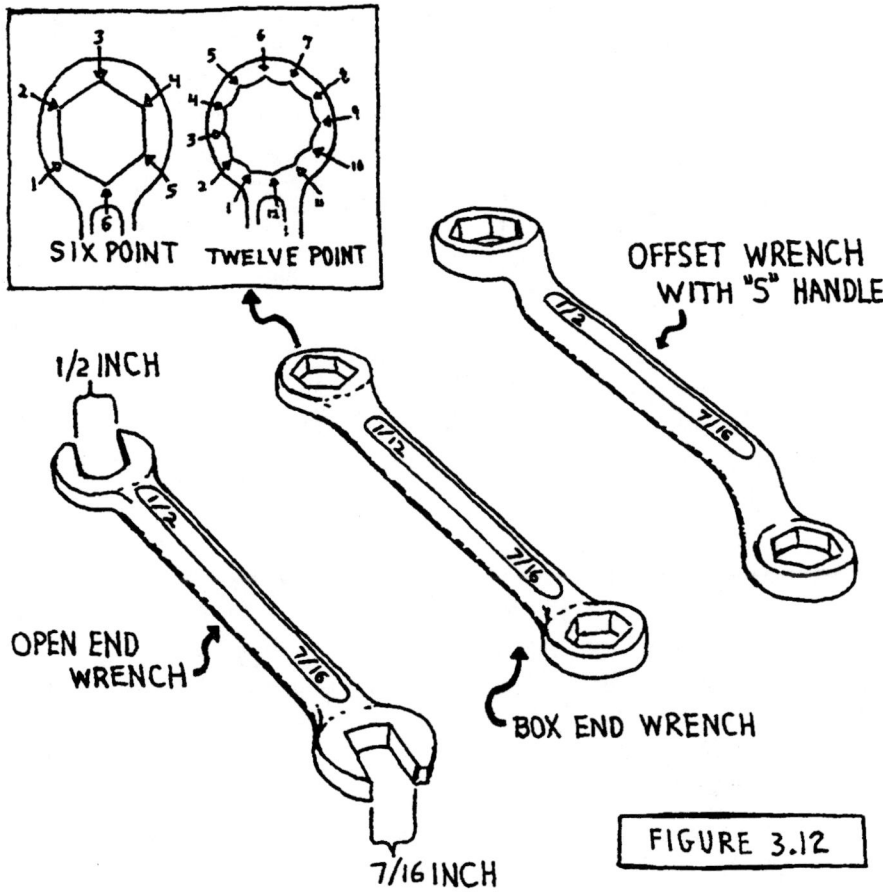

FIGURE 3.12

In your quest for wrenches you may come upon some where the jaws are angled to the handle, sort of like an S curve (shown in figure 3.12). Consider it a major score if you can get one—especially if one end of the wrench is 7/16 inch and the other is 1/2 inch, the most common sized wrenches used in U.S. rigging. These wrenches allow you to get quite a secure hold on a nut and turn it without hitting the rigger stay. This will save you mucho knuckle skin.

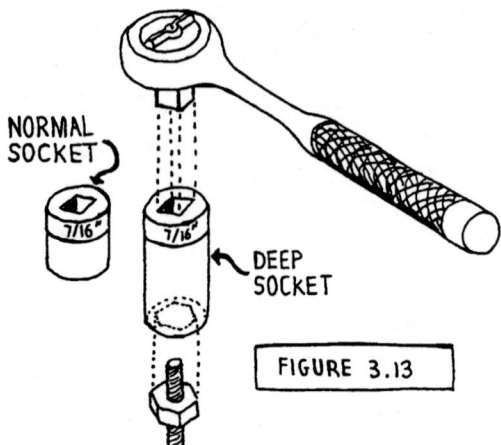

NORMAL SOCKET

7/16"

7/16"

DEEP SOCKET

FIGURE 3.13

On the handle of wrenches you will notice numbers stamped into the metal. This is how you can tell the wrench size. A wrench which has *13* stamped on it is a metric wrench which will fit 13 mm fasteners. One with *7/16* is a U.S. wrench which fits 7/16 in Work.

One of the most ingenious tools you will discover is the **socket wrench**. A socket wrench consists of a round chunk of steel with a hole in one end which fits over a fastener. In the other end is a square hole. Into this square hole goes a driver which allows you to turn the socket and there- fore turn the fastener.

When I say ingenious, it is not because of the socket itself but because of what the socket can do in combination with the driver, which is called a **ratchet handle**. The ratchet allows the socket to be turned quickly, and is reversible. If you are working in tight areas or have a lot of turning to do, the socket wrench will save a lot of tired arms and banged up knuck- les. If the fastener you are working on is in a recessed area, you can put an extension between the ratchet and socket.

You will find sockets most helpful in sectioning of shells (a JOB that is hardly ever done anymore because few sectioned boats are produced nowadays). I suggest you use a "deep socket" if you are going to be sec- tioning (see JOB 18.3, *Sectioning a Shell*).

Be cautious with socket wrenches. People have a nasty tendency to over-tighten the Work with these wrenches. I think it has something to do with the feeling of power they instill in people.

## 3.5 Measuring Tools

Measuring tools specifically help the eyes and brain perform better. No matter how good your eyesight may be, it is extremely hard to judge distances accurately, and in rigging small distances like one half inch or five millimeters can be darned important. All ye skeptics may be saying, "How can those small distances matter?" but you will see in the later chapters that small distances can make big differences.

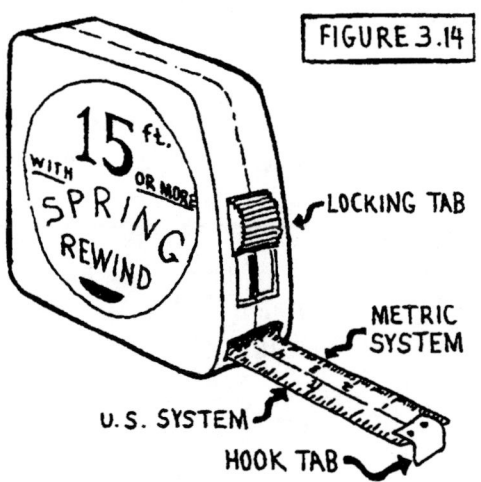

FIGURE 3.14

LOCKING TAB

METRIC SYSTEM

U.S. SYSTEM

HOOK TAB

Your selection of measuring tools is very limited. We have **rulers**, **yard sticks**, and **tape measures**. Rulers are too short to be useful. Yardsticks are too long and inflexible to be handy. But don't despair because tape measures, as Goldilocks said, "are just right."

A tape measure is a piece of flexible steel with numbers painted on it that condenses into a small container. My recommendation, because of the two different measuring systems to which we are slaves, is to buy a tape measure that has both the metric and the U.S. system on it. The tape should be over twelve feet long so you can measure oars without too much hardship. Fifteen-footers are great if you can find them. Get one with a locking tab, which frees up one hand when you need it most, and make sure the paint on the tape is durable and you can read the markings easily. Also make sure the case is sturdy, that it has a spring rewind mechanism, and that the little hooking tab on the end of the tape is not schlock. My favorite make of tape measures is *Lufkin*. They are tough, fit well in my hand, and are not unreasonably expensive. But whatever you buy, go with quality, go with quality, go with quality.

Get the hint?

## 3.6 Holding Tools

Holding tools do just that: They hold things. They help you grip the Work better so you can do what you need to do. As far as the boathouse is concerned, we are mostly talking about pliers: **locking**, **slip joint,** and **needle nose**.

Locking pliers (Vise Grip is a brand of these) are a great all-purpose tool. They take some practice to get used to, so fiddle around with them in your spare time. You will see they are similar to regular pliers, except there is a locking device which will hold the jaws in a set position. This feature comes in extremely handy. A friend of mine, Bobby Joe, is so sold on locking pliers he takes a small pair of them everywhere: trips, work, parties—Bobby always has his locking pliers with him. He says it's his only vise.

Slip-joint pliers (see diagram) have a movable jaw that can slip into two different positions, to grab small or large objects. Rubber-coated handles are nice but not a necessity. Needle-nose pliers will allow you to get into tight areas and pick up small things. These tools will also cut wire and are all helpful in odd and emergency situations, like when you have to remove a crab trap from your propeller, or when your five-year-old has stuck your only car key between the cracks in a cement sidewalk.

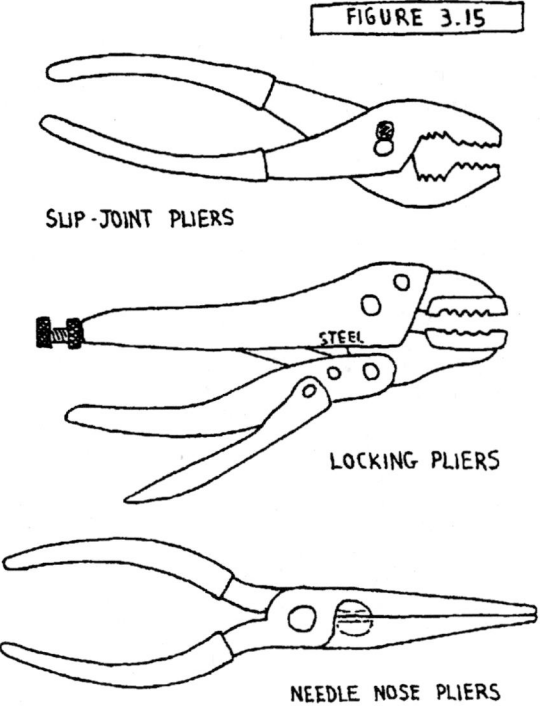

FIGURE 3.15

SLIP-JOINT PLIERS

STEEL

LOCKING PLIERS

NEEDLE NOSE PLIERS

A trick to using holding tools is to use them to grip *but not to turn* your Work. This is an important difference. For example, if you have a frozen nut and bolt, use the locking pliers to grip the bolt while using a turning tool to turn the nut. This will keep you from biting and damaging the nut. This will save the nut, your fingers, and your attitude.

> Do not give pliers to your rowers to use for foot-stretcher adjustments. If you do, you will be repairing and replacing nuts and bolts forever. Instead, get them tools that fit and won't destroy the fastener.

Holding tools tend to be the most abused tools in the boathouse and the ones that can cause the most damage. Used correctly, these tools are a great help; used improperly, these tools can be downright dangerous! I have seen locking pliers used for hammering nails, turning screws, and tightening foot stretcher nuts. *All of these are wrong and dangerous.*

**Clamps** are instruments designed to hold things together. There are three types of clamps you may find helpful. I use large **alligator clamps** to hold the pitch meter onto the oarlock. This allows me to free up a hand and not drop my meter quite so often. Another clamp I used is called a **C-clamp**. I have two six-inch C-clamps I use to help stabilize the shell and for a bunch of odd ball little things. A third type I have and use most of all is called a **quick grip** clamp. Clamps are not necessities, but you'll find that they often come in handy.

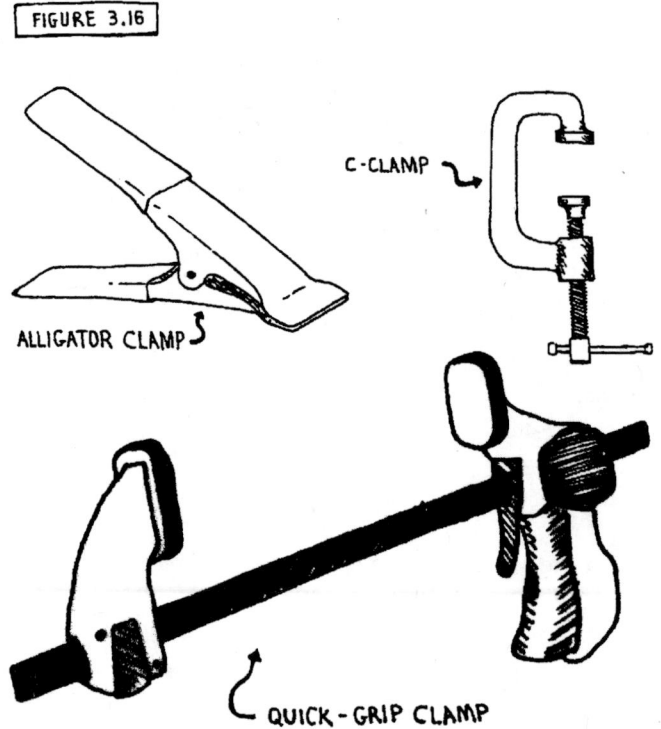

FIGURE 3.16

ALLIGATOR CLAMP

C-CLAMP

QUICK-GRIP CLAMP

## 3.7 Hitting Tools

Let me be right up front and say this about hitting tools: There really ain't a whole lot of hitting that should be going on in your boathouse.

I don't know about you, but the thought of someone wielding a **hammer** in our boathouse around fragile and expensive rowing shells gives me the shivers. I think there is really only one place for a hammer in rigging—tucked safely away inside a **tool box**. You may come upon the rare instance when you need a hammer, not as a "**pounder**" but instead as a "**persuader**." That is what my dad calls them, persuaders, and I think the name fits well. You will find most uses for your persuader will come from trying to loosen stuck or frozen parts where finesse, not power, is needed.

In all honesty, over the years I've found three times when my hammer has come in handy. First, I've used it to lightly tap (*tap*, not pound!) rigger bolts through the knees if they were resisting my efforts. Secondly, I've use it to tap frozen rigger parts in an attempt to loosen them. Lastly, and most importantly, I've used my hammer to intimidate parents who thought they were making helpful coaching suggestions.

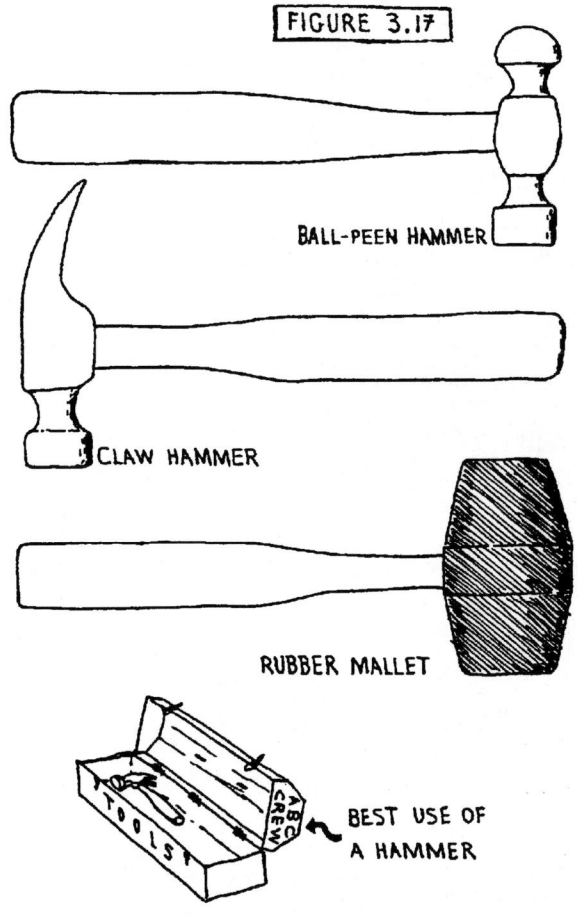

FIGURE 3.17

BALL-PEEN HAMMER

CLAW HAMMER

RUBBER MALLET

BEST USE OF A HAMMER

Other than that, hammers make darn good paper weights. If you feel that you absolutely must have a hammer, then get a good, lightweight one. I suggest one with a metal handle with a no-slip rubber grip, and make sure the hitting surface is in good condition. A rubber mallet would also be a good addition to your tools when you can afford it.

> When using a hammer to strike something, you've got to be careful not to damage it or the material around it. Use soft, gentle blows. No home run, over-the-outfield-wall swings. If you're worried about crunching something you can reduce damage to the Work by cushioning the blows with a piece of scrap wood. You'll still get the force but cut down on the destruction.

## 3.8 Special Rigging Tools

The **height stick** or **rigging stick** is used to measure the height of the oarlock from the seat's top and can be used for a few other things as well, such as a straight edge. Rigging sticks are usually long pieces of material with something similar to a ruler attached to the end (see figure 3.18). There are several makers and many designs, but the important thing is that you will need one to rig. You will find specifics on rigging sticks in Chapter Eleven, including how to make one (JOB 11.1, *Measuring the Oarlock Height*).

> Two types of height sticks I like are Leavitt Rigging Tools' and Potomac Rowing's. Both work well, are easy to carry, and are priced right.

A **pitch meter** is used to measure the pitch, or angle, of an oarlock relative to the vertical plane (straight up and down). More on that later. As with the height stick, there are many makes and models. The best thing to do is to get one with which you are comfortable and that fits your budget. Details are in Chapter Ten.

You must have a pitch meter to rig correctly. There are few substitutes you can use, the least of which is your eyesight.

> My favorite pitch meters are the ones made by Leavitt Rigging Tools and Buffalo Rowing. They are reasonably priced, fit well in the hand, and are durable and quite reliable.

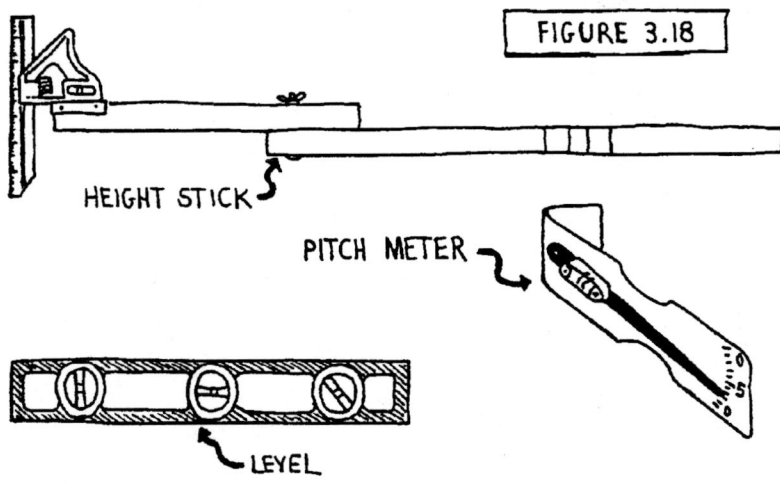

FIGURE 3.18

HEIGHT STICK

PITCH METER

LEVEL

**Rigging cards** and **notebooks** are used to record the numbers of your rigging dimensions. In the beginning, it may seem like a burden, writing all this stuff down, but in the long haul, recording your numbers will save you a lot of time and make life easier. Turn to Chapter Fifteen for the importance of rigging numbers and examples of rigging cards.

FIGURE 3.19

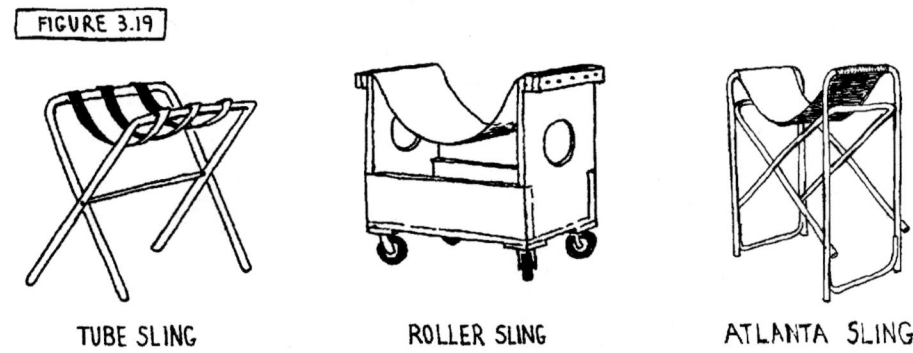

TUBE SLING          ROLLER SLING          ATLANTA SLING

There's not a whole lot of productive rigging you can do when the boat is upside down in the rack. You need to be able to flip the boat seats-up, on land, to work on it. To do so, the gods of the rowing world have given us **slings**. There are many types of slings, from expensive, manufactured slings to homemade versions held together with bubble gum and duct tape. Personally, I like using aluminum tube slings for rigging when on the road or outside of the boathouse, and heavy wooden slings on rollers for work inside the boathouse.

> Don't let the athletes sit in the slings—it is a great way to destroy them. A sling is designed to hold half of a 240-pound boat, not some huge 200-pound rower.

Do yourself a favor and don't ignore your slings. Make sure they are in good condition. Constantly check your slings for overuse and abuse. Look them over well, and if they are damaged or broken, fix them quickly or toss them. If in doubt about a sling's condition, don't use it. By using a marginal sling you set yourself and your boat up for a big letdown.

One final tool to mention here is a rather strange one. It is used to adjust the outward pitch of Euro-style riggers. It is commonly known as a Euro-style Pitch Adjuster; however, I call it the trog-tool (figure 3.20). This tool increases the amount of outward pitch in a Euro-style rigger (more on Euro-style riggers later) by streeeeeettttttccccchhhing the wields of the rigger frame—a rather rough and tumble way to adjust a nice and expensive part of a rowing shell.

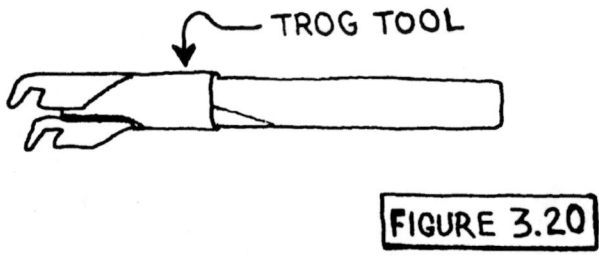

TROG TOOL

FIGURE 3.20

## 3.9 Miscellaneous Tools

There are a few other items you may want to add to your tool collection. In rigging, we use tape for basically two things. One is to hold stuff together and the other is to label stuff. You might find it handy to have a stash of three different types of tape: **duct tape**, **athletic (jock) tape**, and **electrical tape**.

Duct tape is designed specifically to hold things together, and it does it exceedingly well. I had a Volkswagen Beetle I kept in running condition for three years with duct tape. It is water resistant, durable, and a great thing to have when you need to improvise.

Jock tape is slang for white athletic tape. It holds things together fairly well (it held me together in high school) and it is good to write on. Just don't leave jock tape out in the hot sun for a long time because the adhesive will come off the tape and leave a nasty mess.

Electrical tape is made from vinyl. Don't count on it to hold things together. Most people use it for labeling riggers (see JOB 18.2, *Labeling Your Equipment*). You can find a variety of colors that can help spice up things in the boathouse.

Another helpful item is a **tool tray**. Imagine being positively hungry and going to one of those all-you-can-eat cafeterias. They've got everything you could possibly want, except they've run out of trays. To get that huge mound of food to your table you're going to be making a lot of trips back and forth. What a handy little thing a tray is.

Well, why not use one when you rig? A tool tray will save you a bunch of time. Take a peek inside a shell and you'll notice there's really no good place to put stuff. So when you rig, your choice is to either put your tools in your pockets put them on the bottom of the boat, in the sneakers, in the tracks, or on the deck. If you're not a pocket person (and you won't be after sitting on a wrench once or twice), when you're done rigging your tools will be spread all over the shell. When the boat is lifted over the heads, someone will catch the screwdriver you lost in the scull or they'll wrench an ankle. For a tool tray design see JOB 16.5.

A **level** is a simple tool that will tell you whether a surface is exactly horizontal (called level) or exactly vertical (called plumb). Most are made of a piece of metal with a built-in tube. This tube, or vial, is filled with a colored liquid with an air bubble in it. The tube is marked with two lines so that the bubble will come to the center of the vial and show itself between two lines when the surface is level or plumb (see figure 3.21).

I suggest either a carpenter's level or a torpedo level. The carpenter's level is easier to read, being larger (usually 36 to 100 cm) but the Torpedo, being smaller (usually no more than 23 cm long), is easier to use in rigging. You'll find a level handy when trying to balance the boat for checking outward pitches (see JOB 10.3).

If you are looking to get real fancy, you can get yourself an electronic level. I've had one for years and have found it to be very helpful for measuring foot stretcher angles and outward pitch. The one I have cost me about $65.00 and gets some use, but not a lot. Good toy to have if you're looking to impress any engineers in the boathouse.

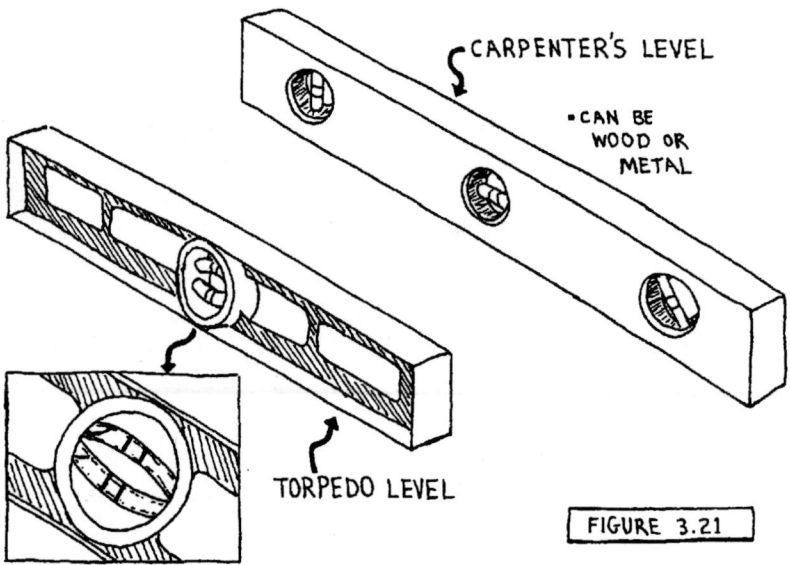

CARPENTER'S LEVEL

• CAN BE WOOD OR METAL

TORPEDO LEVEL

FIGURE 3.21

## 3.10 Getting the Stuff

For a while you might be able to exist by borrowing a few tools. However, there is no better way to sour a relationship than to keep mooching someone's tools, especially if you lose or break them. As the saying goes, "borrow good tools, lose good friends." So keep things cool in the boathouse and motivate yourself to go out and buy your own tools.

Now implant this in your memory before you get tense about having to spend big bucks at the store: You should be able to get all the tools you need for well under $200. Now that may be a lot of bread to you—I know it is to me—but don't worry, you can fix yourself up for less if you are smart and diligent.

A common question most tool shoppers ask is, "Should I buy quality or should I buy inexpensive?" My answer is "Yes!" In today's world of tools you can do both.

For those tools that are critical to rigging and that will get a lot of use, like certain wrenches, I suggest buying a top quality product. Pick one that comes with a lifetime warranty, like Sears' Craftsman or Snap-On. You may pay more initially but the tools will last a long while, and if they break you are certain of a replacement.

For those tools that are going to be suffering a lot of abuse—like a rigger nut wrench—and that will get borrowed and lost dozens of times, I suggest you buy inexpensive tools. If you are just starting your tool collection, a great way to save money and to get a great deal is to buy used tools.

There are several places you can get a good tool at a good price, even at a great price. Most folks buy their new tools at the local department store or at the neighborhood hardware shop. These stores are usually a good place to frequent. Of the two, you'll probably get the best price at the department store, like Sears or Wal-Mart, but you will most likely get the most knowledgeable service from your local hardware store or a place like Home Depot.

For used tools, I've found I can get some bargain prices at places like pawn shops, estate sales, garage sales, second-hand stores, and flea markets. These places can be the sources of some amazing deals, especially if I know what the heck I'm looking for.

Personally, pawn shops aren't my favorite places because I figure whatever is in the shop is there because hard times have befallen someone, and when the person gets it back together, he or she is going to come back calling for the tools. I prefer garage sales and flea markets. They can be a type of social function, and if you don't mind rummaging around in piles of stuff, you just might hit the jackpot and find some brand-name bargains.

> Don't wear your best duds when visiting a flea market or garage sale. Not because you will get dirty, but because if you are dressed up you're going to pay more.

Years ago, I bought a Sears' Craftsman socket set at a garage sale for $10. The same set sells at the store for over $75, and it comes with a lifetime guarantee. As I said, that was years ago, and I'm still using the set. However, not all buys are great.

With that in mind, be cautious before you shell out your hard-earned cash. Too many people think a tool is a tool is a tool—it is more than that. Remember, your tool is going to be an extension of your hand, and you are going to use it on something quite valuable to you—your rowing equipment. So check the tool over well.

A bad tool is more harm than help, and if you buy a bad one you're going to be hard pressed to find someone who will take it back. That's when you will hear the old, "we have your money, you have our sympathy" routine. Before you hit the trail and start building your tool collection read JOB 3.1, *How to Buy Your Tools*, and JOB 3.2, *What Tools to Buy*, of this chapter.

Merely owning the tools is no guarantee of skill as a Rigger any more than the ownership of a Buzz Lightyear doll makes one an astronaut. At the same time, regardless of how much rigging knowledge you have between the ears, there is not much you can do without your tools.

## JOB 3.1: HOW TO BUY YOUR TOOLS.

**Problem:** You need to build your tool supply.

**Needed:** Money, transport to store, common sense, and patience.

Let me serve up my *Six Tool-Buying Principles,* which may help you in your quest for tools:

> **Principle 1:** Make a list of exactly what you need before you leave the house, and then only buy what you *actually* need. Don't let those bucks burn a hole in your pocket. In the first edition of this book I wrote about a wrecking bar I bought 10 years before I wrote the book. I noted that I got a great price but I had only used the thing once in 10 years. Well, it's been 20 years since I bought the silly thing, and I've still only used it once. As they say, "A foolish Rigger and his or her money is soon parted."

> **Principle 2:** Price is not a good indicator of quality. Just because it costs a lot doesn't mean it's a good tool, and just because it is inexpensive doesn't mean that it is not good.

> **Principle 3:** Purchasing a <u>set</u> of tools can oftentimes be cheaper than buying individual tools.

> **Principle 4:** Buy tools that fit well into your hand—if they don't fit correctly, they won't work correctly.

> **Principle 5:** Buy smart. If you need a 7/16 in wrench and also a 1/2 in wrench, why don't you buy a combination wrench? Saves money and space in the tool box.

> **Principle 6:** This is worth repeating . . . **stay away from borrowing tools**. If you must—absolutely must—borrow, then treat the tools as if you owned them, and return them in better shape than you got them in.

## JOB 3.2: WHAT TOOLS TO BUY.

**Problem:** Now that you are armed with all this knowledge, what are you supposed to get?

I have divided up my tool collection into three different kits. One I use for basic rigging around the boathouse, another I take on the water for use during practice, and the third I take on road trips with me. Dividing them up helps me find what I want, when I need it, and keeps me from lugging everything everywhere. Arrange your tools to fit your own needs, but if you want to divide them up into kits, here is what I suggest you have in each kit:

**1. Basic rigging kit**: For rigging, maintenance, and general use.

- ❑ 2 adjustable wrenches: 1 large, 1 small
- ❑ 2 rigger nut wrenches specific for your system
- ❑ 1 tape measure: preferably U.S. and metric
- ❑ 2 screwdrivers: 1 Standard (-), 1 Philips (+)
- ❑ 1 pitch meter
- ❑ 1 height stick
- ❑ 2 clamps: 1 of each type
- ❑ 3 pliers: 1 of each type
- ❑ tool tray
- ❑ 1 level
- ❑ 1 hammer
- ❑ electrical tape
- ❑ utility knife (razor blade knife with snap-off blades)
- ❑ metal file
- ❑ small magnet
- ❑ any other wrenches specific to your shell
- ❑ shims

- ❑ small supply of spare hardware (nuts, washers, etc.)
- ❑ trog-tool

**2. Practice tool kit:** If you think you will never need to make adjustments or repairs on the water during a practice, give me a call. I've got some Enron stock just for you.

- ❑ 2 adjustable wrenches: 1 large, 1 small
- ❑ 2 rigger nut wrenches specific for your system
- ❑ 1 tape measure: preferably U.S. and Metric
- ❑ 2 screwdrivers: 1 Standard (-), 1 Philips (+)
- ❑ 3 pliers: 1 of each type
- ❑ 1 hammer
- ❑ electrical tape
- ❑ small knife
- ❑ any other wrenches specific to your shell
- ❑ cell phone (in case of emergency)
- ❑ pen and paper—for notes and messages
- ❑ shims
- ❑ small supply of spare hardware (nuts, washers, etc.)
- ❑ waterproof container for tape measure, pen and paper, etc. (plastic tennis ball containers work great)
- ❑ spare oarlock, oar button, and seat
- ❑ spare spark-plugs and spark-plug wrench
- ❑ trog-tool
- ❑ spare supply of rigger top bolts or nuts

That last item (a supply of rigger top bolts or nuts) is a critical item to have. Losing one on the water is like someone applying a giant handbrake on your practice. Got a spare—practice continues. No spare—back to the dock with ya (if you're lucky enough to make it there, that is).

**3. Travel tool kit:** This sport involves a lot of travel which means de-rigging and re-rigging boats each time you move. This calls for some special things to stash and bring along (see Appendix Four for a complete travel list check-off sheet).

- basic rigging kit
- slings
- socket wrenches
- sectioning tools
- tape: all three types
- hack saw
- supply of spare hardware
- spare rigger parts (pins, oarlocks, etc.), foot stretchers, seats, fin, and rudder for each type of shell
- flashlight

Once you start accumulating a tool collection, I suggest you keep each kit separately. This will save time spent looking for that lost wrench.

By now the question should have popped into your mind, what exactly do I put all these tools into? I just keep the standard rigging tools on my tool tray instead of putting them away each time. I keep my practice tool kit in an Army surplus ammunition box. It's waterproof, compact and tough as all heck. We keep our travel tool kit in a large Craftsman tool box. It is big and clunky but it holds a lot of stuff, and we don't have to worry about someone wandering away with it—at least not without getting a hernia.

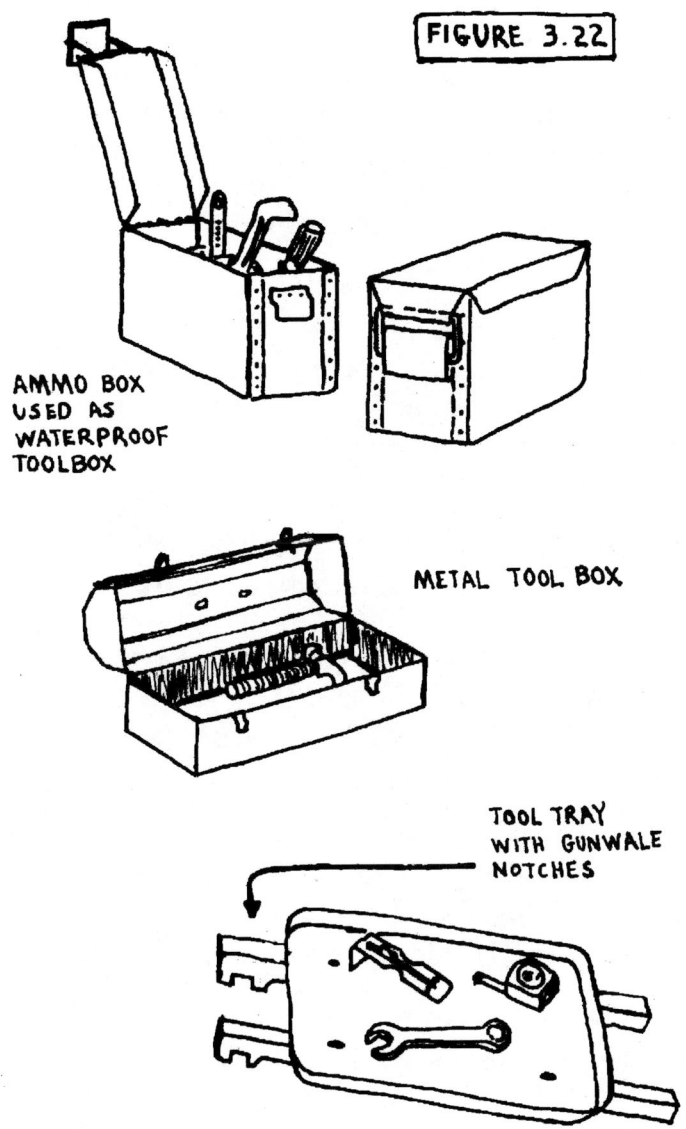

FIGURE 3.22

AMMO BOX
USED AS
WATERPROOF
TOOLBOX

METAL TOOL BOX

TOOL TRAY
WITH GUNWALE
NOTCHES

# JOB 3.3: TAKING CARE OF YOUR INVESTMENT.

**Problem:** You have just gone out and boosted the economy by several dollars. There are a few things you can do to make sure your purchases live a long and useful life.

**Care:** Caring for your tools is fairly simple and quick, yet important. You should clean them regularly. This consists of nothing more than putting some mineral spirits or turpentine on a rag and wiping them clean. Lubricate any moving parts. Keep your tools dry, especially those in your practice tool kit. Most tools are made of steel and will rust quickly. Be nice to them and they will be nice to you, especially in the case of your *Homo sapiens* tool. Be especially nice to it.

**Labeling:** You should mark your tools to identify them as yours. Not because of folks stealing them, but because tools are social things and they like to visit other people's tool boxes, especially on road trips. I have seen three methods used for labeling tools.

One is using colored electrical tape or paint. I like this method since you can mark your stuff with your own design and spice up an otherwise dull toolbox. Another method is to use an electric engraving tool to scratch names into the tools. And still another method is to grind notches into them. This is kind of Troglodytic and you will need a grinder. This method seems to work until you merge with someone who has the same pattern of notches. I like the tape/paint method best because it looks cooler.

**Storage:** I already mentioned where to keep your tools during the season when you will be using them. During the off-season, if not in use, store your tools in a dry area. People who are absolutely into their tools usually hang them from a pegboard with a painted outline around them. I just put mine in a dry place where I can find them when I need them.

If your tools are going to be living at the boathouse, I suggest that you keep them under lock and key. Although I wish we lived in a world where locks and keys are not needed, we don't, so in order to protect your investment this is an important step.

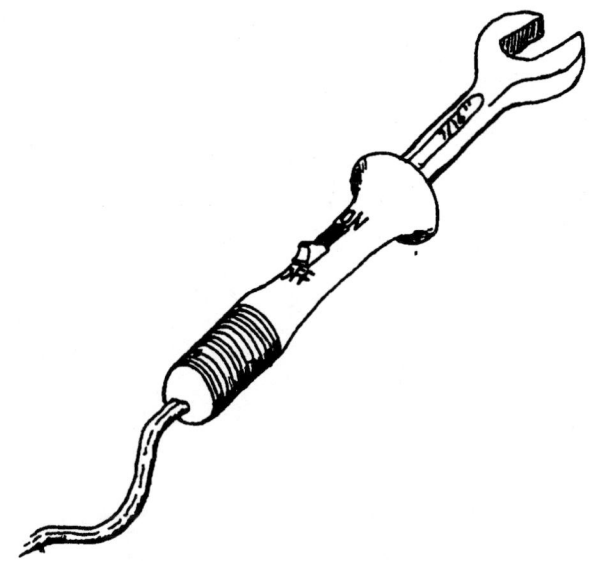

# Chapter Four: The Equipment

A long time ago, when the Troglodytes and Neanderthals were racing for the Flintstone Cup, rowing equipment was much different. Back then, the boats consisted of old chunks of trees that were paddled with sticks. When people finally became civilized, their rowing equipment changed: The logs became shells and the sticks became oars.

Specifically, it is thought that the Phoenicians were the first to take the paddle and turn it into an oar. This is important because a paddle, which has no solid connection to the boat, is only about one-half as efficient as an oar, which is connected to the boat by the **outrigger**. This helped the Phoenicians to become the speed-demons of the Mediterranean.

Since those olden days, the first genuinely big change in the rowing scene occurred around 1600. Until then, rowing usually had been done by slaves or by workers. Competition consisted of fishermen racing each other to get their catch of the day to the market first or of matches between watermen to see whose water taxi was faster. For some reason the upper crust of England decided they were tired of the workers having all the fun. So these folks put down their silver spoons and got into rowing for recreation and competition. In the 1700s rowing became extremely popular in England, and in 1715 the Doggett Coat and Badge Race in England became the first recorded race for recreation.

Considering how long rowing has been around, changes have been few and sparse. There have been improvements, but the basic idea of rowing is the same as it was when the Egyptians were cruising the Nile. There have been four *major* improvements made to equipment in the last 200 years.

These are the **outrigger**, the **sliding seat**, the **swivel oarlock**, and the **keel-less** boat.

The outrigger probably had the greatest effect on rowing. Before the outrigger, the oar was attached to the boat at the **gunwale**. To allow this, the boats had to be wide, sometimes up to four feet wide. You can imagine how much fun those heavy boats were to row. Being too heavy to move, these old boats were left in the water, unlike today's shells. With the invention of the outrigger, boat size was greatly reduced, the weights of the shell dropped, and the boats became faster.

The invention of the sliding seat allowed more power to be applied to the oar. Until this time, the seat had been fixed and most of the oarsman's power came from the upper body muscles. Rowers loved to see the sliding seat because it enhanced their efficiency and reduced injuries. Butt blisters were a common problem with fixed-seat rowing, and many rowers who were training hard literally had to eat their meals standing up.

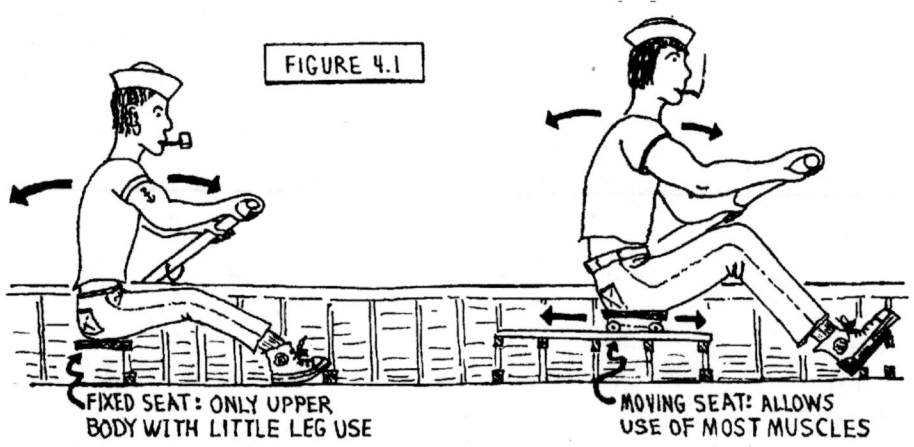

FIGURE 4.1

FIXED SEAT: ONLY UPPER BODY WITH LITTLE LEG USE

MOVING SEAT: ALLOWS USE OF MOST MUSCLES

The swivel oarlock increased the contact between the oar and the boat, improving efficiency. Before the invention of the swivel oarlock, the oars rested between two rigid pins called **tholepins.** The tholepins had a tendency to restrict the movement of the oar and often left gaps between the pins and the oar. This gave the oar an unattached feeling. One reason the swivel oarlock became popular was that it gave the rower a better feel of what was going on with the oar and allowed for a smoother stroke.

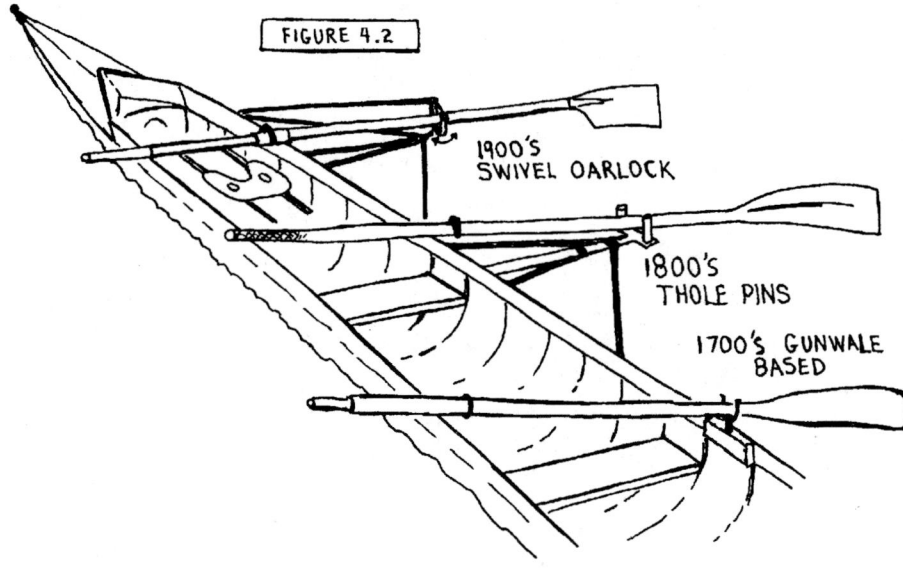

FIGURE 4.2

1900'S SWIVEL OARLOCK

1800'S THOLE PINS

1700'S GUNWALE BASED

Another improvement was the development of keel-less shells. Dropping the keel allowed the hull to be smoother. A smoother hull means less resistance, and less resistance means it takes less energy to move the shell.

FIGURE 4.3

KEEL

WOW!, NO KEEL

NO KEEL

There also has been many *minor* developments made to rowing equipment, with many coming in the last ten years such as: synthetic oars and boats, single action seats, Euro-style riggers, speaker amplifier systems, and speedometers, just to name a few.

Here are some of the other notable developments in rowing:

| | |
|---|---|
| 1810s | First eight raced in England |
| 1828 | Anthony Brown introduces the outrigger: Until this time, oars were attached to the boat on top of the gunwale |
| 1846 | First outrigger used in a race |
| 1857 | First keel-less boat raced |
| 1870 | Sliding seat introduced in America at Poughkeepsie, New York |
| 1870 | Swivel oarlock introduced, replacing fixed tholepin (rowlock) in race on Hudson River |
| 1873 | First sliding-seat boat raced in England |
| 1870s | First oar revolution: shape changes from long and narrow to shorter and wider blades |
| 1875 | Paper boats become popular (no kidding) |
| 1885 | Short slides replaced by long slides that let legs work their full range of motion |
| 1895 | Englishman E. Atkinson loses many friends after he invents first meter that records efforts of rowers |
| 1925 | Fixed-seat rowing finally succumbed to sliding-seat rowing in England, fifty-five years after its introduction |
| 1950 | Adjustment for spread introduced |
| 1960s | Several adjustments became available on equipment, such as adjustable collar on oar, pitch, and work-thru |
| 1960s | Second oar revolution: Macon style became the standard blade |
| 1968 | First synthetic boat raced |
| 1970 | Lateral pitch adjustment and movable foot stretchers become standard in shells |
| 1976 | First synthetic oar introduced |
| 1992 | Third oar revolution in the making, Big Blades are the new standard. |
| 1996 | Euro-style rigger becomes popular in the U.S. |

As you can see, new ideas were not quickly accepted. It took almost fifty years before the sliding seat totally replaced fixed-seat rowing. Some of this was due to stubbornness on the part of coaches and manufacturers, and some because people did not know how to use the new equipment.

An Eaton coach was quoted as saying he believed the new swivel oarlocks were a good idea, but he felt he could not teach rowers how to use them. Every time there has been a new development in equipment the art of rigging has had to change. In the past rigging was kept a deep, dark secret because of the intense rivalries in the sport. It was not uncommon for three teams rowing out of the same boathouse to have three different rowing styles and three different rigging techniques, all kept as secret as possible. It has just been in the past few years that rigging techniques and rowing styles have become standardized. This is mainly because national governing bodies, such as USRowing, are doing all that they can to promote and develop rowing in their countries. Rowers and coaches are thinking, and acting, more on a national and global level.

## 4.1 Tour of the Equipment

Before we try to tackle the mechanics of rowing, let's introduce you to the equipment.

**Finding your way around.** The first time around a shell can be very confusing. In rowing we don't deal with **left** and **right**. Instead we give directions by saying, **"Port,"** and, **"Starboard."** We don't use **front** and **back**; instead we have **bow** and **stern**. And when we move and store a boat it's upside-down. Not only that, but we identify the different positions in the boat by numbers. They start with the number *one* which is in the front (bow) of the boat and count upwards as you approach the back (stern) of the boat. And to top that off, in some places we don't even use numbers, but throw names in there instead—like stroke or bow-person.

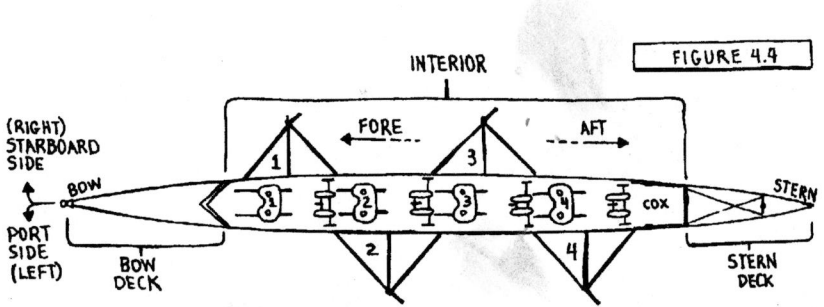

Confused? No sweat: here are a few helpful hints. The stern is the back of the boat. That is easy to remember because the stern is usually where the coxswain (person who steers) sits and they tend to be stern people. The front of the boat is the bow and it may help you to remember that when you bow, you lean forward.

Go to the bow of a seats-up boat and face the stern. Raise your right hand. Which side are you pointing to, port or starboard? Those of you who said, "Port" pat yourself on the back; those of you who said, "Starboard" read on.

When you are in the stern and looking towards the bow of ANY boat, port is always on your left. And it will always be in the same place regardless of where you are facing. This system came about a long time ago so sailors would always have an easy reference point. If Captain Bob came up, looked a sailor in the eye, and said, "Quick sailor, we're sinking, jump off the ship!" the sailor could easily get confused. "But captain, which side of the ship should I jump off, the left or right? And since we are facing each other, would that be your left, captain, or my left?" By using port and starboard instead of left and right, the sailor and captain know exactly what places they are talking about, and the sailor knows exactly where to jump.

Three more terms: **aft** means towards the stern, **fore** means towards the bow and **midships** means around the middle of the boat. You will see these terms many times. Don't expect to catch all of this in your first outing. As a matter of fact, I have been around rowing for thirty years and I still stumble over port vs. starboard.

## 4.2 The Parts

When you look at a boat you'll notice everything is in plain sight and easy to see. Follow along on Pete's sketch (figure 4.5) to get an idea where the parts are located.

**Shell** is the common name for any rowing boat, whether it's used for sweep rowing or sculling (although sculling shells are often called "sculls"). The term came about because the **hull** (**outer skin** of the boat) used to be as fragile as an egg shell (I'm not making this up). All shells are basically the same. The hull is what separates the insides of the boat from the outside world.

To help the hull keep its shape, there is a framework structure inside the boat for support. In most boats, this **superstructure** consists of pieces of wood that extend from one part of the shell to another. The horizontal pieces are called **braces**. Extending upward, from the bottom of the boat (called the **keelson**) to the top of the hull, are vertical pieces which are called **ribs**. The top part of the rib is called a **knee**.

Now take a couple of steps away from your boat and look at the whole thing. Notice how it appears to be divided up into three sections. At either end, bow and stern, you have closed areas called **compartments.** In between the compartments is the **interior** where the **seat assemblies** and **foot stretchers** are.

Although the bow compartment and the stern compartment look like a waste of space, they actually serve two purposes. The first is that they extend the total overall length of the boat. This is important because there is a critical relationship between the boat's length and its speed. The second is that they provide watertight compartments which are used for floatation in case the boat swamps. The top part of a compartment, when the boat is seats-up, is called the **deck**, and this can be made of either hard or soft material.

Where the interior and the compartments meet is a wall. These walls are called **bulkheads**. Either in the bulkhead or on the deck, there should be a **hatch** and **cover**. The hatch allows access into the compartment for inspection, repairs, or drying.

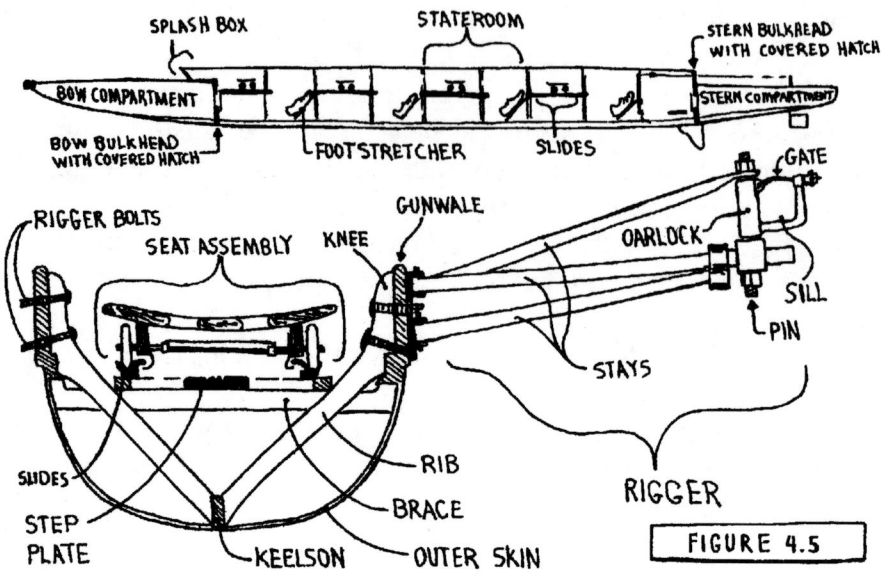

FIGURE 4.5

> When the boat is not in use, leave the hatch covers open. If you have a good watertight seal, damage might occur to the hull or deck if pressure builds up or decreases greatly inside the compartment. This tends to happen when the boat is out in the sun. Make sure the hatch is closed when the boat is rowed to ensure flotation.

The braces and ribs together form a platform upon which sits the **slides**, **runners**, or **tracks** (any of these names can be used). The seat assembly moves back and forth on these tracks. Between the tracks, on top of the braces or deck, is a spot, usually identified by tape or markings, called a **step plate** where the athletes step when getting into and out of the shell.

Using the step plates keeps the rowers from putting their weight on the bottom of the hull and letting the outside world (water) into the shell. You might find your boat does not have this bracing and instead the inside looks like one solid platform with holes cut into it. This is called a monocoque seat deck and is basically the same as the bracing system but just different in design, although structurally stronger.

Aft (toward the stern) of the seat assembly, between the braces and ribs, are the **foot stretchers**. The area from one foot stretcher to another is called the **stateroom**.

At the upper edges of the hull, on both sides of the boat, are the **gunwales** or **gunnels** (again, both terms are okay). On top of the bow deck there is a small extension of the gunwale called the **splashbox**. Its purpose is to keep water from riding up on the deck and into the interior. In the older shells you will probably see all of the gunwales made from wood, but on the newer, synthetic boats they are made from the same materials as the outer skin. If that's the case with your boat you may not even be able to tell where the hull stops and the gunwale begins.

Extending horizontally outward from the gunwale are the **outriggers** or **riggers.** The riggers are constructed of tubes called **stays.** These stays function as supports. At the end of the rigger is the **pin** and sitting snugly around the pin is the **oarlock.** There are a lot of variations of rigger designs. Regardless of design, the riggers are attached to both the gunwales and the knees by long bolts called **rigger bolts**. You will notice each rigger connects to the gunwales at two or possibly three different places, depending on the make of the boat.

A problem you may stumble upon is the lack of standardization of names between shell makers for rigger parts. For five different types of riggers you might have five different names for the exact same part. To avoid some confusion I have named the parts common to all five riggers (i.e. the top rigger stay) with names that identify them easily. For those parts specific to a certain type of shell I will use the manufacturer's part name.

The **oar** is what moves a shell. The difference between an oar and a paddle is that the oar is attached to the boat by a **rigger**, while a paddle is not attached. The oarlock is where the oar resides. The oar sits inside the oarlock resting on the **oarlock sill**, secured in place by the **gate** or **keeper**. Over the years, oars have undergone many changes, even though they don't look that much different. The size of the blade has become shorter, fatter and more curved and the length of the oar has decreased. We discuss this more in the later chapters.

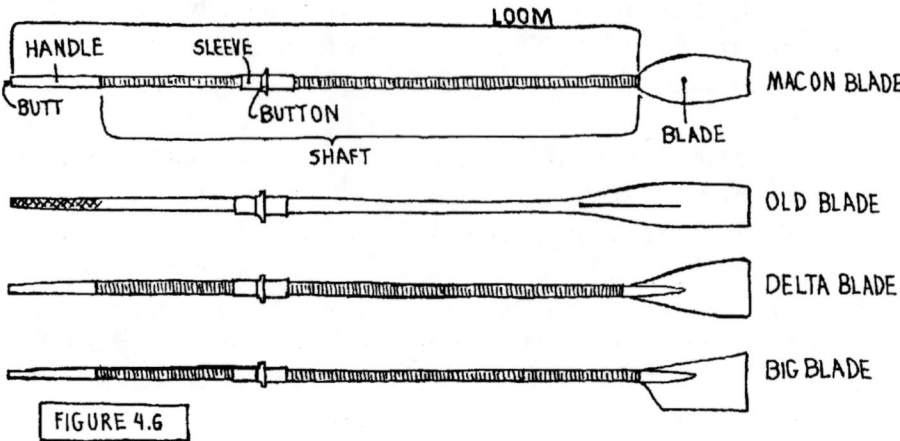

FIGURE 4.6

Oars always seem to be going through an evolution. One of the most significant changes has been in the materials used in making the oars. At one time, all oars were made from wood, but in the mid-1970s composite oars, made from graphite and fiberglass, hit the scene. This revolution has been led by a very innovative company called Concept II, <http://www.concept2.com>. Nowadays, wooden oars are slowly becoming collectors' items. As a rower I like the feel of wooden oars, but as a coach the synthetic (composite) oars are a dream. They are tougher than the woodies and need a lot less tender loving care from the Rigger.

The oar is made up of six parts. The **handle** is what the rower holds. This is usually a wooden piece; however, composite handles are being made and used today. The handle is usually fairly rough to assist the rower's grip when it gets wet. The end of the handle is called the **butt**. The **shaft** extends from the handle down to the **blade** or **spoon**. Between the handle and blade is a **sleeve** upon which is the **collar** or **button**. The collar fits up against the oarlock and keeps the oar from extending outward. This is the only place where the oar contacts the shell.

When the oar is in the oarlock, there are a few positions you can put it in. Positioning or placing the blade in the water is called making a **catch**; removing the blade from the water is called making a **release** or **finish**; when the blade is held **perpendicular** to the water, it is said to be in the **squared** position; and when it is held **parallel** to the water, it is in the **feathered** position.

Now look at the outside of the hull. Somewhere along the bottom of the boat is the **skeg** or **fin** (once again, it's proper to use both terms). The fin helps the boat track in a straight line in the water and resist sideways forces, like wind. To steer the boat there is a **rudder**, also along the bottom (not all shells have rudders). The rudder may be in combination with the fin or they may be separated by some distance. In either case, the rudder will always be aft of the fin.

There are two places the rower contacts the shell: the **seat assembly** and the **foot stretchers**. The **seat** is the top part of the seat assembly (may be wooden or fiberglass), and is designed to fit the human backside fairly well—although there have been many practices after which I would disagree with that statement. The fore (bow) part of the seat has an indentation for the lower spine (coccyx) to fit in. It looks like a half-moon. Underneath the seat is the **carriage** upon which are connected the **wheels,** which allow the seat to roll on the slide. Depending on the make of boat, you will find different carriages and wheel designs. A great new design being produced now incorporates ball bearings with the seat carriages—a great innovation.

The seat assembly is removable and if you get confused as to which way it should go, always have the half-moon towards the bow (see JOB 7.86, *Seat Assembly in and Out)*. The foot stretchers are attached to the braces by **notched channels.** These channels allow the foot stretchers to be moved fore and aft, and then secured. Most boats today will have sneakers on these stretchers. They are usually attached by nuts and can be easily exchanged for fit or repair.

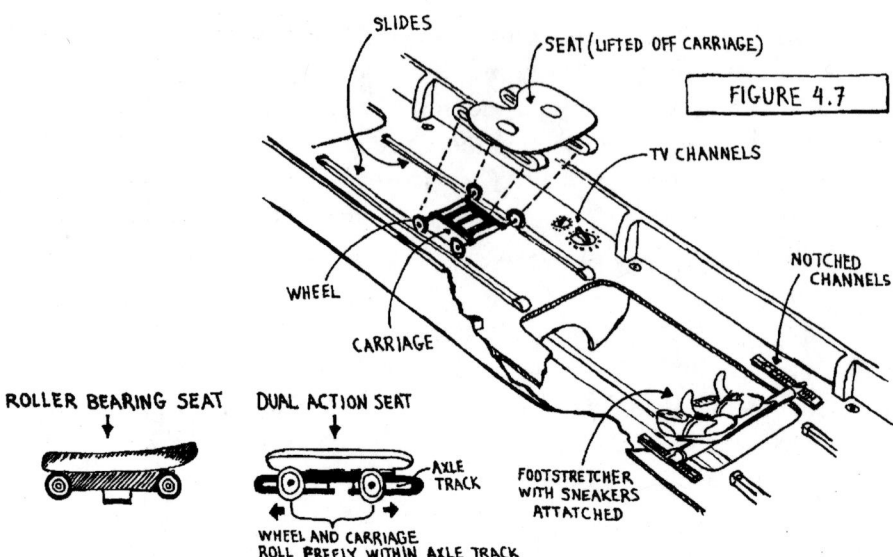

One last note: some of the larger shells, mainly eights, may come with the ability to be split into two or three pieces. These boats are called **sectional** boats and this is done to make transporting the shell easier. It's easy to tell if a shell is sectional. Look inside the boat for a large reinforced area that is bolted together, or if the shell is seats-down, look at the hull for a seam line. The sections are usually at midships, but not always. See JOB 18.3 on how to section a shell. Now that the tour is over, let's move on to the mechanics of rowing.

## 4.3 How It Works

This section won't make you a rigging genius, but it will help you understand some of the mechanical mysteries that happen in your boat as you glide along the water. I'd like to say that the mechanics of rowing are easy to explain. I'd like to say that, but I can't. As a matter of fact, it's rather difficult to explain the theory of rowing, which is how a rower, an oar, a rigger, and a shell all function together.

But let's give it a shot.

There is one basic principle that will help you understand how all of the parts work together in rowing, and that is:

> In rowing, the power of the rower is applied through the oar to the water by means of the rigger.

When a rower sets the oar in the water and pushes against the foot stretcher (which means he or she is also pulling on the oar) there is a force exerted upon the rigger. The rigger transfers this force to the shell, which in turn is moved through the water. This may sound simple—it's not actually—but it's worth trying to understand.

**First- and Second-Dimensional Riggers.** If you are in either the First or Second Dimension of rigging I wouldn't get too worried about the nitty-gritty details of the theory of rowing. It's not that you can't handle it, but there are other more important items that need your attention. Trying to grasp the theory of rowing would be like going to the local high school to take a beginner's driver's education course, only to be taught race strategy for the Indy 500. Kind of a waste of time.

Instead, I suggest you do this: Focus on learning the parts and how they interact and then get competent in adjusting them. This will give you a good dose of reality before you tackle the theory. When you feel comfortable with this, you will find the theory of rowing will come easier. In fact, you will already understand the basics of it.

**For Higher-Dimensional Riggers.** Well, I've got good news and bad news. The good news is that if you're reading this then you're doing well with your rigging and you're now ready to discover the intricacies of the theory of rowing. The bad news is that you are not going to learn them here. The theory of rowing is a real handful. Let me show you an example of what I mean.

There are two different ways to look at the mechanics of a rigger and an oar. One is to assume that they work together as a first-order lever and the other is to assume they work as a second-order lever.

As a first-order lever, the oar moves the water but not the boat. As power is applied to the handle of the oar, the spoon is moving the water in front of it. The fulcrum, or point on which the oar turns, is the pin and oarlock. As a second-order lever, the oar moves the boat and not the water. As power is again applied to the handle, the boat moves instead of the water.

This time the fulcrum is at the water and not the oarlock. You can look at the rigger and oar either way, and either way is right! It can get confusing.

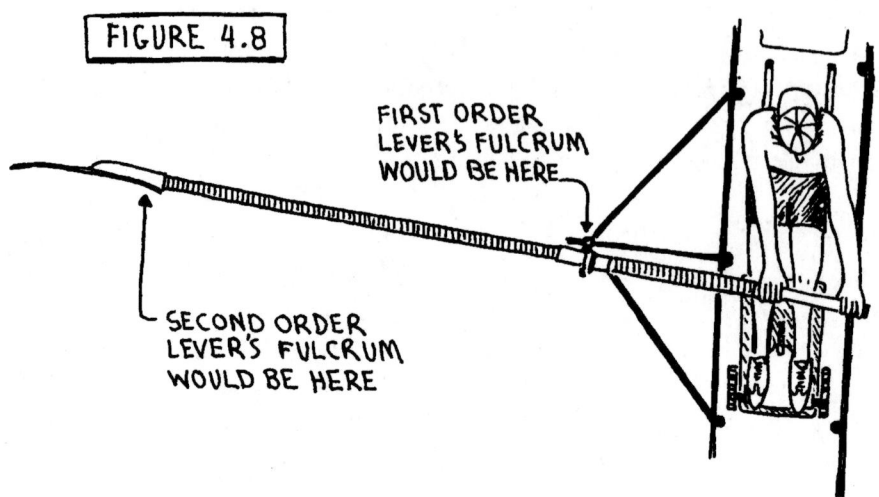

FIGURE 4.8

FIRST ORDER LEVER'S FULCRUM WOULD BE HERE

SECOND ORDER LEVER'S FULCRUM WOULD BE HERE

This is just a tidbit of the theory, which should give you some indication of how involved rowing mechanics are. As a matter of fact, to do it justice would take a book in itself and that's exactly what several people have done. Many of these folks have done a superb job of putting the complete theory of rowing into words and I am going to refer you to their books. Call this a cop-out if you want, but these folks will give you a better education on this subject than I could. The books are: *A Textbook of Oarsmanship*, by Gilbert C. Bourne; *Rudern*, by Dr. Ernst Herberger; and *The Complete Steve Fairbairn on Rowing*, by Ian Fairbairn. Complete citations can be found in Appendix Three, along with other suggested books.

I highly recommend Anu Dudhia's Web site FAQ: Physics of Rowing, <http://www.atm.ox.ac.uk/rowing/physics.html>. It has a wealth of information about the physics and mechanics of rowing. Well worth a view.

**For all Dimensions.** All of the specifics of rigging, like height, pitch, leverage, etc., are covered in the individual chapters of this manual. There you will find a little theory and a lot of the reality. By reading the chapters and the suggested books you should be able to get a basic idea of how a rower works with his or her equipment.

One last thing, there is not one "set-in-stone" theory of rowing. Most coaches and Riggers agree on the basics of what moves a rowing shell, but there are many different views on how it is best implemented. This is evident by all of the different rowing styles. As you become more involved in rowing you will probably even develop your own theory or style.

# Chapter Five: Rigging Safety

Since I first wrote this book, I've done many rigging clinics across the country. The topic of safety is one that I always bring up, and it tends to generate a very typical reaction—people get a glazed-over look and I can tell that they are "tuning out." This usually happens from folks who have never seen someone get seriously hurt while rowing or who themselves have never been hurt.

Let me be right up front with you here: A great many people think that rowing is a super-safe sport and that very few, if any, people get hurt while doing it. I'm here to tell you that it is not (super safe) and people do (get hurt). The same can also be said about rigging—many folks think that rigging is super safe. Well, I've got to tell you that it too is not (super safe) and people do get hurt (while rigging).

Okay, to be honest, there're not a lot of injuries in rowing and rigging (especially compared to contact sports) but there are more, probably many more, than most people know.

So with that thought in mind (that you *can* get hurt rigging and that people *do* get hurt while rowing), it is a really good investment of our time and energy to talk about **safety**. A good place to start is to pin down what exactly "safety" is. I put it in these terms: Safety is limiting the possibilities that something harmful will happen. That's it—rather simply put.

> Safety is simply limiting the possibilities that something harmful will happen.

Safety and "being safe" do not mean that you will never have an accident or an injury or a problem or a hassle or a bad experience. Those things can happen, and if you rig and row long enough they will most likely happen. But safety and being safe do mean that you are doing all you can do to limit the possibilities that something bad will happen.

Now that brings up a question which is darn difficult to answer: "What do you need to be safe while you're rigging?" Not only is this question tough to answer, but it's difficult to decide what you need to be safe while doing almost anything. The reason why is because safety is a **value judgment**—a judgment about what is an acceptable level of risk for *you*. This value judgment can be a downright difficult decision to make.

Cigarette smoking is a prime example of how difficult this decision is. Everyone knows how dangerous smoking is. Some folks decide to keep smoking because, to them, the pleasures outweigh the risks. Another example is seat belts. It's a fact, a well-known fact, that seat belts save lives. But many people still don't wear them because they have made a value judgment that the risk of not wearing a seat belt is acceptable to them.

What makes these value judgments difficult is that if you have never experienced the bad that can happen from a decision (lung cancer, car accident), then how can you be sure you are making the correct choice when it comes to safety? I wonder how many non-seat-belt wearers become seat-belt wearers after they have been in, or have seen, an accident? As Barry LePanter told us, "Good judgment comes from experience, and experience comes from bad judgment."

With that in mind, please follow along with what comes next—it could be important to your own health and well being, and that of other folks.

No glazed-over looks allowed.

## 5.1 Super Rigger

Let's try this—imagine yourself as a superhero. Let's call you Super Rigger (yeah, yeah, I know it sounds hockey, but humor me here). Your job, Super Rigger, is to do three things.

Your first order of business is to *reduce the incidences of injuries and accidents while someone is using rowing equipment.* You see, the world changes greatly once you push away from the dock, and rowers tend to be a very trusting group—trusting that nothing bad will happen and the gods of their rowing site will protect them. But things do happen, and you need to try to reduce how often those bad things occur.

When you rig, focus on rigging the equipment for efficiency and comfort for the rower, while at the same time look at the equipment from a safety perspective. Search out faulty equipment. When you find something that is broken, fix it or replace it immediately—and don't row it until it is fixed.

Although you don't have x-ray vision, like your cousin Superman, look at things extremely closely. Make educated guesses about the quality of the equipment. If a top stay is badly bent from a crab or is unusually corroded at the attachment point, then replace it—now. If the wheels on a seat assembly are brittle, worn or cracked, then change them—now.

Besides looking for bad equipment, be cautious when making adjustments. When you make changes, don't make radical ones to the equipment all at once; do it gradually. Rowers get used to the way a shell is rigged and when there are changes it usually takes a break-in period to adjust to those changes. If the equipment is changed dramatically then there is a good likelihood that folks are going to get hurt.

Your second order of business is *to protect the equipment itself.* You will be surprised, or maybe you won't, at how easily rowing equipment is damaged. Considering all the hazards your equipment goes through—practices, moving back and forth to the docks, transporting to races, novice rowers, First-Dimensional Riggers, storage—the equipment is actually pretty tough. But it does get damaged.

What you must do, Super Rigger, is to use your powers to protect the equipment from all of these dangers. This is easier said than done. Two of your superpowers that will help the most are **prevention** and a good **maintenance program**. Prevention, using your brain to think ahead to avoid problems, is critical to a Rigger.

For example, a crew is coming off the water from practice and they need to put their boat into slings for attention. The slings are of questionable quality. If you were to put the boat into the slings inside the boathouse it will be left there all day and will get shoved around as people move other boats. Think ahead to the worst case scenario—the slings collapse and your boat slams into the floor. As Super Rigger you can prevent this.

For instance, make alternative plans for rigging the boat, like putting it on a rack and rolling it into slings just before the next row. Or, fix the boat now when you know there will be people there to move it as soon as you are done. Prevention, prevention, prevention.

---

According to one insurance company, the two most common causes of damage to rowing shells are (a) falling off of racks, and (b) being damaged in transport.

---

Another power that you have and need to make use of is a maintenance program. This is the least used of all the Rigger's resources. Most people give their equipment a minuscule amount of attention and when it breaks down they usually get torqued out, act surprised, and get upset.

Why?

The stuff needs attention, it doesn't last forever, and it breaks. For some Riggers and rowers this is a very foreign concept.

Shells, oars, and the assorted equipment need a lot of tender loving care. A maintenance program is a fairly small investment of your time and it can reap you great rewards (see JOB 18.1, *Tune-Ups*, for a suggested program). Good maintenance will add to your superhero reputation and keep your equipment in motion. For more information on equipment maintenance, turn to Chapter Eighteen: *Keeping Your Equipment Alive.*

Your last but certainly not your least order of business is *to protect yourself.* There is absolutely no need for people to get hurt while rigging, yet they do. Again I need to ask,

Why?

The three most common ways Riggers get hurt are: (a) moving boats, (b) bashing themselves on a rigger, and (c) using tools. A quick talk about each method of destruction might be helpful. I'll keep the graphics to a minimum. I promise.

First, I truly think some folks believe they actually do possess superhuman strength the way they try to move shells in a boathouse. I have seen (and, okay, I admit I have done this) two people move a fully rigged eight from a rack onto slings. What a great way to rearrange your skeleton or the shell! Moving a boat can be hazardous; be careful. It takes two things to move a boat safely: brains and brawn. Both are needed. Get both and stay healthy. Forget one and something or someone is going to get trashed.

Second, a place that I constantly see people get dinged and dented while rigging is when something soft and organic (i.e., human body part) meets something hard and inorganic (i.e., a shell's rigger). This can be tough when the rigger is stationary and the human body part, like a head, is moving. (You stand up and bash into the rigger that is on the rack just above you.) However, this can be downright brutal and possibly even devastating when the rigger and the human body part are both moving—like when a shell is being carried to the dock and connects with an unaware spectator (can anyone say *Magazine Beach?*).

Third, I think that some people really believe that tools have brains of their own—and as soon as they pick one of them up the tool knows what it should or shouldn't do.

Tools are dangerous, even something as simple as a wrench. You need to be careful when using them. Ah, I see you are using your superpowers to detect a lecture ahead. Now you are catching on.

## 5.2 Being Safe with Tools

No one in their right mind wants to get hurt when using tools and certainly no one plans on it. But people do get hurt. I divide up the injuries that occur with tools into two categories: **accidents**, in which something totally unavoidable happens, and **screw-ups**, in which the operator did something dumb and avoidable.

As far as accidents go, you can't prevent all of them, but you certainly can cut down the risk of many of them happening. A simple step like keeping your tools in good shape, free of dirt and grease will help a lot. Dirty tools breed accidents. And damaged tools will only end up breaking, ruining the Work or hurting someone. Be smart: when using a hitting tool or power tool, wear safety goggles. When using a wrench, always pull it; never push it. This will save a lot of scraped knuckle skin. Don't hammer on a wrench to loosen a frozen bolt. See Chapter Sixteen for tips with fastener problems. When using pliers, watch out for your skin becoming pinched between the handles.

> Have you heard about the price of eyes? It is out of sight. Wear safety glasses!

As far as screw-ups are concerned, to help avoid them, be smart. Use each tool only for the job it was intended for. Don't use a holding tool as a turning tool. **DON'T**, I repeat **DON'T** use non-hitting tools as hitting tools. A locking pliers makes a lousy hammer, so do wrenches and screwdriver handles. Don't hold the Work in one hand while you use a screwdriver in the other. Too many people get holes in their hands this way. Use a vice.

Also, it's okay to use your screwdriver as a can-opener, chisel, paint stripper or crowbar. Okay that is if you don't mind breaking the driver, screwing up whatever you are fiddling with, and getting hurt.

One last item about tools. Tools are revenge oriented—in other words, if you mistreat a tool, it will, sooner or later, get back at you. I speak from experience.

The absolute best prevention for screw-ups is common sense. Without a doubt, common sense is one of the most important items in terms of safety that you can have around the boathouse. Yet, I've got to admit I really think that common sense is disappearing from the face of the earth just like Judge Crater did. And it seems that there are several reasons for its disappearance.

One of those reasons is pressure, especially *peer pressure*. Simple sayings like, "Ah, come on you can do it," "What's the matter with you? Everyone else is doing it," "Try it; just a little bit won't hurt," seem to be sucking the common sense right out of people.

Another type of pressure, *performance pressure*, also seems to be destroying any common sense it meets. This pressure can be devastating in our sports-oriented society, and it affects rowing just like any other sport.

All too frequently, rowers and coaches don't use their common sense because of pressure applied on them to perform (and most often this pressure is applied by no one else but themselves). For instance, the pressure to have fast crews lead some coaches to subject their teams to hazards that common sense would recommend against. Because of performance pressure of upcoming competitions, rowers have rowed in conditions, and with injuries, when common sense would dictate otherwise.

Another reason is *ego*. Rowing attracts people who often have high expectations for themselves, who are driven, and who like to achieve. Nothing wrong with that. However, sometimes this drive, this effort to please our inner-selves (our ego), can make us do things we know we shouldn't do—if we would only stop and use our common sense.

> Common sense could prevent a great many divorces, but, on the other hand, it could also prevent a great many marriages.
> —E. C. Mckenzie

## JOB 5.1: GETTING MORE COMMON SENSE.

**Problem:** You want to juice up your supply of common sense.

Right up front, let me tell you this: We all have common sense. Inside each and every normal brain there sits a whack of common sense. But some of us just don't use it. There are many reasons for this, some of which we just discussed above.

Before we go any further, it is important to note how common sense can help you rig better. You see, common sense is simply the knack to view things as they are and then to do things as they ought to be done.

That's it. Pure and simple.

When we use our common sense, we tend not to get overwhelmed by the effects of peer pressure, egos, and emotions. We act a little more logical in situations—rather Mr. Spock-like. This can help you rig better, especially during a pressure-ridden racing season.

If you have a hard time using your common sense, it is possible to improve. Here is a way you could try: Put yourself in a situation in which you need to make a decision. For example, zip on down to your favorite gas station and fill up the car with gas. Before you put the gas in the car, you have a decision to make: "How much gas do I buy?"

Pretty simple steps to answer that question: (a) your mind gathers information, (b) it weighs it, (c) it makes a decision, and then (d) common sense might speak up if it disagrees with your decision.

In this specific case, you gather the information about how much cash you have on you, or if you have a credit card, or if the station takes checks. Then your mind weighs the information, and makes a choice. Now, before the mind tells the body to pay the guy behind the counter, common sense speaks up if things are wrong. For example, if you've only got three dollars and you plan on putting five bucks into your car, chances are that your common sense will want to have a little talk with you. You should listen to it, and that's that.

But what goes on in today's world is that a lot of folks just don't listen to their common sense. So, often it talks, and folks just don't hear.

I know this sounds very simplistic, but if you want to have your common sense work for you, then you need to listen to it. Try to look at it this way—your common sense is pretty much similar to a muscle. Like any muscle in your body, it needs to be used to stay healthy and grow. If it's not used, it atrophies and becomes flabby, limp, and pretty much useless. Use your common sense, and it becomes stronger. Don't use it, and it becomes weak.

> Learn more about common sense at:
> <http://www.wikipedia.com/wiki/Common_sense>

## JOB 5.2: HOW SAFE SHOULD YOU BE?

**Problem:** You need an answer to that question.

Let me ask you this, "Can you be safer?" My answer: "Yup, you definitely can!"

Regardless of how safe you are now, you can be safer. However, there are two factors here that need to be considered: Do you want to be safer, and can you afford to be safer?

Remember, safety is nothing more than limiting the possibilities that something bad will happen. There comes a point where the amount of time, effort, and money you invest in limiting the possibilities can be too much. You should do all that you reasonably can do, but if safety ever becomes the main focus of your rigging, then you may be doing too much.

You see, safety should be a component of your rigging, not the focal point. Safety should not be invasive. If it becomes that way, then you diminish your experience, your rigging becomes less fun and less enjoyable, and you stand the chance of having a backlash against safety.

There is this invisible line that separates being safe and being unsafe—and that line is what is *reasonable*. Paying someone to follow you in a launch while you row in the pond in your front yard that is 200 meters long, 200 meters wide, and three feet deep could be considered unreasonable. At the same time, not rowing with someone following you on a river where the water is 45 degrees, choppy, filled with powerboats, and foggy could also be considered *unreasonable*. You have to decide what is reasonable and what is not. If that decision is difficult for you to make, and often it is, there is help (see Step 2).

Well then, I'm going to suggest two simple steps you can take to help determine if you need to be safer.

**Step 1. Track:** A rather simple way to decide if you need to be safer is to track injuries and accidents that occur as you row/rig. This is one thing that a great many sporting groups do to help make their sport safer.

So I'm going to prompt you to ask this question: "Are people getting hurt while rowing/rigging in my boat shack?" If the answer to this question is yes and injuries are happening, then you need look at the cause of each injury and determine if it was preventable. If it was preventable, then take immediate steps to prevent it from occurring again.

**Step 2. Follow The Rules:** A sign of a civilized society is that we hire or elect people to make some safety value judgments for us and to help us determine what is reasonable. For instance, many states have now passed laws making seat belts mandatory. They have seen what car accidents can do and have decided that you don't want to be in one without a seat belt on and that it is reasonable for you to wear one. The same is happening with cigarettes in the work place.

As far as rowing is concerned, there are some recommendations, requirements, and suggestions made by folks who have been around water, rowing, and rigging long enough to make some wise decisions that you might find helpful. Finding these folks may not be as simple as it sounds, but the time and effort to get the information they have to offer is usually very well spent. Here are a few resources you could turn to:

| Safety Concern | Resource |
| --- | --- |
| Using tools . . . | Manufacturer |
| Using rowing equipment . . . | Manufacturer |
| Safety at rowing events (practice, regattas) . . . | USRowing |
| Motor boat safety . . . | USRowing, US Coast Guard |
| Boathouse safety . . . | Your insurance agent |

# Chapter Six: Your Rigging Environment

Rowing is both an outdoor sport and a water sport. Two pretty darn-simple concepts. And just about every coach, rower, and Rigger that I've ever met is well-versed in both those notions. So why, why, why is it that so many of those same rowing folks forget these simple concepts when it comes time to actually row or rig?

I see coaches, athletes, and Riggers who just seem to ignore that we do our thing out-of-doors in what is commonly know as the environment—and they seem oblivious to the fact the environment plays a very big factor in what we do and how we do it. Let me clue you in on something—as a Rigger, the environment is going to have an enormous impact on what you do and if you want to rig well you will be best served to keep that in mind.

## 6.1 How the Environment Impacts Your Rigging

The environment—in essence your surroundings—will impact your rigging in basically three ways. To help you be an ace in your rigging, we should briefly discuss all three.

The first way the environment is going to play a factor is by the level of *PRE*. "What the heck is PRE?" you ask. Simply, PRE is short for *Positive Rigging Environment*, and it is absolutely essential to rigging well. The best way to explain what PRE is is to look at it in terms of minimums and maximums. The level of PRE is usually the greatest when:

- ➢ The <u>knowledge</u> you have about your rigging is at a maximum
- ➢ The <u>mental pressure</u> on your rigging is at a minimum.
- ➢ The <u>time</u> you have to do your rig is at a maximum.
- ➢ The <u>distractions</u> on you while you rig are at a minimum.
- ➢ The <u>tools</u> you have for your rigging are at a maximum.

Seems pretty simple, doesn't it?

Regardless of how simple it may seem, oftentimes the mental environment we surround ourselves with is far from conducive to good rigging. It boils down to this, when the mental environment is positive, when you have control of those five items (pressure, time, distractions, tools, knowledge) almost everyone seems to do a much better job of rigging. When the rigging environment is not positive—look out. JOB 6.1, coming up in a few pages, details how you increase your level of PRE.

The second way your rigging can be impacted by the environment is by the *SRE* (yes, I know . . . another acronym). SRE stands for *Safe Rigging Environment*. As we discussed in Chapter Five, safety should be a critical component of your rigging; however, often folks (especially Riggers) tend to forget about safety. I'm not going to belabor that point here, but I wanted to tell you that JOB 6.2 in this chapter details what you can do to maximize a safe rigging environment.

The third way the environment can impact your rigging is that it can produce factors that may well dictate changes in your rigging. One of those factors is wind. Wind generates waves, and waves and rowers—like oil and water—don't mix well.

Waves can demand that you adjust your rigging heights or do some creative rigging (which I call McGyver-rigging after that enormously famous TV show starring, who else, a guy named *McGyver*). For instance, at the 1995 World Championships in Tampiere, Finland, I spent hours McGyvering splashguards for many of the US teams boats because (in theory) it was supposed to be a very windy and very wavy race course In reality, it turned out to not be that windy and not that wavy.

Another factor is that water currents can affect your leverage, and in turn affect your rigging. Basically you can look at water currents like an invisible force that is pushing your rowing shell in a certain direction. This force might necessitate that you adjust your leverage.

Yet another factor is the quality of the water itself. Is it polluted, does it contain salt?

All of these items: wind, current, water quality are addressed in JOB 6.3.

## 6.2 How Your Rigging Impacts the Environment

It seems only far that if the environment can impact your rigging that your rigging should be able to impact the environment. Okay, fair is fair. Your rigging can impact the environment, especially in ecological ways.

We as people whose work, play, and dreams are often focused on water should take a leadership role in keeping our rivers and waterways clean. If we don't the day may soon come when the environment has been so used and abused that we can no longer row in it. To steal a phrase, we need to think globally and act locally (especially in the boathouse and on the river).

I'm a true believer of the "Seventh Generation" philosophy, that we should look at what we do by the impact it will have on those who follow us in seven generations. With that said, any choices you make in terms of disposal of equipment and materials (e.g., paper, cardboard, motor oil, paints, etc.) should be looked at in terms of how it is going to impact future rowers, coaches, and Riggers. In JOB 6.4, the last JOB in this chapter, I discuss some of the ways to lessen our impact upon the environment.

## JOB 6.1: CREATING A POSITIVE RIGGING ENVIRONMENT (PRE).

**Problems**: How do you create a positive rigging environment?

I'm sure you've heard the saying that "It is all between the ears." Well, that is exactly what I am talking about with PRE—how your rigging surroundings impact what is going on between your ears. I've found that when my rigging environment is positive, what goes on inside my head tends to be positive; and when that happens I do a much better job of rigging.

As we discussed previously, there are basically five items that will impact the level of PRE. I'm not going to go into a detailed discussion on each of those items, its not needed. But I did want to relate that I've often found that just telling folks that these items are going to impact their rigging is usually enough for them to control them and do a better job of rigging.

**Step 1. Max Your Knowledge:** Simply put, the more you know, the better you'll rig. I discussed in Chapter Three how to become more knowledgeable about rigging. So flip there if you are on a knowledge quest and you have some time to read.

However, if you are out of time and in one of those ugly, panicked situations, you know—*I've-got-to-get-this-done-right-now-and-I-don't-have-a-clue-what-the-heck-I'm-doing* types of situations—ask for help. Get on the phone, email, fax, whatever-the-heck-you-have, and communicate with a peer/mentor/manufacturer/rigging-czar. In my opinion, that is one cool thing about our sport. People are helping each other all the time. You go to a big championship regatta, an all-or-nothing-race, and you can find coaches from competing teams helping each other rigging shells and lending each other tools. A model for the rest of the world.

**Step 2. Minimize Your Mental Pressure:** When the pressure is great, such as I just described in the previous paragraph, rigging effectiveness usually goes downhill quickly. Some people love pressure situations, but most just wilt. The pressure gets in the way of thinking straight and being effective, and usually pressure rears it ugly head on race day.

So how do you control the pressure on your rigging? That depends on you and your situation, but you might find this one tip helpful—don't do any rigging on race day except for *maintenance-rigging* (turn to Chapter Two for info on the different types of rigging). Do your race-rigging days before your race, and don't do, and this is really hard (and important)—don't do race-rigging on race day at the race site.

Joe Murtaugh, who wrote the foreword of this book, has given his boatman, a big-hulking-biker-type-guy named Brad, standing orders. If Brad sees Joe going near one of his teams boats with a wrench on race day—in an attempt to do some race-rigging or peace-of-mind-rigging—Brad is to flatten him. Stand right on his chest till he whimpers.

Get the picture?

**Step 3. Maximize Your Time:** As you probably well know, dealing with time is not easy. It is something we all must do so wouldn't you tend to think we would be very good at it? Usually we aren't.

If you are going to be involved in rigging for the long haul, you will need two things to help you handle the time it takes—you're going to need organization, and you're going to need discipline.

Rigging demands that you structure your time. For instance, there are certain times of the day when it's best to rig because of the weather. There are certain times of the day when it's best to rig because of people's schedules. And there are certain times of the day when it's best to rig because of equipment usage, coaches' schedules, boat house hours, etc. To fit into these best times you will need to be organized.

Rigging also demands a large quantity of time, much more so than most people think. And it seems that the more you give it, the more it wants. If you plan on balancing your life with rigging and not alienating the rest of your world, you are going to need to be disciplined in the amount of time you are willing to give to rigging.

Maximize the time you have for rigging, and you'll do a better job. There is a direct correlation between the time you have to rig and the quality of job you'll do—mostly because it relates to the pressure on you. Over the years I've found that this ratio usually holds true:

> ➤ If you're a First-Dimensional Rigger: it will take three times as long to rig as you first estimate.

> ➤ If you're a Second-Dimensional Rigger, it will take you twice as long to rig as you first estimate.

> ➤ If you're a Third-Dimensional Rigger: you can pretty well estimate exactly how long your rigging job will take.

**Step 4. Minimize The Distractions:** Distractions, distractions, distractions. Our world is full of distractions. And if you are not careful they will gobble up your time, and quickly redirect your focus from what you are doing. Here is a solid rule of thumb:

*The more important the rigging, the more interruptions you'll get.*

Do your best to organize your work space so you can putter along with a minimum of distractions and hassles. To reduce your distractions find some way to get peace and solitude so you can concentrate. For instance unplug the phone, rent a junk-yard dog, eat onions, play *Oxford Blues*. Do what you've got to do to focus. One friend of mine has a motel's "Do Not Disturb" sign she hangs on the bow ball so her rowers know not to bug her until she's done.

**Step 5. Maximize Your Tools:** Lack of tools is one sure way to bring a rigging job to a dead-stop. In fact, I've seen the final event of a championship regatta held up for over an hour as a coach tried to replace a broken skeg on his boat, but couldn't get it done because of lack of the right tools.

Before you go diving into a rigging job, take a couple of minutes and get everything ready. Find your tools (JOBs 3.1–3.3), set the equipment up (JOB 7.3, *Preparing To Rig*), and sling your shell (JOB 7.4, *Slinging A Boat*). If you think that you are lacking a tool to do the job correctly, get it. There are times when it is okay to beg and to borrow, but not to steal.

## JOB 6.2: CREATING A SAFE RIGGING ENVIRONMENT (SRE).

**Problem:** You want to reduce the chances of you, someone else, or your equipment getting hurt while rigging.

**Needed**: Your eyes, ears, and that special thing between your ears known as the *gray matter*.

Okay, in the previous chapter we just spent a fair amount of time discussing safety, getting hurt while using tools, and the importance of using common sense. There is another factor we should discuss and that is your rigging environment. It can play a significant factor in how "healthy" your rigging is. There are several specific items worth chatting about.

**Lighting**. Good lighting can make the difference between rigging well and rigging poorly; between spending an hour looking for a washer that you dropped and finding it in a second; between redoing your work because the wrong-rigger-ended-up-at-the-wrong-seat and getting your work done quickly. The definition of good lighting is varied, but I'll put it in these terms, "If it is light enough for me to see an ant on my shoe, then it should be light enough for me to rig."

If you are constantly rigging in poor light, go to the hardware store, get one of those big mama lantern (ignore the little flashlights that run on two "D" cells—they won't last long) and fire it up. Or find another solution that is more solid, like a long extension cord and a trouble light. Sometimes you might find yourself with a need to be a little more creative in your lighting—like rigging a boat for an event at a midnight regatta (you know, the race that's been postponed for about eight hours because no one in the world could get the novice eights lined up in that fifty-mile-an-hour wind).

This happened to us and we just brought over a few cars and we did a little "headlight rigging." A hint here—just make sure the cars are in *Park* with the parking brakes on so the Ford doesn't meet the Vespoli. (I won't into details why, just trust me on this one.)

**Ventilation**. Fresh, clean air is important to our health, you know that. And rigging usually is done in places with lots of clean air. Usually. However, sometimes we need to do rigging that requires us to muck up the air, and that can cause problems. Specifically I'm talking about making repairs using chemicals like epoxy. Be careful, epoxy and solvents can be very toxic to the body. Read all directions. Open doors and windows and get a lot of air flowing. This is especially important when dealing with gas for launches.

**Wind**. Once you venture outside of the warm, snuggly place we call the boathouse things change quickly. When rigging outside, you are at the mercy of Mother Nature, and let me tell you that old Mom Nature can change a peaceful rigging experience into a hellish rigging nightmare quicker than Steve Irwin (of Crock Hunter fame) can say, "Danger, Danger, Danger."

It happened to me. I will spare you the gory details, but just let me say that at the beginning of the rigging session I had an hour to get a four and a single "fine-tuned" for a race. Seconds later I had a four that was broken in half and a single that was absolutely obliterated. Smashed, crushed, destroyed. No exaggeration, two boats taken out in less time than it takes you to read this. A lot of heartache spread all around.

Things like the gory-story I just mentioned can happen quickly when you rig outside and the main culprit is the wind. Set an eight seats-up in slings and walk away, and odds are pretty darn good some hurricane is going to come along and do its best to knock it over.

When boats are seats-up they really want to be seats-down, they are more comfortable that way. So, if you need to leave a boat seats-up in slings outside—strap it down. Take two straps, put one over the bow and one over the stern. Connect them in such a manner that the boat doesn't rock in the slings. It is the rocking motion you are worried about, when they rock—they can flip. Strap it, grab a rigger, and try to rock it. Make sure it is stable, and then keep a darn close eye on it. The two minutes it takes to strap the boat can save hours and hours of repairs.

**Some hate it hot.** Another culprit to watch out for when rigging outside is the temperature. Cold is not too much of a worry. Wear gloves when it is gets frosty and don't stick your tongue to a rigger when it is below freezing and you should be cold-okay. Hot is a different story.

You need to be hot-aware. If you're into rowing you are probably knowledgeable about the dangers of heat and sun on folks, so no lecture here on that. But did you know that rowing equipment does not really like the heat and lots of sun?

Over the years I've had a couple of interesting problems from heat/intense sun. One was when I got a pretty good sized second degree burn on my hand when I put it on top of a Resolute eight (black hulled) that had been outside in the hot summer sun at the 1996 Olympics. The other was when we had an eight actually "melt" in slings from the sun (that was an older eight, not much of a worry now with the newer boats). So, be cautious about heat and rowing equipment.

**Rain**. When it rains, it pours—pours right into a boat that is seats up, that is. One gallon of water weighs about eight pounds. Let a shell get a few gallons in it and chances are pretty darn good that your slings aren't going to appreciate it. I've seen it happen—boats left seats-up in the rain, and about 30 minutes later one coach had two broken eights.

**Lightning**. Not much doubt about it—lightning is a killer. It kills approximately 150 people per year in the United States. The bottom line is this, if you are caught in a lightning storm, get out of the storm quickly. If you are rigging outside, get inside. If you are on the water, get off the water, pronto! If a crew cannot make it to the docks, get them to shore and get them off the water anywhere you can. A broken fin, dented hull, scraped paint is a small price to pay for a crew's safety.

Following are a few questions to ask yourself about your rigging environment to see how safe it is:

- ✓ Is the area free of obstacles (e.g., holes, things to hit your head on)?
- ✓ Is the area well lit?
- ✓ Will rain/lightning be a factor in your rigging?
- ✓ Is/are the boat(s) strapped down?
- ✓ Is a first aid kit handy?
- ✓ Will heat/intense sun be a factor?
- ✓ Are the slings of good quality?
- ✓ Is the area well ventilated?

## JOB 6.3 ASSESSING THE IMPACT OF THE ENVIRONMENT ON YOUR RIGGING.

**Problem:** You want to know how the environment is going to impact your rigging.

**Needed:** Same as in the previous JOB: your eyes, ears, and that special thing between your ears known as your brain.

Let me start by saying this, the environment is going to have an impact on how you rig your equipment. It may well influence how you set up a few adjustments on your boat, such as your height or the leverage (spread, inboard). And it may require you to do take some other steps.

Now that I've said that, let me give you the bottom line—if you are a First or Second-Dimensional Rigger, don't worry about this impact. Just stay to the recommendations I make in JOBs 15.1 or 15.2, and you will be just fine. If you are a third dimensional Rigger, read on.

For you Third-Dimensionals, you need to know that the environment is going to have an important impact, and it is one that you should not ignore.

For example, if the place you row is wavy, then that will have an impact on your heights (you will probably have to raise them). If the place you row has a strong, continuous current you may (*may*, not *will*) want to adjust your leverage. I discuss both those items later in the chapters specific to those adjustments.

But you also need to take other things into consideration. For instance, what is the water quality like where you usually row? Is it brackish (has salt in the water)? Is it polluted? Those things may require you to take steps to care for your equipment in different ways. Is equipment stored outside in the direct sun? Again, this means steps you should take to help the equipment.

So, how do you tell if you should make rigging changes due to the environment? One of the best ways is to go for a walk. Yup, get up and go. Put shoes on, get off the chair and go cruising. Best destination, head for the dock (just keep in mind, if it is a short dock don't go for a long walk).

What you are mostly interested in is the prevalent conditions. If the water is only choppy once a month, or there is current only for two days every Fall when they drain the damn upriver, then no worries. You want to know what are the customary conditions. For example, if your team only races once in salty water, that may require only a good washing after the race. However, if you constantly row on salty water, then you need to do things differently for the sake of your stuff. Another example is storing your equipment outside. If it only happens once-in-a-great-while, no worries. If it is a daily occurrence, then action is needed.

So take a walk and make a list. Once you've got items written down then turn to the specific chapters that come later in this book for steps you might need to take. To learn more about the maintenance aspect of things turn to Chapter Eighteen, *Keeping Your Equipment Alive*.

# JOB 6.4 BEING AN ECO-RIGGER.

**Problem:** How to lessen your negative impact on the environment.

An **Eco-Rigger** is someone who takes care to lessen his or her negative impact on the environment. Being an Eco-Rigger can be simple, yet at the same time it can be difficult. Not as confusing as it may sound—let me explain.

It can be simple in the aspect that you don't need to take drastic measures or spend money to make a significant difference in your impact on the environment. And often the effort that needs to be spent to make a difference can be small. The difficult part comes because you may be bucking habits or oftentimes you are going against the status quo.

For what it is worth, in my opinion the world gets polluted due to three reasons. First, people think that they are saving a buck. Second, people think they are saving time. Third, people want to do things easier. I see it all the time, "Hey man . . .it's too much of a hassle to take this old motor oil to the recycle center, I'm just going to pour it right here onto the ground."

Things have gotten somewhat better in the environment since the first edition of this book, but not good enough. And the word from many of the experts is that unless we get it together soon (like now!) the degrading of the environment is going to continue to accelerate. So what can you as one person do? Here are two simple things that will have a big impact.

**Step 1. Take Ownership:** I don't know about you but I get overwhelmed when I look at the big picture of the environment and what is going on. What helps me keep things in perspective is to look at the smaller picture. I just focus on my surroundings, and then I take ownership of the impact I have on my immediate area.

Simply enough, I take responsibility for the environment around my office, boathouse, race site, and home. From there I focus on lessening my impact and my team's impact.

For example, in the boathouse we recycle our old batteries from megaphones and flashlights, or when we can we use rechargeable. We strive to make sure trash is recycled and hazardous waste and toxins are disposed of properly—not poured directly into places that drain into waterways. We recycle all of our cardboard (when a new set of oars comes, there is a lot that gets recycled). We reuse as much of our fasteners and hardware as possible. We try to be extremely careful of the damage that our launches propeller, fuel, and wake can do. And we make efforts to buy from environmental-conscious manufacturers. When we travel with the team to away races, we bring trash bags for our recyclables, and we bring them home to be recycled.

These are simple steps, but they quickly add up in their impact. And I've noticed over the years that the athletes involved in our program not only learn from our efforts but they often come up with some great new suggestions and ideas.

**Step 2. Take Action:** Ever thought of doing an environmental project? A bunch of rowers/coaches/Riggers are. Here is one example, relayed by Liza Dickson, facilities director at Miami Beach Rowing Club.

> "Miami Beach Rowing Club and the University of Miami team up once a year to clean up about three miles of Indian Creek. Since our creek is in the city, it fills up with debris. The week before our head race we do a six hour clean-up with all of our rowers—about 80 university rowers, 30 master rowers, and 20 juniors.
>
> We divide all of the rowers up into 'teams' with group leaders and send everyone to a specific area either on the water or on land. We have pulled out furniture, parts of docks, boats etc. We also keep a couple of teams at the boathouse so that it gets cleaned up as well. We get support from the county—they provide us with nets, gloves, and plenty of trash bags. Then we call the city and they come and pick up all of the trash for us.
>
> At the end of the day, we order out for pizza and feed all of our hard workers. It's usually a fun day, it helps everyone to get to know each other better, builds a spirit of cooperation between the club and the university and helps our boathouse and waterway

look beautiful for our Head of the Indian Creek Regatta the next weekend."

Efforts like this (and there are many more that go on around the country each year such as a great one at Three Rivers) are great—and critical.

Why?

Face it, we are an outdoor sport. We are on the water, we are in the water, and the water is often on, and sometimes in, us. Also part of the beauty of rowing is being out in the environment. I don't know about you, but rowing along and seeing five empty beer cans go floating by ain't my definition of beauty.

# SECTION TWO
# RIGGING SPECIFICS

# Chapter Seven: The First Steps Of Rigging

So here we are, all ready to start. As you know, all journeys begin with the first steps, and that is exactly what this chapter is all about—showing you the first steps to take to become a competent, comfortable, able Rigger.

This chapter will introduce you to many new items, terms, and numbers. Don't let any of it throw you for a loop—they're not too complicated, and any math that is needed is easy. We also tackle some of the first JOBs you'll need to do as a Rigger. Before we get going, there are a couple of things we must discuss.

## 7.1 Rigging Procedure

When you rig you, will be best served if there is a method to your madness. I have a plan I follow when I rig and it has helped me keep my sanity when everything around me has gone nutty. The first step is to . . .

**Determine and identify problems.** Before you lay a single tool upon your equipment, there should be a darn good reason for it. Change, just for the sake of change, is a waste of time. You should be trying to accomplish something when you make adjustments, whether it is the correction of a diagnosed problem, routine maintenance, or experimentation. Remember these oh-so-profound words, "Don't fix it if it ain't broke." So determine that there is a problem or a reason to rig (see JOB 7.3, *Preparing to Rig*) and then . . .

**Get tools, information, and equipment needed.** The next step is to gather the necessary equipment. This will probably consist of tools (see JOB 3.2), information—specifically your rigging numbers (see JOBs 15.1–15.4) and your equipment specifics (see JOB 7.2). This will also include any other items you may need, such as a helping hand, java, tunes, etc. Once you have this stuff, it is time to . . .

**Prepare yourself, the rowing equipment, and your tools.** Make sure your environment is a safe and positive one in which to rig. Do you have enough time to do a good job? Are your surroundings safe? Are the shell, oars, etc., prepared to be worked on? See JOBs 6.1 and 6.2. If everything is all set, then you're cruising, and it's time to . . .

**Adjust the mechanics.** This is the meat of the beast. Whether you are doing one or two adjustments or a complete rigging JOB (adjusting all of the mechanics at once) the order in which I recommend you make your adjustments is as follows:

| | |
|---|---|
| 1. Set the Leverage | See Chapter 9 |
| 2. Set the Pitch | See Chapter 10 |
| 3. Set the Height | See Chapter 11 |
| 4. Adjust the Arcs | See Chapter 12 |
| 5. Set the Minor Adjustments | See Chapter 13 |

This is only a suggested order. Make your adjustments in any order you want; however, I've found this order works well and causes me minimal hassles, especially with the new Euro-style riggers. One thing to grasp when making adjustments is that a change in one area might affect another area. For example, on older Vespoli riggers, if you change the height of the oarlock (without removing the top stay) the pitch of the oarlock will also be affected.

Go through and make your adjustments and then record them for future reference. (See JOB 15.7 concerning recording your numbers and changes.) Afterwards, it's off to a step most people ignore . . .

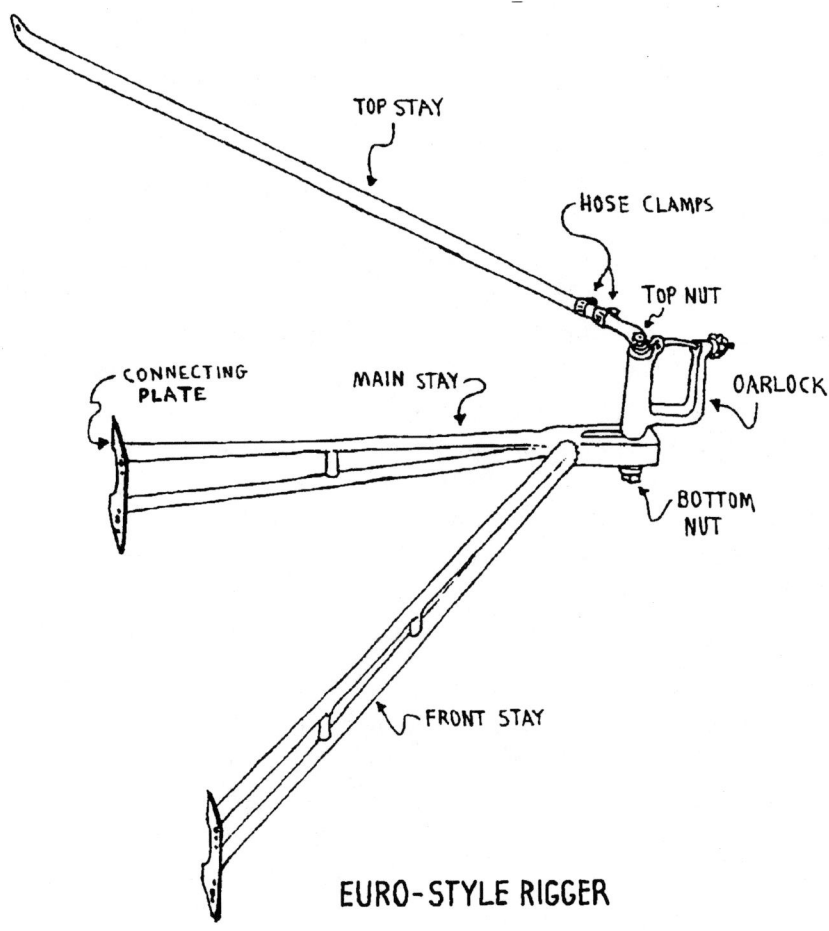

TOP STAY

HOSE CLAMPS

TOP NUT

CONNECTING PLATE

MAIN STAY

OARLOCK

BOTTOM NUT

FRONT STAY

**EURO-STYLE RIGGER**

**Check your work.** You've done your adjustments and now your work is done, right? Not quite yet. Remember how your teachers always stressed to check your work before you passed it in? In rigging, you would be well advised to follow that lesson.

Here is an example: At an international race, the U.S. team I was working with lent a four to the Romanian women's team. Since the Romanians had never rigged that make of shell, I went with them to lend a hand and did most of the rigging of the boat. Things went fairly smoothly and it was just about launch time for the qualifying heats. I wanted to go through the boat to double-check my work, since it had been done fairly quickly. But the Romanian head coach wanted nothing of it and would not let me get near the riggers.

We stood there arguing back and forth in English and Romanian, which must have been entertaining, since I don't speak a speck of Romanian and he did not speak any English. Finally, he threw his hands up in disgust. I thought he mumbled something about "pushy Americans" and then he let me proceed. It turned out that one of the nylon rigger clamps had not been tightened. If they had attempted to row the rigger the way it was, the oarlock pin would have slipped, and there would have been several mad Romanian rowers with revenge on their minds. Instead, they won their heat and went on to win the gold medal. Ahhhaa . . . pushy Americans indeed.

So after you check your work, which I hope you are now motivated to do, go . . .

**Row the boat.** Put the boat in the water and see the results of your work. If you were rigging to correct a problem, hopefully it's gone. If it was maintenance rigging you should feel good knowing your boat will last longer and it likes you better for the tender loving care you are giving it. And if you were doing peace-of-mind rigging hopefully you have found it. And lastly . . .

**Clean up.** Put away your tools, equipment, and toys. You'll be a better Rigger if your work area is organized and tidy. Also, be careful about what you throw away. Recycle and reuse whatever you can.

Remember to be cool, kind, and flexible and you'll be on your way to rigging greatness in no time. As a review, here are the seven steps we just discussed:

---

### Procedure for rigging

1. Determine that you need to rig.

2. Get tools and equipment, find numbers and information.

3. Prepare area, yourself and equipment.

4. Adjust the mechanics and record changes.

5. Check your work.

6. Row and readjust if needed.

7. Clean up your mess.

---

Now that you've some idea of what lies ahead, here are a few thoughts to help you down the path:

## RIGGING COMMON SENSE

✓ Don't blame the rigging for all of your problems. It is not as big of a culprit as you might think.

✓ Double-check your work and record your dimensions every time you rig. The few minutes this takes could save you hours of hassles later on.

✓ Plan on making mistakes. You're going to make mistakes, you're supposed to make mistakes, you WILL make mistakes! It's going to happen, so plan on it—don't let it bug you. If you're not making mistakes, you are not learning!

✓ When you make a mistake, don't get mad, swear a lot, and throw a wrench. If you work with someone who, when they make a mistake, gets mad, swears, and throws wrenches, remember to duck.

✓ Don't bash the messenger when a rower comes to tell you about a rigging problem.

✓ Be respectful of your equipment. Treat it like you would a good friend. And like good friends, equipment has a memory. Mistreat it and it will get revenge. Count on it!

✓ Be consistent in your work. Always take measurements from the same place, and when you get information from other sources, know where the measurements were taken from.

✓ Never be afraid to ask for help, advice, or sympathy. It's usually there if you ask for it.

✓ If you notice faults not previously seen in your rower's technique, check your rigging . . . that may or may not be the problem.

✓ To reduce injuries, make rigging changes gradually. Usually, make no leverage changes greater than 0.5 to 1.0 cm at a time.

## 7.2 Rigging Numbers

As I have mentioned, there are numbers—a lot of them—involved in rigging. Specifically, there are two types of numbers. **Equipment measurements** are those numbers (dimensions) concerning your equipment and are part of the equipment's design—for example, the length of the shell. For the most part, these measurements are nonadjustable.

**Rigging measurements** are those dimensions you use for the various parts of your rowing equipment. They are usually adjustable. Following is a brief description of all of the measurements I've ever encountered in rigging, some of which you'll use a lot, some of which you may never see.

> Don't let the terms "numbers," "measurements," or "dimensions" (with a small "d") confuse you. As far as we are concerned they are interchangeable.

Before you proceed, I must offer a word of caution: Don't get overwhelmed. Depending on your Dimension of Knowledge, some of these numbers are critical, some are important, and some you don't need to worry about in the least. We will sort all that out in the following chapters.

## 7.3 Rigging Numbers of the Foot Stretcher

The foot stretcher is one of the few areas a rower connects with the shell, and this makes it a critical piece of equipment. If the settings for the foot stretcher are not correct then the rower will not be comfortable. Also, if the adjustments are off then the athlete's feet and lower legs will not be in position to be efficient. The rigging numbers you may run into are:

- ❖ **Foot stretcher angle:** this is the slant of the foot stretchers toward the stern; normal range is 38 to 42 degrees.

- ❖ **Foot stretcher location:** not quite so obvious. This is where the foot stretchers go in respect to the pin, and this is an extremely critical adjustment.

❖ **Heel cup height:** height of sneaker heel cup measured from the top of the seat, normal range is 14 to 20 cm.

❖ **Opening angle:** angle the sneakers turn from each other, normal range is 25 degrees.

❖ **Sneaker size:** pretty obvious.

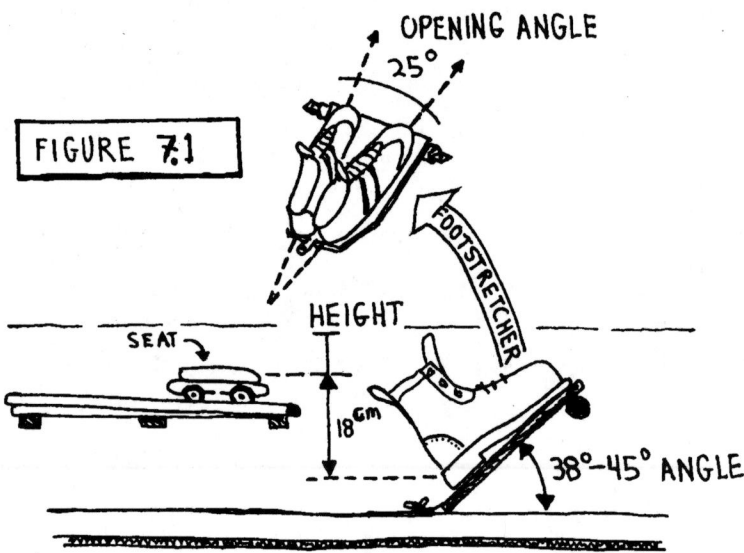

## 7.4 Rigging Numbers of the Oar

Everything in this sport hinges on the oars. The measurements are vital, and there are several you need to be concerned with.

❖ **Blade surface area:** this is the area of the blade, and it varies considerably.

❖ **Deflection:** this is the flexibility of an oar under pressure; normal range is 5 to 8 cm.

❖ **Handle size:** one of the options you'll now be offered when you purchase oars is the diameter of the handle. They usually range from small to extra-large. This is an important number, especially for rowers with smaller hands.

❖ **Inboard:** the length of the oar shaft from the butt of the oar handle to the water side of the button; normal ranges are from 111 to 118 cm.

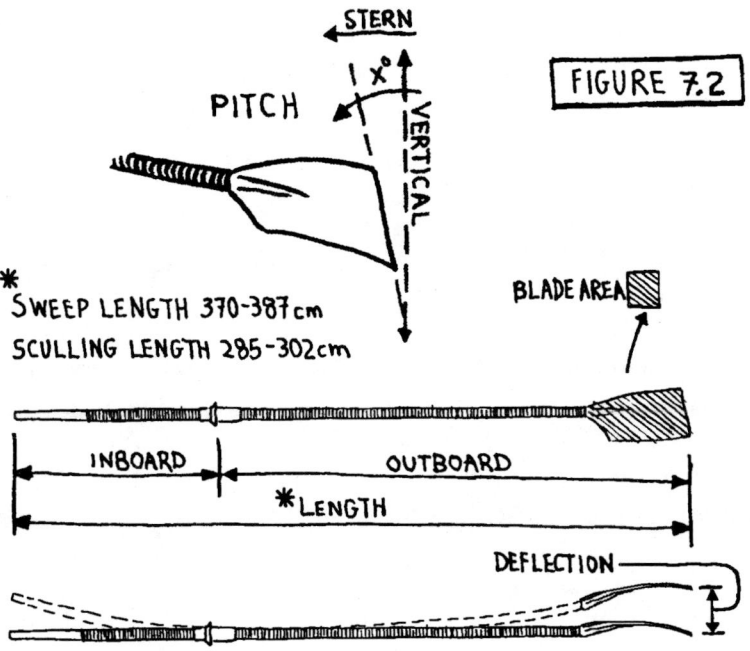

❖ **Length:** total length of oar from butt to blade tip. Normal sweep oars range from 363 cm to 380 cm, and normal sculling oars range from 280 cm to 300 cm. Shorter oars seem to becoming more common as blade shapes change.

❖ **Oar balance point:** center of gravity of oar, which is important since the boat's balance can be upset if the balance point is not identical on both sides of shell.

❖ **Outboard:** the distance from the oar's button to the blade tip.

❖ **Pitch:** sternward inclination of the oar during the drive phase. In other words, the tilt of the oar when it is vertical in the $H_2O$. Positive pitch is toward the stern; negative pitch is toward the bow.

❖ **Position number:** this is the number or letter that identifies where the oar goes on the shell.

❖ **Serial number:** sets of oars are usually identified by the manufacturer with serial numbers. Most are engraved into the shaft of the oar. The serial number can be very helpful to keep sets together and in locating replacement oars if one were to break.

## 7.5 Rigging Numbers of the Rigger

The rigger connects the oar to the boat. Measurements here are critical and affect the power applied to the oar and greatly impact the comfort and efficiency of the rower. The measurements you may see are:

❖ **Arc:** the distance an oar moves; two types: inside and outside, measured in degrees; normal range is 70 to 85 degrees.

❖ **Catch angle:** when the oar is at the catch, this is the oar's angle from a line perpendicular to the shell. Normal range is from 42 to 56 degrees.

❖ **Catch length:** make a line perpendicular to the shell from the pin. From there, the distance to the butt of the oar handle when it is at the catch is the catch length. Normal range is from 80 to 96 cm.

❖ **Finish angle:** the same as catch angle, only measured when the oar is at the finish.

❖ **Finish length:** the same as catch length, only measured when the oar is at the finish.

❖ **Height:** here, we are talking about the distance from the bottom of the oarlock sill (called the horizontal flat) to the top of the water's surface. Normal range is 24 cm from the water or 14 to 18 cm from the seat top.

❖ **Lateral pitch:** the angle of the oarlock away from vertical, usually 1 to 2 degrees.

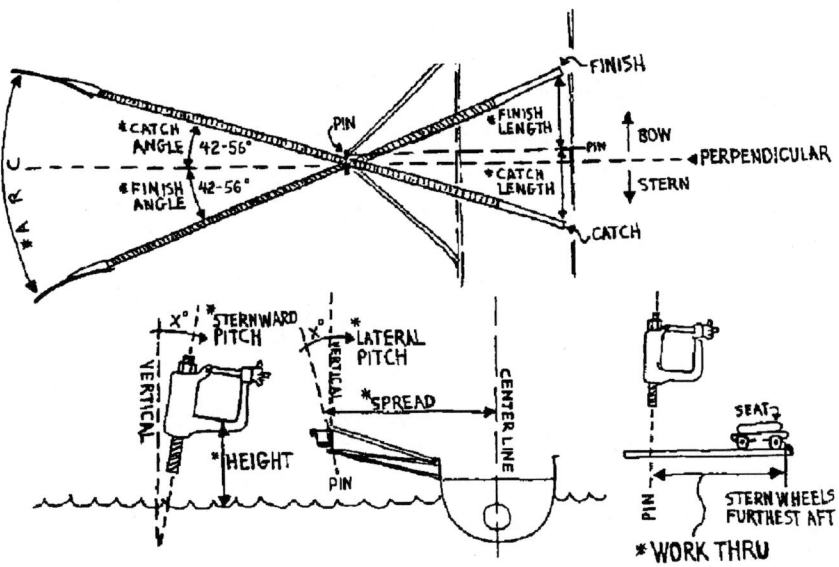

❖ **Leverage:** a balance between the resistance a rower feels (load) on the oar and the efficiency of the rigging.

❖ **Seat position:** each seat in a shell usually has a specific rigger that fits it exactly. Putting the wrong rigger on the wrong seat can be trouble. Most riggers are stamped where they should fit.

❖ **Span:** the distance from the center of one pin to the center of the other. Used only in sculling.

❖ **Spread:** the distance from the center of the shell to the center of the pin. Spread can be used in both sweep and sculling. Normal range is 80 to 85 cm.

❖ **Sternward pitch:** angle of the oarlock away from the vertical, usually 4 to 8 degrees towards the stern.

❖ **Work-thru the pin:** distance from a perpendicular line through the center of the pin to a perpendicular across the front-stops.

# 7.6 Rigging Numbers of the Shell

Your shell is your chariot, and here are the measurements describing your chariot, oh, great Caesar . . .

❖ **Beam:** the width of the shell at its widest point.

❖ **Centerline of shell:** an imaginary line drawn lengthwise that splits the shell in two. Used to determine the spread.

❖ **Depth:** vertical distance at the deepest part of shell from the top of gunwale to the bottom of shell.

❖ **Designed waterline:** planned distance of how deep the boat will sit in the water.

❖ **Draft:** the distance from the designed water line to the shell's bottom.

❖ **Freeboard:** distance from top of gunwale to water's surface.

❖ **Girth:** distance at widest part of shell. Measured from the top of one gunwale, around outside of hull, to the top of the other gunwale.

❖ **Oarlock perpendicular:** this is an imaginary line that extends from the oarlock pin perpendicularly into the boat and intersects the centerline; extremely important when talking about arc and work-thru the pin.

❖ **Size of shell:** the weight category of the shell.

❖ **Skeg and rudder size:** some manufacturers offer skegs and rudders in different sizes. This can affect performance and definitely affects drafts.

❖ **Track length:** the length of the tracks on which the seat assembly moves.

❖ **Weight of shell:** how much the shell weighs, when fully rigged.

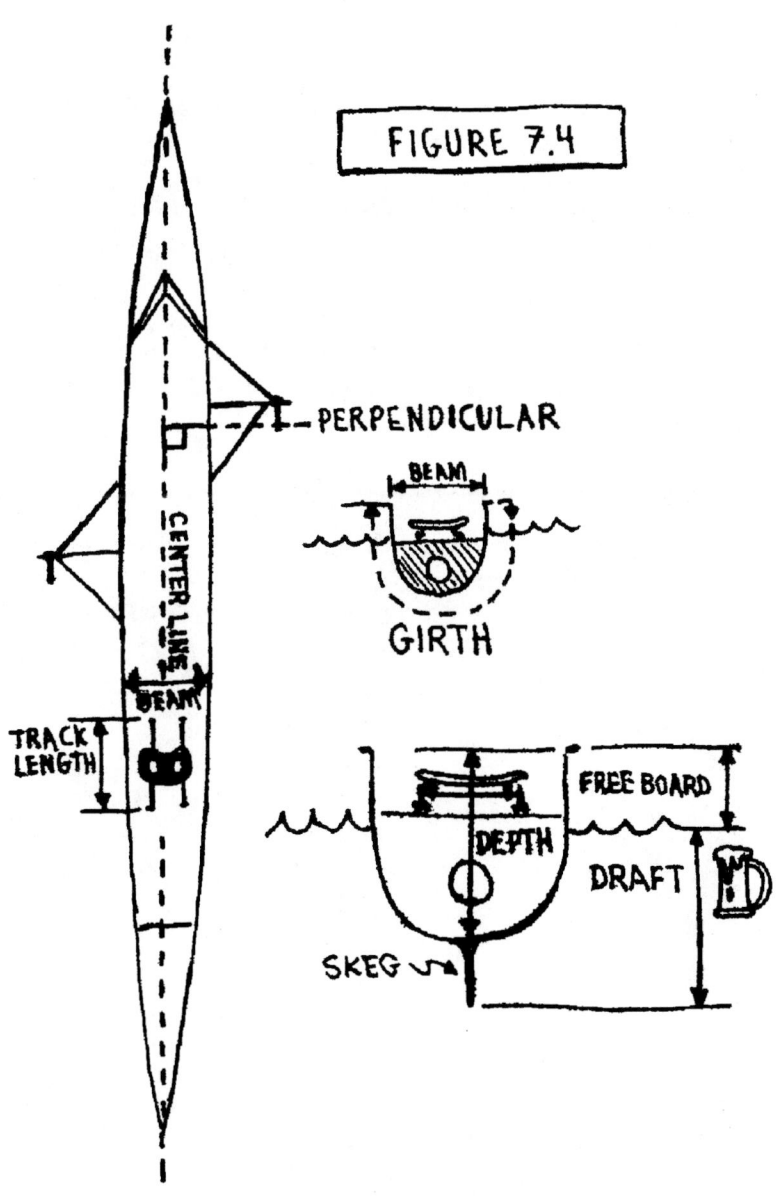

FIGURE 7.4

## 7.7 Miscellaneous Numbers

There are a few other numbers that are important.

- ❖ **Crew's average weight** is critical to determining the height adjustment and how comfortable the rower(s) is/are.

- ❖ **Gender** of the crew is important, since women will be rigged differently from men.

- ❖ **Length of race:** you should have different leverage numbers for different lengths of races.

- ❖ **Prevalent environmental conditions:** the conditions you row in will make a difference in the numbers you pick, especially in leverage and height.

- ❖ **Rower's skill level:** the closer a rower gets to one million strokes, the better (supposedly) he or she is. Knowing this can affect how you select such other numbers as leverage pitch.

Well . . . there you have it: over forty different rigging numbers.

# JOB 7.1: DETERMINING THAT YOU NEED TO RIG.

**Problem:** You're not quite sure if you need to rig your equipment.

**Needed:** Your body, brain, and possibly a stopwatch.

Knowing when to rig your shell should be a kind of sensual experience. By this I mean use your senses to help figure out when to pick up your tools and get busy. You should be using your sight, hearing, touch, smell, and memory to identify any problems.

If you are coaching a crew, *look* at them for problems. Do you *see* washing out, oars hitting the water, over-compression, different catch angles, feathering under water, crabs, and a myriad of other technical problems? In other words, does the rowing look bad? If so, then it might be a good time to check the shell.

> **A word of caution**: If a rower has had good rowing technique and it has suddenly gone bad, it may be due to the rigging. If the rower has never been able to row well, it's probably not due to the rigging.

If things move too fast for you at practice to notice any problems, use a video with a good slow-motion control. When the boat is in the slings look at the riggers. Pull out your tape measure and see if the dimensions are what they are supposed to be. Are the back stays bent? (A sign of crabs.) Eyeball the oarlocks. Do they look worn, deformed, out of kilter? When all the oars are in the rack, look at the buttons. Are they all the same?

Can you *hear* any problems? If you're in a launch you may find it rewarding to stop your motor, sit quietly, and just *listen* as the shell rows by. Notice any clicking, clanking, grating, banging? How about any sounds out of the ordinary? Heard any boats hit riggers in the boathouse? Also, listen to your athletes. Ask them for input on how the rigging feels. The rowers can give some interesting, and important, feedback.

Can you *feel* any problems? We had one guy at practice who was always complaining about the pitch on his oarlock no matter how many times it got adjusted. After several days of listening to his grumblings the coach stopped practice, motored up next to our boat, put the rower into his launch, got into the shell, and then rowed with us for about five minutes. The outcome was that the rigger was indeed off, the coach corrected it, and the rower went on to complain about other things.

Can you *sniff* out any problems? Don't actually use your nose, especially around all those old sneakers, but can you play detective and detect rigging problems? For example, you are doing timed, full pressure, 1000-meter pieces on a windy day. If the times into a head wind are the same as those with a tail wind then there is possibly something funky going on. It might be the rigging, but then again, it might not.

Can you *remember* the last time you rigged your equipment? Like most people, you probably have a lot on your mind, but somewhere in that memory bank of yours should be stored the last time you made adjustments. How long has it been? I usually check the boats for my experienced rowers every two weeks and the ones for beginners every one to two weeks.

So what do you do if while using your senses you notice a fault? You throw the boat in slings and tear apart your rigging, right? Maybe yes, maybe no. When a problem is detected, like a boat is slow, team morale is down, the stock market is crashing, most folks blame the rigging first. But remember, *there are four other things that are more important to boat speed than rigging* (see Chapter Two). So, keep an eye on your rigging, but look more closely at your rowers, training, technique, and equipment. I would suspect them first before I go blowing apart the rigging.

# JOB 7.2: DETERMINING YOUR EQUIPMENT SPECIFICS

**Problem:** There are a couple of things you need to know about your equipment so you can find your rigging numbers.

**Needed:** Tape measure, pencil and rigging card, friend.

In the measurements section of this chapter, we described all of the dimensions of your rowing equipment. Of these, there are certain dimensions you must know to help you find your rigging numbers. If you record this information you'll only have to do this JOB once.

### Shell

**Category of shell:** As we mentioned before in JOB 7.2 you need to know the category of your shell. There are five categories of sweep rowing shells in use today, and they are classified by the numbers of rowers in the boat. They range from two to nine rowers. Specifically, the designations of <u>sweep</u> boats are:

> pair without coxswain, a.k.a. straight pair (2–)
> pair with coxswain, a.k.a. pair-with (2+)
> four without coxswain, a.k.a. straight four (4–)
> four with coxswain, a.k.a. four-with (4+)
> eight with coxswain, which, surprisingly, is called an eight (8)

A popular boat in the late nineteenth century which is no longer rowed today was the six-without-coxswain.

There are basically five categories of <u>sculling</u> shells you will run into:

> recreational single, a.k.a. rec. single (rec. 1X)
> single scull, a.k.a. single (1X)
> double scull, a.k.a. double (2X)
> quadruple scull, a.k.a. quad (4X)
> octet, a.k.a. octuple (8X)

It's a cinch to determine what category of *sweep* shell you are dealing with. Just count the number of riggers on the boat and this will tell you what you've got. For *sculling* boats just count the riggers and divide by two. Next, to see if it is a straight or coxed boat, just look for a coxswain's seat.

Many are in the stern but some, especially in elite-level boats, are in the bow. In this case, the coxswain will be lying down and not sitting upright as in the stern designs. This is done to lower the center of gravity of the boat and to help the balance. Don't assume a rudder is an indication that a shell is coxed or not. Straight boats (coxless) may have rudders also. It will be attached to one of the rower's shoes and they steer by moving the foot side to side.

**Weight classification of shell (weight class).** It used to be that boat manufacturers built their boats in about three separate weight classes. The smallest boats (*lights* as they were sometimes called) were usually used for women's and lightweight men's crews. These boats were designed to carry crews whose total average weight was about 130–160 pounds. The next division was called the midweight, and these boats were for crews whose average weight was 160–185 pounds. The third level was for heavyweights, and these boats were designed to carry crews of 185–210-pound averages.

But that was then, and this is now.

Buying a boat today is a lot like buying a computer. In other words, there are a lot of options you can get with your money, and if you're not careful it can get wickedly confusing because there are no longer just three weight classes—there are tons of them. And there doesn't appear to be a standard weight classification used by all the manufacturers. That means that when you go to buy a boat, or to identify the weight class of boat you already have, you might get some drastically different weight ranges and "names."

For example, for their eights, Vespoli USA uses initials such as "DS" to designate a boat designed for 130–165 pound crew average, "DM" for 160–175 average, "DL" for 175–195 average, and "DXL" for 195–220 average. And that works great, simple and clear.

However, those same weight ranges are not the applicable for their other sized boats (a "DM" for their four is a 165–180 average). Which still is fine and dandy, if you are only dealing with Vespolis. The confusion can really set in when you might have more than one make of boat you are dealing with.

For example, Empacher has five different weight classes for their eights (85–100 kg, 85–95 kg, 75–85 kg, 75–85 kg – short version, 70–80 kg) and they use "K86" to identify their 75–85 average boats. But that's just for eights. And Pocock has different weight class system that are identified by ranges such as "< 180," and so forth.

So what to do?

You should treat each boat as an individual entity. Realize that if you have three different makes of singles in your boat house (or eights, or pairs) that you can no longer say, "They are all made for midweight." Nope, you are going to be dealing with a lot of different ranges and names.

The easiest way for you to tell the exact weight class of your hull is to talk to the manufacturer. They won't remember your boat off the top of their head, but if you have the serial number they can look it up for you. This may be the easiest way for you but not for them; they are busy folks. Turn to Chapter Thirteen, JOB 13.3, *Determining Weight Classification of Shell*, if you need help determining your boat weight classification.

---

In some cases, the serial numbers can provide a lot of information, depending on the manufacturer. For more information on locating serial numbers see my Web site article archive.

---

## Oars
**Length of oar.** A friend can be very handy when measuring the length of an oar. Take the tape measure and have your friend hold the start (called the *dumb end*) of the tape at butt of the handle. Holding the tape (the *smart end*), pull it to the tip of the blade. If the tape is not long enough then extend it out as far as it will comfortably go, mark the spot and remember the distance, bring the start of the tape to this new spot, measure

to the tip of the blade, and add up your distances. Record the number so you won't have to do it again.

> When measuring the lengths of oars it is best to measure the whole set of oars and not just one or two. Frequently sets get mixed up, especially if they are not well labeled. If that's the case, they may not all be of the same length. Be sure to check them all.

**Type of blade.** Determining which type/model/shape of blade you have used to be a cinch. All you had to do was look at it and chances was it was either a "Macon Blade" or a "Big Blade." But things have changed significantly in the past ten years.

Macon blades are all but gone, there are a bunch of different sizes for Big Blades, and new models/shapes such as "Smoothies," "Vortex," and "Apex" are appearing. So how do you tell?

You could ask someone who you think knows, or you can check your files if you bought the oars. However, if you want to know exactly what you have the absolute best way to tell is to find and record the serial number and then call the manufacturer.

## Miscellaneous

There are a couple of other items you may want to know about your equipment. These bits of info can come in handy. Let's discuss them here.

**Make of oar.** Look at the label on the shaft (**loom**) of the oar. There is most likely a label there with the manufacturer's name on it. If you're in the U.S., most carbon fiber sweep oars are made by **Concept ll** or **Drehr** (most, but certainly not all). Another great make of oar, from Australia, are those made by **Croker**.

One reason it's good to know the make is to keep the sets uniform because of the varying **deflection** of the oars (see JOB 13.2).

**Shape of hull.** If you were to cut your shell in half you would get a cross-section profile of the hull. A profile that looks deep and narrow will have less wetted surface when the boat is in the water. This will lead to less resistance between the boat and the water and is supposedly a faster hull design, yet at the same time this design will make the boat a less stable platform.

A hull profile that is more rounded and flat-bottomed will have more surface in contact with the water. This design will tend to be slower through the water; however, at the same time, it is more stable. The tendency is to put beginners in the latter and the more experienced crews in the former.

To tell the shape of the hull, you don't have to actually cut the boat in half. Instead, when the boat is resting on sawhorses or slings—seats down—go to the bow of the shell and sight down the hull. You should get a good idea of what type of hull you have.

Now, exactly what you do with this info is up to you. This is something you should definitely think about *before* buying a shell. See Chapter Twenty, JOBs 20.1–20.3, for suggestions if you're about to fork out money for a shell. However, once the shell is yours, there is little you can do with this info. Remember, usually (usually—but by no means always) novice crews tend to be put into flat-bottomed hulls and experienced crews into the narrower hulls.

**Girth of shell.** The girth is one of those specifics you probably won't ever think about. It is the distance from the top of one gunwale, around the outside of the hull, to the top of the other gunwale at the widest part of the boat.

To measure girth, go to the middle of the shell, take your tape measure and secure it on one gunwale. Pull the tape around the hull to the other gunwale and see what you've got. Girth will give you some idea of the size of the shell but I find that depth is a better indicator of shell size. If you find a good use for the girth dimension, please let me know.

**Beam of shell.** This is the distance from the top of one gunwale to the top of the other at the boat's widest point (usually amidships). But unlike girth that is measured *around* the hull, the beam is measured *straight across,* between the two gunwales. This could actually be called the width of the boat, but that's not nautical enough. I have found this to be informative in comparing different designs of hull shapes. And it becomes very, very, very important for those wide folks who end up rowing in narrow-beamed bow and stern seats.

**Weight of shell.** The weight of your boat when rigged is something you need to consider, but at the same time it is something you can do little about. On the elite level of rowing, shells are weighed at regattas. This is because the concern is with **minimum weight**. If a shell weighs below a set standard then weight will be added until it reaches the minimum. But shell weigh-ins don't happen at most high school, club, or collegiate races. Thank goodness—you've got enough to worry about on race day.

So actually your only concern should be **maximum weight**. One researcher estimates that for a 10% increase in weight of the boat, there could be about a 2% reduction in speed. That could average out to be a lot of speed. There are a variety of thoughts on this, but the rule of thumb is that the more the boat weighs, the more energy it takes to get it to go fast. But like I said, there is basically little nonradical stuff you can do about your shell weight, except get another boat.

Following is a chart of the minimum weights of shells allowed at international regattas.

### Minimum Shell Weight

| Category of shell | Minimum weight (kg.) | Minimum weight (lb.) |
|:---:|:---:|:---:|
| 1X | 14 | 30.87 |
| 2X | 27 | 59.54 |
| 4X | 52 | 114.66 |
| 2- | 27 | 59.54 |
| 2+ | 32 | 70.56 |
| 4- | 50 | 110.25 |
| 4+ | 51 | 112.45 |
| 8+ | 96 | 211.67 |

You might notice that there is no difference in minimums for women's, men's, or lightweight shells, which I feel is a little unfair—a women's lightweight crew has to row the same weight shell as a men's heavyweight. Maybe in the future that will change.

**Make and age of shell.** When we're driving along the highway, my wife prides herself on being able to point out any car she sees and telling me the make and model. This is kind of aggravating because she is usually right. Once you've been involved with rowing for a while it should become second nature for you to do the same with shells. But if you're new to the sport and unsure of what is what, it's still easy to tell the makers of boats.

Of course, the first thing is to look for the label. Manufacturers are seldom shy about what they make and they like to display the labels in prominent places. But where the label is placed will vary not only between the different makers, but also between shells of the same company.

I have found labels on the inside of gunwales, on the outside of gunwales, on the coxswain's seat, on the wash box, on the bulkheads, and in some cases not at all. If you can't find it, keep looking; it should be there. If not, then try to find a boat that looks just like yours by comparing characteristics of the boat (color of hull, design of riggers, shape of wash box, anything that stands out) with other boats in the boathouse. When you have found one that looks the same, check the label of the boat. If that fails, swallow your pride and ask someone.

The best way to tell the age of a shell is by the serial number. Locate it, and write it down. Again, it may be located in a multitude of locations. Some numbers will have the year the boat was made. If you are not positive then take the number and call the manufacturer (again, see my Web site article archive for more information about serial numbers).

**Draft of shell.** Draft is how far the hull extends below the surface of the water. This dimension may be important to you if you row in shallow areas or if you are building a boat rack. Measuring the draft is very easy to do with the boat seats-up on slings, after it's been rowed a few times.

When the boat comes in from practice, don't wash or wipe off the hull. Take your tape measure and start at the top of the gunwale at amidships. Extend the tape straight down towards the ground. Measure to the bottom of the hull. You might think the bottom of the hull is where you would stop but look back at the stern. Does your fin extend down further? If it does, try to estimate how much more the fin adds to the distance. This total distance, from the top of the gunwale to the tip of the fin, is what I call the **true boat depth.**

The reason that you don't wipe the hull clean, which you should normally do, is so you will have a waterline mark on the hull. This mark is the point where the hull sits in the water. Find this line and then measure from the top of the gunwale to it: the distance is your **freeboard**. If you subtract the freeboard from your true boat depth you will have your draft. See Figure 7.5 for help.

**Freeboard.** As we just explained, freeboard is the distance from the top of the gunwale to the water. It is important when considering how rough the water conditions are where you row. Hulls with more freeboard will not be affected by rough water as much as hulls with less freeboard. If your shell has a small amount of freeboard you may want to consider splash guards for when the conditions get rough (see JOB 16.5).

Although you can measure your freeboard with the boat in slings I suggest you measure it when the rowers are in the boat. It's the simplest way to get the most accurate reading. Be aware that the new wing riggers won't really affect your freeboard, but they might make rowing in rough water easier—at least less splashy.

## JOB 7.3: PREPARING TO RIG.

**Problem:** You are absolutely, positively, rock-solid certain that you need to rig, and you've got your numbers. Now let's get down to business.

**Needed:** PRE (positive rigging environment), SRE (safe rigging environment), rigging cards, and your tools.

There are three things you need to prepare when it's finally time to go to work: yourself, the equipment, and your tools.

**Yourself.** If this is one of your first times rigging, then I suggest you definitely spend a couple of minutes getting yourself ready. The hardest part is what happens between your ears. It is usually best to start off when the boathouse is empty. It doesn't help to have people looking over your shoulder if you are a little nervous. You're going to make mistakes, so get ready for them.

To get going, try some of the easier tasks first. The first time you rig can be a madhouse because even a small adjustment might change several other dimensions. Don't try a complete rig JOB (Chapter Fourteen) on your first outing. For suggestions on constructing a positive rigging environment, flip to Chapter Six, JOB 6.1, before you begin.

Then, before you get going, make sure you have read Chapters Three (*Karma of Tools*) and Five (*Safety*), and all the information in the chapter specific to the JOB you want to do. If you're a First-Dimensional Rigger you need to get comfortable with your equipment. Take a piece of paper and pencil to the boat-shack and sketch your rigger, foot stretcher, and oar—then label your parts. This will give you a good idea of what's what.

When you're ready, turn to the JOB index at the beginning of this book, find the JOB you need to do, grab some patience and a dose of positive mental attitude, and you'll do just fine. If you happen to get stuck, turn to JOB 16.1 for tips.

**Equipment**. Put the equipment in the best location that you can. Find a comfortable setting where things are easy to get at, the lighting is good, the temperature is comfortable, the shell is at the right height (so you bend and crawl as little as possible), you are safe, and set up any little extras such as tunes or snacks. (Turn to JOB 6.2, for tips on constructing a safe rigging environment). Always make sure the rigger bolts are tightened before you check the rigging of the boat. See JOB 16.2, to prevent overtightening.

> An age-old debate in boathouses centers on whether you let rowers use tools. Many coaches live in constant fear of the damage their athletes can do with a wrench, while others have their rowers do all the rigging. It depends on what you are comfortable with. In our boathouse, we limit our tool-use to our coxswains. Of course, we keep a good eye on them.

**Tools**. Try to have all your tools ready before you start. Read through the JOB once before you begin. This will give you an idea of exactly what you will need and what is going to happen. A tool tray can help you save a lot of time looking for lost tools (see JOB 16.5 for suggestions on a tool tray design).

Now you should be ready to rig, so turn to the JOB you need and get going. If you're working on a shell, it's easier if it's in slings, so . . .

## JOB 7.4: SLINGING A BOAT.

**Problem:** You need to put a shell into slings.

**Needed:** Someone with basic knowledge of commands; rowers, friends, or hired help enough to roll the boat; a solid pair of slings.

The goal here is to put your boat into a position so that you can comfortably work on it. First, prepare the area and make sure it is well lit. You don't want to walk away from this JOB needing glasses. Also make sure the area is clean. It's no fun spending an hour looking for that "doodad" you just dropped.

I'm not going to sit here and tell you my commands for moving a shell. I have found rowing commands are basically the same everywhere, but there are enough differences to make one person's command another person's confusion.

Therefore, how you move and roll your shell is up to you since there are a multitude of ways to do it. Whatever your commands, before you move a boat, make sure everyone knows their role. It's not a good time to have a mutiny when you've got a $25,000 shell hoisted over your head. If you're not comfortable giving commands, then beg, borrow, or steal someone who is. Listen to them a few times, write down the commands if you need to, and memorize them.

Before you move your boat, check the slings for quality. Don't use them if they look suspicious in any way. You could totally demolish a shell by having it fall off slings, although I have seen one or two fall with only slight damage.

Next, make sure you have enough folks to move the shell. For a maximum, I suggest you have as many helpers as there are riggers. I leave the minimum amount of help up to your discretion. Just keep this in mind—a shell may seem fairly lightweight, but when you put it in motion it can be terribly awkward to handle. The more people you use, the easier and safer moving a shell will be.

If your helpers are not experienced, show them where to grab the boat. I have actually seen people try to pick up a boat by grabbing a seat and trying to lift. This can be dramatic, but not helpful. When placing a boat into slings I always prefer rolling it down to the waist first and then placing it into the slings. Rolling the boat directly into the slings may work for you, but just be cautious of someone bashing the boat onto the top of the sling and damaging the hull. Also, watch out for the fin and the rudder or any speed-measuring devices that may be attached to the hull.

Once you have rolled the boat to the waist make sure the slings are in the proper place. You want to have about one-third of the boat overhanging from both slings. For example, to give proper support for an eight the slings should go under the two's and the seven's foot stretchers. For a four, the slings should go under the bow and stroke seat, and for a pair, they should go under the wash box and by the fin. If you're in doubt take a few steps back once the boat is in the slings, take in the whole picture, and adjust the slings if you need to.

When you think it's time to take the boat out of the slings, I suggest you pick it up to waist height and then walk away from the slings a small amount before you roll it overhead, if you have clearance to do so. This will keep you from hooking the slings on any riggers when the boat is turned and lifted. Also be cautious of anything hanging over the shell. You will be surprised at how high the riggers extend upward on a boat being rolled.

The trick to moving boats smoothly and safely is technique, and that comes from practice.

## JOB 7.5: RIGGERS ON AND OFF.

**Problem:** It is time to either put the riggers on or to take them off.

**Needed:** Basic rigging kit, shell and riggers, labeling supplies (tape, marker).

Sooner or later, you will need to either remove riggers from, or attach riggers to, a shell. This usually happens when traveling to and from races, but you may also need to do it for repairs or for changing the rig setup in your shell.

**Labeling.** One of the benefits of having adjustable riggers is they are interchangeable when you need them to be. They will fit any position on the same side with a few adjustments and a few types will even fit the opposite side with some minor changes. This can be a help when you want to arrange your rowers in different positions, but it can be a pain in the neck if whoever is putting the riggers back on the boat doesn't know what they are doing.

To save yourself a lot of time and hassles, it is important to label your riggers in such a fashion that you know exactly which boat they are for and exactly what position they belong to. Most manufacturers will stamp a number on the rigger to identify where it goes, but often these numbers are hard to read and sometimes the rigger will not be used for the position marked. I suggest you use either tape or paint to mark the riggers. Try to color code your equipment or come up with a number/boat name system.

For example, "Q 6" might stand for the six-rigger of the "Quackenbush" shell. Use any method that works for you. Just be sure to mark each rigger clearly and make it semipermanent, so you can change it if you have to.

We use colored electrical tape to mark our stuff. Some folks prefer athletic tape but the adhesive leaves a mess and the cloth breaks down in sunshine after a short period of time. A nice feature of colored tape is that you can color-coordinate your oars and riggers with matching colors. This will make yours and the rowers' lives easier. Put a wrap or two of tape around the riggers and oars and then put a piece of the same color tape at a visible spot on the boat. Now people can tell what riggers and oars go to which boat. If you want to be slick, put some tape on the boat rack and then the coxswain will know exactly where the boat goes. These few wraps of tape and a waterproof marker can help solve a lot of mix-ups. See JOB 18.2 for more suggestions on labeling equipment.

**Riggers off.** Once you are sure everything is labeled, begin loosening your riggers. Take your rigger wrench and turn all the rigger nuts counterclockwise to loosen them.

> Most rigger nuts will be 7/16 inch; however, some will be 10 mm. if the boat is foreign made. This should not be a problem as long as the nuts are same as all the other rigger nuts on the boat. If you have odd sizes then standardize when you can and get rid of any of the odd ones—it will make your life much easier.

Once they are finger-loose, take them off by hand. Put the nuts and washers in a secure place—like the sneaker's heel cup. You should be using washers, either plastic or metal, on your boat. This will protect the rigger stays and help secure the riggers better. The plastic washers may need a little bit of persuasion to come off. They are designed to collapse to prevent overtightening, which causes compression of the knee. They do this well, but when they're compressed those washers can be a royal pain to remove.

As you remove the nuts, be sure to support the rigger with one hand or else gravity may grab it and it will crash. What you are doing is open heart surgery on your rigger, so take your time, doctor, and be patient. If a surgeon had his hands in your chest would you want him hurrying because he had a golf game to scoot off to? I don't think so.

When the nuts and washers are off, slide the rigger away from the gunwale and off the rigger bolts. This may take a little bit of persuasion as well. Once it's off, place it in a safe place out of harm's way.

At this point pull out your pencil and rigging card and record any specifics for that rigger, like if it is shimmed—or a quick hint as to which stay goes to which bolt. Pack the cards away so they will be where you will need them. If you are preparing for a trip see Chapter Seventeen for suggestions.

Inspect the rigger stays at the attachment points for corrosion and replace any damaged nuts, bolts, or washers.

**Riggers on.** The important trick to putting riggers on is to make sure you know what goes where. It helps to have the correct rigger going to the right position and that the riggers are placed right side up. I know of one rower who had the wrong riggers on his shell for three months because they were not labeled. When you've figured out what is what, begin by removing any nuts and washers that are on the rigger bolts.

Pull out your rigging card for any notes you may have scribbled about the rigger. Then put the foremost stays of the rigger on their proper rigger bolt. This is where a lot of people run into difficulties. If you are confused as to which stay goes to which bolt, try checking out another boat for guidance.

---

Sometimes riggers with only one front and one back stay make it tough to decide which stay goes to which rigger bolt. If you're confused, look towards the stroke seat for clues. Often there will be only one bolt for the aft-most stay and this should help you figure out which stays go where.

---

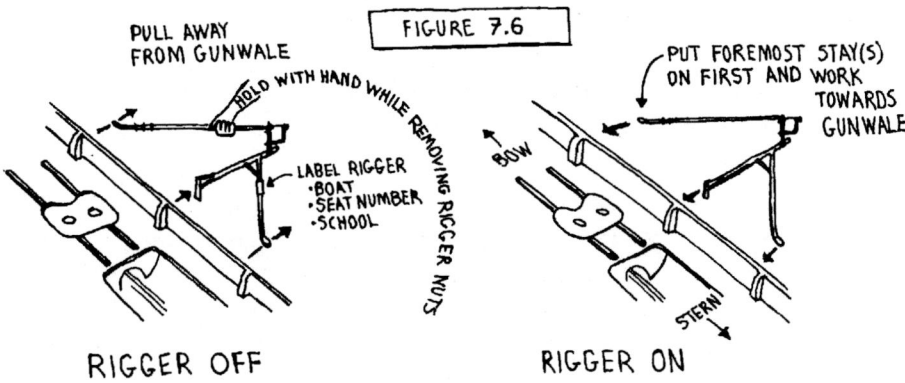

**FIGURE 7.6**

PULL AWAY FROM GUNWALE

HOLD WITH HAND WHILE REMOVING RIGGER NUTS

LABEL RIGGER
·BOAT
·SEAT NUMBER
·SCHOOL

RIGGER OFF

PUT FOREMOST STAY(S) ON FIRST AND WORK TOWARDS GUNWALE

BOW

STERN

RIGGER ON

If the boat is seats-up, it helps to keep the rigger pointed slightly downward until all of the bolts and stays are lined up. If the rigger has previously been adjusted for the position you are placing it on, it should slip right on when you gently raise it up. If the rigger has not been adjusted for the position it may be a difficult fit. If it is, remove the rigger and loosen any rigger clamps that are tight. Adjust the stays so they are loose and try again.

Once the rigger is on, replace the washers and put on the nuts and finger tighten them. Tighten to **two-finger tight** (see JOB 16.2) all the nuts with your rigger wrench, being cautious not to over tighten. Be careful about letting athletes do this before a big race; it is amazing what a dose of adrenaline can do.

> Serious damage to the shell can occur from overtightening the rigger nuts. Make sure the person(s) doing the work understands this. Don't let unknowledgeable people tighten the nuts or you may be facing some major repair work. Instruct them to use the two-finger method described in JOB 16.2, or do the JOB yourself.

## JOB 7.6: SEAT ASSEMBLY IN AND OUT.

**Problem:** Your seat assemblies are not where you want them; it's time to put them in or take them out of the shell.

**Needed:** Seats, shell in either seats-up (easiest) or seats-down (hardest) position, possible container to collect seats in, good pair of hands. These steps are simple to do but usually cause confusion the first few times. Athletes seem to have a real hard time with this.

**Take seat assembly out.** Make sure any retaining devices (straps or hooks) are loose. You will have either two types of seat assembly: (a) ones with retaining clips or (b) ones without. Retaining clips are small bits of angled metal or plastic that ride under the tracks to hold the seat in.

If you don't have them, then the seat assembly should lift right out. If so, then make sure you have labeled the seat assembly in some manner so you know where it should go.

Normally, seat assemblies from the same boat are identical and you can switch them between positions. But seats from different shells, even of the same manufacturer, may not be the same. So label them well to avoid hassles. I like to put the boat's name, our school's name, and the position number under the seat with a waterproof marker. I've also seen them engraved with a wood-burning tool.

If the seat doesn't lift out easily then it probably has retaining clips and you need to roll the seat assembly as far aft as it can go. All seats will come out towards the <u>stern</u> and not towards the <u>bow</u>, except for a few vintage-types of boats.

You will basically have two types of seats to deal with: non-roller bearing (a.k.a. dual-action seats) and roller bearing (a.k.a. single-action seats).

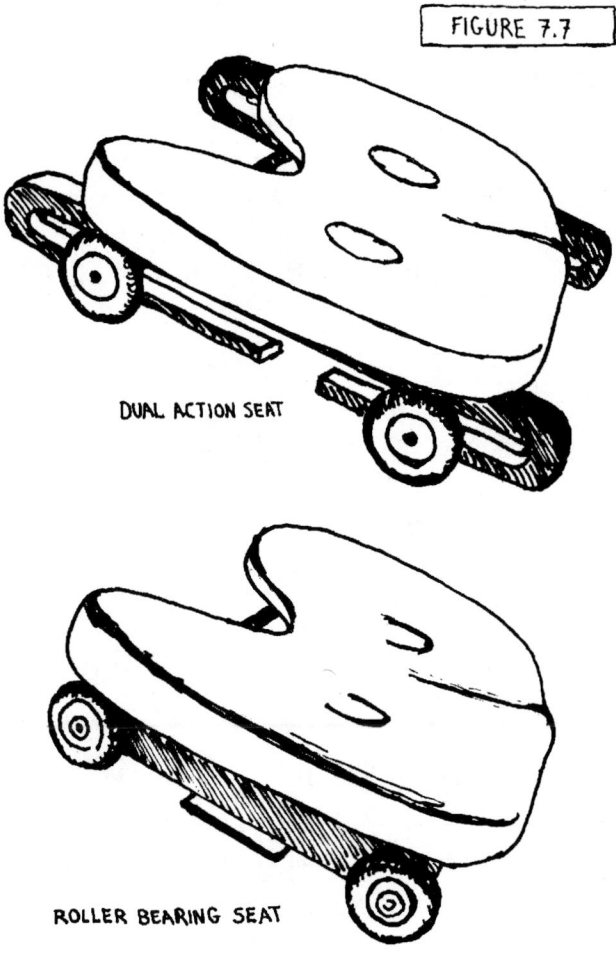

FIGURE 7.7

DUAL ACTION SEAT

ROLLER BEARING SEAT

**For non-roller bearing seats.** If you're on the port side of the shell place the wheels of the carriage against the front stops with your right hand while keeping the seat-top towards the bow with your left hand (see Figure 7.8). Gently push or tap on the seat top with your left hand until the assembly rides up and over the front stops. Keep your right hand close, but out of the way, in case the seat assembly pops out. Once both sets of wheels are clear of the front stops then take the seat assembly out and make sure it's labeled.

**For roller bearing seats.** Roller bearing seats are just a little different to take out than non-roller bearing seats. Do all the steps as you would for the non-roller bearing seat (previous step); however, realize that there won't be a carriage underneath the seat sliding back and forth—just retaining clips. That's good, not having the carriage is what makes these seats superior. It also means when you take them out you'll have to have everything lined up just right, and that your "gentle push" or "tap" of the seat will have to be a little heftier and at the right time and the right place.

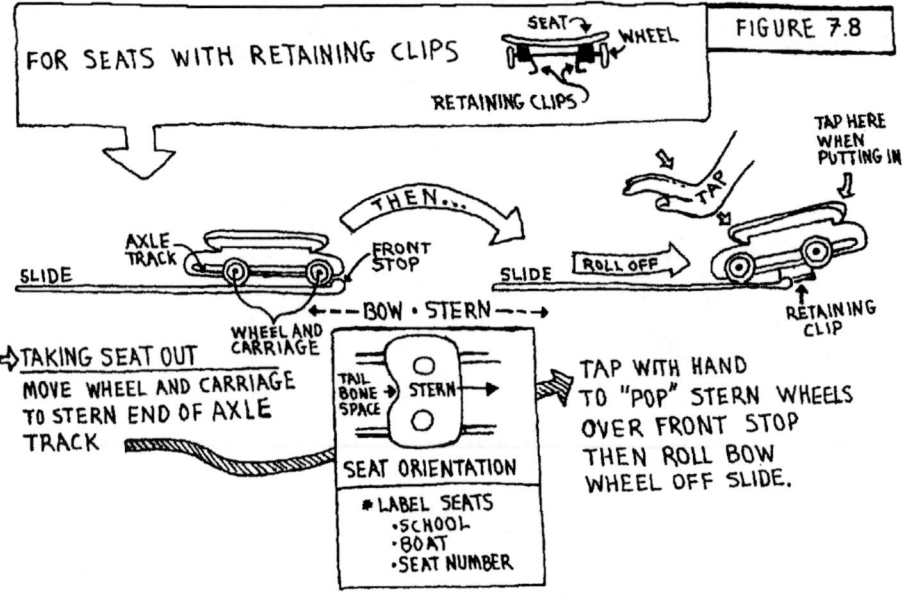

**Put seat assembly in (non-roller bearing types).** The seat assemblies often go in a lot easier than they come out. Again, if you're on the port side of the shell hold the seat assembly with your left hand, grasping the bow axle (that is the axle under the half-moon part of the seat) and your right hand holding the seat top (you can do this on the starboard side; just change hands). Line up the assembly with your left hand towards the bow. Place the bow axle's wheels into the tracks and gently push the seat assembly fore until the retaining clips come snug against the bottom of the front stops. Now tap or gently push the seat top fore with your right hand until the clips are past the stops. Check the wheels to see they are all on the tracks and they roll freely. If not, repeat the process.

**Put seat assembly in (roller bearing types).** This should be a pretty simple process; however, if things are not lined up just right it won't work.

At the stern end of the tracks, place the bow wheels of the seat onto the tracks. Now begin to push the seat towards the bow, making sure that the retaining clips under the seat are both under the tracks. As the stern wheels of the seat get to the stern end of the tracks you will need to apply gentle, but firm, pressure on the seat to get those wheels up and over the tracks' front stops. Once the seat is on the tracks, place firm pressure on the top of it and roll it back and forth to make sure that the wheels are in the tracks and the retaining clips are under the tracks.

---

The whole process of removing or inserting the seat assembly is done with <u>easy</u> pressure. This is no time for Troglodytic strength.

---

# Chapter Eight: The Arcs

Imagine a rower sitting in a shell preparing to take a stroke. Try to picture just the rower's body and nothing else.

At the catch, the body is located towards the stern. The knees are bent and the angle between the shin and femur (thigh bone) is about 50 degrees. This is called the *knee angle* and a 45–50-degree knee angle puts the rower's shins almost vertical relative to the water.

The upper body, specifically the chest, is leaning forward along the top of the thighs and the arms are extended. The rower is ready to take a stroke.

Now stick an oar and oarlock into this picture. The oarlock will be located slightly behind the rower's hips. The oar extends from the rower's hands, through the oarlock, and then out toward the bow. Our imaginary rower is ready to row and puts the oar into the water.

With the oar in the water the rower takes a stroke and two things happen at the same time. The blade at the end of the oar is going to travel, *with respect to the shell*, from the bow to the stern. Also the oar handle, at the other end of the oar, is going to travel, *again with respect to the shell*, from the stern to the bow. As these two parts of the oar rotate around the oarlock pin neither of them moves in a straight line. Instead they move in a circle, or actually part of a circle.

This part of a circle is called an **arc**, and the oar forms two arcs. One is called the **inside arc**, which is the distance traveled by the butt of the oar handle. The other is called the **outside arc**, and this is the distance traveled by the blade.

## 8.1 Rigging and the Arcs

When I first started rigging I had a difficult time trying to picture exactly what the heck I was doing. All I did was adjust the equipment according to "the book" and what people told me to do. I never really understood what I was doing; I just did it. I was a Second-Dimensional Rigger!

Then one day, a friend who was rigging a shell began to chat about what she was trying to accomplish with her rigging. She started talking about this funky subject she called "arcs," and I got her to explain it in detail.

She sat me down at a desk. In my right hand she gave me a pencil, had me put it on the desktop and told me to hold it around the middle with two fingers. She said my fingers holding the pencil represented the rigger, the eraser end of the pencil was the oar handle, and the pointy end of the pencil the oar blade. Then she told me to grab the eraser with fingers on my left hand and gently move the pencil back and forth—like an oar.

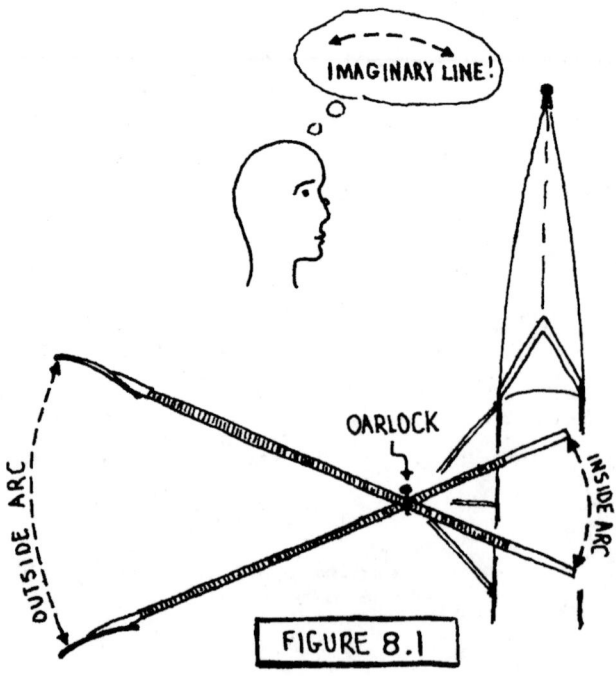

FIGURE 8.1

As I moved the eraser, the pointy end moved just like an oar blade, with both ends of the pencil describing arcs as they moved. Then she had me slide my right fingers along the pencil to different places, wiggle it again, and took notice how the arcs changed.

Suddenly it dawned on me what she was trying to demonstrate. When I moved the rigger, which in this case was my fingers holding the pencil, the arcs changed. As simple as it sounds, this is almost exactly what you are trying to do when you rig: *adjust the rigger to locate the arcs exactly where you want them*. So what does this mean to you? To be honest, this concept of arcs is going to make your life as a Rigger a whole lot easier.

Let me show you how.

## 8.2 Outside Arc

If you've been around rowing for a while you've probably heard remarks about how a rower is either "too long" or "too short" in the water. These are references to the length of the rower's outside arc, which is a critical dimension in rowing. This *length* is going to have an impact on how "heavy" the boat will feel to the rower as the oar moves through the water. And that will affect how hard it is for the rower to propel the boat, how high the stroke rating can go, how efficient the rower is, and in the long run how much boat speed can be generated. Pretty important stuff (more detail coming up in the next chapters).

Let's get kinda scientific for a moment and talk about *propelling the boat*. You and I both know the boat is moved by the rower applying power to the oar. But did you know that if we break down the mechanics of the stroke we find the most powerful part of the stroke is when the oar is perpendicular to the shell? At this position, called the **mid-drive**, the rower is biomechanically in a very strong setting. The legs are almost all the way down, the arms are straight, and the back is getting ready to surge on.

To be a successful Rigger, you'll need to have a fairly good imagination because we use several imaginary things. For example, both of the arcs don't actually exist; they are imaginary. Neither does the centerline, which divides the boat in half from bow to stern, nor the perpendiculars, which intersect the centerline at ninety-degree angles. You have to be able to "pretend" in the real world of rigging.

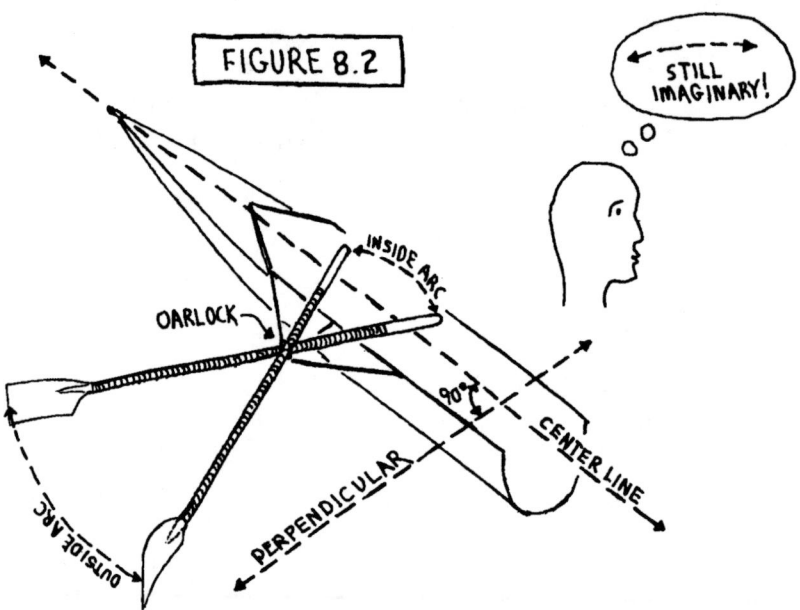

Besides the rower, the oar itself is at its most efficient position. At the mid-drive the oar is 90 degrees to the centerline. Here all of the force applied to the oar is being used to propel the boat forward (called **propelling force**). But, you might ask, isn't all of the power applied to the oar used to move the shell forward no matter where the oar is located?

Nope.

If you locate the blade away from this perpendicular position, either aft or fore, the stroke becomes less effective. That's because some of the propelling force is not moving the boat forward but instead is directed into a sideways force, called a **turning force**. And as you can see in figure 8.3, as the oar follows the arc and moves away from the perpendicular, the propelling force lessens quickly and the turning force becomes greater.

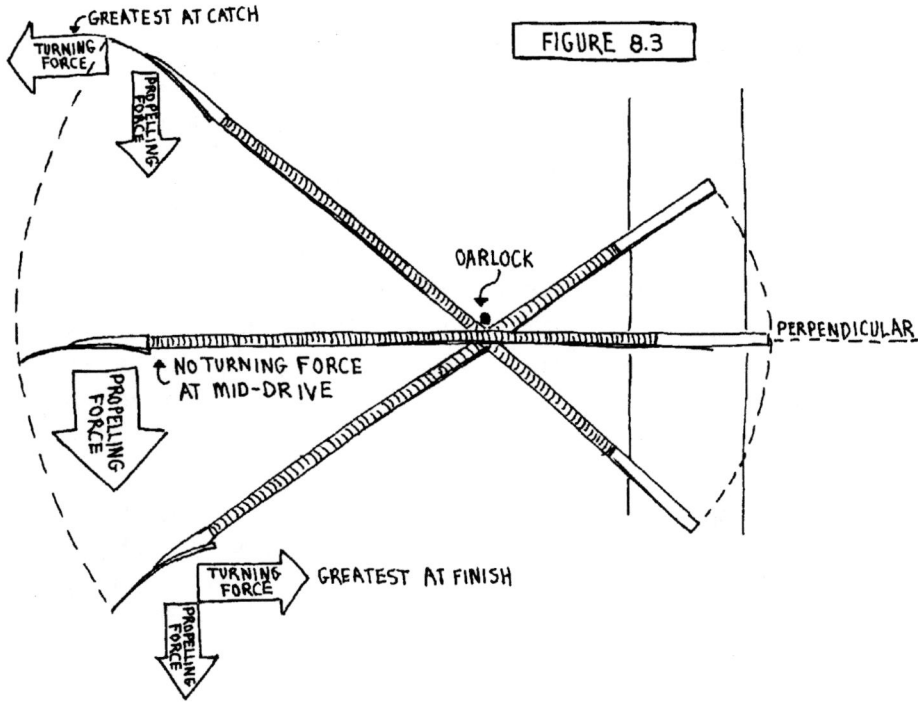

FIGURE 8.3

So when you rig, if you have located the outside arc too far aft when the rower makes the release, a lot of the propelling force will be changed into turning force. Instead of driving the boat forward, this turning force will pull the shell towards the blade. This effect is called "**pinching**." The same effect can happen at the catch if the arc is located too far towards the bow, but in the bow the turning force pushes the shell away instead of pulling the shell towards the oar.

Okay, let's catch our breath here a second. What does all this mean?

First off, if the length of the outside arc is too long (or too short) then the feel, or load, on the rower will be too heavy (or too light). Second, it means that if the outside arc is not located correctly, then the propelling force will be diminished and the turning force will be greater. This means there will be pinching of the boat, the boat speed will be reduced, and the steering of the shell may be affected, especially for smaller boats (for more on pinching, see Chapter 12, JOB 12C, *Measuring and Marking the Catch Angle*). In both cases, it means that if the outside arc is not adjusted correctly then the efficiency of the rower will be lessened and boat speed will suffer.

## 8.3 Inside Arc

Now let's look at the other end of the oar. The butt of the oar handle describes an arc inside the shell called the inside arc. People pay great attention to the inside arc—which they should because it's important. Just like the outside arc, the length and location of the inside arc are quite critical.

You see, when rowers are either at the catch or the release, there is a certain position in which their bodies are most efficient. The inside arc can have a great impact on whether a rower can achieve this position. If for whatever reason the rowers cannot attain this position, the efficiency of their stroke decreases quickly.

For example, I mentioned how at the catch the compression of the legs should be about 45 degrees for the angle between the calves and hamstrings. If a rower compresses this area more than 45 degrees (called **overcompression**) and the calves and hamstrings are closer together, the leg drive will be less powerful.

If the rigger is adjusted so the *length* of the inside arc is too long, the rower will be forced to compensate by doing one, or all, of three things. First, he or she may have to reach out farther at the catch to compensate for the extra length which will cause the overcompressing we just mentioned. Second, he or she may have to lay back farther at the finish, which will cause too much layback. Or third, he or she may just row with a shorter stroke, which means less effectiveness.

If the rigger is adjusted so the length of the inside arc is made too short then again the rower will have to compensate. Only this time the compensations will be shortness at the catch (called **undercompression**), not enough layback, or rowing too long in the water. Either way, the compensation will decrease effectiveness.

The *location* of the inside arc is also important. As a rower takes a stroke, the hands and the body generally follow the arc of the oar handle. The hands follow the arc a lot more closely than the body does, depending on the rower's style. If we adjust the rigger so the inside arc is moved a few inches closer to the oarlock pin, this new arc may cause the rower to lean towards the rigger. If the relocation of the inside arc is too great this can have the effect of throwing both the athlete and boat off balance and can make a big difference in the comfort of the athlete and the speed of the shell.

> It may be helpful to think of arcs in this way: changes to the inside arc will affect the biomechanics of the rower; changes to the outside arc will affect the propelling force of the oar.

## 8.4 Importance of Arc

So how is all this information going to help you become a better Rigger?

My rigging greatly improved when I realized most of the major adjustment I did when I rigged had an effect on the arcs. As soon as I grasped this concept, everything about rigging seemed to fall into place and I made the step from Second-Dimensional to Third-Dimensional Rigger.

Following, you can see how each adjustment involves the arcs, specifically the two critical characteristics of the arc: the length and the location.

| ADJUSTMENT | | EFFECT ON ARC |
|---|---|---|
| Work-thru the pin | > > | Moves arc around perpendicular |
| Catch length and angle | > > | Changes location of arc |
| Leverage (spread and inboard) | > > | Changes length and location of arc |
| Foot stretcher location | > > | Locates arc around perpendicular |
| Height | > > | Changes height of inside arc |
| Pitch | > > | Changes angle of oar during arc |

Each adjustment has an effect on the arcs. In the following chapters we will discuss the effect, what it means in terms of performance, and how you as a Rigger can make the adjustment.

# Chapter Nine: Leverage

You've been sitting at a red light for a couple of minutes when it finally turns green. You press down the gas pedal, shift gears, and scoot off in your car. What allows this act of modern-day transportation to happen is a device located between your engine and the tires. It's a box full of gears, nuts, and bolts called the transmission. The transmission takes the power from the engine, modifies it, and then transfers it to the wheels. Whether you realize it or not, rowing shells also have a transmission—it's called the rigger and oar.

When a rower takes a stroke, power is generated. The oar and rigger work together to modify and then transfer this power from the rower to the end of the oar just like a car's transmission. Also, like a car, a shell has different gears, but shifting gears in a car transmission is a lot easier than shifting gears in a rowing transmission. When zipping along in your car you shift whenever you need to (uphill, passing, stopping at the mailbox, etc.).

However, things are a little different in the world of rowing: You start off in one gear and stay there. To shift gears in a shell, the boat has to be stopped, taken out of the water, put in slings and the riggers adjusted. Shifting gears in rowing is called *rigging*.

What gear you're in (in our case, how the boat is rigged) is called **leverage**. There are four critical items which make up the leverage: **spread** (**span** in sculling), **length of the oar**, **inboard**, and the **blade surface area**. I'm not being too radical when I say these are the most critical dimensions in rigging.

The spread is the distance from the centerline of the shell to the center of the pin (see figure 9.1). The oars are divided into two lengths: the **inboard**, which is the length from the butt of the handle to the blade side of the button, and the **outboard**, which is the length from the button to the blade tip. These two combine to give the total length of the oar. The blade surface area is just what it sounds like—the size of the blade's area.

How you rig these four items (shift your gears) will determine your leverage, and this will dictate how hard or easy it is for the rower to use the transmission.

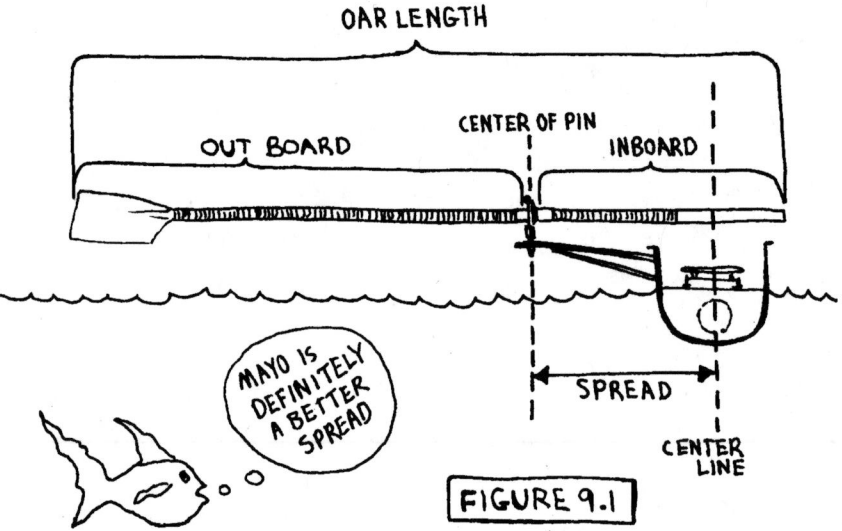

FIGURE 9.1

## 9.1 Leverage and the Balancing Act

For example, let's say this fellow who we'll call Bob is rowing in the three seat of an eight, and his rigger is set up so there is not much leverage. This could be due to several things, such as a small spread, a short inboard, a long oar, possibly a large blade surface area, or any combination of these.

The small leverage makes it hard for Bob to transfer his power when he takes a stroke, and this will make the rigging feel *heavy* to him. Ralph, Bob's identical twin brother, is rowing in the three seat in an eight next to Bob's. Everything is exactly the same in both boats, except that Ralph's rigging has a little more leverage. Since Ralph has more leverage, it's easier for him to transfer his power and the rigging will feel *light*. These feelings or demands that both Bob and Ralph are experiencing are called *load* and this is what every oarsperson feels when he or she rows. Load can be thought of as the resistance felt when a stroke is taken.

Now here's where it can get tricky: The less leverage there is, the harder it is on the rower to transfer the power, and in turn, the heavier the load feels. The more leverage there is, the easier it is to transfer power, and the lighter the load feels. This might help:

**< leverage = heavier feeling**
**> leverage = lighter feeling**

That's part one.

Here is part two: Leverage also determines something else—how **efficiently** the rigger and oar transfer power from the rower to the blade. So, in essence, there are two things you have to be concerned about when dealing with leverage: the *load* and the *efficiency*.

This shouldn't seem too foreign to you, I hope; it's something that you do every day when you drive. You see, when you're in your car zipping along the highway, all the shifting you do (or that the car does for you if you have an automatic transmission) is nothing more than an attempt to put the transmission in the most appropriate gear so it can transfer the maximum power from the engine to the wheels. You don't try to take off from a red light in fourth gear and you don't try to drive fifty miles-per-hour in first gear. Neither would be efficient, and you'd probably end up destroying your engine.

Well, it's the same in rowing.

When you rig you, are attempting to put the transmission in the most appropriate gear so it can transfer the maximum power from the rower to the blade. In other words, so it can be as efficient as possible without destroying the rowers.

Rigging the leverage is actually a balancing act. You must try to find the perfect mix between load and efficiency. Remember Bob and Ralph? Well

Bob's boat, rigged with little leverage, transferred a lot of power for each stroke taken, but the demand (load) on Bob was great. The heavier the load, the greater the demand; the greater the demand, the quicker Bob tired. So Bob had an efficient leverage, but he paid a price for it because he was under a heavy load. On the other hand, Ralph's shell had more leverage. Ralph wasn't transferring as much power per stroke as Bob, but he also wasn't under such a great load. Ralph wouldn't tire as fast, but his rigging is not as efficient as Bob's.

So what the heck do you do—rig the leverage to feel heavy or light? For more power or less? You balance by finding the perfect mix!

You do this by selecting the right leverage numbers (see JOB 9.5, this chapter). To get a better idea of how important leverage is, let's look at the four dimensions in detail.

Don't start worrying about this balancing act of *load* vs. *efficiency*. Most of it's already been done for you. Many rigging charts, like the ones in Chapter Fifteen, are based on years of research and experimentation by coaches and Riggers, and the dimensions printed take into account this balancing act.

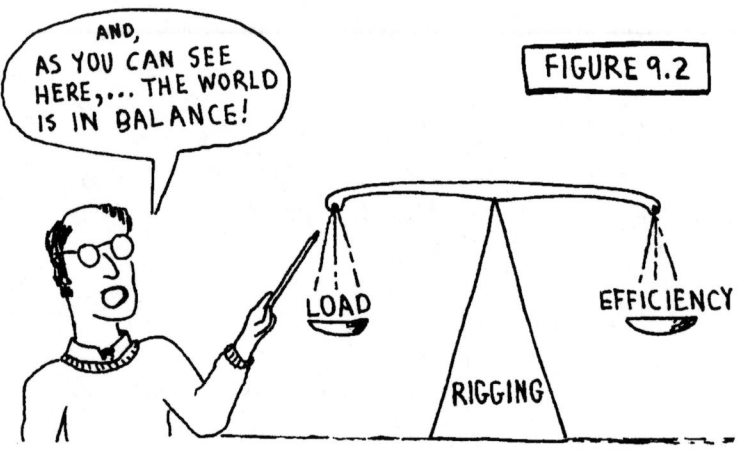

## 9.2 The Four Dimensions (Not a Rock Group)

Time for a little kitchen experiment. Find a smooth table top, dig up a ruler and grab three different sizes of full bottles or cans. A two-liter bottle of soda or anything about 64 ounces works great for the largest size and work down from there. Set things up like figure 9.3.

What you're constructing is a lever—your finger in the middle is the fulcrum and the bottle is the load. Start off with the largest bottle and put your finger at the 6 inch mark on the ruler. Pull the free end of the ruler toward you and watch what happens to the bottle. Reset the lever and move your fulcrum finger so this time it's only 2 inches away from the bottle. Pull the ruler and watch the bottle again. Reset once more and move your fingers 10 inches from the bottle, pull and watch.

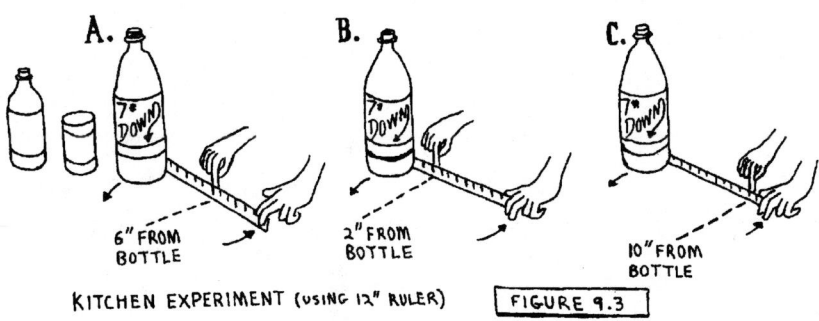

KITCHEN EXPERIMENT (USING 12" RULER)    FIGURE 9.3

With a little imagination (which you need to be a Rigger), you'll see that you've just made a working model of a rigger. The ruler is the oar and your fulcrum finger is the oarlock pin. The bottle represents the resistance the rower feels (load), and the end of the ruler being pulled is the oar handle. Every time you pull on the ruler you've just taken a rowing stroke!

With each stroke there are two important things you should have noticed. First, the farther your oarlock pin (fulcrum finger) was from the bottle, the harder the bottle was to move. Second, the closer your fulcrum finger was to the bottle, the easier it was to move—but the closer your finger was the less distance the bottle traveled.

> Notice that this is your balance of *load* vs. *efficiency*. The heavier the load (fingers were close), the more efficient you were but the harder it was to pull. This is leverage.

With these first couple of pulls on the ruler, you've just witnessed the effect of **adjusting the spread** on a rigger. Moving your finger along the ruler is the same as moving the oarlock pin on an actual rigger and you've just seen and felt how that affects the leverage. Changing the spread (moving the pin) is the most important adjustment you'll make in rigging. There are two reasons for that. First, the location of the pin has the greatest effect of any of the leverage dimensions. Second, changes to the pin affect all the other major rigging measurements. In fact, pin location is so important that changes of 1/2 cm are sometimes critical.

Try our experiment again. Take a stroke, feel the resistance, and watch the bottle move. Keep 4 inches between your two sets of fingers, slide them both 1 inches closer to the bottle, and set up again: there should now be 1 inches of ruler extending past your pulling fingers (like "B" in figure 9.3). Now take a stroke, feel, watch. Slide your fingers 2 inches closer to the bottle and take another stroke (you should now have 3 inches sticking out). You should've noticed the closer your fingers got to the bottle the less resistance there was, but when the bottle moved it traveled a shorter distance.

You've just seen the *effect changing the length of the oar* has. The shorter the oar, the greater the leverage but the less the load. For this reason, oar length is the next most important adjustment you can make concerning leverage.

Set the experiment up as before and, using the ruler, put your fulcrum finger 8 inches from the bottle. Take a stroke. Now set up again, but this time substitute something several inches longer for the ruler. Be sure to keep those fingers 4 v apart (like "C" in figure 9.3). Take your stroke. What did you notice?

The resistance should have felt greater with the new oar and the bottle should've traveled farther. You've just experienced the *effect shortening the inboard* has on the leverage. Inboard is the distance between the button on the oar and the butt of the oar handle, or in our model the distance from your pin finger to the pulling end of the ruler. When you substituted for the ruler you did the same thing as shortening the inboard on an oar. If you were to increase the inboard (use something shorter than a ruler) the result would have been opposite.

Put your ruler down for a minute. There are two fairly strange but quite important relationships between the spread and inboard that we need to discuss.

The first relationship is that changes to the inboard make changes to the length of the outside arc, making it shorter or longer by very small amounts. When you adjust the spread, you adjust the location of the outside arc, moving the arc closer to or farther away from the centerline. Both these adjustments effect the leverage, but adjusting the inboard has less effect than adjusting the spread.

As far as the leverage is concerned, there is a 3:1 ratio between the spread and the inboard. This means changes in the spread have three times the effect as the same change to the inboard, so moving the pin 1 cm is the same as moving the inboard about 3 cm.

> Because of this ratio (3:1), major adjustments to the leverage can be made to the pin and minor adjustments can be made to the inboard.

The second relationship is that in sweep rowing the inboard is usually 30 cm longer than the spread. This is so the butt of the oar handle will extend about 30 cm past the centerline (actually it is 30 cm ± 2 cm) and this overlap allows the oar handle to be in a better position so the rower will be able to comfortably grasp the oar with the outside hand. This is called the **Thirty-Centimeter Rule**. (See figure 9.4.) In sculling, we aren't worried about this—instead we're concerned with how much the handles **overlap**.

> The Thirty-Centimeter Rule is a critical rule to remember. It says the inboard should always be about 30 cm (give or take a couple) longer than the spread.

Let's do our experiment one last time. Go back to the ruler and place your fulcrum finger exactly 8 inches away from the bottle but this time change bottles. First, use the smallest one. Take a stroke, feel and watch. Now try the middle bottle, take a stroke, and observe. Both loads moved the same distance, but the smaller load was easier to pull, right? Now try the largest bottle. Again the same distance but harder to pull, right? This is the *effect changing the blade surface area* has on the leverage. The largest bottle represented a large blade; the smallest bottle, a small blade.

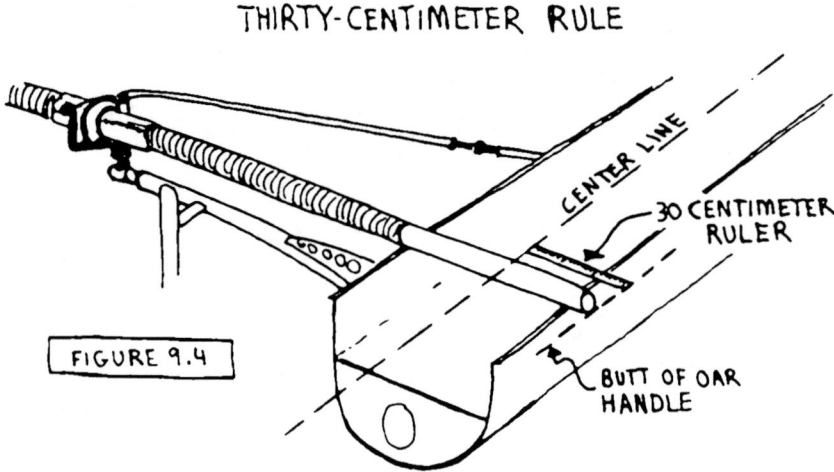

Out in a shell, a larger surface area makes it easier for the blade to grip the water and this increases the efficiency of the power transmission, which is good. But increasing the blade surface area also increases the resistance as the blade moves through the water and decreases the amount of slippage. This increases the load on the rower, and whether this is good or not depends on what cardiovascular shape the rower is in.

Riggers normally have an efficiency of 65 to 75 percent. Studies have been done showing that increasing the surface area of the blade improves this efficiency by about 5 percent, which might give a crew 1/3 length advantage over a 2,000-meter race course. But only if the crew is not already rowing at top efficiency. If they are already going as fast as they can, with no improvement possible, increasing the surface area can actually make a crew slower, unless the length of the oar is shortened at the same time. Okay, put away your stuff and let's focus on the arcs.

## 9.3 Leverage and the Arcs (Not a Rock Group Either)

What you should've noticed from your kitchen experiments with your homemade lever is that whenever a change was made to the spread, to the inboard, or to the oar length, it had an impact on the location and lengths of both arcs (changes to the blade surface area have little impact on the arcs). Specifically, there are two things regarding the arcs you need to be concerned about when making leverage changes: (a) how the changes will affect the location of the inside arc, and (b) how the changes will affect the length of the outside arc.

The exact location of the inside arc is critical for the rower's comfort and function. In most cases the inside arc is located almost on top of the centerline (see figure 9.5). When a rower slides back and forth on the tracks there is basically little potential for body motion from side to side due to the hands holding onto the oar as it follows the inside arc.

If the inside arc were to be greatly shifted to either side of the centerline, then the rower would be forced to shift the body to one side or the other to follow the arc. This could cause drastic leaning, which would result in major balance problems in the boat setup. This is where the Thirty-Centimeter Rule comes in handy. The spread should always be about 30 cm less than the inboard. This will assure that the inside arc is located 30 cm to the outside of the centerline at the mid-drive and that it is in the proper location for the rower.

The length of the outside arc is critical because it directly affects the load on the rower and the efficiency of the rigger. Any changes to the spread, to the inboard, or to the oar length will change the length of the outside arc. The longer the outside arc, the longer the stroke. The longer the stroke, the farther the boat moves each time the oar is pulled. But we know what this will result in: a greater load on the rower. So once again we're back to the balancing act. But as I mentioned before, don't worry about it: It's already handled by the dimensions of the rigging charts.

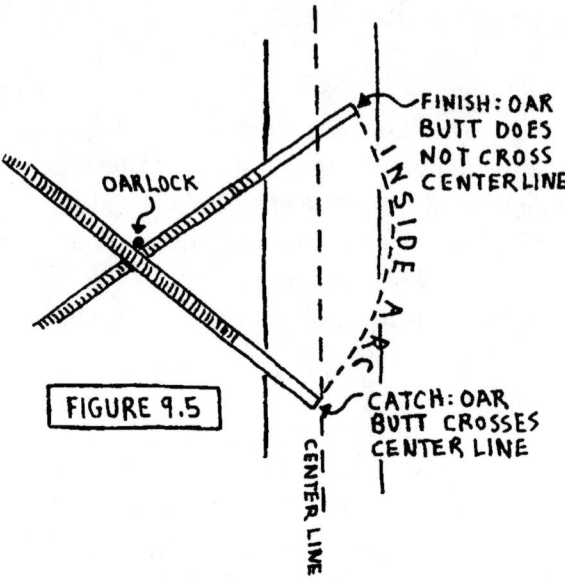

FIGURE 9.5

As you're puttering with your equipment and making a leverage change, there are a couple things to watch for in your rower's technique which can tip you off that the arcs aren't correct. A rower leaning may be a clue the inside arc is off, but also watch the rower's hands. If you notice 1 or 2 inches of oar handle sticking out past the rower's outside hand, this might mean the inside arc may be shifted too far away from the rigger and the rower is compensating by shifting the hands down the oar handle.

A tip that the arc is shifted too close to the rigger would be the rower's pulling the oar away from the oarlock at the catch and/or release. Watch the blade in the water for clues about the outside arc. After a leverage change look to see if the rower's catch or release timing is suddenly different than the rest of the boat. If it is, it may be due to the outside arc length being too long or too short. This could be a big problem, especially in a pair or four.

## 9.4 Slippage

For you folks in the Third Dimension and aspiring Second-Dimensionals, here is an important message from Mr. Physics. When a stroke is taken, the blade not only moves fore to aft, but it also moves sideways away from the boat. This is called **slippage** (see figure 9.6), and it's an important concept to grasp because it affects your leverage balancing act. To illustrate, let's say it's winter, the river is frozen solid, and things have gotten a little boring in the boathouse. To liven things up, you and your pair partner decide to try a little ice rowing. You strap skates onto the bottom of your pair and affix ice picks onto the oars. You launch your ice-shell and get ready to fly. You and your buddy come up to the catch and set the ice picks into the ice. You both take a stroke but something strange happens—the boat doesn't move! You try again and pull and pull and pull with all your might but the boat doesn't budge.

Why not?

The reason why is pretty simple. When you both pull at the same time the oars can't slip sideways so your ice-shell literally has nowhere to go. The blade (fulcrum) is fixed and both sides of the boat are pushing against each other. In this case, you have no balance in your leverage; you have maximum load but no efficiency in your rigging. As you can guess, ice rowing isn't destined to be a very popular sport.

Thank goodness things are different when the boat is on non-frozen water. When the blade is set into the water at the catch, it tries to fix itself as in our ice-shell, but it can't because water flows. The blade slips through the water as shown in figure 9.6 (notice the blade movement away from the centerline). So when you row in water your blade is able to slip sideways: you can achieve a balance and the boat can move. But you don't want too much slippage—it would be a waste of power.

It's important to note that slippage has caused a revolution in oar designs. The days of the long oars with the narrow flat blades are gone, and those oars have been replaced with shorter oars with stout, curved blades (Big Blades, Apex, and other designs). The reason why is that the long oars had too much slippage and the short oars slip less in the water—and with reduced slippage you can increase the load.

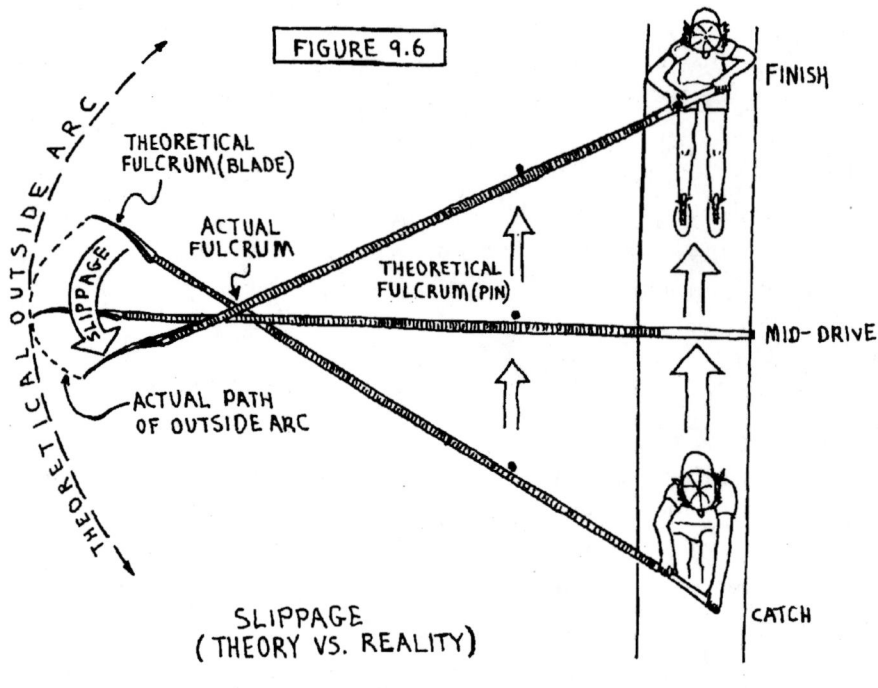

**FIGURE 9.6**

SLIPPAGE
(THEORY VS. REALITY)

For an excellent discussion on slippage, load, and gearing see *Rudern*, or Concept II's Web site at <http://www.concept2.com>.

Okay, enough talk; just remember any adjustments you make to the leverage are going to result in drastic changes in what the rower feels. So when making changes, do them gradually to prevent injuries—make no Mega-Changes.

## JOB 9.1: MEASURING THE BLADE SURFACE AREA (B.S.A.), OAR LENGTH, INBOARD, SPREAD.

**Problem:** You're dealing with a couple of unidentified dimensions you want to measure.

**Needed:** Just a tape measure, scrap paper, rigging cards.

### Part 1: Measuring the Blade Surface Area

What we are concerned about is the amount of surface area on the blade of the oar. It's important we know it for two reasons: first, to see if it is the right size for our rower(s), and second, to see if the oars are all the same—it's not helpful to have an unmatched set of oars.

Actually, we don't need to figure out the exact surface area. Instead, if we focus on three simple dimensions we can find out what's important and skip doing a lot of math. The dimensions are: **A**, the width of the tip; **B**, the width at the middle of the blade; and **C**, the length of the blade. These will give us enough info to make sure we have the right size blade and also to compare blades to make sure the set is identical.

**Step 1. Setup. All types:** A little organization is going to be a big help here. Get your tape measure and a piece of scrap paper. On the paper, draw a chart with four columns, with the first being for the number of the oar, the second for dimension **A**, the third for dimension **B**, and the fourth for dimension **C** (see sample chart). Find yourself a fairly quiet area and lay out your set of oars. Having a friend replace each oar into the oar rack after you measure it will help keep things straight.

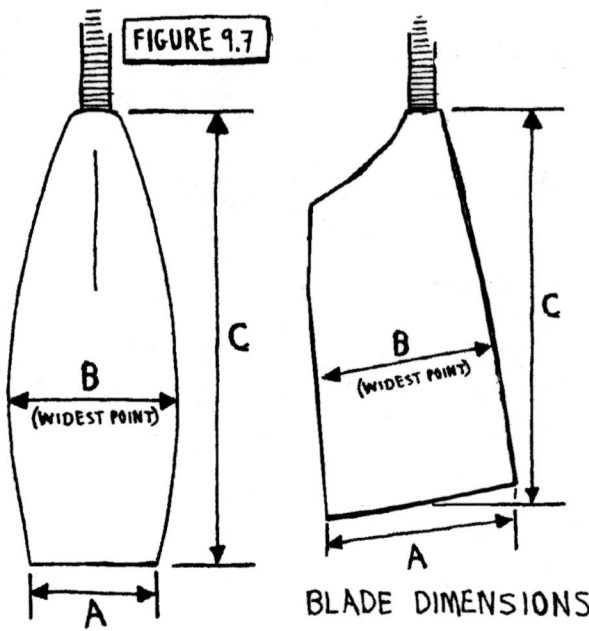

**BLADE DIMENSIONS**

**Step 2. Measure Away:** Fill in the first column with the number of the oar. Now measure dimension **A**, the width of the tip, and write it down. Measure dimension **B**, the middle width. If it's a Big Blade style blade measure at the widest part of the blade, usually close to the middle. Fill in the column. Now put the hook end of the tape measure on the tip of the blade and measure the length, dimension **C**, and enter it on the chart. Replace the oar in the rack and finish measuring the set.

## Chart Of Blade Measurements

| Oar | A | B | C |
|-----|---|---|---|
| 8 | | | |
| 7 | | | |
| 6 | | | |
| 5 | | | |
| 4 | | | |
| 3 | | | |
| 2 | | | |
| 1 | | | |

For oars with different shapes, such as the "Apex," you should contact the manufacturer to see what dimensions they use.

**Step 3. What Have You Got?** Quickly scan the chart to see if all the oars are the same. If you're using Concept II oars, compare your dimensions to the Blade Specification/Size Comparison Chart that's on the next page to see what size blades you have. If you're using other oars such as Drehr or Croker, contact the manufacturer for the specifications. If you need to change the blade surface area or oar length, on to JOB 9.2.

You might notice from the specification chart that Macon oars are listed. Yes . . . they are still made, sold, and rowed. Concept II states that about 2% of sweep oars and 8% of sculling oars, purchased from them, are Macon oars (as of 2002).

## Blade Specification/Size Comparison Chart
## For Concept II Oars
(Adapted with permission from Concept II)

| | Blade/Size/Model | Width at Tip "A" | Max Width "B" | Length "C" |
|---|---|---|---|---|
| | | (all dimensions in centimeters) | | |
| **Sweep Oars** | Smoothie | 25.5 * | 25.5 | 54.5 |
| | BB 25x55 mold '87 | 25.0 * | 25.0 | 55.5 |
| | BB 25x52 mold '87 | 25.0 * | 25.0 | 52.0 |
| | BB 25x55 mold '94 | 25.0 * | 25.0 | 55.5 |
| | Macon Medium | 16.5 | 20.0 | 58.0 |
| | Macon Large | 18.0 | 20.0 | 58.0 |
| | Macon X-Large | 18.0 | 21.0 | 58.0 |
| **Sculling Oars** | Smoothie | 21.0 ** | 21.0 | 46.0 |
| | BB 21x43 mold '87 | 21.5 ** | 21.5 | 43.5 |
| | BB 21x46 mold '94 | 21.5 ** | 21.5 | 46.5 |
| | Macon Medium | 14.0 | 17.0 | 50.0 |
| | Macon Large | 14.5 | 18.0 | 50 |

* This dimension is 19.5 with Vortex Edge

** This dimension is 17.0 with Vortex Edge

## Part 2: Measuring the Oar Length

It's darned important to have all oars in a set the same length. Mismatched sets can cause major problems with balance, steering, and technique. So let's measure them. . . .

**Step 1. Find Your Dimensions:** See the rigging charts in Chapter Fifteen to find the best oar length for your crew.

**Step 2. Setup:** Find an area where you can lay down a few oars without getting them, or you, trampled. Organization will make this JOB easier and so will a friend to horse the oars while you do the cerebral stuff. On the scrap paper draw two columns: one for the oar's number and the other for the length. This will help you keep your place when some crisis comes up and you need to run off.

**Step 3. How Long?** On your first blade, hook the end of the tape measure to the tip of the blade. Now measure the length of the oar. If you've got a ten-foot tape, you'll have to measure out ten feet, mark the shaft, roll up the tape, measure the rest, add it up in your head, and mark it down on your scrap paper.

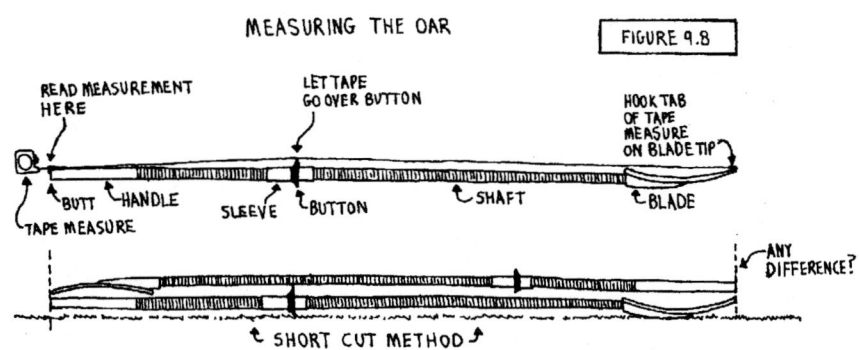

MEASURING THE OAR — FIGURE 9.8

**Step 4. Compare:** There is a shortcut to finding the lengths of the other oars without having to measure them all. With the first oar still on the ground take your next oar and place it on top of the first, but flip-flopped so they are handle-butt to blade-tip. Match up one end and check the other end to see if the second oar is longer or shorter. If it's different, measure the difference, add or subtract it from the first oar, and you've got your length. Of course, the other way is to measure each oar separately but that's boring: so be daring, take a shortcut, and wow the crowd. If you discover you've got a mismatched set, a little grumbling is okay.

**Step 5. Record And Mark:** Your oar lengths should never change unless there is a saboteur in your boathouse. Or unless you have adjustable handles, and they get adjusted. Once you've got the lengths, mark the oar sets distinctly (see JOB 18.2, *Labeling Your Equipment*) and record the info on your rigging cards.

## Part 3: Measuring the Inboard

Measuring the inboard is a lot like measuring the oar length except you're concerned about a much shorter distance.

**Step 1. Find Your Dimensions:** Turn to Chapter Fifteen and review the rigging charts to find your inboard dimensions.

**Step 2. Setup:** Same as for oar length.

**Step 3. How Long?** Hook the end of your tape measure onto the butt of the oar handle. Sometimes the butts of the handle will get worn or are rounded, so make sure the tape measure is sitting squarely on the end. Now measure the distance to the blade side of the button. This is your inboard. On the scrap paper write down each oar with its inboard. A rule of thumb for sweep oars is that the inboard should be 30 ($\pm$2) cm more than the spread.

**Step 4. Compare:** When measuring, be accurate; a half centimeter makes a difference! Because accuracy is important, don't get lazy and try to eyeball the inboards and guess what they are. Measure each oar individually, no shortcuts here! Put the correct ones back and leave the others to be adjusted.

**Step 5. Record And Mark:** You've got to understand that inboards change all the time. Sometimes on purpose, sometimes not. It's not uncommon to have buttons slip because of the wear and tear of practices or the bump and grind of traveling. Or adjustable handles move and never get put back to their original spot. Check the inboards weekly. And save yourself some major headaches by making sure that once you've got your numbers you write them down. That way if the inboards do slip, it's a cinch to adjust to the right place again.

### Part 4: Measuring the Spread

Spread is the most critical ingredient of the "gearing" (leverage), and because it's so important you've got to know what it is—exactly. Measuring it is a breeze, just take your time and do it right. One thing though, don't measure the spread while eating a large pizza with extra cheese and onions: it's hazardous. I know from experience.

**Step 1. Find Your Numbers:** Once again, the rigging charts in Chapter Fifteen are the best place to find your spread ranges.

**Step 2. Boat Seats-Up:** Get your boat rolled into slings with the seats up. Take a peek to see if any rigger washers were put in the wrong place—like between the connecting plate and bolt shield instead of between the nut and connecting plate. If they're in the wrong place (it happens more than you'd believe), take a moment and right the wrong. Once you're done, go through the boat and snug up the rigger nuts.

**Step 3. Make A Centerline:** Grab your tape measure. At the seat position where you want to know the spread, measure perpendicularly across from the outside of one gunwale to the outside of the other. Do this as close to the mid-drive rigger bolts as possible. What you are measuring is the width of the shell. Now take this distance and divide it in half. This number tells you where the centerline of the shell lies. Measuring the centerline is a lot easier to do if you're using metric (hint, hint).

**Step 4. Out To The Pin:** You're looking for the distance from the centerline of the shell, which you just found when you divided your width, to the center of the pin. To get it, you need to place your tape measure so the number you just calculated is on the outside of the inside gunwale (the gunwale with the rigger on it). Now hold the tape measure in place on the gunwale with a thumb and extend the tape out to the center of the bottom of the oarlock pin. The place where the pin intersects the tape measure is your spread. Remember, you want the center of the pin, not the side of the pin nor the side of the oarlock. If you're not in a hurry, take a few moments and check all the riggers.

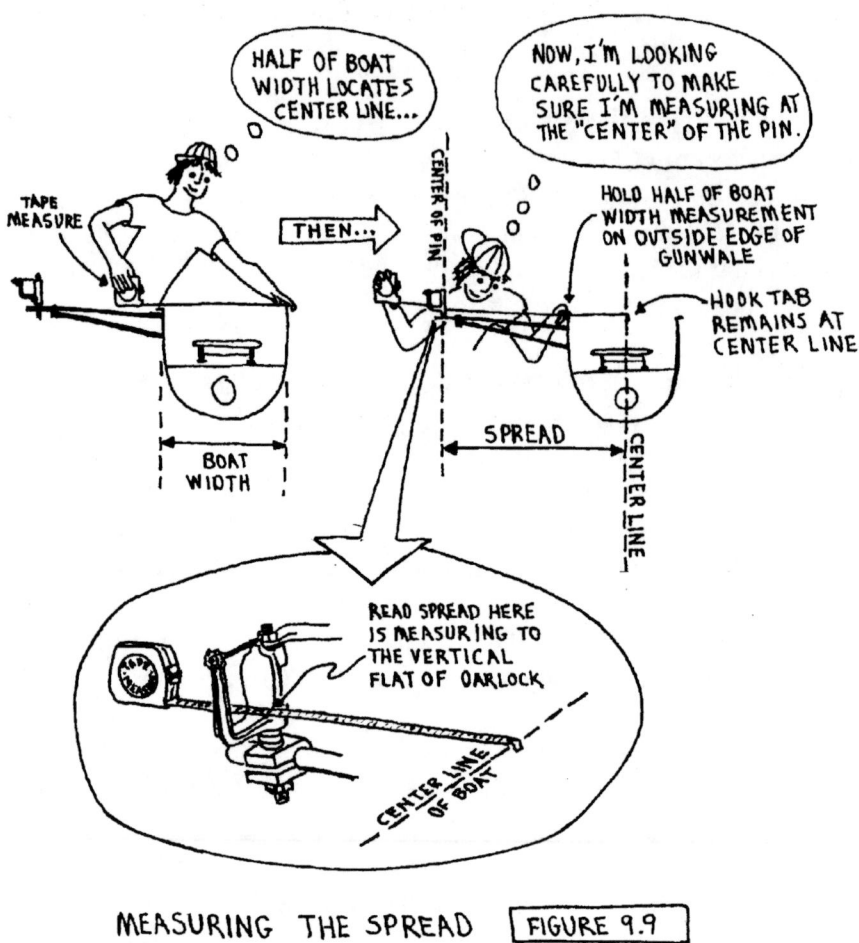

MEASURING THE SPREAD  [FIGURE 9.9]

Some folks measure the spread to the side of the vertical flat of the oarlock. This can shorten your measurement from 1–2 cm. That's fine, as long as you know that's where the measurement was taken from. When looking numbers up in charts, comparing them with friends, or discussing them with other Riggers, make sure you know where the measurements are taken from.

**Step 5. Enter The Data:** Record the spreads you've gotten even if you're going to change them. If the new dimensions you try don't work, you may want to come back to these original numbers.

# JOB 9.2: ADJUSTING THE BLADE SURFACE AREA AND OAR LENGTH.

**Problem:** You need to change your blade surface area and/or oar length.

### Part 1: Adjusting Blade Surface Area

There are three ways to change the blade surface area of your oar if you're not happy with it.

**Easiest method:** Before the oars ever get to the boathouse is the best time to adjust blade surface area. If you're placing an order for a set of oars, talk to the manufacturer about the size of blade and design that would be best for your team. They know the equipment better than anyone else and usually have some good advice.

I suggest that if you are happy with the equipment you already have, try to keep future purchases similar to what's already in the boathouse. This will make rigging easier, but at the same time, don't be afraid to experiment. But if you are not ordering oars and you've got to do something, try the . . .

**Next best method:** If you've measured your set of oars and notice some irregularities, the solution may be as close as the oar rack. Sometimes, especially if they are not marked well, oars get switched around and out of order. You might have the wrong oar in your set, which also means another set has the wrong oar. If that's the case, pull out the oars and measure the blades. Make sure that if you make any switches you mark the oars to stop any more mix-ups. If this doesn't work, you can . . .

**Get the kit.** Some blades are changeable by using a kit from the manufacturer. For instance, we changed a set of Concept II Big Blades to Vortex Blades by getting a kit from them and adapting the blades. It wasn't difficult at all. However, this option is only available to a few specific types of oars. To find out which are adaptable call the maker directly.

**Pain-in-neck method. Composite oars only:** I don't recommend this method unless you like hard work and have a bunch of free time. On some makes of composite oars, the blades are detachable from the oar shaft. This allows you to remove the old blades and replace them with different ones. Sounds like a good idea, but those blades can be a nightmare to get off and on, and when the new blade is finally attached you've got to worry about whether the pitch is set right. I've only had to do this once, when replacing a broken blade on a set of oars we needed, and it was enough to make me want to go out and buy a new oar. But if this is the direction you must take, then call the manufacturer (see *Suppliers* in back of book) for advice.

## Part 2: Adjusting Oar Length

If you don't like the length of your oars, there are four methods to change it.

**Easiest method:** The best time to take care of problems with your oar length is when you buy them. When you order oars, my suggestion is to standardize—try to have all the oars in the boathouse the same length. That way, if an oar breaks, or if an oar is forgotten on a road trip, or the wrong oar is taken out to practice, all you have to do is shift an inboard. Check what length oars you already have, and if you're happy with them, order your next set the same length. The standard range for sweep oars is 378.5–386 cm. But if you need to do something about the length right now try the . . .

**Next-best method:** Adjust the adjustable. Did you buy or inherit adjustable oars? If you did, it's your lucky day.

Adjustable oars are designed to do exactly what you need to do: change the length of the oar. This is done by sliding the oar handle into or out of the shaft of the oar. Two things will tip you off that you have adjustable oars. First, the handles are not wood, they are usually made of either metal or a composite material. Second, there will be some sort of re-straining hardware close to the handle.

Adjusting an adjustable oar is not difficult, just a little tricky. Grab the tool you need to loosen the restraining hardware (usually a Philips screw driver), your tape measure, and get ready for a change.

Put the oar in a comfortable position. I've found that having it lying on the floor/ground works best. Measure the oar first, then loosen the re-straining hardware. Be careful here. The trick is to *loosen* the hardware, not to remove it. If you unscrew the bolt too much, the doodad inside the oar handle that keeps it from slipping will fall off, inside the oar, and then you have got a time-consuming hassle to get it back on.

Once the hardware is loose, slide the handle in/out, and measure until you get the length you need. You might need to do a little twisting or a little taping of the handle to get it to move. Tighten up the hardware, check the length again, tighten again. And off you go.

**Next-next-best method:** Change your oar's length by switching oars. If your set has an odd length oar there might be one in the oar rack that can solve your problem. You'll have to measure a bunch of oars, but you may just stumble upon a solution. But if this doesn't work and you're stuck, there is always the . . .

**Troglodyte method:** If anyone asks, tell them you heard about this in some back alley, not from me, okay? If you've got to shorten your oar length, I mean you've positively, absolutely, really got to shorten it, then this may be your method. If this is the way you've got to go, then pull out your handsaw and prepare to operate. (This method only works on wood handles!)

The plan is to trim the extra length off the oar handle; you should be able to cut several centimeters off and still have a workable oar. Measure the length you want removed, make a mark, make a clean cut, sand the rough edges and hide, but save (see TIP below) the evidence. Just be cautious not to get radical and shorten your handles too much. Again, only do this with wooden handles!

---

Well, Doc, if you've decided to make the cut, keep the pieces you cut off. I saw a guy cut about an inch off a set of oars. The next day his buddy took the scraps back to his boathouse and glued them to his set of oars to make them longer. True friendship.

---

## JOB 9.3: ADJUSTING THE INBOARD.

**Problem:** Your inboard's not right and needs to be adjusted.

**Needed:** Tape measure, screwdriver, and rigging cards.

**Step 1. Find Your Dimensions:** Same as JOB 9.2, Step 1, this chapter.

> For help in finding how all your leverage numbers should fit together, see Chapter Fifteen.

**Step 2. Setup:** Same as JOB 9.2, Part 3, Step 2.

**Step 3. Measure them:** Same as JOB 9.2, Part 3, Step 3.

**Step 4. Adjust Buttons:** Look at the button on your first oar. There should be one or two fasteners securing it. The fasteners should always be on the oar handle side of the button, so the flat side is against the oarlock. Depending on the age of the oar and how well the oars have been treated these fasteners will either loosen easily or be a major hassle to turn.

Just loosen them. No need to remove the button unless it needs replacing. On the new oars the button is designed so the nut is held in place while the bolt head rotates. Get your screwdriver and loosen the bolt. If it's frozen, which happens, go to JOB 16.3, *Stuck Fasteners*, for help. If the nut turns while you rotate the bolt head place another screwdriver between the nut and button to lock it and try again.

> Don't hold the oar in your lap while doing this JOB. The screwdriver can easily slip off the bolts, which is a great way to ruin a pair of pants—or a leg.

With all the fasteners free, you should be able to wiggle the button. Move it to where you think you want it. Most oars will have indentations in the sleeve and each indent is usually about 1/2 cm. Measure to see if you've got what you want, tighten down the button, making sure not to over-tighten the fastener, and measure once more to see if it slipped. Now onto the next one.

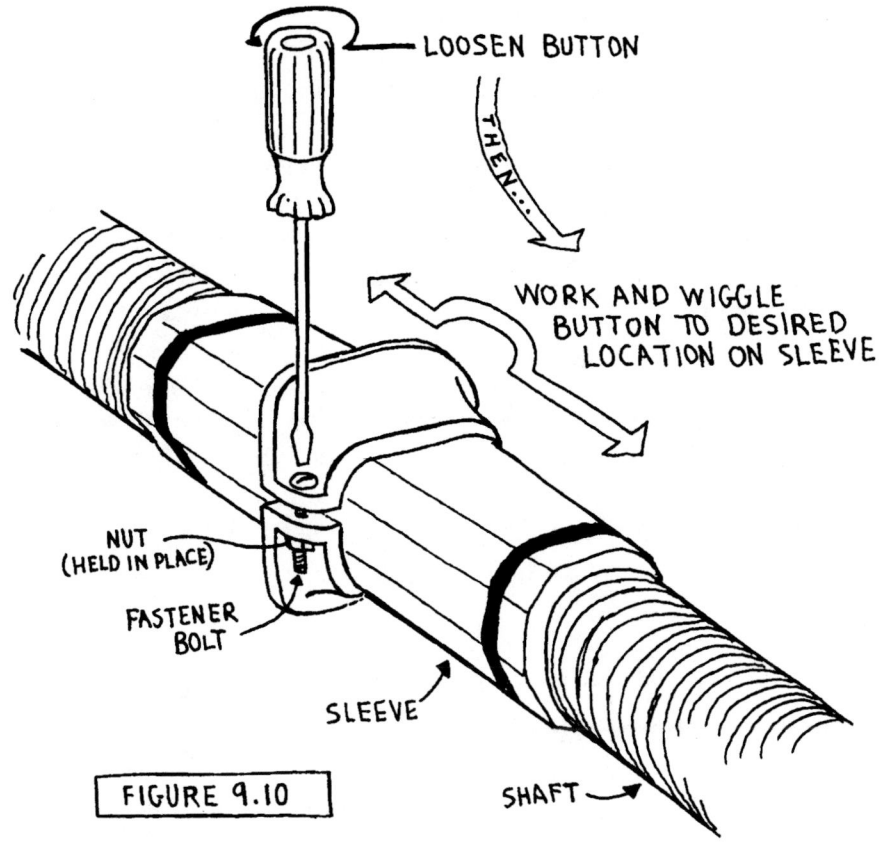

FIGURE 9.10

**Step 5. Record And Replace:** When you're done with an oar, put it in the rack, send it to the dock, or just get it out of your way. Then record the new inboard dimension. I say it all the time and there is a reason for it—you will need the info sooner or later.

## JOB 9.4. ADJUSTING THE SPREAD OR SPAN.

**Problem:** According to your measurements, the spread (or the span) needs adjusting, or you need to replace the oarlock pin.

**Needed:** Basic tool kit, rigging cards, access to the Web.

A brief sidebar: there was a time, not long ago, that I actually could outline all the steps for adjusting the spread of all the most popular sweep rowing shells; and I could accomplish that in only a few pages. Ah . . . but times have changed. Boats, riggers, and the adjustments have become much more specific, and to outline all of the steps for adjusting the spread in all of the more popular sweep shells and sculls (or most of the other adjustments) would be a book in itself. And those boats, riggers, and adjustments are changing significantly almost on a yearly basis. So . . . this is what I've done. . . .

To give you access to the best and most current information possible I've created documents on my Web site <http://www.helpingcoaches.com> that you can download specific to many of the JOBs you will need to do. Those documents are in PDF files (portable document format) and can be read right on any computer, or printed out to use at the boathouse. Yes, technology comes to the world of rigging.

## JOB 9.5: FINDING YOUR RIGGING (LEVERAGE) NUMBERS.

**Problem:** What the heck are your rigging numbers supposed to be?

**Needed:** Chapter Fifteen, pencil, paper.

Chapter Fifteen is set up exactly for this question. Go directly there. Do not pass *GO*, do not collect $200.00.

NOTE: DO NOT TRY THIS AT HOME

# Chapter Ten: Rigger Pitch

Have you ever wondered why an oar doesn't sink when it's rowed? It is buoyant, of course, but when someone is yanking as hard as possible on an oar handle, floatation isn't enough to keep the blade from going straight to the depths of Davy Jones' locker. An oar usually stays close to the surface, and pitch is why.

When an oar is placed into the water at the catch, there is a slight motion down on the **blade**, due to the lifting up on the oar handle. If the blade were to enter the water perfectly vertical, this downward motion would tend to carry the oar deep, and when force was applied to the oar it would go even deeper. Back in the olden days, someone figured this out and they devised a way to stop it. They put a slight **slant** on the blade. This slant, which we today call **pitch**, keeps the oar from going deep and bugging any submarines cruising below.

## 10.1 Types of Pitch

In our realm of rigging, there are two types of pitch. **Stern pitch** is the inclination of the blade away from a true vertical perpendicular during the drive phase of the stroke (see figure 10.1). In plain terms—stern pitch is the slant on the blade towards the stern when the oar is in the water. This slant is important because it keeps the blade from diving.

**Outward pitch,** also known as **lateral pitch**, is how far the oarlock pin tilts away from the centerline of the shell. Although the pin never tilts very far, it still tilts enough to make it an important measurement. As the blade moves through the water, the outward pitch works in combination with the stern pitch to give the blade a varying amount of slant. Outward pitch is a relatively new adjustment added to riggers and today most riggers usually come with the outward pitch already built into them. On several types of riggers you will find you can change the outward pitch if you need to.

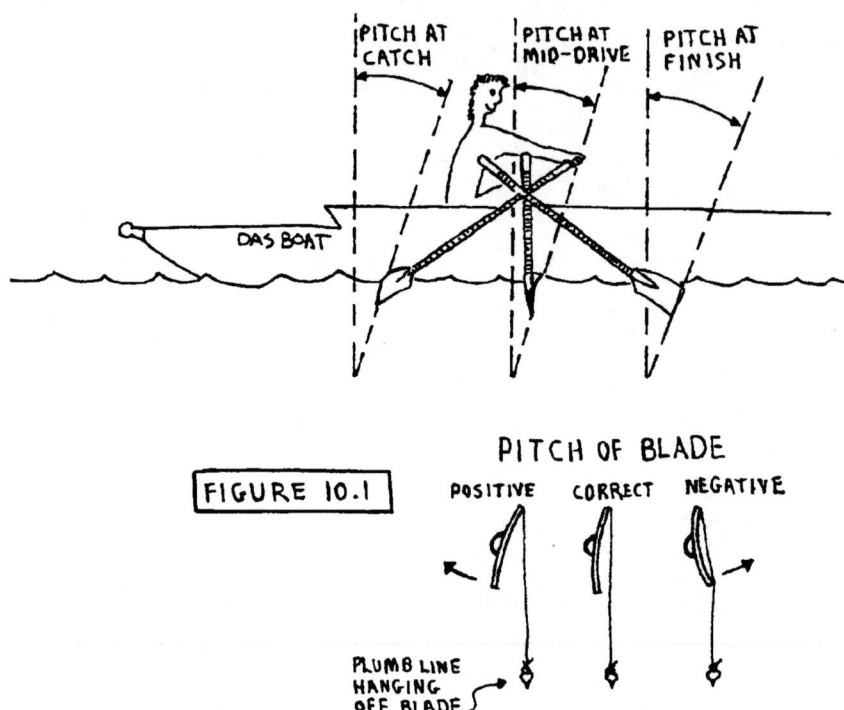

10.2 Where Pitch Comes From
The pitch can come from three different sources: (a) pitch in the oarlock, (b) pitch in the oar, or (c) pitch in the oarlock pin (or a combination of any of these). Let's quickly discuss each.

**Pitch in oarlock.** Pick up an oar and look at the shaft. About one-third of the way between the handle and the blade there should be a **collar** and **sleeve**. The sleeve is a protective tube around the oar shaft and the collar (button) is the small ring around the sleeve, which will rest against the oarlock when the oar is in it. One side of this sleeve is flat, called the **sleeve flat**.

Now look at an oarlock. Notice how there are two flat surfaces in it: one sits parallel to the water, the **horizontal flat,** and the other sits perpendicular to the water, the **vertical flat.**

An oar and an oarlock are good buddies, and just how close they are is apparent when the oar is inside the oarlock. The sleeve flat always rests against one of the flat surfaces of the oarlock: against the horizontal flat when the oar is feathered or against the vertical flat when the oar is squared.

> There are several different names for the *horizontal flat*, *vertical flat*, and *sleeve flat*. Call them whatever you wish, but check out figure 10.2 to make sure we're talking about the same things.

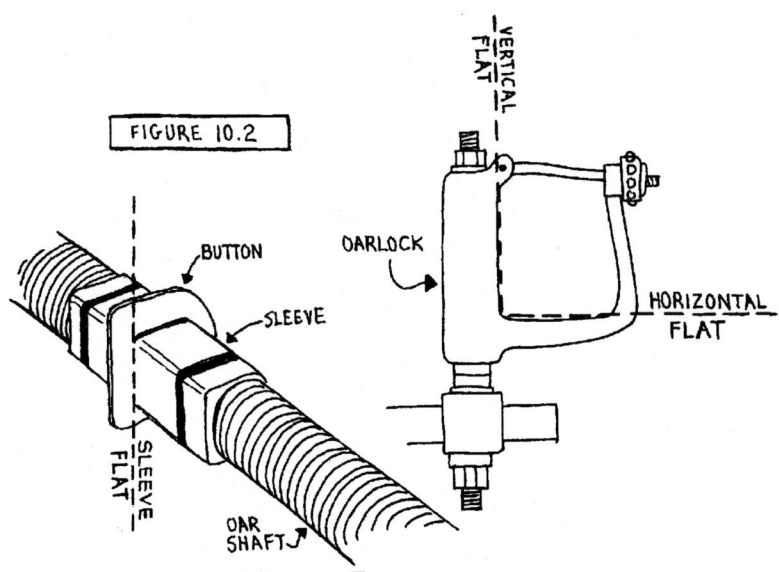

FIGURE 10.2

Can you see how the vertical flat and horizontal flat are slightly tilted? It's hardly noticeable so look closely. This tilting of the oarlock flats does two things. First, when the oar is feathered, the tilt of the horizontal flat gives the bow edge of the blade a small slant upwards. This helps the oar skim across the water when it's rough. Second, and most important, when the oar is squared, the tilt of the vertical flat helps give the oar pitch. And this tilting is what accounts for the pitch in your oarlock.

**Pitch in oar.** An oar itself can have pitch. This is due to any angling between the sleeve flat and the blade. If you're buying new oars you can order them with a wide variety of pitch built into them, although most folks order them with 0 degrees pitch. If a new set has just arrived, wood or composite, measure them just to make sure you got what you ordered.

The newer composite oars are a blessing as the pitch in these oars will hardly ever change with age. Wooden oars are a different story. They have a tendency to twist as the wood gets old and over a period of time this twisting may change the pitch. Regardless of the make of oar, you must know its pitch to figure out the stern pitch.

Some of the early types of composite oars had problems holding their pitch. This was usually due to the sleeve slipping on the shaft—not the oar twisting. Changes in design and production have all but eliminated this problem.

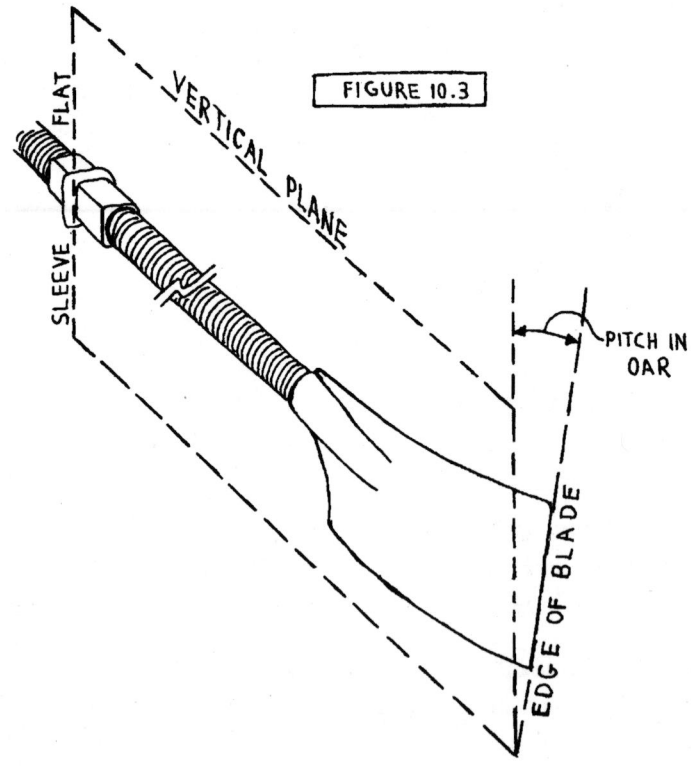

FIGURE 10.3

**Pitch in oarlock pin**. Oarlock pins are rarely straight up and down: they usually have some degree of stern and outward pitch. On all of the newer riggers, the stern pitch is adjustable and on some the outward pitch is too. Most Euro-style riggers do not come with outward pitch adjusters. That's where the Trog Tool comes in handy.

How much stern pitch the pin gets depends on how much pitch is in the oar and the oarlock itself. The amount of outward pitch will depend on what you as a Rigger determine you need for proper performance of the oar.

## 10.3 Importance of Pitch

The pitch helps direct the transmissions of power from the blade to the water; therefore, it has a major impact on the efficiency of the stroke. If there's too little or too much pitch, there are going to be efficiency and load problems.

There are two major reasons riggers have stern pitch. One is to help keep the oar just below the surface of the water during the drive. That's where you want it, just below the surface. The farther the blade goes under the surface, the higher the oar handle will rise. If the blade goes too deep (called **rowing deep** or **diving**) the oar handle will go so high that power application is difficult for the rower. It will also make getting the blade out of the water extremely frustrating. If the blade doesn't go deep enough it will begin peeking up above the surface. If that happens, the blade will be rowing air instead of water (called **washing out**). Unfortunately rowing air doesn't move the boat.

> During the drive, if the pitch is off greatly, the oar handle will rotate while the oar is pulled. The rower will have to spend strength and energy fighting this rotation. I call this the battle of "the hands vs. the oar handle." It's a fight the oar handle wins every time, and often results in crabs or wicked bad blisters.

The other reason for stern pitch is to help with boat balance. When a stroke is taken, the oar generates an upward force (it's a small one but it's there). This upward force pushes the rigger slightly towards the sky and pushes the opposite gunwale down. If this small force is not the same on both sides of the boat there can be balance problems. An eight has four ports and four starboards. If only the four ports were rowing, with nothing happening on the starboard side, the upward force would pick up the port riggers and drive down the starboard gunwale, giving the boat a **starboard list** (a leaning of the boat to starboard). But when both sides are rowing, the force upward from starboard should cancel the force upward from port. If all eight are rowing and someone is underpitched (so they're going deep), the upward forces won't balance and the underpitched rigger will actually generate a downward force. This added to the unbalanced force will give a healthy balance problem. The opposite will happen when a rigger is overpitched and the oar washes out.

There is one good reason for outward pitch: we don't want the same amount of stern pitch during the whole stroke.

As the oar moves through the outside arc, it's actually desirable to have the stern pitch decrease slightly from the catch to the release. The same amount of stern pitch that keeps the blade from sinking at the catch (due to the oar handle lifting) would make extracting the oar from the water difficult. You want to decrease the stern pitch as the oar nears the release. Outward pitch acts like a mentor for the stern pitch telling it when to change. The more positive outward pitch in the oarlock pin the greater the decrease in the stern pitch from catch to release.

## 10.4 Pitch Problems

No doubt about it, the most sensitive rigging measurement on a shell is pitch. A tricky thing about pitch is that it's hard to see with the naked eye (or even a dressed one) if you've got a pitch problem. In fact, the pitch is so sensitive you need to use a meter to measure changes in it.

Another tricky thing about pitch is that it doesn't take much to mess it up. A slight crab, a run-in with the boathouse door, or an oar slammed hard into an oarlock can cause a change in your pitch. And any change, even a little one, can result in big problems with the stroke and possibly with the balance of the boat.

Which brings up the point of how do you tell if you have a pitch problem? Three ways. First, follow your routine maintenance checkup (JOB 18.1): this will help you cut off problems at the pass. Second, keep an eye out for problems as the oar moves through the water—such as the blade's going deep (possibly not enough pitch) or the blade's washing out (possibly too much pitch)—especially checking the pitch immediately after you see or hear of any crabs. And third, listen to the rowers.

But don't listen too hard. . . .

After a hard day of slaving over a hot rigging stick, I was hanging out at the boathouse watching the sunset. The boss came around the corner and said one of his guys was complaining about the pitch in the rigger. To appease the boss, and to satisfy my curiosity, I got the boat down and checked the rigger and oar. No problem with the pitch—in fact, it was just a whisker away from perfect. We told the rower this and he replied, "No, my rigger is not off, it's Bob's rigger. It's got to be off at least one forth of a degree!"

This guy was telling us that from the two seat he could tell the six seat's rigger was out of pitch, and by some tiny margin no less. We did the only thing possible in this situation: laughed it off and banished the rower to an ergo-
meter for a short prison term. It's important to listen to the rowers, but unless you're dealing with topnotch elite rowers, take "pitch-bitching" with a grain of salt.

## JOB 10.1. USING A PITCH METER.

**Problem:** Ya gotta figure out this fancy-dancy tool with the neat bubble in it.

**Needed:** Pitch meter, a boat seats-up, and about five minutes.

The best way to determine pitch is with a **pitch meter**. The meter can be a little intimidating at first, but after using it a few times you'll get very comfortable with it. Figure 10.4 shows a common design for pitch meters.

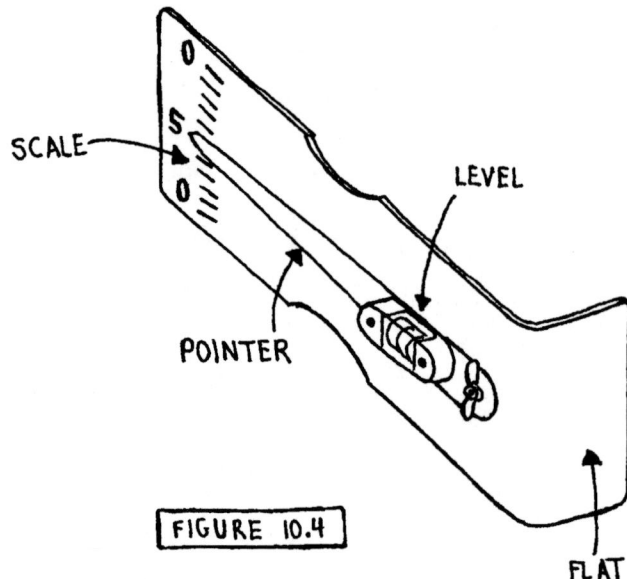

SCALE

LEVEL

POINTER

FIGURE 10.4

FLAT

**Step 1. Getting To Know You:** The first thing to do is pick up the meter and check it over. There are basically four parts to the meter: the scale, the flat, the level (bubble), and the pointer. If it's out-of-the-box new, read the directions. If it's used or borrowed, check it out to make sure the flat and pointer are straight and the bubble is not broken (There are several different pitch meter designs. I use the more common one here for the figures.)

**Step 2. Check Your Surfaces:** When you measure the pitch of something, you are comparing how much tilt there is in it compared to a true vertical or true horizontal line (called the **reference surface**). To get a good reading, the surface(s) you're going to measure and your meter need to be clean and undamaged. A gunwale with a big chunk missing is going to screw up your reading.

Finding a reference surface for a shell is a snap; all we need to do is place the meter on some surface in the shell that is level in respect to the bow and stern. The keel, lip along the gunwale or top of the gunwale (if it's in good condition) are prime sites. The tracks aren't a good choice because they slant slightly from bow to stern (check how the seat rolls aft). It doesn't matter if the shell is level, on a hillside or upside down, the meter will account for it (pretty smart little tool).

**Step 3. Zero The Meter:** Place the pointer on the lower zero, it should slide easily along the scale. Put your thumb on the pointer and firmly hold it at zero. Now place the meter on the reference surface you've chosen for your true horizontal line. Muster up all your coordination and while holding the meter on the surface and the pointer on zero adjust the bubble so it's between the two lines scratched in the tube. If the bubble is fairly small in relation to the space between the lines, adjust the bubble so it just touches one line and then be sure to use the same line in the next step.

> I like to have the meter facing me when I take a pitch because it is easier to read. But that is my preference—you can have it facing the other way if you want. It's just critical the meter is always facing the same way at the reference surface and of the oarlock.

**Step 4. To The Oarlock:** Carefully take the pitch meter and hold the vertical base onto the vertical flat part of the oarlock. An oarlock with many years of use will be pretty worn so check the vertical surface to see if it's flat and not damaged. If you've got a large alligator clamp, use it to clamp the meter in place instead of holding it. Keep the base in good contact with the oarlock, making sure it is not resting on rounded corners at the top or the bottom. Now slide the pointer until the bubble centers itself between the two lines and read the number at the pointer—that's your oarlock pitch.

**Step 5. One More Time:** Take your meter off the oarlock and walk around the shell, enjoy the scenery, grab a sip of soda and relax. Let's try it once more to see if we really know what we're doing. Set yourself up at the same rigger and measurement again.

You should be right on the money, 1/2 degree off is acceptable for First-Dimensional Riggers, but you'll get more accurate with experience. Got the same number? Great, go to the store, pick yourself up your Pitch Meter Merit Badge, and proudly wear it. Got a major difference? Check your steps and try again—you're probably just moving too fast.

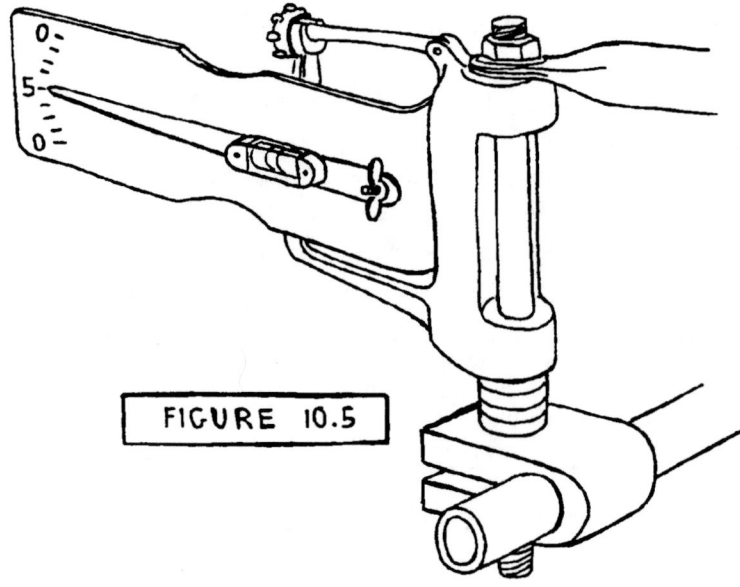

FIGURE 10.5

## JOB 10.2: HOW TO MEASURE YOUR STERN PITCH.

**Problem:** You need to check out your stern pitch.

**Needed:** Pitch meter, boat seats-up, rigging card (**helpful extras:** large alligator clamp, carpenter's level, two C-clamps, sawhorse, three-foot-long chunk of wood [not too wide], rigging stick, adhesive tape, rag, friend.)

There are two different types of pitches we need to fret over. Stern pitch is the degree of tilt the blade has when it's perpendicular in the water. This tilt can come from three places, a twist in the oar, a slant in the oar-lock pin aft or fore, or angling built into the oarlock itself. Or it might be a combination of all three. To find out exactly what your stern pitch is we'll need to measure them all. The other pitch is the outward pitch, if that's what you need go to JOB 10.3.

The pitch is a key measurement. To quote that world-class mooch Goldilocks, "It has to be just right." Too much pitch or too little pitch can cause all sorts of trouble, especially with transmission of power from the rower to the blade. First we'll start off with the oars.

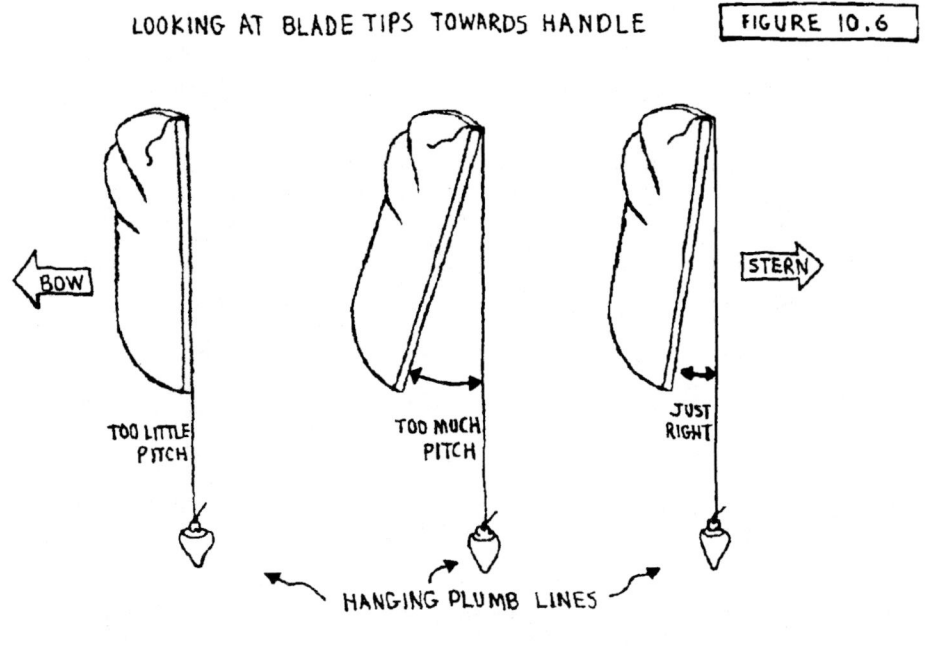

LOOKING AT BLADE TIPS TOWARDS HANDLE

FIGURE 10.6

When you measure the pitch, be accurate. We want to know the pitch to half a degree. That's a small amount, but it can make a big difference.

## Part 1: Measuring the Oars

**Step 1. Set Up The Oars: All Types:** Composite oars hold their pitch well with age, so you should have to measure their pitch only once. Wooden oars don't hold up as well, so you're going to have to measure them frequently, maybe once a year or even more often. Before we touch the shell, we need to know what the pitch is in the oars. If you know the pitch, and are sure what you know is right, then go to Step 4.

To measure the oars, you'll have to lay them out flat, so give yourself some room. Set your sawhorse up so it's stable; if it wobbles toss it out and get another one. Set the rigging stick on top of the horse and secure it with tape. There are two places on the oar you're going to measure: the blade and the flat part of the sleeve (sleeve flat) that sits against the oar-lock face (vertical flat) when the oar is squared (see figure 10.7). Take your rag and make sure both places are clean; a little bit of gunk under your pitch meter can screw up your readings. Place two small pieces of tape about 8 inches apart on the rigging stick: this marks the space where the oars go (when you're doing a lot of oars, this will help your sanity).

---

The folks at Concept II used to ship their pitched oars with colored bands around them (they no longer do that). This was for quick identification that the oar has pitch. A green band denoted starboard pitch, a red band port pitch and a plain band was zero pitch.

---

**Step 2. Measure Away:** Now lay your pitch meter flat between the pieces of tape and zero it (see previous JOB if you need help with using the meter).

Take your first oar, feather it, and place it between the two pieces of tape. Make sure the sleeve flat is on the rigging stick. Have your friend press slightly down on the sleeve to make sure it stays level. With your buddy stabilizing the oar, take your pitch meter (which is zeroed!) and place it on the blade, while keeping the meter parallel to the sawhorse. Remember to have the meter facing the same direction as when you zeroed it. Place the meter about one third the length of the blade from the blade tip and center the bubble by moving the pointer. Read the scale; what you see is your oar pitch.

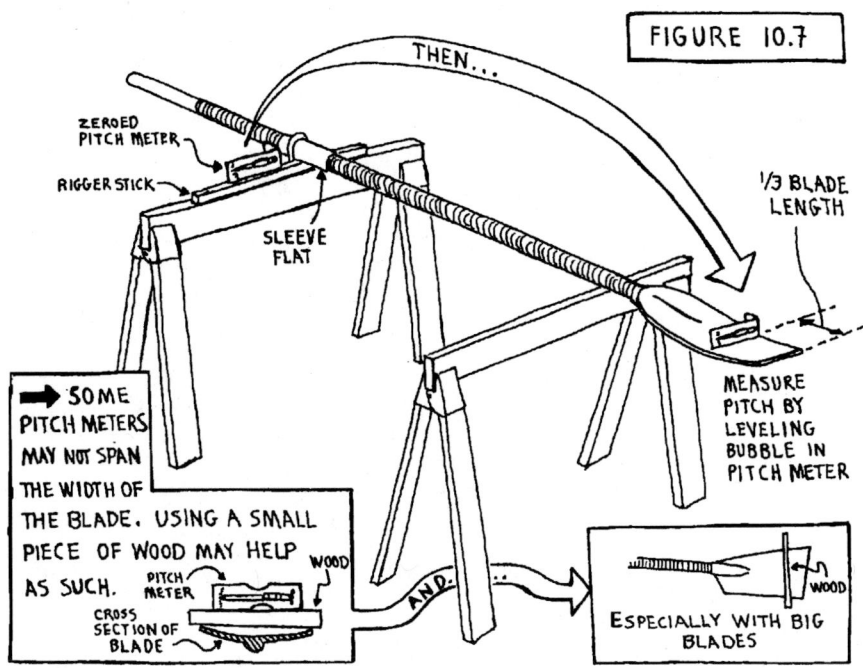

**Step 3. Keep Track:** Let's think ahead and try to save ourselves some time down the line. We need to mark down this pitch, either on the oar itself or on your rigging cards. The easiest way is to mark the pitch with a waterproof pen on the same label that identifies the oar. If that won't work, pull out the rigging cards and write it down. Wooden oars have a tendency to change their pitch with age, so I'd suggest you measure them every season or so; composites don't seem to change much so once every year or two should do.

## Part 2: Measuring the Oarlocks
**Step 1. Stabilize the shell: All types:** Now on to the shell. We'll measure the oarlock and pin at the same time. Place your boat in slings in an area where it is going to be relatively out of the way. Accuracy counts, and the last thing you need is a bunch of geeky rowers bumping into your shell as you try to get your pitches.

Tighten all the riggers. After you've set the boat up, it's going to help your cause greatly to stabilize it so it doesn't rock freely from side to side. If you are a pro at taking pitches, or in a hurry, this step is not necessary, but if you are a First- or Second-Dimensional Rigger, take a few extra minutes and stabilize the shell well. A stable shell is a necessity for doing outward pitch, regardless of how experienced you are.

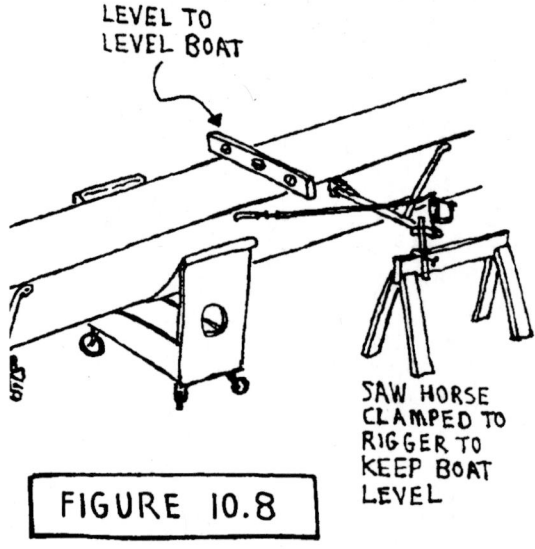

LEVEL TO LEVEL BOAT

SAW HORSE CLAMPED TO RIGGER TO KEEP BOAT LEVEL

FIGURE 10.8

There are several ways to stabilize a shell. My favorite is to place a sawhorse under one of the riggers. With my two handy-dandy clamps I fasten a small piece of wood to the sawhorse and clamp the other end to the main rigger stay. Doing this on only one rigger should give plenty of stability and doesn't take up much room.

When you clamp onto the stay, do so on the gunwale side of the oarlock pin so that if you have to adjust the spread, you will not have to remove the clamp. Before you tighten down the clamps, you need to level the boat. Take your carpenter's level and place it across the gunwales perpendicular to the centerline. Have your friend ready at the clamps, and when the boat is balanced (the bubble is centered), have your pal tighten down the clamps.

> If you don't have a carpenter's level, you can substitute your pitch meter. Find a place you know to be level (door frames usually are). Zero the pitch meter on it, place your rigging stick perpendicular to the centerline across the gunwales, and put the pitch meter on top of it. Now balance the boat so the bubble is centered and tighten the clamps.

If you can't be quite as fancy with your setup, you can place a strap or two over the boat and snug it down to the sling. Or place an oar in both the port and starboard side oarlocks and then let the oars rest on the ground. You will find your boat is fairly steady. You will also find you've made a great roadblock and are bound to have half a dozen people tripping over your oars.

One of the worst methods I have found to keep the shell from rocking back and forth is to have someone lean against it and try to hold it in place. This works about as well as giving a five-year-old child an ice cream cone and telling him not to lick it.

**Step 2. Zero The Meter:** Grab a rag and clean all the goobers off of the oarlock. Take your pitch meter and, keeping it parallel to the centerline, zero it somewhere on the boat. Gunwales, monocoque decking, and braces work well if they are smooth and not damaged—tracks do not work because they are slightly inclined and will screw up your readings. Keeping the meter facing the same direction, bring it out to the oarlock, and place the vertical face of the meter against the vertical flat surface of the oarlock (see figure 10.9) and secure it with your alligator clamp. Make sure the meter face is even against the vertical flat.

> **Oarlocks wear.** If the vertical flat of your oarlock is worn, it can make accurate pitch readings hard to get. Try to hold the meter against the part of the flat the oar is most likely to rest against. Replace worn oarlocks as soon as you can.

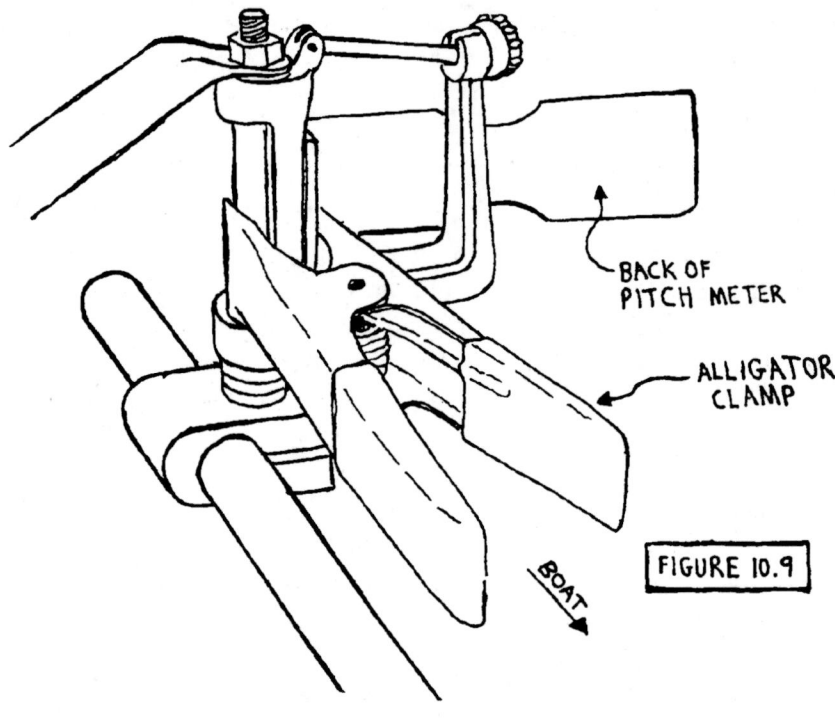

BACK OF
PITCH METER

ALLIGATOR
CLAMP

BOAT

FIGURE 10.9

Some people measure the oar pitch and oarlock pitch at the same time. They put the oar into the oarlock and holding it steady move the oar into the different positions, then take their readings at the blade. I've never had much luck with this system: it takes up too much room and I have too little coordination.

**Step 3. Catch Your Pitches:** You're ready to get your pitches. There are three different places you want to find the stern pitch: the catch, the mid-drive and the release.

Turn the oarlock to the catch position (where an imaginary oar handle would go just aft of the foot stretchers). Slide the pointer until the bubble is centered and read the pitch off the scale. Now turn the oarlock to the mid-drive position (the oarlock is parallel to the centerline of the shell), slide the pointer, and read the pitch again. And finally to the finish position, slide the pointer and find your pitch there. Be careful that with all this turning and twisting the clamp doesn't slip and you drop your meter. If it does, or if you think you have messed up the bubble, you'll need to zero the meter again. In fact, you should zero it every time you move to a new rigger.

**Step 4. Add It Up:** To find out what your stern pitch is, add your oar pitch to the measurements you just got from each oarlock's position. The normal range from catch to release is 6 to 4 degrees. If you find the stern pitch does not decrease from the catch to the release then you may have a problem with your outward pitch. If you need to change either the stern pitch or the outward pitch, get ready for an operation. If you're happy with what you've got, grab a cookie and move on to other things.

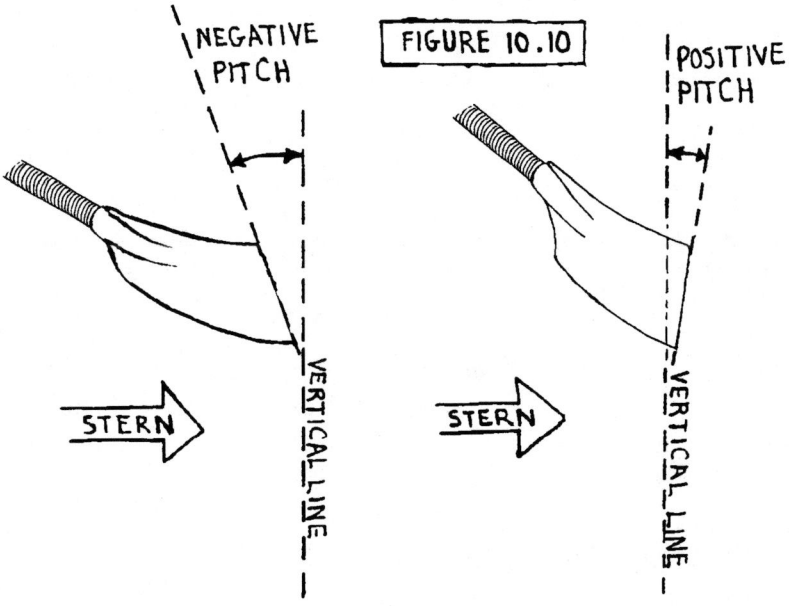

**Step 5. Write Everything Down:** I know I keep nagging, but write down your numbers. If you're doing more than one rigger, you'll forget them.

# JOB 10.3: HOW TO MEASURE YOUR OUTWARD PITCH.

**Problem:** You need to determine what's going on with your outward pitch.

**Needed:** Pitch meter, saw horses, pencil and paper, access to the Web.

**Outward pitch** is the slant of the oarlock pin leaning away from the centerline of the shell. This tilt of the pin will cause the stern pitch to change slightly as the oar is rowed through the outside arc. An outward pitch of 0 to 1 degrees (which is the now the norm—it used to be 1 to 2 degrees) will cause the stern pitch to decrease by 0 to 1 degrees from the catch, through the mid-drive, to the release. A larger stern pitch at the catch helps keep the blade from diving deep, and a smaller stern pitch at the finish helps with extraction of the oar.

> For more detailed information on combined effects of stern and outward pitch I suggest reading the C.A.R.A. *Level Two manual*, pages 77–82. Also Purcer, in *Rigging*, has a layout chart that compares the stern pitch at the three positions for half-degree changes in the outward pitch. Both give good ideas of how changes in the outward pitch affect the stern pitch.

Measuring the outward pitch is similar to measuring the stern pitch, except that it's critical to have a level boat. You're trying to measure a tiny, yet important item and a level boat will make it a possible chore. You won't have to measure the outward pitch frequently because you can use the stern pitch as a trip-wire to inform you that the outward pitches are off. If you get some funky stern pitch readings, like the pitch at the catch is less than the pitch at the finish, then you know it's time to check the outward pitch.

## Quick Method
There is a quick and simple method to measure your outward pitch, one that doesn't involve taking the rigger apart. Here it is.

**Step 1. Stabilize Boat.** (See JOB 10.2, Part 2, Step 1, *Measuring the Oarlocks*.) I strongly suggest you use the sawhorse method to stabilize the shell. Ever notice how a lot of tools are named after animals? For example, monkey wrenches, sawhorses, alligator clamps—but hardly any are named after vegetables? Aah . . . never mind. Make sure your riggers are on tight; a loose rigger is a waste of time.

**Step 2. Measure Away.** Now measure the stern pitch at all three positions (catch, mid-drive, release). Your numbers should read something like the following:

> catch = 5 degrees
> mid-drive = 4 degrees
> release = 3 degrees

Now grab your pencil and paper. Time to do a little math.

Subtract the mid-drive pitch number from the catch pitch number. Then subtract the release pitch number from the mid-drive pitch number. Now add these two numbers you have left, divide that number by 2 and that's your outward pitch. If you do your math and your measurements correctly, your number should be between 0 to 1. If it is not, do the measurements and math again.

If the outward-pitch number looks reasonable (between 0 and 1) and your catch-pitch number is the same or slightly greater than your release-pitch number, you're golden. If the outward-pitch number is greater than 1, negative, or your release-pitch number is greater than your catch-pitch number, you might have outward pitch problems.

### Detailed Method
There is a more specific method to measure the outward pitch of a rigger; however, it involves talking the rigger apart and can be tedious. Each make of rigger is different, which means the detailed method is different for each make of boat.

To get the detailed method for your make of boat, check out my Web site, <http://www.MaxRigging.com>. There you will find a series of downloadable PDFs with information about many different types of boats and measurements.

## JOB 10.4: HOW TO ADJUST YOUR PITCH.

**Problem:** One, or all, of your pitches isn't right.

**Needed:** Access to the Web.

At this point, things are not right with your pitch. It is time for some serious surgery on your oar(s) or rigger(s). What you need now is specific information about your equipment. Go to my Web site, <http://www.MaxRigging.com>, download that specific information, and get ready to operate.

## JOB 10.5: FINDING YOUR PITCH NUMBERS.

**Problem:** You need to know what numbers to use for your pitches.

**Needed:** Chapter Fifteen, and/or a reference source (book, friend, Web site).

If you don't already know your pitch numbers, then turn to Chapter Fifteen. I've included Rigging Charts there that have numbers you can use for pitch adjustments.

You'll notice that the numbers come in ranges and are not specific. Why a range? So that you can adapt the pitch for an individual or a group.

Novice rowers tend to row fairly rough. To help them control their stroke, especially to make a clean release, rig them in the higher range of stern pitch. More stern pitch is helpful in keeping the oar close to the surface of the water and making a clean release. Elite rowers tend to row more smoothly—that's what comes from rowing a million or so strokes. These folks tend to need less help from the pitch. So rig them towards the lower range of the stern-pitch numbers. Reducing the stern pitch will reduce some of the slippage of the blade during the drive. This helps the blade get a better bite on the water.

If while watching a person row, or while doing it yourself, a blade appears to be "ripping" through the water (not holding the water during the drive), or complaints arise about the oar "feeling like it's not grabbing the water," try rigging with less stern pitch. The unofficial rule with pitch is the better the technique of the rower the less stern pitch you need to give. The better rowers need less help.

# Chapter Eleven: Rigger Height

**N**ow it's time to focus on a different element of rigging, the **height.** If you read some of the older or more technical writings, you may see this measurement called **oar height**, **oarlock height**, or even **height of the swivel**. All of those names are pretty official, and by now you should be on fairly friendly terms with your rigger, so let's simply call it *rigger height*.

Understanding height can be a little tricky, but once you have a good grasp of it, life as a Rigger will be much easier.

In theory, height is the distance from the **horizontal flat** of the oarlock (a.k.a. **oarlock sill**) to the top of the water's surface. The horizontal flat is the bottom support of the oarlock, which is where the oar rests.

It would be downright inconvenient if we had to put the shell in water every time we wanted to measure the height. So to make life a little simpler the top of the seat can be substituted for the water's surface. This works because shells are designed so that when they are in the water the seat top is usually a consistent distance off of the water's surface.

Therefore, in reality, the height is the distance from the horizontal flat to the top of the seat. Got it? Check Pete's diagram; it'll help.

You adjust the height by moving the oarlock up and down, which is usually a simple JOB. What isn't so simple is knowing where your heights should be adjusted to. The height needs to be set correctly for two reasons. First, on the recovery phase of the rowing stroke, proper height adjustment allows the rower enough room to extract the blade cleanly from the water and gives the oar enough clearance to go over the puddles of the other rowers or over the waves on the water. Second, height affects how efficient the rower is during the drive phase. If the height is not adjusted correctly, then the rower won't be able to properly apply power.

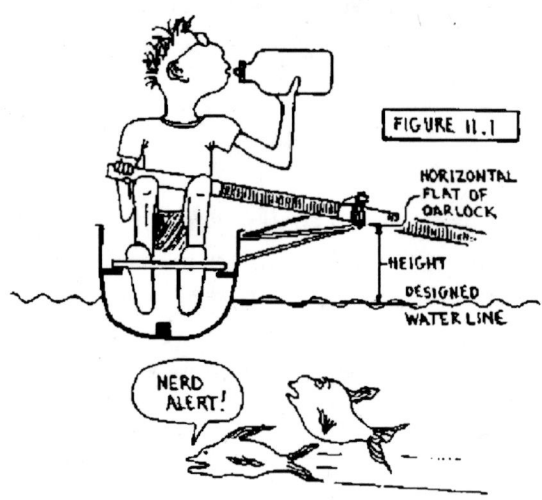

## 11.1 The Zones

When you think of height, two words should pop into your head: *comfort* and *efficiency*.

Picture this: You and the family have gone to Aunt Mabel's for the annual Thanksgiving feast. When the time comes to sit down and eat, you're short one chair. Being well mannered, and very hungry, you volunteer to go without a chair and sit on the only thing around, a milk crate. There you are, sitting at the table on this little milk crate and feeling sort of low (literally) . . . but things are getting better because here comes the food.

After a couple of minutes you begin to notice something: because you're sitting so low on a milk crate, you can't reach out very far and all the great food is passing you by. You're uncomfortable and starting to starve. Being intelligent, and getting hungrier, you put another milk crate on the first one. This sits you high enough to dig in . . . finally your plate is full . . . but now you're sitting so high you have to lean forward to eat, and your back begins to hurt—and because you have to lift your spoon so high, the soup keeps spilling off it. Once again you are uncomfortable and now famished.

The measurement of height can be looked at the same way. The height of the oarlock determines how high the oar will be carried during the drive. If the height is not adjusted correctly, then the rower will be uncomfortable and inefficient (remember, a rower will always be hungry—regardless of the height).

Let's take this thought of comfort and efficiency one step farther and name two zones after them. I call them the **comfort zone** and the **efficiency zone.**

**Comfort zone** is a ballpark area of height in which the rower feels comfortable during the drive and especially comfortable at the finish. If the height of the oarlock is in the comfort zone then the rower will have neither excessive strain on the upper body (due to pulling in the oar too high) nor excessive strain on the lower back (due to pulling in the oar too low).

The rower will also have enough room on the recovery so that the oar will be off the water and the handle will clear the top of the thighs. A decent rule of thumb *is the higher the rigging, the more comfort for the rower* (to a certain point). The comfort zone varies with each individual rower due to varying body types.

**Efficiency zone** is the area of height in which the stroke is the most efficient. Basically, *the lower the rigging, the more efficient the stroke (*to a certain point) because the blade will hold the water better. Also, the oar, which will be carried lower during the drive, will form a better lever. Well then, sounds like you should set the height high for comfort and at the same time set it low for efficiency. So what do you do? Go for both!

Try to set the height so you are getting the best of both zones. This will happen at the union of the comfort and efficiency zones. Trying to determine where this union is located is not easy. JOB 11.3 is all about helping you to determine where the proper height (and this union) is.

## 11.2 Bits and Pieces

Let's take a look at your rigger and the pieces that are important to height. You know by now that the oar sits in the oarlock, but what you might not have noticed is that in several riggers, especially Euro-style riggers, the oarlock itself sits on top of small plastic rings called **spacers**. These spacers go around the **oarlock pin** like rings on a finger. In riggers that use spacers the oarlock pin is attached at the base to the rigger **mainstay** and at the top to the rigger **lock stay** (top stay).

Adjusting the height is simply a matter of shifting these little spacers from the top of the oarlock to the bottom or vice versa. This raises the oarlock up or down.

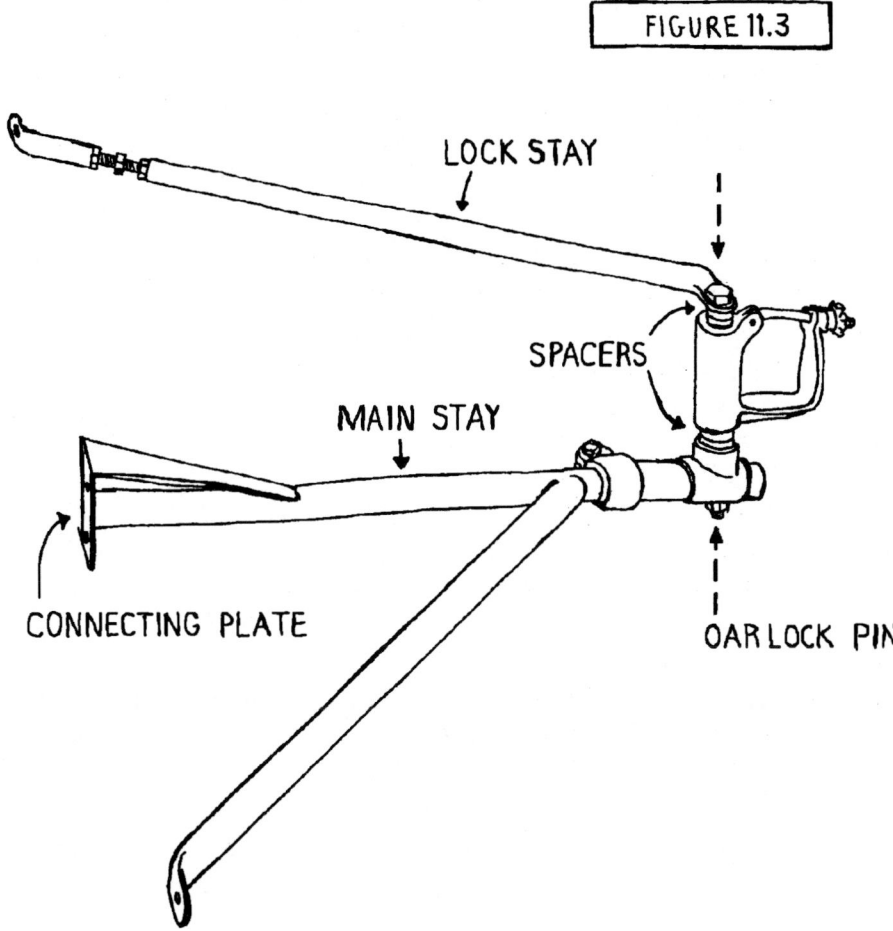

FIGURE 11.3

LOCK STAY

SPACERS

MAIN STAY

CONNECTING PLATE

OARLOCK PIN

Some makes of riggers, for instance older Vespolis, do not use the spacer system. Instead, the oarlock pin has been threaded so that the pin itself can be raised or lowered by rotating it through the rigger mainstay, as shown in figure 11.3. This in turn moves the oarlock, which then adjusts the height. It is a fairly simple procedure, but be wary: *when the height is changed on these riggers, the pitch can also change* (that is if you do not remove the lock stay when adjusting the pitch).

Some older Empacher riggers use a different system altogether. While there are a few spacers on the pin for small height changes, in their Excentric oarlocks, there are no spacers but instead a couple of large washers. On those riggers, major height changes can be achieved by actually moving the whole rigger. Three different sets of holes have been put into the **con-**

**necting plate**, where the rigger attaches to the shell. This allows you to put the rigger onto the boat at different height settings. In conjunction with the metal spacers (or washers), this system allows you to get a wide range of height adjustments. Some Kaschper models adjust this way too, except they only have two holes at the connecting plate instead of three like the Empachers.

Now don't lose your cool if your rigger is one of those really old, antique types that are basically nonadjustable. Unlike some of the other measurements for these riggers, in which there is nothing you can adjust, you can adjust the heights to some degree.

## 11.3 When to Adjust?

Knowing when to adjust the height of a rigger is just as important as knowing how to adjust it. There is a very simple test you can do to see if your heights are set in the correct spot—it's called the *height check*.

Have your crew launch and find a relatively calm spot of water. The rowers should then sit at the release position with the blades square in the water. The hands should be placed lightly on the handles, and the blade of the oar should be allowed to find its natural depth.

At this release position, the handle should just be touching into the rower's chest area. It is important that the shell is on an even keel, so I recommend you do this test with at least one pair (in sweep) or one rower (in sculling) keeping the shell balanced.

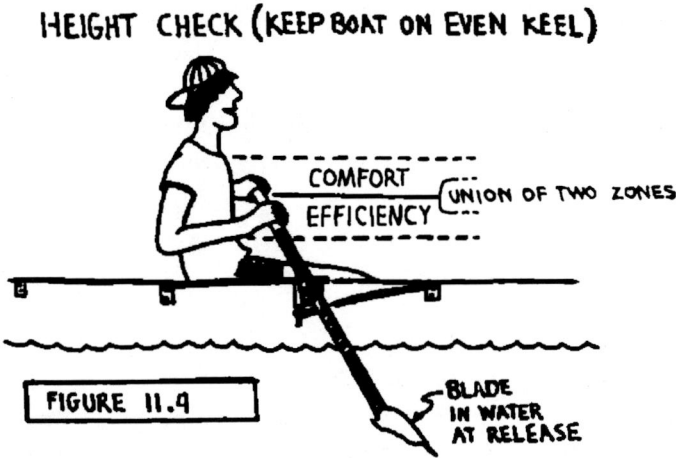

Now check where the oar handle touches the rower's chest. If the height is properly adjusted, the butt of the handle should be just an inch or two above the **xiphoid process,** which is the bottom of the rower's sternum (chest bone). This point usually turns out to be within the union of the comfort and the efficiency zones. If the butt of the oar handle is not near this area of the chest, then you need to readjust.

> Just remember, the boat must be on an even keel and the oars buried for the height check to work. Keep checking these two points before you decide your heights are out of whack and you get in a huff.

The height check will give you a pretty good idea if your heights are right, but there are two other signs to keep your eyes and ears alert for that may signal you that the heights need adjusting.

One is when a rower complains of *discomfort*, especially in the small of the back or in the shoulders. Complaints like this are signs something is wrong. I have found if a rower complains about the rigging they usually snarl about the height and bitch about the pitch. At the collegiate level I usually ignore most "pitch bitching" but I definitely listen to complaints about the height because it's important that the rowers are comfortable. If you do get complaints, hopefully it's the rigger and not an injury. Be extremely careful.

The other sign of height trouble is when a rower has difficulty extracting the blade cleanly from the water. This may be due to something else, such as pitch or a technique problem, but having trouble at the release (such as rowing it out or feathering underwater) is a fairly good sign you need to check the height.

Now don't be surprised, or overwhelmed, if you end up adjusting a rigger several times before you get the height right. A good rule of thumb is **adjust, row, observe**, then **readjust**. Just like the shampoo, rinse, and repeat routine. Adjusting the height tends to be a constant process and may take a couple of tries before you get it perfect.

## 11.4 Generic vs. Brand Name

Early in the season most coaches begin with a generic rig, where all riggers are set at basically the same dimensions. As the season progresses and seat selections are made, coaches then begin to have an idea which rowers will be rowing consistently in which seats and the riggers are then set to the individuals. When this is done, the height is usually one of the major adjustments made because the upper bodies of people vary greatly.

A change of only inches in someone's upper body height can change their comfort and efficiency zones greatly. The spread, pitch, and work-thru remain fairly constant throughout the boat, but the height needs to receive some special attention.

> I've heard it said by several notable coaches that about 60% to 80% of riggers have the height adjusted too low. I tend to put my own rigging in the upper extremes of the comfort zone.

## JOB 11.1: MEASURING THE OARLOCK HEIGHT.

**Problem:** You're here to measure the height of a sweep oarlock. (Scullers—read this JOB and then refer to Chapter Twenty-One for more info.)

**Needed:** Rigging stick (or a long straight edge), tape measure, something to clean oarlock with.

This JOB is a lot easier if your shell is seats-up. In a pinch it can be done upside-down, but that's a great way to get a stiff neck. Before we touch the boat, we need to discuss two things:

**What to measure:** It's important we have an understanding about where to take the readings. Look at the oarlock. We are going to use a point on the horizontal flat (sill) that is midway between the vertical flat and the front of the oarlock. The height is always taken with the oarlock in the mid-drive position.

The seat top is the other reading point. We measure from the lowest point on the seat which is at the bow end right before the half-moon (where your tail bone would be).

Any part of the seat top will work for your height measurement. When comparing notes, just know what spot has been used. Different spots will give slightly different readings.

**What to use:** Are you one of the fortunate sons who can afford a **rigging stick** (see Chapter Two)? Good. Pull it out and make sure it is in good shape. They tend to get beaten up when traveling or in storage. Make sure the ruler is clean and easy to read.

If you don't have a rigging stick, or if you're in a pinch, you can make out quite nicely with a **straight edge**. Find yourself a long, clean piece of whatever. I've seen wood, plastic, and metal used. It needs to be about four or five feet long, in good shape, and easy to handle. If you're using a two-by-four, do yourself a favor and remove any nails in it.

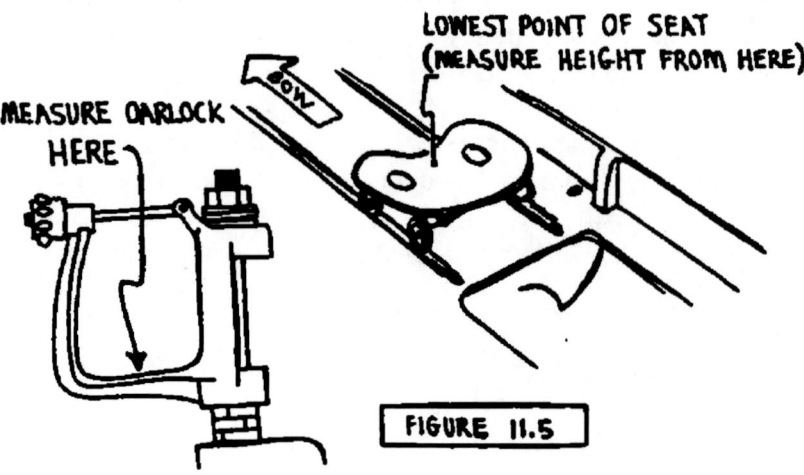

FIGURE 11.5

Hold the straight edge in one hand and look down the end, just as if you were looking down the barrel of a gun—which of course you wouldn't do! Look at the edges. They should be straight and curveless. If they are, then you've got your piece. Are the edges wavy? Return it where you got it, especially if it's holding up the roof, and try another piece. Be picky; get a good one. Also get a good tape measure, preferably one with both metric and U.S. systems on it.

### Rigging Stick Method

**Step 1. Measure Once:** At the shell's position you want to measure, roll the seat to the stern end of the tracks. Place your rigging stick perpendicular across the gunwales and pull the ruler down so it just touches the seat at the right spot. Lock your ruler so it won't slide.

**Step 2. Measure Twice:** Take your rag and clean off the gunk growing on the oarlock. Get it nice and clean, especially if you are doing this on Sunday morning in your good suit. Place the oarlock so it is parallel to the centerline of the boat (mid-drive position). With your rigging stick still across the two gunwales (perpendicular to the centerline), push its end out to the oarlock. Take your ruler and place it at the end of the rigging stick and move it so it touches the oarlock. Read the number where the ruler touches the mid of the horizontal flat. That's your height.

> **Watch out!** Make sure both sides of the rigging stick are still touching the gunwales. If your rigger has a front stay, the stick may get hung up on it causing it not to sit flat on the gunwale. This will give you some wild readings.

## Straight Edge Method

**Step 1. Measure Once:** If you're using a straight edge, set it up the same as the rigging stick. Take your tape measure and measure down from the <u>top</u> of the straight edge to the seat. Now mark the intersection of the tape measure and straight edge. I usually place my thumbnail at the spot or just remember the number.

**Step 2. Measure Twice:** Now slide the tape out to the oarlock end of the stick. Hold the tape against the rigging stick with the number you just measured right at the <u>top</u> of the stick. Keep the oarlock at the mid-drive, bring together the tape and oarlock and read the number where the middle of the horizontal flat and the tape intersect. That's your height. Is it where you want it? Great, clean up, and you're done. Not what you want? Then on to JOB 11.2.

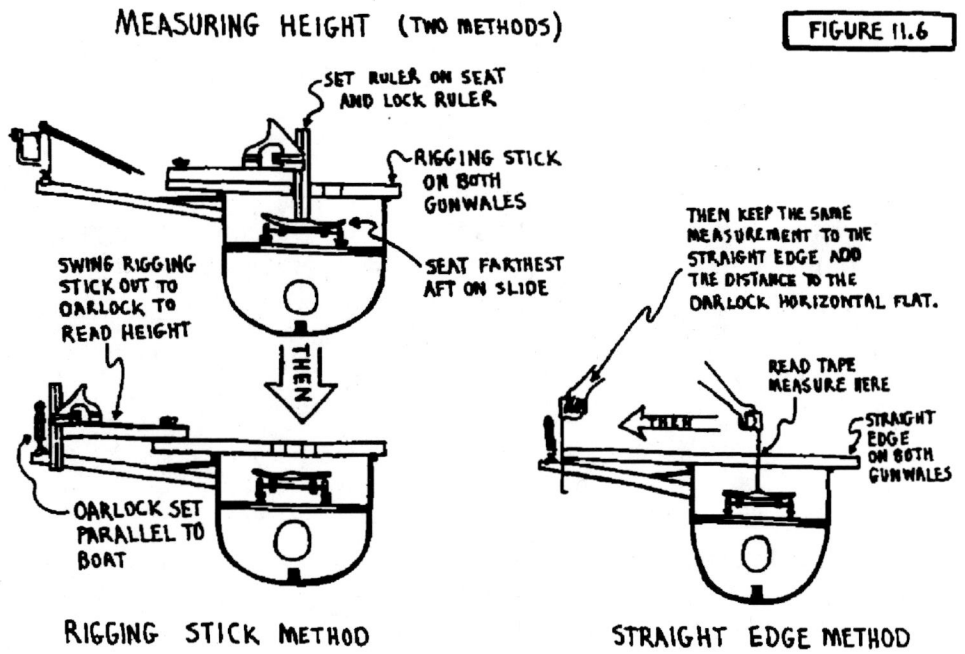

MEASURING HEIGHT (TWO METHODS)            FIGURE 11.6

SET RULER ON SEAT AND LOCK RULER

RIGGING STICK ON BOTH GUNWALES

SWING RIGGING STICK OUT TO OARLOCK TO READ HEIGHT

SEAT FARTHEST AFT ON SLIDE

THEN

OARLOCK SET PARALLEL TO BOAT

RIGGING STICK METHOD

THEN KEEP THE SAME MEASUREMENT TO THE STRAIGHT EDGE ADD THE DISTANCE TO THE OARLOCK HORIZONTAL FLAT.

READ TAPE MEASURE HERE

STRAIGHT EDGE ON BOTH GUNWALES

STRAIGHT EDGE METHOD

## JOB 11.2: ADJUSTING YOUR SWEEP HEIGHTS.

**Problem:** You're here because your heights are not where you want them.

**Needed:** Basic rigging kit, height numbers, clean rag, shell seats-up (this can be done upside-down, but why kill yourself?), access to the Web/phone.

At this point, things are not right with your height. It is time for some serious surgery on your rigger.

**Step 1. Change The Spacers:** A great many sweep riggers today use spacers to change the rigging height. Look at your rigger. Are there spacers? Are they easy to get too? If you have a Euro-style rigger you're golden with this step. (If not, off to Step 3.)

If so, then remove the top nut/bolt and shift your spacers around. Then, put things back together correctly, with a three-finger tightened top nut/bolt.

**Step 2. Re-measure:** After things are back together double check the rigger height. Then go row to see how it feels.

**Step 3. More Difficult:** If it looks like your height is going to be more difficult to change due to rigger design (and many riggers are) I'm going to suggest two things. First, experiment. Go ahead, give it a shot, but only if you think that your chance of success is pretty darn good.

If experimenting isn't meant for you today, then go to my Web site <http://www.MaxRigging.com> and see if there are any resources there for you. If so, download the specific information for your boat, and get ready to operate.

**Step 4. No Luck:** If experimenting isn't for you and you cannot find a resource on my Web site, pick up the old telly-phone and give your mentor or the builder a call. Ask for help, adjust the rigger, and off to bigger and better things.

# JOB 11.3: DETERMINING YOUR HEIGHT NUMBERS.

**Problem:** What numbers should you use to rig your height?

**Needed:** Pencil and paper, rigging card, Chapter Fifteen.

My sixth grade teacher was fond of saying, "There are two ways to do something, Master Davenport: the easy way and a better way." In this case, I agree with Mrs. Gatlingun; there are two ways.

**Easy way:** If you are a First- or Second-Dimensional Rigger you'll want to keep things simple and concise until you get your feet on the ground. This is a quick and easy way to pick your range of height numbers.

**Step 1. Book It:** Refer to Chapter Fifteen for your height numbers.

**Step 2. Adjust, Row , Observe, and Readjust:** Adjust the rigger according to the above numbers (see JOB 11.2, for how to adjust). Send the boat out, try the height check, watch the rowing.

Any problems? Nope. Great—you're done.

Got problems? Try again.

**Better way:** I woke up one night in a sweat, believe it or not, worrying about the heights of my shell. I had a dream and in it Archimedes was trying to explain his thoughts on bodies submersed in water. It was so weird I woke up my roommate and told him about it; then we spent most of the night developing a formula to help find rigger-height numbers.

That was the last time I ate pickled-herring pizza.

We came up with a formula that has been a helpful guide and has gotten me through a few hectic times when my head was spinning. The formula takes into account some things you may not consider when picking your height numbers. Using the formula may take a little more effort on your part, and a better grasp of what's going on (a Third-Dimensional Rigger)—but the results are usually good and you might save some time in the long haul.

There are four things you need to worry about when picking height numbers. The first two are the shell's **weight classification** and the **average weight** of your crew—truly important stuff we briefly touched on in JOB 7.2.

Think hard now, where do we measure the height from? The seat top to the center of the horizontal flat, right? And remember, so we can use the seat top, we assume the distance from the water's surface to the seat top is always consistent. Well, it may not be consistent if you start mucking around with the boat's weight classification and your crew's average weight.

What Archimedes was trying to explain to me (and I admit I slept through it) was that any body immersed in water will sink until an equilibrium is found between its mass and the mass of the $H_2O$ it displaces, and then it will float. This is how boat-builders find their weight classes. They take the weight of the boat and the estimated weight of the rowers (and coxswain), and from this info they know their designed water line (how low the boat will sit in the water).

So, for example, if you row a heavyweight men's 8 designed for crews whose average weight is 185–210 pounds, everything will be fine and dandy (height-wise that is) if the crew's average weight is between 185–210. The distance from the designed water line to the seat top is just where the manufacturer planned it. But if you throw midweights (160–185 pounds) into the boat, things won't be okay.

Realize that the shell with midweights in it will not be carrying as much total weight as it was built for. With the midweight rowers, the shell will be sitting higher out of the water because of this weight difference—there is less mass so the boat sits higher. The distance between the designed water line and the seat top is greater than it should be. The seat is higher out of the water, so is the horizontal flat, and therefore so is the oar.

Even though you set the heights correctly off of the seat top, the heights are not correct in respect to the designed water line because you have changed what the builder took as a given—the average weight of the crew.

It works the other way also. When you try to row a heavy crew in a shell designed to carry a lighter load the boat will sit lower in the water because there is more total weight in the boat than the manufacturer planned for. The seat top and water are closer than they should be, and the oar height is therefore lower. Got it?

The amount of boat touching the water is called the *wetted surface*. When the weight of the crew is less than what the manufacturer had planned for, there will be less wetted surface. This might make the boat a little slower, and a little less stable because of the change in the surface contact area. This is something you might want to keep in mind when selecting a boat for your crew.

Another thing to worry about is **water conditions**. The distance from the horizontal flat to the water's surface is the important thing, right? When the water is rough and wavy then this distance is constantly changing. Sometimes it's less (when a wave goes by) and sometimes it is greater (when a trough goes by).

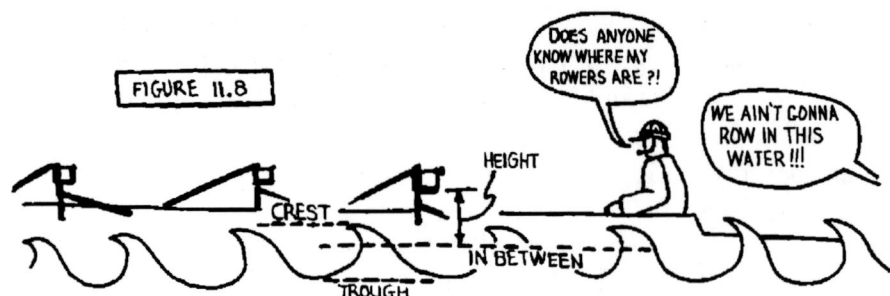

When you are rowing in very rough water, raise your oarlocks to maintain your heights clear of the waves. Hopefully this will keep your rowers happy and efficient (just think "high and dry"). For a suggestion about rowing in rough water, see Chapter Sixteen, JOB 16.5, for a tip on **splashguards**.

The last item to think about is **body size**. Every once in a while, you may have a rower whose body size makes your rigging difficult. The most common problems are extra-large thighs or very short upper bodies. I tend to add .64 cm (1/4 inch) for big thighs (they've got to be truly big) and subtract .64 cm (1/4 inch) for a short upper body.

With all that in mind, here's the formula:

**Step 1. Book It:** Look up the height number that corresponds to your crew's size. Write it down.

**Stop 2. Shell's Class:** Know your shell's weight classification? If yes, next step. If not, see Chapter Seven, JOB 7.2. When you find it, also write it down.

**Step 3. Crew Average:** Determine the approximate average weight of your crew—to the nearest 10 pounds should do just fine. Subtract .96 cm (3/8 inch) from the book number for every weight classification your crew is under your shell's class. Add .64 cm (1/4 inch) for every class the crew is over.

For example, if your boat is a heavyweight model (185–210 pounds) and your crew's average is in the midweight class (160–185) then subtract .96 cm (3/8 inch) from your height number.

**Step 4. Surf's Up?** Rough water? If so, then add about .64 cm (1/4 inch) to the book number.

**Step 5. Body Size:** Got a rower with huge legs or small torso? Add or subtract .64 cm (1/4 inch) respectively.

**Step 6. Total Them Up:** Time for a little math. Take your book number and do this:

- ✓ add/subtract .64 cm (1/4 inch) if you're rowing in a different weight classification
- ✓ add .64 cm (1/4 inch) for rough water
- ✓ add/subtract .64 cm (1/4 inch) for mutant bodies.

Here's an example for a large-thighed, midweight rower in a heavyweight shell, rowing in rough water:

$$17.15 \text{ cm} - .96 \text{ cm} + .64 \text{ cm} + .64 \text{ cm} = 17.5 \text{ cm}$$

or in U.S. system

$$6 \ 3/4 \text{ inch} - 3/8 \text{ inch} + 1/4 \text{ inch} + 1/4 \text{ inch} = 6 \ 7/8 \text{ inch}$$

Once you get good at finding your height numbers you'll be able to pick them right off the top of your head. Remember two important things here. One, getting the correct height is a constant adjusting process. Two, as soon as it is convenient, you should do a height check after you have adjusted the riggers to double-check yourself.

# Chapter Twelve: Work-Thru

As we've discussed, the oar generates two forces: a **propelling force** and a **turning force**. Because of these forces, it's very important that we are careful about how far fore and how far aft we locate the inside and outside arc. That is what Work-thru is all about—locating the arcs.

We want to get as much of the propelling force as possible and at the same time as little of the turning force as possible. Work-thru will help us do that. And there's also another reason that the arcs fore and aft location are important, and that reason is going to have a major impact on your boat speed.

## 12.1 Why Place the Arcs Correctly?

Let's look at a person rowing in an eight. Her name is Jane and she is in the bow seat.

Jane comes up to the catch position, sets her oar in the water, takes a stroke, makes the release, and stops. From Chapter Eight we know that as Jane took her stroke, her blade drew an arc in the water: the outside arc (remember, that is in theory; the oar does not really draw an arc in the water). But did you know the outside arc needs to be located differently for different sizes of boats?

It all has to do with hull speed.

When Jane is rowing, her eight moves along fairly fast. At the split second when Jane sets her oar in the water, the boat is moving faster than her oar.

This is because Jane has just shifted her body from moving sternward to moving towards the bow and she hasn't had time yet to get her oar, or body, moving. Once she has made her catch and started her drive, it takes Jane time to accelerate her oar up to the speed of the boat.

Her oar won't be doing much good until it starts moving faster than the boat—then it will begin to accelerate the hull. What would be best for Jane, and her boat, is if she could have her oar moving as fast as possible by the time it is perpendicular to the hull (called the mid-drive position). That is where the oar is most efficient (see figure 12.1).

So if you were rigging Jane's rigger you'd want to locate her outside arc so the oar would have enough distance to accelerate up to the hull speed by the time the oar is about perpendicular to the boat.

Actually, the most efficient area for the oar is 20 degrees to either side of the perpendicular. I call this the "prime acceleration area." Herberger explains it in detail in Chapter Two of his book *Rudern*.

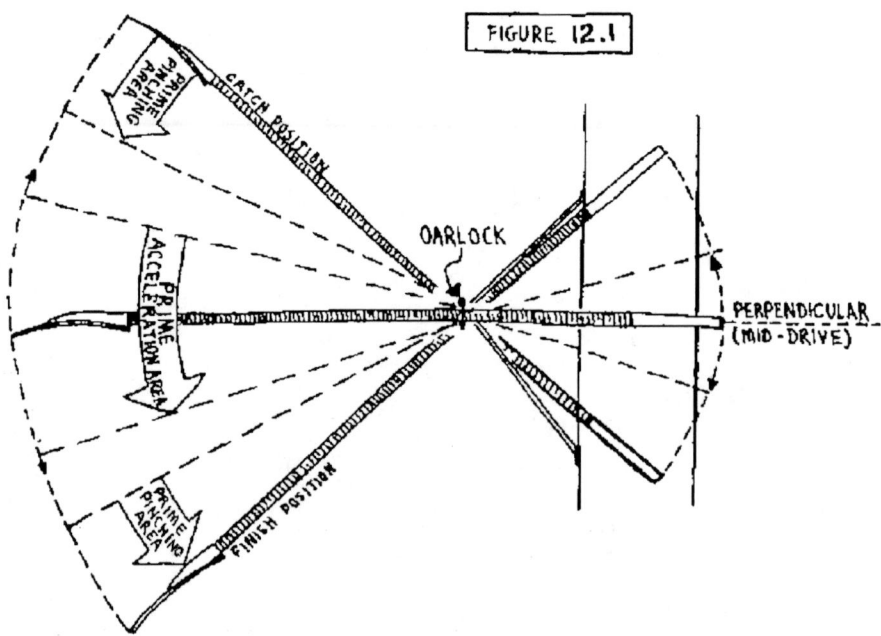

The next day Jane is rowing in a pair. When she comes up to the catch and takes a stroke, her oar makes an arc just like that in the eight, and again it takes time for Jane's oar to accelerate up to the speed of the boat. But the difference is that the pair has a slower hull speed than the eight. So when Jane's oar is in the water it's going to take less time (and distance) for her to accelerate her oar up to the speed of the pair's hull than it did in the eight.

If you were adjusting Jane's rigger in the pair, you'd want to give it enough distance so her oar could get up to hull speed by the mid-drive. Since the pair is a slower boat than the eight, this distance will be shorter in the pair's rigging than it was in the eight's rigging.

A little review music, Maestro.

So what we try to do when we rig is have the outside arc in the right spot to give the rower's oar enough time to accelerate up to hull speed by the prime acceleration area. This way, when the oar reaches its most efficient position, it will be moving faster than the hull and can accelerate the boat. The slower the boat, the less distance toward the bow you have to locate the outside arc to achieve this.

On the other hand, the faster the boat, the greater the distance toward the bow you have to locate the outside arc. So a men's eight would have a greater distance into the bow than a men's four because the eight is faster. This distance is called the **work-thru**. Following the same logic, a four's distance (work-thru) would be greater than a pair's. The same adjustment of the outside arc holds true for women's rowing.

Let's look at the other end of Jane's oar for a second. As she rows along, the butt of her oar handle makes an arc inside the boat called (you know this) the **inside arc**. Where we place this inside arc is important because it can have an effect on the technique of the rower. Rowers have a comfort zone when they row in which they are efficient and comfortable.

Whenever you change the location of the inside arc, it will affect this comfort zone and force the rowers to compensate for this change. Usually, the compensation is something as simple as adjusting the foot stretchers, but sometimes the rower compensates for changes in the inside arc by altering the technique (i.e., changes body angles, leaning). This may force the rower to be inefficient or uncomfortable, which is something you definitely want to avoid. Just remember, the oar is a solid object, and because it is any, change to the outside arc will cause a change to the inside arc, and this will affect the rower.

## 12.2 Ways to Locate the Arcs

So how do we locate the arcs fore and aft? The best way is with an adjustment called **work through the pin**, which is the long version of work-thru. It is also known as **distance through the pin.**

There's not much controversy in rigging, but if you're going to see an argument, it's probably going to be over the topic of work-thru. There's no consensus on exactly how to measure work-thru, and believe me, there are a bunch of different ways to measure it. Work-thru is the distance between two perpendiculars, the first one usually going through the oarlock pin. That's where most folks start, from an imaginary line through the pin and perpendicular to the centerline—that's also where any agreement ends.

From here, some folks measure the work-thru as a distance from this oarlock pin perpendicular to another perpendicular line going *across the front of the seat when it's aft.* Others measure to a perpendicular across the *center of the wheels,* some to a *perpendicular across the center of the holes in the seat,* others to a *front-stop perpendicular,* and some even measure to the *aft of the rear wheels of the seat assembly.* All of these methods work well but, but, but, as you might guess, each way of measuring is going to give a different number.

A hotbed of controversy, huh?

I've tried all these methods and I don't think one method works any better than any of the others. I use the front-stops' perpendicular just because that's the way I was taught. As far as you and I are concerned, and we'll let everyone else grumble, we'll measure the work-thru from the center of the oarlock pin to a perpendicular across the foremost part of the front-stops. Therefore, our definition of work-thru is *the distance from a perpendicular line through the center of the oarlock pin to a perpendicular across the front-stops.*

The reason we use work-thru is to help us locate the outside arc so the oar has enough distance to accelerate to hull speed by mid-drive, with an inside arc that is comfortable and efficient.

Work-thru is the distance from a perpendicular line through the center of the oarlock pin to a perpendicular across the front-stops. That is my definition. Feel free to use your own.

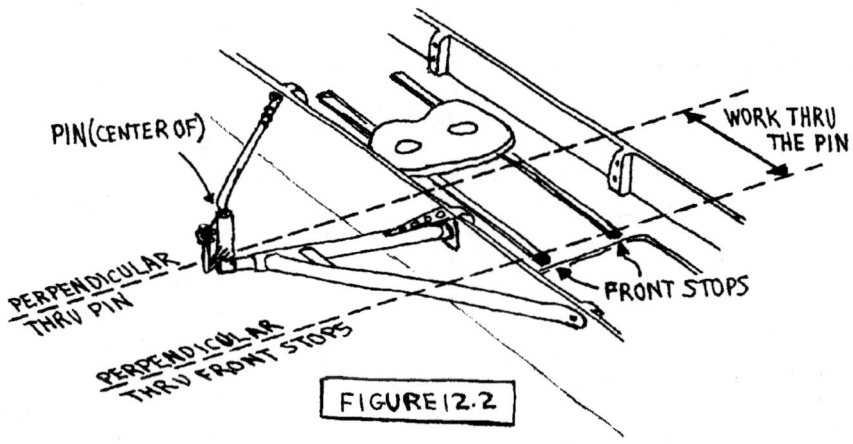

Work-thru is a lot simpler than it sounds and is a very easy adjustment to make. Don't worry about using these imaginary lines. When you measure the perpendiculars, you will be using your rigging stick (or straight edge) and this will give you something tangible to measure.

## 12.3 Fine-Tuning the Fore and Aft Location of the Arcs

Work-thru is the best way to locate the arcs fore and aft; however, there are several ways to fine-tune their location once you have them about where you want them. Which method you use will depend on your skill-level of rigging.

**First-Dimensional Rigger:** I have been holding off discussing the foot stretcher location until we got to a point where we had a fair amount of background info. If you are in the First Dimension, and we've all been there at one time or another, you'll find the foot stretcher adjustments are a helpful way to fine-tune the work-thru.

The correct foot stretcher adjustment will determine if the rower can get the full range of motion on the **track** (slide), and it will help locate the inside and outside arcs. The foot stretchers are a very critical part of rigging and very simple to adjust, but at the same time, they are one of the most overlooked adjustments in rigging. For more information on the foot stretchers see JOB 13.1.

If you look inside a shell, you'll notice the foot stretchers are separated from the front-stops of the tracks by a certain distance. When you adjust the foot stretchers, you are fine-tuning this distance for the individual rower so he or she can be efficient as possible.

I mentioned before that when a rower is at the catch, the most efficient knee angle is 45 degrees (45 degrees is approximate depending on the individual). Well, if this angle is greater than 45 degrees, the rower will not get the full compression at the catch. This means the oar will not be moving through the normal outside arc length. This is called rowing **short**. If the angle is less than 45 degrees then the calves and hamstrings are too close together and this means the leg drive will be weaker. This is called **over-compression**.

> Most track lengths are between 62 cm (24 inches) and 71 cm (28 inches), except in some of the older shells. The average person only uses between 41 cm (16 inches) and 52 cm (20 1/2 inches), which means there should be plenty of track length for you to adjust the foot stretchers.

Some people are skeptical if over-compression really weakens the leg-drive. If you're one of them, try the following.

Stand next to a tall wall. Squat down until you have an angle about 45–50 degrees between your calves and hamstrings. Then jump as high as you can and touch the wall at the top of your jump. Now try it again but this time compress way down so the angle is much smaller. Jump and touch.

You should find you have not jumped as far, or if you have, then it took you a lot more energy to get there.

Exciting stuff, huh?

Rest your weary legs and check JOB 12.3A for how to adjust the foot stretchers.

To check for proper foot stretcher adjustment, try to get a side view of the shell while it is being rowed. Look for under-compression or over-compression of the legs, a sign of improper foot stretcher adjustment. For correct compression, the rower's shins should be *slightly bow-ward* (but not greatly bow-ward) of perpendicular at the catch. If the compression is not right, stop the boat, and have the rowers adjust their foot stretchers.

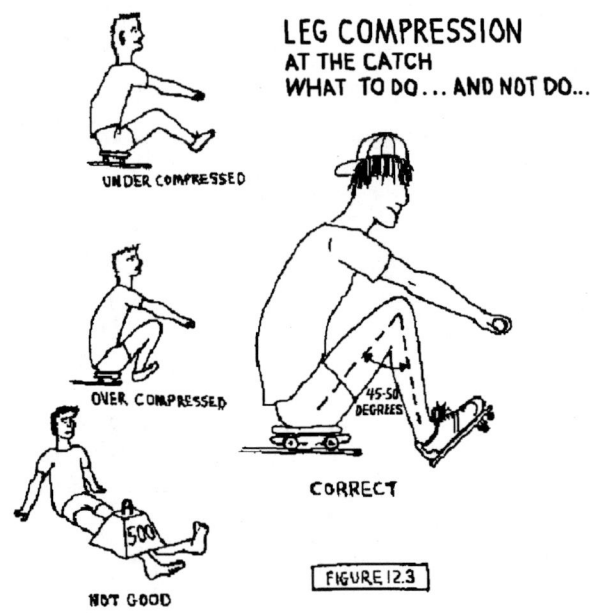

**Second-Dimensional Rigger:** An even better method to fine-tune your location is with a measurement known as the **catch length**. Catch length is the distance from the oarlock pin perpendicular to the farthest point the butt of the oar handle extends to at the catch (which is the aft end of the inside arc), but along a straight line instead of a curved one. This straight line is called a **chord**.

So how is this helpful? When a person is rowing, it is very hard to tell if he or she is making the catch at the right point. When you measure catch length you put a marker on both gunwales of the boat. This gives you a landmark to check the location of the stern end of the rower's inside arc. The marker will assist you in making sure the catch is in the proper place with the work-thru you've set. See JOB 12.3B, this chapter, to measure and mark the catch length.

**Third-Dimensional Rigger:** If you want to take your fine-tuning one step farther, then try a measurement called **catch angle**. With it, you can measure the angle between the oar and the oarlock perpendicular when the rower is at the catch. This is going to be a great help for two reasons.

First, *when we use work-thru, we assume all of the rowers are the same in body types.* But that's clearly not the case in this imperfect world; rowers are of different builds and different flexibilities. If you've got a boat-load of people of different sizes and abilities, you'll find the outside arcs at the catch won't be located in the same places. And of course you remember the pinching effect produced by the turning forces, right?

If the outside arcs start in different places, there will be varying amounts of turning forces at each rigger, and this is going to impact the boat's course.

Let's say you need to rig a four and the two port rowers reach out farther at the catch than the two starboards. This means the ports' outside arcs are closer to the bow than the two starboards', and at the catch, the ports will be applying a greater turning force. The boat will be pushed to the starboard side.

At the release, the ports will not be as long in the water as the starboards, and now the starboards will be applying a turning force to the boat pulling the stern towards the starboard side. To keep this boat on a straight course there is going to be a lot of rudder action needed. This is not what you want since every time the rudder is used it acts like a brake, slowing the boat down. Common sense should tell you this is something you want to avoid.

If the catch angles are identical, then all of the rowers will be entering the water with the outside arc located at the same place. The turning forces on port will balance those on starboard and the boat should travel a straighter course.

Second, *the slower the hull speed of a shell, the less work-thru we want.* Another way to look at it is: the slower the boat, the closer you want the angles on either side of the oarlock perpendicular to be. To see what I mean, look at figure 12.5 and you'll see I've divided the outside arc into two sections, the **fore section** and the **aft section**.

In an eight, with a large work-thru, the fore section is greater than the aft section. In a pair, the fore section will be closer to the size of the aft section—the slower the shell, the closer the angles are. Normal outside arc ranges are usually 70–85 degrees for sweep and 85–100 degrees for sculling. The catch angle will help you find these angles (see JOB 12.3C).

---

Don't give yourself ulcers worrying about the size of the outside arc. Just remember two important things: *the slower the hull speed, the smaller the size of the fore section* (so, the smaller the catch angle), and *fine-tune the arcs with catch length or catch angle markers* so you can check the rower's catch position.

---

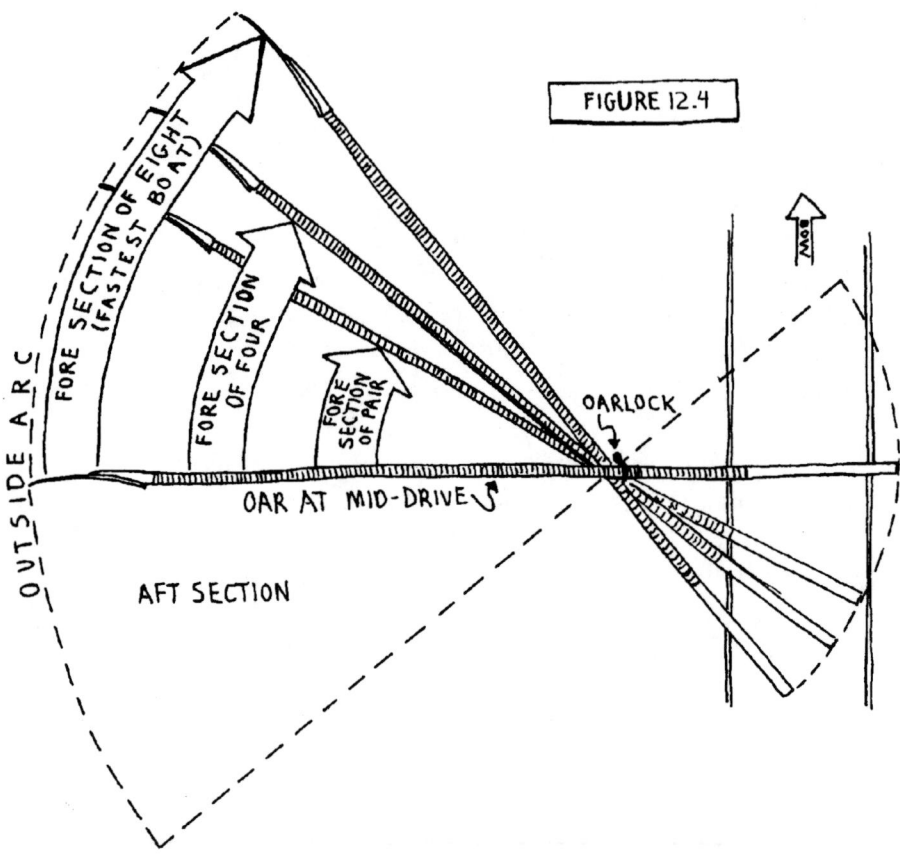

Oh, there's one thing you and I need to discuss while the First and Second-Dimensional folks ramble around in other parts of this book. The oar doesn't really make an outside arc.

Huh?

Yeah . . . I know . . . I've talked about this outside arc *ad nauseam*, but instead of an arc, the blade carves a design in the water more like the letter *J* (see figure 12.5). I've found it helps new Riggers (it helped me) get a grasp on what they are trying to do if they think the oar is just moving through the water making a big arc. But it actually doesn't—the oar slips sideways through the water.

Don't let this bit of news change your thinking about how to rig; everything is still the same. It's just important you know this, especially as

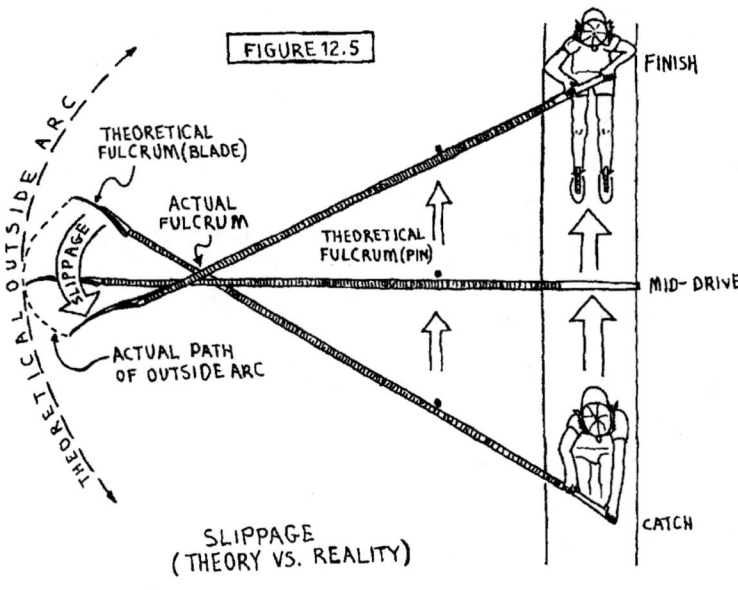

FIGURE 12.5

THEORETICAL OUTSIDE ARC

THEORETICAL FULCRUM(BLADE)

ACTUAL FULCRUM

SLIPPAGE

THEORETICAL FULCRUM(PIN)

MID-DRIVE

FINISH

CATCH

ACTUAL PATH OF OUTSIDE ARC

SLIPPAGE
(THEORY VS. REALITY)

you get comfortable with the Third and try to leap up into the Fourth Dimension. (See section 9.4 for more information about *Slippage*.)

## JOB 12.1. HOW TO MEASURE YOUR WORK-THRU.

**Problem:** You need to find out what your work-thru is.

**Needed:** Rigging stick or long straight-edge, tape measure, boat in seats-up position, rigging cards.

The work-thru is the distance from a perpendicular through the center of the oarlock pin to an imaginary plane (not a new defense weapon) which goes across the bow part of the front-stops. The easiest way to measure it is to extend a make-believe line out from the front-stops, which forms a perpendicular to the centerline; then measure the distance from this line to the pin's center. No problem.

Make sure your rigging stick, or straight-edge, is long enough to rest across both gunwales and extend out to the distance of the pin, about four feet.

**Step 1**. **Prepare Seat And Tracks:** If you have adjustable tracks, make sure they are both even. To do this, put the seat assembly aft and look at the stern wheels. Do they both touch the front-stops equally? Or is one front-stop offset? If so, then you will measure from the fore-most front-stop since that will be where the wheels of the seat will stop.

**Step 2**. **Measure:** Take your tape measure and measure the distance from the perpendicular through the pin to the fore of the front-stop. It's easiest to do this right along the track. Again, if the tracks are not equal, then measure to the one that has the front-stop closest to the mid-drive knee. Remember this distance.

**Step 3**. **Locate Front-Stops Perpendicular:** Now place your rigging stick perpendicular across the gunwales just over the top of the front-stops. Place the end of your tape measure at the top of the mid-drive knee and measure out the front-stop distance you just got. You're measuring to the fore side of your rigging stick.

Measure this distance from both knees to make sure your rigging stick is sitting square to the gunwales. You have just made a perpendicular. If it's your first perpendicular, pat yourself on the back, give out a "whoopee," and let's get back to work. Make sure the rigging stick extends out to the pin. What you have just done is to extend an imaginary line, which represents the front-stops, out to the side of the boat. If you have a friend handy, have him or her hold the rigging stick in place so it won't wiggle around.

**Step 4**. **Find Your Distance:** With your tape measure, find the distance from the center of the pin to your rigging stick. Make sure you are measuring to the same side of the rigging stick you measured to from the knees. This distance is your work-thru. If your pin is located on the bow side of your rigging stick, which is usually where it should be, then your work-thru is positive. If the pin is stern of the rigging stick, your distance is negative. If the center of the pin and front-stops are even, then you have zero work-thru.

**Step 5**. **Compare:** Take this distance, write it down and compare it to the number you want (see JOB 12.5 on how to calculate your work-thru dimension). Got the work-thru you need? If so, then clean up and you are done. If not, then on to JOB 2.

## JOB 12.2. HOW TO ADJUST YOUR WORK-THRU.

**Problem:** You've measured the work-thru and it's not where you want it.

**Needed:** Boat seats-up, riggers on tight (see JOB 7.5, *Riggers on and Off*), basic rigging kit.

Think of an oarlock as a big letter *D*. This letter *D* kinda hangs around the outside of the shell. What's neat about this *D* is that you can move it in any direction. You can move it fore and aft; you can move it closer to the boat or farther away. You can tilt it towards the stern or the bow, and you can even tilt it sideways.

What we are concerned about with work-thru is moving this letter *D* fore or aft in respect to the front-stops. Depending on your type of shell, there are different ways to do this. You need to check out your shell to see which method to use.

First, you need to know if the tracks are adjustable. Easy enough. Feel around underneath the tracks where they appear to be connected to the bracing of the boat. What you're looking for is a small threaded bolt that goes through the bracing and connects the track to the boat. It should have a nut on the end of it, most likely a **wing nut**. Usually they have one in the stern and one in the bow end of the tracks. Get your hand down there and dig around, sometimes they are tough to find. If you find any then you have adjustable tracks (most makes will have them—Schoenbrod Intercollegiate won't). Didn't find any? **Nonadjustable** tracks for you.

Second, you want to know if the rigger is adjustable fore and aft. Easiest way to tell is look at the connecting plate where the rigger attaches to the shell at the mid-drive knee. If the connection between the mainstay and the connecting plate is solid then there is no fore/aft adjustment to your rigger (I call this a **limited-adjustable rigger**). If the connection is a movable joint then there is fore/aft adjustment. Use the following directions depending on what type of equipment you have.

### Nonadjustable Tracks with Limited-Adjustable Rigger (Some Pre-1970 Shells)

Before the late 1960s the rigger adjustment of work-thru was not standard on most riggers. Boat builders built their boats with a standard work-thru and left it at that. If you needed to change the location of your outside arc you did so with the foot stretcher adjustments. With a limited-adjustable rigger and nonadjustable tracks, you have a set-in-stone work-thru and you have basically got to live with it. Measure it and see what it is. If it is not quite what you want, don't despair, there may be help.

### Nonadjustable Tracks with Adjustable Rigger (Schoenbrod Intercollegiate)

When coaches finally convinced the manufacturers that they needed a work-thru adjustment, they started seeing fully adjustable riggers offered on shells. These riggers allow the oarlock pin to be moved freely in any direction (including fore and aft), and this allowed the outside arc to be moved a greater distance than before. What a happy day for some Riggers.

With the Schoenbrod Intercollegiate and similar types, the tracks are set, and this means the front-stops will not move, but you can still get a wide range of work-thru adjustment by moving the rigger.

**Step 1. Get Your Numbers:** See JOB 12.5, this chapter.

**Step 2. Locate And Loosen Adjustment Clamps:** On the rigger, locate the adjustment clamps: you're trying to free-up the stays so you can move the mainstay. If it's a Schoenbrod, there will be three clamps to loosen, one each on the top stay, aft bottom stay, and fore bottom stay. With your 1/2 inch wrenches, loosen these clamps.

**Step 3. Find Front-Stops Perpendicular:** This chapter, JOB 12.1, Steps 1–2.

**Step 4. Adjust:** With the rigging stick still in position, slide the rigger fore or aft to move the oarlock pin into the position. Recheck your stick because they have a tendency to move. With your tape measure, put the pin where you want it; remember to measure to the middle of it. Tighten the two bottom stay-adjustment clamps. Re-measure once more to make sure you've got it where you want it.

**Step 5. Check Other Measurement:** Since you've moved the oarlock pin, you've probably changed the spread and pitch of the rigger and you need to check them. From here, it's on to check the spread (JOB 9.1, *Measuring the Spread*) and the pitch (JOB 10.2, *How to Measure Your Stern Pitch*).

### Adjustable Tracks with Limited-Adjustable Rigger (Euro-style Riggers)

You've got a fixed rigger as far as fore and aft adjustments are concerned so your only option with this type of setup is to move the front-stops, and this works just as well as moving the rigger.

**Step 1. Get Your Numbers:** See JOB 12.5.

**Step 2. Set Tracks:** Remove the seat (see JOB 7.6). Then loosen the tracks. Most adjustable tracks I've seen are held with two fasteners, one fore and one aft—but yours may have more, so check well. Find these fasteners, which may be a lot harder than it sounds. In shells with brace construction it is usually not a problem to loosen and tighten these wing nuts.

The nuts most likely will be plastic so don't crank them down too hard. In shells with monocoque decks it can be a little more difficult. You may get lucky and have an inspection port nearby that allows easy access to the nuts. If not, you may have to move some foot stretchers to get at them. Once you've found them, loosen them so there is a good 1/4 inch between the nut/washer and the contact surface.

With all fasteners loosened, slide the track to the desired position. You may need to apply some "gentle" persuasion to move them, especially if they have not been moved in a while. Remember, the key word here is **gentle**. Try tapping it with a hammer, <u>not your tape measure</u>, to loosen it up.

If they don't move freely, I suggest you remove the nuts and take the tracks out of the shell. Try to find the problem and clean the tracks. If you have never seen what they look like, you should take them apart at least once to get an understanding of what holds these tracks in. When you get it moved, adjust the other track.

To find your new work-thru position, locate the perpendicular through the oarlock pin with your rigging stick, measure the distance you need out on the gunwales (toward the stern), and put your rigging stick at this new location on the gunwales. This is now your imaginary plane for the work-thru. Look down to see if the front-stops break this plane (or measure from the mid-drive knee to the front-stops).

> Instead of just looking down from the rigging stick to check if the front-stops are right, measure them. Determine the distance from your rigging stick, along the top of the gunwale, to a landmark (e.g., mid-drive knee). Take this distance and place your tape measure along the tracks and measure out from the landmark to the front-stops an equal distance. Now you know exactly where your front-stops should be.

Once you've moved the tracks, check to see if both of them are in the same position by putting the seat on and rolling it to the front-stops. If both tracks are equal, the wheels on both sides of the seat will be touching the front-stops. Check your measurement, tighten the nuts—being very careful not to overtighten—and move on to the next position.

**Step 3. Adjust Foot Stretchers:** You're only half way done and this is where some people flame out. Since you've changed the front-stops' location you **must** adjust the foot stretcher position. See JOB 12.3A, and don't give up. If you don't adjust them, you may be in for some technique changes you don't want. You haven't touched the rigger, so all the other adjustments should be the same.

**Step 4. Check Your Work:** After the first couple rows, visually check the tracks to see if they may have slipped. Sometimes they will move when jarred by a seat hitting the front-stops.

### Adjustable Tracks with an Adjustable Rigger (Kaschper)
With this setup, you've got two options for adjusting your work-thru: you can move the tracks or move the rigger. So what do you do? I favor moving the tracks. It's simpler, easier, quicker, and moving the tracks

gives you a wider range of adjustment than changing the rigger. Additionally, by not changing the rigger, you haven't messed up any of the other measurements. The only time I change the rigger is when the rigger is way out of whack, like with a brand-new rigger, or when switching riggers to different positions.

**Step 1. Get Your Numbers:** See JOB 12.5.

**Step 2. Move The Tracks:** If this is the way you decide to go, which as you can probably tell gets my vote, then see the preceding JOB, steps 2–4.

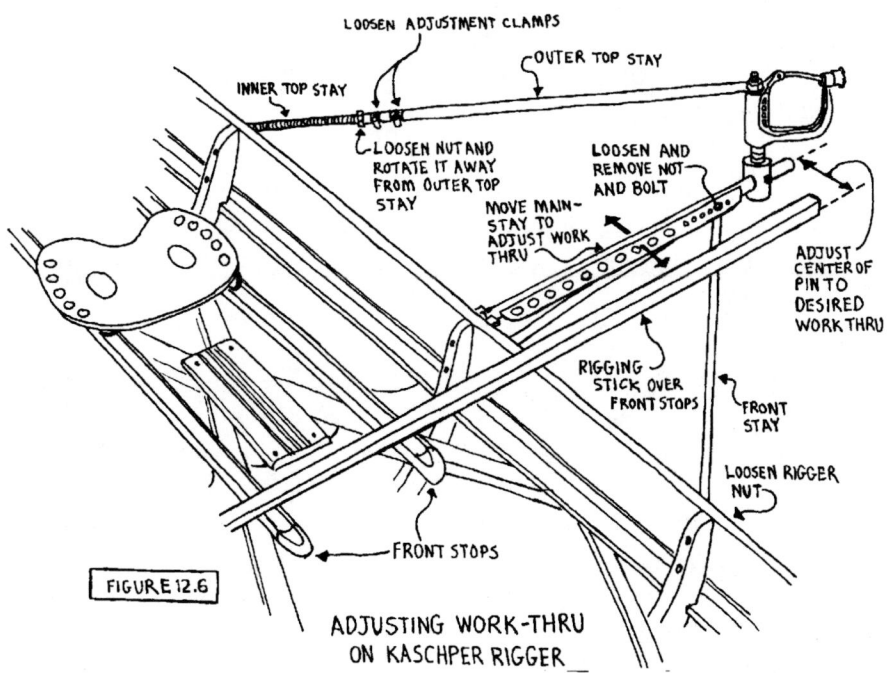

LOOSEN ADJUSTMENT CLAMPS

OUTER TOP STAY

INNER TOP STAY

LOOSEN NUT AND ROTATE IT AWAY FROM OUTER TOP STAY

LOOSEN AND REMOVE NUT AND BOLT

MOVE MAIN-STAY TO ADJUST WORK THRU

ADJUST CENTER OF PIN TO DESIRED WORK THRU

RIGGING STICK OVER FRONT STOPS

FRONT STAY

LOOSEN RIGGER NUT

FRONT STOPS

FIGURE 12.6

ADJUSTING WORK-THRU ON KASCHPER RIGGER

**Step 3. Change The Rigger:** Are you sure you want to do it this way? If it is, then you'll need to go to my Web site for the specifics. Go there, download the correct file, and come back here.

# JOB 12.3A: HOW TO ADJUST THE FOOT STRETCHERS.

**Problem:** You need to adjust your foot stretchers correctly and/or you are a First-Dimensional Rigger and you want to fine-tune your arc location.

**Needed:** Boat seats-up, tools to loosen fasteners, gentle touch.

Take a look at your tracks. Notice at each end there is a small block. These blocks keep the seat wheels from sliding off the tracks. The blocks in the bow are called **back-stops** and the ones in the stern are called **front-stops** (slightly confusing, huh?). The distance from these front-stops to the foot stretcher is critical, but first let's focus on where the front-stops are located for a moment.

The location of the front-stops is important for two reasons. First, the front-stops can, and will, stop the seat dead in its tracks. This has a positive side—the front-stops can act as a guide and help a novice rower get the correct compression.

When a rower makes a catch, the momentum aft needs to be stopped and redirected towards the bow. This is a pretty difficult maneuver to do, and you can never be quite sure the rower is doing this with the seat at the right place. So if the foot stretchers are adjusted correctly, the front-stops can be a helpful landmark, there to remind the rower when to stop the seat and make a catch.

But there is also a negative side. If the foot stretchers are too far away from the front-stops, they can act as a barricade, blocking the rower from getting the compression needed. With each stroke, the rower will bang into them like a jackhammer—but at least keeping the seat on the tracks!

Second, tracks are coming in some very long lengths nowadays. If you have long tracks, you need to be aware that if they extend too far towards the stern, they could possibly dig into the back of the rowers' calves. The front-stop-to-foot-stretcher distance is critical. So how do you tell when you've got the right distances? Judge by the angle of the rower's legs at the catch.

**Step 1. Survey The Scene:** Look at the tracks and locate the front-stops. They should be in good shape, relatively clean, and free of tape and junk. Check out the foot stretchers and make sure that you know the parts and that they also look in good shape. Before you proceed, make sure your work-thru is set correctly (see this chapter, JOB 12.2).

> Sometimes the front-stops will bruise or even cut into the rower's calves, especially in smaller boats, regardless of your best adjustment efforts. This should worry you because of the possibilities of infection. Try padding the front-stops with tape (keeping it out of the tracks) or having the rowers wear protection on their calves (such as the top half of socks).

**Step 2. Rowers In Boat:** With the shell in the water, have the athletes get in and have them put their feet into the foot stretcher sneakers.

**Step 3. Check Foot Stretcher Adjustment:** With the boat on an even keel (most likely this means the boat will need to be away from the dock) have the rowers come to the catch position with the oar extended. Have the rowers compress until the aft wheels of the seat assembly are just touching the front-stops. If the boat is unsteady, have several rowers set the balance.

Now we need to check the rowers' shins.

FOOT STRETCHER ADJUSTMENT

When the wheels are at the front-stops, look at the rowers' shins to see what angle they form with the water. (To get a good view, you shouldn't be too close). The shins should be almost straight up and down (perpendicular). If the shins are angled past perpendicular (towards the stern), then there is probably not enough foot stretcher/front-stop room for the rower and most likely they will overcompress at each catch. If the shins are not up to the perpendicular, then there may be too much foot stretcher/front-stop room for the rower, and every time they come to the catch they will hit the front-stops.

**Step 4. Change The Foot Stretcher**: If you think a change is called for, then have the rowers loosen the fasteners holding the foot stretchers, remove their feet from the sneakers, move the foot stretcher, feet back in, and check again.

Save yourself a lot of hassles and make sure the rowers take their feet out of the foot stretchers when they move them. If they don't, they tend to use caveman-like leg strength to move the foot stretchers instead of gentle hand strength, and things are going to get demolished.

> You should know that every time you move the foot stretcher, there is an impact on the inside arc, but there is triple the impact on the outside arc. So if you move the foot stretchers aft 1 inch, this moves the inside arc aft 1 inch, but at the same time moves the outside arc towards the bow about 3 inches.

**Step 5. On Your Way:** If the placement looks okay, then tighten and get a rowing. If not, then adjust again, observe, and adjust until you've got them where you want them.

> Your sneakers on the foot stretchers should have two small strings attached to their heels. These are used to attach the heels to the foot stretcher. In case the rower needs to get out of the shell quickly, as in a capsizing, these strings secure the heels and help the rowers slip their feet out of the sneakers. Be safe, and make sure these strings are tightly tied to the footplates.

# JOB 12.3B: HOW TO MEASURE AND MARK THE CATCH LENGTH.

**Problem:** You want to use the catch length to fine tune the arc fore/aft location.

**Needed:** riggers on tight (see JOB 7.5), basic rigging kit, tool tray, tape measure, colored tape, rigging stick, helping hand (nice, but not a necessity).

As we discussed, it is often very hard to tell if the rower is making the catch at the correct spot. You'll find the catch length a great coaching aid because you can observe from a launch if the rowers are making the catch at the right place. By marking these lengths not only can you fine-tune the work-thru of a lone rower but you can do the whole boat at one time.

**Step 1. Find Your Oarlock Perpendicular:** See JOB 12.1, this chapter, Step 1–3.

**Step 2. Determine Your Measurement:** Check with Chapter Fifteen to find out the catch length you want.

**Step 3. Measure And Mark:** We begin where the perpendicular through the oarlock pin meets the gunwale opposite the rigger. At this intersection point, hold the end of the tape measure and measure aft along the gunwale. When you've got your length, mark the distance with a piece of colored electrical tape. Use a highly visible color because you will be trying to see this tape from the coaching launch—the brighter the better.

Now measure the same distance along the other gunwale, and mark the length. Do the same thing with all the positions. You have just marked out your catch length on the gunwales.

I also use brightly colored wire-ties. You can find them nowadays at almost any hardware store. When taped to the gunwales, they stick up, which makes it easier for the rowers to find the mark and easier for me to see the marks from the launch.

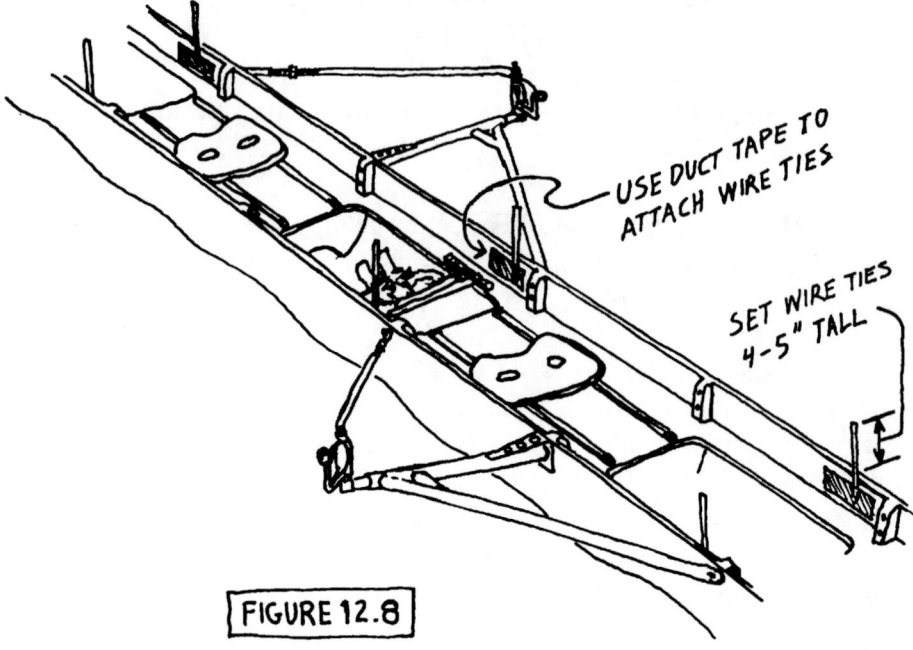

USE DUCT TAPE TO ATTACH WIRE TIES

SET WIRE TIES 4-5" TALL

**FIGURE 12.8**

**Step 4. Observe:** Take the boat for a spin and focus on the catch length. As the athletes are rowing, motor along the side of the boat in a launch and see if the butt of the oar handle is breaking the imaginary plane between the two tape markers. If for whatever reason the rowers are not reaching your markers, or are overreaching them, you know they are not achieving the work-thru you want.

> If things move too fast for you at practice to get a good view of this, or you've got lousy eyesight, then videotape your rowers. Play back the tape in slow motion to get a good idea of what is going on.

**Step 5. Adjust:** Stop the boat and have the rowers adjust the foot stretchers accordingly so at the catch the butt of the oar handle will be just breaking the plane of the tape markers. When this happens, you know the rowers are at the correct work-thru.

# JOB 12.3C: MEASURING AND MARKING THE CATCH ANGLE.

**Problem:** So you want to tackle the catch angle. This is definitely a Third-Dimensional JOB.

**Needed:** Boat seats-up, large protractor, tape measure, markers, adhesive or duct tape, a helping hand (a necessity).

**Step 1. Find Your Numbers:** Check the charts in Chapter Fifteen.

**Step 2. Locate Oarlock Perpendicular:** See this chapter. JOB 12.1, Steps 1–3.

**Step 3. Measure Angle:** I truly suggest some peace and solitude when you first try to measure the catch angles, not because it's difficult but it might get a little confusing in a crowd.

Measuring and marking the catch angle is similar to measuring and marking the catch length, except instead of using tape for a marker, we use something that extends up from the inside gunwale (gunwale closest to the rigger). Now when the rower takes a stroke, the oar will physically touch the marker. This gives the rower instant feedback—on every stroke, they can see and feel, unlike the catch length where the oar passes through an imaginary plane and the feedback comes mainly from the coach.

The first rigger is the toughest; the others are easier. Start where the perpendicular through the oarlock pin meets the inside gunwale. At this intersection point, slide your rigging stick out to the pin and place the protractor on top—the protractor needs to be next to the oarlock pin.

Once you've done this, put the oar into the oarlock and have your friend balance the oar and boat. Watch out for the oar's swinging wildly. Make sure the button is against the oarlock and bring the oar to the catch position.

Looking down on the oar shaft, line up the stern side of the oar with the proper angle on the protractor. Now mark where the oar intersects the inside gunwale. This is where you are going to put your raised marker.

Make sure you have it marked well, remove the oar, and get your adhesive tape and raised marker.

Put the marker at the exact intersection point and tape it in place so that it extends above the gunwale about 4–5 inches. To make things easier at the other riggers, measure the distance from the oarlock perpendicular to this marker. Measure out and mark this distance with all the positions. You have just marked out your catch angles on the gunwales.

> Measuring and marking catch angles is darned difficult. If you have problems (or no protractor), try this: mark your catch length, have a buddy hold the oar in the oarlock and steady it, place the butt of the oar at the imaginary catch length plane and mark where the stern side of the oar intersects the inside gunwale—that's your catch angle. Measure the distance from the oarlock perpendicular to this mark on the inside gunwale, and mark the remainder of your riggers.

Some folks get a little fancier and cut out large templates they can place right on the boat to find their angles. It's a good idea, especially if you think you'll be measuring a lot of catch angles. All you need is a little trigonometry, a protractor, and a large chunk of cardboard. This method will be a little more accurate than the above method—but it is just a different method for the same thing.

> You can use several different things for raised markers. I use plastic ties (wire ties) that are colored. They're rugged, cheap, bright, and flexible enough to withstand lots of abuse and keep on working. Most hardware stores carry them.

**Step 4. Row, Observe, Adjust:** Now that you've set things up, have your rowers go for a spin. What you are looking for is if the oar shaft "touches" the marker consistently. If it does touch, then you're all set. If the shaft is either short of the marker or goes past it have the rower slide her foot stretchers fore or aft respectively so at the catch the marker is touched.

## JOB 12.4: DETERMINING YOUR STROKE LENGTH.

**Problem:** You're not quite sure the oar is going through the complete length of the arc.

**Needed:** Rigging charts, marking tape, launch, and video camera—if available.

We've spent quite a bit of time discussing arc length and a question may have dawned on you—how do you know if the rower is rowing the whole stroke? From my experience, the rower will usually attempt to row the stroke you rig. But sometimes they don't, and it's usually due to some physical limitation.

Some people just don't have the flexibility, length, or strength to achieve the same rowing stroke as the others in the boat—for some, the rigging is just wrong. This is something you need to know, not so you can holler at the rower, but so you can fix the problem.

### First- and Second-Dimensional Riggers (Sweep Only)
There is a fairly simple method to tell if the rower is rowing the complete arc. It consists of two parts. First we measure out and mark the inside arc on the outside gunwale (the one opposite of the rigger). The arc will consist of two parts: the catch length and the **finish length.** You should be acquainted with the catch length (remember, it is the distance from the oarlock pin perpendicular to the farthest point to which the butt of the oar handle extends at the catch). The finish length is the distance from the same perpendicular to the farthest point to which the butt on the oar handle extends at the finish. Both these distances add up to the length of the stroke.

Then we watch the athletes row and see if they are rowing the stroke. Simple enough. What you then do with the info isn't quite so simple. Let's get on with it.

**Step 1. Mark The Catch Length:** See JOB 12.3B, this chapter.

**Step 2. Mark The Finish Length:** Turn to Chapter Fifteen and find your finish length. From the perpendicular you used for the catch length, mark out the finish length on the outside gunwale. Make your mark with something highly visible—colored electrical tape, for example. The finish length marker is usually harder to see than the catch length marker because the rower will be behind it and may obscure it.

**Step 3. Observe:** Send out the boat and watch them row. Check out both markers. If you have a hard time telling what's going on, I suggest you videotape the rowing and play it back in slow motion. It should help you easily identify problems. If you don't have a camera, use your best judgment.

**Step 4. Now What:** It's extremely critical that your rowers follow the arc and length you've rigged for them. Just one rower's being off the mark can cause balance and flow problems. Well, if a rower is missing the marks, what do you do?

If the rower is rowing short (not reaching a mark) or rowing long (going past a mark), maybe it's just a case of adjusting the arc location. Try using the fine-tuning JOBs in this chapter (JOBs 12.3A–12.3C) to fix the problem. Or maybe there is a serious problem, like an injury or poor technique. If there is a problem, you should put effort into correcting it. If you're lost for a solution, try JOB 16.1 for help.

### Third- And Fourth-Dimensional Riggers (Sweep Only)
If you're really interested in the stroke length, I suggest that you check out Purcer's book *Rigging,* Chapter Three, "Individual Rigging." He focuses more on the length that the oar travels through the water, instead of the inside arc chord length that we have just discussed. In the book you will find a detailed account of determining the stroke length by more scientific means.

## JOB 12.5: CHOOSING YOUR WORK-THRU, CATCH LENGTH AND CATCH ANGLE NUMBERS.

**Problem:** You need the numbers.

**Needed:** Rigging charts (Chapter Fifteen), knowledge of boat's class, and rowers' gender.

Finding your numbers is as simple as turning to Chapter Fifteen and looking it up. But—and there are always buts—you'll notice the numbers come in ranges. Where you plan on setting your measurements will depend on two items: the rowers' individual characteristics and the relative hull speed for the class of shell you are using.

For example, you may find a suggestion of a work-thru for an eight of 8 to 12 cm. You're offered a range because rowers come in a variety of different shapes, sizes, and abilities, and you may have to tailor the rigging to a specific rower.

When contemplating adjusting the work-thru you're trying to give the athlete enough room so the oar can achieve hull speed by the mid-drive position. With rowers of greatly different sizes this may take some fiddling around to get things perfect. A position rigged with a work-thru of 10 cm for a rower who is 6' 4 inches tall won't be as efficient for someone substantially shorter (or less flexible). This is where the catch length and catch angle come in handy because they help you fine-tune your work-thru.

The hull speed of the shell is something you want to keep in the back of your mind. There is a fairly wide range of hull speeds for the fifteen classes of shells we are considering in this book. If we were to take the same level of rowers over a 2000-meter course, the following chart illustrates their ranking from faster to slower:

### RELATIVE HULL SPEEDS

| | MEN'S | WOMEN'S |
|---|---|---|
| | | |
| Faster | eight (8+) | |
| | quad (4X) | eight (8+) |
| | four-without (4-) | quad (4X) |
| | four-with (4+) | four-without (4-) |
| | double (2X) | four-with (4+) |
| | pair-without (2-) | double (2X) |
| | single (1X) | pair-without (2-) |
| | pair-with (2+) | single (1X) |
| Slower | | |

There is some comparison between the two columns. For example, a men's four with (4+) is about the same speed as a women's four without (4-); that is, if the rowers are of the same experience level (junior, senior, etc.). Therefore, you would tend to think the work-thru is the same.

Yup.

# Chapter Thirteen: The Minor Adjustments

W ell, we're done with all the major rigging stuff. Now let's get on with a couple of the minor parts of rigging, focusing specifically on the foot stretchers, oars, and a couple of shell dimensions. This is a small chapter, but don't let it fool you; it's crucial.

## 13.1 Foot Stretchers

The foot stretchers are as important to a rower as tires are to a cyclist and skates are to a skater. They form the platform that the rower pushes against. If there is something wrong with this platform, the performance of the rower during the whole stroke, drive and recovery, will suffer. You already know about the most important adjustment of the stretchers, the location (see Chapter Twelve). However, there are four minor foot stretcher adjustments that are almost as critical to rigging. In large part they determine the rower's comfort, and if the rowers aren't comfortable, they won't row well.

There are two ways to secure a rower's feet in the shells. The older method, which you won't see too often uses clogs, which are basically open shoes built on top of the foot plate. This was quite popular way back when; however, now you might only see clogs in recreational singles.

Today, most builders are now installing sneakers in their boats. Nothing affects the rower's comfort as much as how their feet feel, and sneakers are enormously more comfortable than clogs. Regardless of whether you have sneakers or clogs, all the following measurements pertain to both types.

The distance from the top of the seat to the bottom of the heel cup (inside the sneaker) is called the **height of the heel cup**. Rowers move backwards and upwards during the drive. This means the feet need to be lower than the seat so the legs can be in a good position to drive. When the heel height is adjusted properly, the rower's feet and legs will be in the right spot for a comfortable stroke. When it's not adjusted correctly, it can make the rower feel off-balance and awkward.

If you take a good look at the foot stretchers, you'll notice the sneakers pronate out from the centerline. This is called the **opening angle**, and it allows the legs to open naturally as they push. In sweep rowing, the outside leg tends to flair out slightly, depending on the build of the rower. The opening angle lets this outside leg be comfortable when flared. The angle is not meant to be adjusted and comes standard around 25 degrees. In sculling, the legs do not flair so you will find the opening angle substantially less.

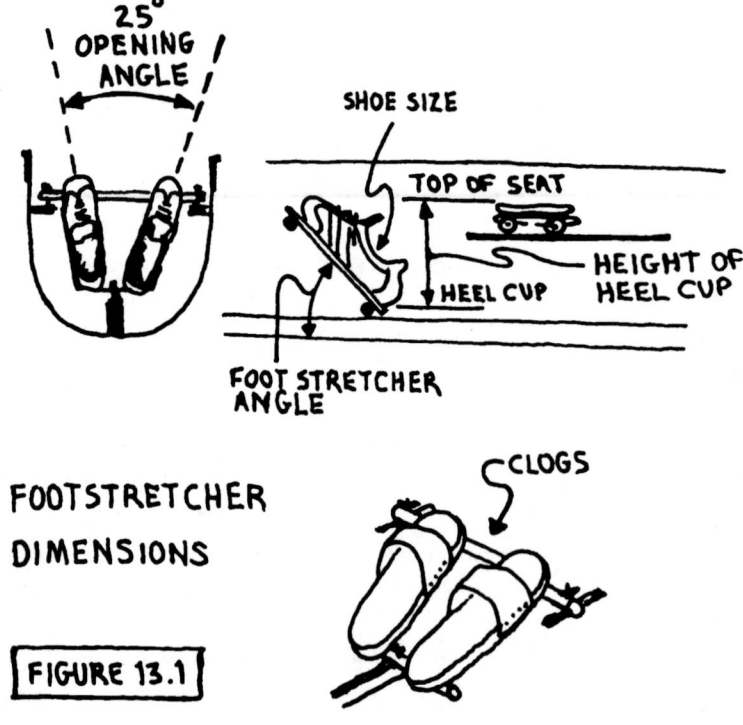

FOOTSTRETCHER DIMENSIONS

FIGURE 13.1

Foot stretchers are tilted up from the keel and this tilt is called the **foot stretcher angle** or **rake of stretcher**. This angle is important because of the flexing required by the rower's ankles at the finish and catch. The normal range of 45 degrees seems to accommodate most feet, but you may stumble upon someone with flexibility problems who will need the angle changed. If that's the case see JOB 13.1, this chapter.

I'm not going to waste time discussing **sneaker size** except to say if you've ever rowed with sneakers too small you know how miserable life can be. One day I stumbled upon a poem left on a foot stretcher by some rower/poet who apparently was upset about the sneaker size. It read:

> I am tall—
> Too large is fine.
> These are small—
> No longer mine (please).

## 13.2 Oars

We've already discussed the two major oar dimensions—oar length and inboard (see Chapter Nine)—but there are two other dimensions of oars you need to know about, neither of which you can adjust.

Despite what you may think; the shaft of an oar is not solid, it is hollow. One reason for this is so the oar can bend when it's rowed. Oars are designed to bend, even though some people think that is a sign of weakness or a manufacturer's defect. The bend helps the rower make the release and enhances the rower's feel of what's going on during the stroke.

However, not all oars bend the same amount. They range from very stiff to very flexible. The amount an oar bends is called the **oar deflection**. Problems occur when sets are mixed with oars of different deflection. See JOB 13.2, this chapter, for how to measure the bend in your oars.

When you place an oar into an oarlock, about one third of the oar ends up on the inboard side of the pin and the other two thirds on the outboard side. This means more of the oar weight is located outside of the pin. When your rowers have their oars up off the water this oar weight plays a major role in the boat balance. This is where the **oar balance point** comes in.

Each oar has its own balance point, which is usually about halfway down the shaft. It's helpful if all of the oars in your set have the same balance point. Unless you're doing some important Third-Dimensional Rigging, I wouldn't spend much time worrying about the oar balance point. If the oar length and inboards are the same throughout your set, then the balance point will take care of itself.

## 13.3 Shell

In a perfect world, each crew would row only in a boat built just for them. It would be the right size, length, shape, color, and have a refrigerator full of ice cream.

But this isn't a perfect world, and unfortunately most rowers end up rowing whatever boat is available in the boathouse. This can cause problems because boat-builders build their shells to carry an average weight of a crew, and sometimes a crew's average weight is different than what the builder planned for. Turn to JOB 13.3, to find out if your crew is in the right **weight classification** of shell.

## 13.4 Stiffness

I was taught to row in an old wooden eight that was many years older than our coach. Over the years, the poor boat had suffered a lot of wear and tear and much of the bracing was loose. It was so loose and the boat wiggled so much we could have a port list in the bow seat (a *list* is sailor-talk for when a boat leans), starboard list at four, another port list in the stroke seat and the coxswain's seat would be perfectly balanced. We called the boat "Slinky." There was no stiffness left in ol' Slinky and it was impossible to row more than four people at a time.

Like most novice we didn't know about stiffness: we thought that was the way all boats were supposed to be.

Stiffness is how tightly the boat is constructed. Think of it as how well the builder connected all the staterooms, and this connection helps rowers in one stateroom feel what goes on in another. This ability to feel what's going on is important in a sport in which you can't look around to see what's happening.

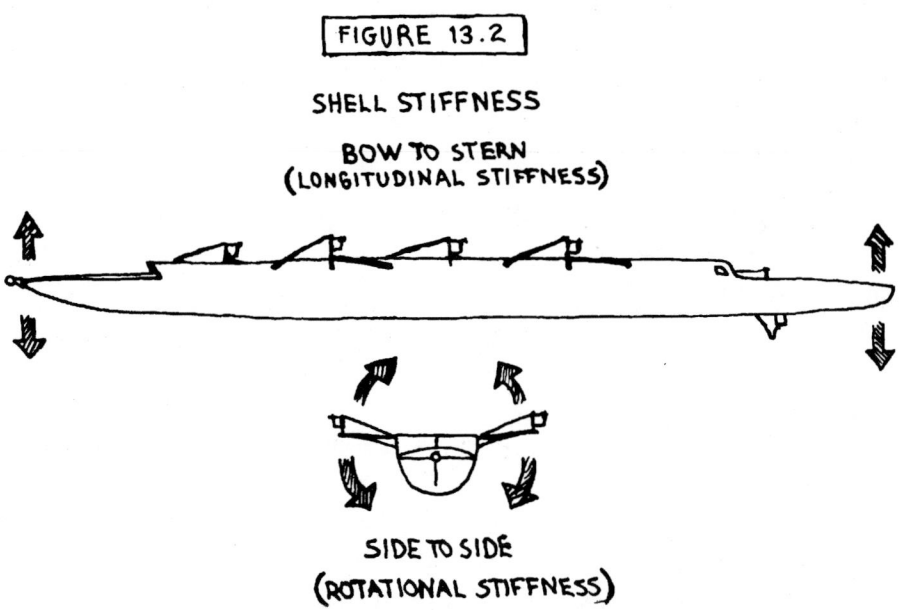

**FIGURE 13.2**

**SHELL STIFFNESS**

**BOW TO STERN
(LONGITUDINAL STIFFNESS)**

**SIDE TO SIDE
(ROTATIONAL STIFFNESS)**

In a stiff boat the stroke should be able to feel what is going on in the bow. In boats that aren't stiff, it's hard for the rowers to work together as a team, the balance will be bad, and the boat speed will suffer. The more competitive you want a shell, the stiffer it should be. Speed ahead to JOB 13.4 if you want to check your shell's stiffness.

If you're a First-Dimensional Rigger, skip the rest of this chapter; no offense, but you don't need it. This stuff is trivial compared to the big picture you should be worrying about. If you're a Second-Dimensional, read on to get a feel for what's cooking, but don't stress over it. This stuff will come in time. If you're in the Third Dimension, you should feel comfortable with what's ahead.

# JOB 13.1: MINOR FOOT STRETCHER ADJUSTMENTS.

**Problem:** You need to figure out what's going on with your minor foot stretcher dimensions.

**Needed:** Rigging stick, rigging card, protractor, waterproof marker, rowers for feedback.

### Part 1: Measuring and Adjusting Height Of Heel Cup

There are two sources I rely on to see if the heel cups are in the right spot: (a) the tape measure, and (b) the rower. I look at the tape measure and both look at and listen to the rower. What the rower says is more important than what the tape measure reads.

**Step 1. Measuring The Heel Cup:** The distance you want is from the seat top to the bottom of the heel cup. At the shell's position you want to measure, slide the seat aft. Lay your rigging stick across the gunwale—over the seat, and measure down to the lowest part of it (same spot we use for height). Note the distance. Now slide your rigging stick over to the top of the heels of the sneakers.

Push the sneaker flat against the foot plate and measure down from the rigging stick to the bottom of the inside of the heel cup. Subtract the two numbers, and you've got your heel cup height. The normal range is about 17–19 cm, but remember, some rowers aren't normal (or is it most?). So use the rower's feedback to see if the height is right. To get reliable feedback, try a **dock check.**

Here is how a dock check works: With the shell at the dock, have the rowers get in. One at a time, have the rowers come to the catch, while the others keep the boat balanced—if the catch length or catch angle is marked, they should get as close to it as possible. At the catch, and then at the release, ask how their legs feel.

If the heel cup height is too small their legs will feel too high—they'll feel like they just can't reach out far enough at the catch. If the height's too large their legs will be too low—they'll feel like they're off balance and leaning too far forward at the catch. Also, if it's too large the rowers may not be able to extend their legs completely at the release. If you need to make a change, onto Step 2. Just remember, rowers are built differently and what feels "right" for one may not feel "right" for another.

MEASURING HEIGHT OF HEEL CUP

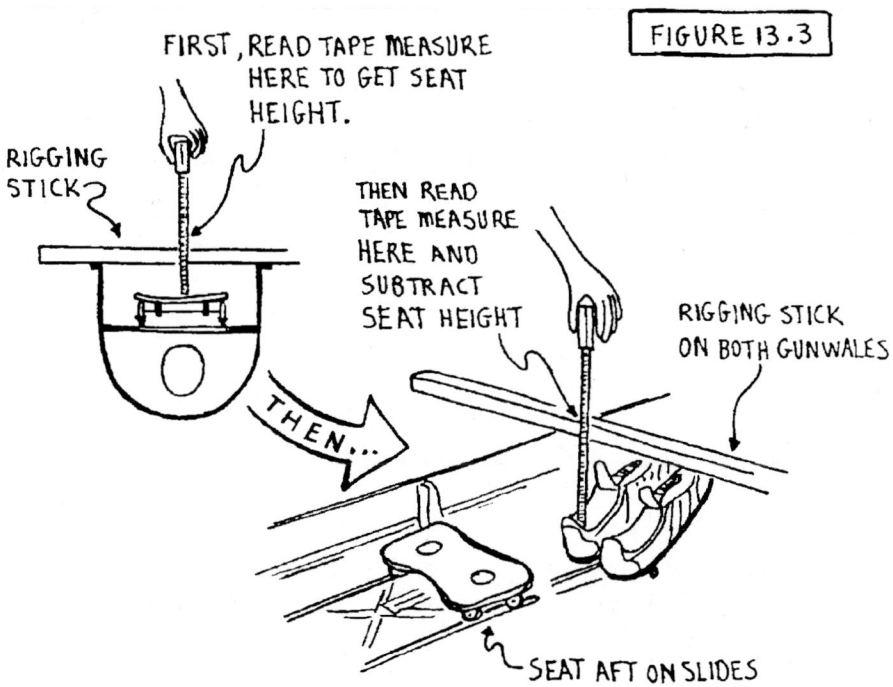

FIRST, READ TAPE MEASURE HERE TO GET SEAT HEIGHT.

FIGURE 13·3

RIGGING STICK

THEN READ TAPE MEASURE HERE AND SUBTRACT SEAT HEIGHT

RIGGING STICK ON BOTH GUNWALES

THEN...

SEAT AFT ON SLIDES

> Always take rower's feedback with a grain of salt. If you go searching for problems most rowers will be happy to oblige. The more experienced the rower, the more useful the feedback. I feel that the closer the rower has come to rowing one million strokes, the more valuable the feedback is.

**Step 2. Adjust The Heel Cup: Clog Types:** If your boat has clogs, you have two options: either they're adjustable or they aren't. Look at your foot stretcher; take it out of the shell if you need to get a good look. You'll find a variety of designs for the heel cups, ranging from simple three-screw adjustments to nonadjustables. There are so many varieties that have popped up over the years I've got to say you're on your own here. See what you've got; if it's adjustable, move it, and if it's not, you may need to call the manufacturer for advice.

**Sneaker types:** If your boat has sneakers, your choice is simple: relocate the sneaker on the foot plate. Usually the sneakers are attached to a plate that has several holes in it that is then attached to the foot stretcher. Usually—not always. If yours is attached that way, just unscrew the fasteners of the plate, relocate the plate either higher or lower, and tighten up the fasteners.

If your sneakers are attached differently, you'll have to determine how they are attached, and if they are movable. My suggestion here: take out the entire foot stretcher, and look it over well. If it is not obvious how to relocate the sneakers, make a call to the manufacturer, especially before you go ripping things apart.

**Step 3. Check Your Work:** After you've made the change do another dock check just to see how your work turned out. Hopefully you were successful. If not, keep fiddling with the heel cup heights.

## Part 2: Foot Stretcher Angle

Usually with foot stretcher angle, what you see is what you get. Most boats come with the angles fixed. Most, but not all, and that's fine because the standard angle built in usually fits everyone. But you might find yourself having to change the angle due to the rower's flexibility. Problems pop up if the angle is either too steep or too flat for the rower to get their feet comfortably situated.

**Step 1. Check The Angles:** There are two ways you can check the angle: (a) measure it, or (b) watch your rower. Measuring is simple. Find yourself a protractor, a simple little device for measuring angles. Leave the stretchers in the boat and set yourself up like figure 13.4.

Ballpark the angle as best you can—you've got a couple of degrees of error to play with, so don't get too stressed over accuracy. The normal range is from 38–45 degrees, with the standard angle about 42 degrees.

You might want to try this: Instead of a protractor, I use an electronic level that also measures angles. This little handy-dandy device lets me measure the angles of an entire eight in about 60 seconds. Is it worth getting one of these things just to measure angles? No, not really. A protractor will work fine; however, if you have access to an electronic level, give it a try.

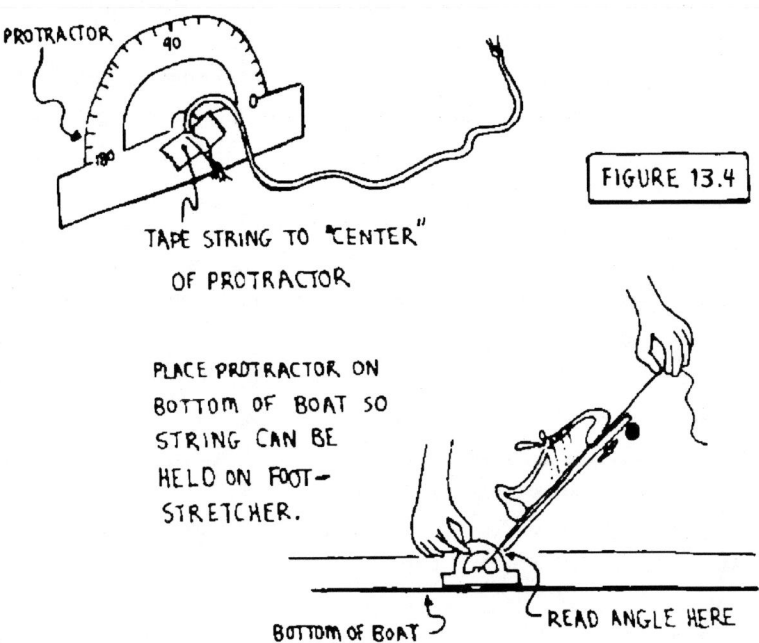

I've found that watching the rowers is a more reliable method than measuring the angles—plus you don't have to go digging around for a protractor. Do your dock check just like Step 1 for the heel cups. At the catch, look at the distance from the bottom of the rower's heels to the **footplate**. If the angle is set properly the rower's heels will come up just slightly from the foot plate at the catch until the drive starts, then they'll be flush against it. If the angle is too step, the heels will be too far up from the foot plate and the rower may end up driving off the toes. If the angle is too flat, then the heels won't lift off the foot plate at all.

Have the rower go to the release; if the angle is too flat, the legs may not be able to extend completely—almost the same as problems with the heel cups. If you see anything funky, ask the rower how the stretcher feels. If you think you need to make an adjustment, check to see if your stretchers are adjustable. If they are, on to Step 2. If they aren't, don't panic; there might be a few things you can do.

**Step 2. Adjusting The Adjustable:** If you've got to change the angle and it's your lucky day, then you've got foot stretchers with built-in adjustments. Before you adjust anything, measure the angle with your protractor. If you make a mistake it's good to know where you started. Now look at the foot stretcher and identify the moving parts. To allow adjustment, either the ends of the top-cross support will turn or the footplate itself will turn on the top support. Loosen the fasteners, make a small adjustment, re-tighten, and get the rower's feedback.

**Step 3. The Nonadjustable:** If you've got to move the angles and the stretchers are nonadjustable, you might be able to fudge things enough to get what you need. I've only stumbled upon this situation twice. In one case, I replaced the sneakers with a pair with more heel cushioning and that solved the problem. The other case involved a Schoenbrod Intercollegiate foot stretcher. I had to take it completely apart, re-work it, and then reassemble it. Turned out to be a lengthy JOB—drilling a bunch of new holes and all that. If this is the direction you think you're headed, I suggest first picking up the phone and calling the manufacturer. They may have some handy-dandy suggestions.

## Part 3: Adjusting the Sneaker Size

The nice things about clogs is that they fit a wide range of rowers. But they have two disadvantages compared to sneakers. First, you might find those people with tiny feet or really big ones have a fit problem. Second, clogs aren't comfortable (don't see many clog dancers, do you?). Sneakers, on the other hand, are comfortable, easily changeable, and come in a ton of different sizes.

**Step 1. Mark Them:** You can save yourself some hassles down the road by marking all the sneakers in your shell with waterproof markers. Mark on the sole, or on the toes. Put on the size and what boat they go to; that way you'll know where they came from and be able to keep like sizes together. The only thing worse than rowing with sneakers too small is rowing with two different-sized sneakers.

**Step 2. Remove Them:** Before you change any sneakers, make sure you've got a replacement pair. If your luck is still hot, you'll have a spare pair that already has the holes drilled with the correct number of bolts in them. If it's not your lucky day, keep reading.

Remove the complete foot stretcher from the boat (by removing the nuts attached to the stretcher bolt), especially if this is the first time you've ever done this. Then look at the bottom side. You should see one or two fasteners holding the sneaker to the foot plate. Loosen and remove these.

Remove the sneakers, being sure to note which holes in the foot plate the bolts go through. Some foot stretchers have several different sets of holes and each set makes a difference in the heel cup height. If you're here to change the heel cup height, moving the bolts to different holes is what you want to do.

If your replacement sneakers don't have bolts, then you'll need to remove the bolts from the old sneakers, drill holes in the new sneakers, and slide the bolts into them. If you feel comfortable with a drill, it's pretty easy. Just line up the old sneakers, mark the bolts and drill away—you will need to go all the way through the sneaker bottom. If you need replacement bolts try using stainless steel **elevator bolts**. They are used on some household appliances to level loads and can be found in many appliance and hardware stores—just make sure you use stainless steel.

**Step 3. Replace Them:** Replace the old sneakers with new ones (or if not new, then better ones). If you're keeping the old ones, tie the laces together and stash them. When tightening the fasteners, make sure there's a washer between the nut and foot plate. This will save the foot plate from a lot of wear and tear and stop the nuts from working loose.

---

I use plastic wing nuts to secure the sneakers, if they are bolted from underneath the foot stretcher. They prevent over-tightening and cut a few ounces of weight. They are easier to adjust than regular nuts and the rowers can tighten them by hand with the stretchers still in the boat.

---

**Step 4. Measure The Heel Cup:** A different sneaker size can move the heel cup height by a few centimeters. If you've changed the sneaker size, measure the height to check you're still in the range you need.

**Step 5. Rower's Feedback:** Go for a row and then get feedback from the rowers on how the sneakers feel. You're not only checking the size but also checking the opening angle and heel cup height—they may have changed. If you've got sneakers too big, see if having the rower wear an extra pair of socks (or two) makes a difference. If they are way too big, or too small, you should change the sneakers.

If you're buying replacement sneakers, I strongly suggest you get ones with Velcro fasteners instead of shoe laces. In case of mishap, the Velcro makes emergency exit from the sneakers easier. Also, make sure that there are heel ties on the sneakers, and attach them to the foot stretcher securely.

## JOB 13.2: MEASURING OAR DEFLECTION (STIFFNESS).

**Problem:** You want to compare the deflection in your oar set.

**Needed:** Sawhorse, measuring device, weight, and small piece of rope.

You can't change the oar deflection, but it's something you need to know—you want all the oars in your oar set the same. Remember, we are talking about stiffness. If your set has a variety of stiffnesses you're going to end up with all sorts of funky balance and technique problems, which you and the rowers don't need. Measuring them is fairly simple once the setup is done, and a set of eight should only take you fifteen minutes to do.

**Step 1. Setup :** You'll need a setup like in figure 13.5. I suggest you use a sturdy sawhorse for the fulcrum point and something quite solid to stabilize the handle, like the rack of a trailer or something secured to a wall.

Depending on who you talk to, or read, there are several variations on how to measure the deflection: for example, how much weight to use for the load **A,** where to measure distance **B**, and the length of distance **C**. If you're only measuring your oars to compare them with each other you can use any weight and measure any distance that works for you, as long as you're consistent.

At our boat-shack I use a twenty-five pound weight from an old barbell set for the load, with a chunk of rope strung through the hole in the middle. I use an old yardstick found in the trash to measure the distance. Recycling at its best! I'll assume you're using similar stuff, but limit yourself to a weight no greater than twenty-five pounds. If you're comparing your deflection to manufacturer's specs, you'll need to contact them for their specifics of A, B, and C.

**Step 2. Measure Away:** Lay out your first oar. With the weight not attached yet, measure and record where the blade tip comes to on the yard stick. Now slip the rope attached to your load over the blade until it sits almost in the middle of the spoon. Let the load hang free, and now measure where the blade tip is on your yard stick. Subtract the two distances and you've got your deflection. Record this number and do the rest of your set.

**Step 3. What Ya Got?** When you're done the set, compare the numbers and see what, if any, variety you've got. I usually get about a 1–2 centimeters variety in my sets, but that's probably due to the way I measure things. I can't tell you what to expect, except that you should see a pattern between oars and try to put as many like oars together as you can. I suggest you measure sets once every couple of years to keep track of things.

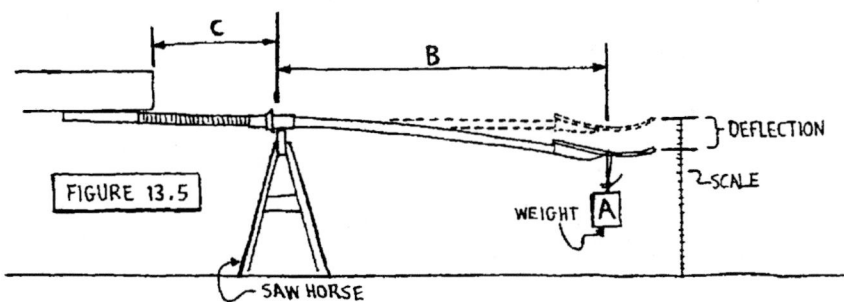

FIGURE 13.5

## JOB 13.3: DETERMINING WEIGHT CLASSIFICATION OF SHELL.

**Problem:** You need to know your shell's weight classification (the average weight of rowers it's designed to hold).

**Needed:** Rigging stick, tape measure, rigging card.

Most boats used to come in basically three different weight classifications (sizes): **heavyweight** (for 185–210 pound average crew weight), **midweight** (160–185 average) and **lightweight** (130–160 average). That was in the olden days, oh . . . say in the 1990s.

Today, there are more choices, and with more choices you have the need to make more decisions and you have more chances to make mistakes. What you are interested in with weight classification is pretty simple: trying to get the correct size crew in the correct size boat (see Chapter Seven, JOB 7.2, for more info on this).

Each size boat will have different dimensions. There are two dimensions that change the most between the different sizes: **depth** and **beam**. But there is variety as far as these dimensions are concerned, and two heavyweight shells from the same builder may have different depths and beams.

One reason is that customers may want different options that change the dimension of the boat, and models change from year to year as the builders experiment to come up with better and faster shells. Also, the building processes change over time with new methods and new technology, and that may mean different dimensions, too.

So how do you tell what shell size a boat is? First, you need the depth and the beam dimensions. Get your tape measure and go to the midships of the shell. This is where the hull should be the deepest. Set your rigging stick or straight edge across the gunwales. Now measure down from the bottom of the straight edge to the bottom of the inside of the hull. That's your hull depth. At the same point—which should also be the widest part of the boat—measure from the inside of one gunwale to inside of the other for the beam. These numbers will be a guideline to help you find the shell size. Second, you may need your serial number (see

<http://www.MaxRigging> for info on locating different serial numbers). Armed with this information, you've got three ways to tell the shell size:

**Good method:** Eyeball comparison. If you've been around this sport long enough you'll be able to tell a shell's size just by looking. If you're in a boathouse, and need a little help, take a few steps back and compare shapes with another boat you know the size of. If this doesn't help, try . . .

**Better method:** The best way to tell a shell size, with the least amount of hassles, is to already have the measurements (beam and depth) of a boat whose size you know and then compare the boat in question to those numbers. There are two ways to get these numbers. One, of course, is to call the builder and get the **beam** and **depth** for a size and category (eight, four, pair) of boat. The other way is just to measure a boat. Either way, make sure the numbers are from the same manufacturer.

Don't try to compare a Dirigo's measurements to a Pocock's—the measurements vary drastically between different makes of shells. Generally, heavyweight shells will have larger depths and beams than midweights, and midweights will be larger than lightweights. But don't be surprised if there is not a lot of difference in dimensions between sizes. In fact, different classes might have the same beam or depth. If this won't work, try . . .

**Best method:** Take your measurements and the serial number and head to a phone. You need to call the builder. This may cost you a few pennies, but you'll find out positively what size shell you've got.

I know all this may sound like a lot of hassle, but for good rigging you need to know what class a boat is.

## JOB 13.4: MEASURING SHELL STIFFNESS.

**Problem:** Trying to find out how much wiggle you've got in your shell.

**Needed:** The boat in question, preferably slinged, seats-up.

What we're interested in finding out is how tight, or un-tight, your shell is. We are going to check in two directions: side to side, and bow to stern. I use a reliable, but a fairly unscientific method. Definitely check the stiffness if it's a used shell you're thinking of buying.

**Step 1. Setup:** It's best to try checking stiffness when the boat is in slings. For an eight, place the slings under the two and seven seats. If you can't sling it, you can still check the bow to stern stiffness in the rack.

**Step 2. Side To Side:** Make sure your rigger nuts are tight. Go to the fore-most rigger and press down with a gentle motion. Notice what happens to your aft-most rigger on the opposite side. When you press down the other rigger should go up the same amount, and at the same time. Now gently rock the bow rigger up and down and see what happens. There should be little or no time delay between the two riggers moving, or any swaying occurring in the boat. The more sway you have, the less stiff the boat.

**Step 3. Bow To Stern:** Now we're going to find out if the boat is tight from end to end. Go to the bow, about two feet from the bow ball. Cradle the hull in both hands and wiggle the shell up and down. Nothing drastic—just a subtle motion. Careful of the soft decking if you've got it. Look at the stern and see what's happening. Are things tight, or does the boat wiggle like a bowl of strawberry Jell-O? (See figure 13.2.)

If the boat is in the racks, there's another test you can do. Go to the bow, about halfway between the bow ball and wash box. Cradle the sides of the boat and gently lift up. Watch your back; grab a friend to help if you need it. When you lift, look at the racks and notice if the shell moves as one unit or if it sags in the middle. If it sags, it's not stiff—the more the sag, the less the stiffness.

**Step 4. Now What?** You've looked at sag and sway so now you know something about how stiff your boat is. What do you do with the info? Your choices are fairly simple. If the shell is tight and solid, keep rowing it. If the boat wiggled, it may be time to either do a major repair JOB, such as tightening up the bracing, or take the boat off of your competitive racing-boat list and start using it as a training shell. If it's a used shell you're thinking about buying, lack of stiffness is a warning there might be problems.

> Purcer's *Rigging* goes into more detail about a boat's stiffness. It shows two more scientific methods to check how tight the boat is.

# Chapter Fourteen: Putting It All Together

This chapter is about doing a complete rigging JOB. Previously we've been doing one JOB at a time, but often you'll come upon a boat in which the whole rig needs to be done. This makes things a little more complicated, but doing it step by step makes it easy.

## JOB 14.1: THE COMPLETE RIG JOB.

**Problem:** It's time for the *big rig*.

**Needed:** Basic rigging kit, boat in slings, rigging cards, rigging numbers, mellow place to work, time, PRE (positive rigging environment), SRE (safe rigging environment).

It seems everyone has a different method for doing a complete rig JOB, and what works best for you is the way that you should proceed when faced with the big rig. I'm going to present here for you the way that I do it. Feel free to use this or venture out on your own.

The following steps are the way I was taught. I remember asking my rigging mentor why we were doing things in this order. The answer was, "Because, grasshopper, it flowed." And he was right, it flowed. There should be a flow when you rig and everything should feel comfortable with a minimal amount of back tracking over steps. If you're a First- or Second-Dimensional try this way. When you're a Third, you'll be ready to develop your own.

**Step 1. You've Got To Do It:** All signs are saying that it's time to rig. If you're not quite sure that you need to get to work, then see Chapter Seven, JOB 7.1, *Determining That You Need to Rig.*

**Step 2. Find Your Numbers:** Here's where you start because there's not much you can do without numbers. You need to know three things: the size of some specific equipment, the average weight of your crew (this can be an estimate), and the numbers you will want to adjust your equipment to. Check your sources, measure your stuff, and find your numbers. For help, turn to your favorite reference book or Chapter Fifteen. Once you've got your numbers, write them down and keep them handy (see JOB 15.7). You'll be surprised how hard it is to keep all those figures straight in your head, especially when every little half-centimeter counts!

**Step 3. Prepare To Rig: Setup, Tools, Game Plan:** Before you go diving into things, take a couple of minutes and get everything ready. Find your tools (JOBs 3.1 and 3.2), set the equipment up (JOB 7.3: *Preparing to Rig*), sling your shell (JOB 7.4, *Slinging a Boat*), construct your rigging environment (Chapter Six), and organize your work space so you can putter along with a minimum of distractions and hassles.

The more important the rigging, the more interruptions you'll get. Find some way to get peace and solitude so you can concentrate, like unplug the phone, rent a junkyard dog, eat onions, play Oxford Blues. Do what you've got to do to focus. One friend of mine has a motel's "Do Not Disturb" sign she hangs on the bow ball so her rowers know not to bug her until she's done.

---

When rigging a complete boat I suggest you do the same JOB to all the riggers before you move on to the next JOB. So, for example, go through and do all the leverage adjustments, and check them before you move on to the next measurement (for sculls do both riggers of a position at the same time). This saves a lot of tool-switching, and you can compare the riggers to see if they all fall within the same range. A complete rig JOB may take several hours, depending on the equipment's need and your skills. Start at one rigger, such as the stroke's, and use that for a landmark. It will help you with your flow.

---

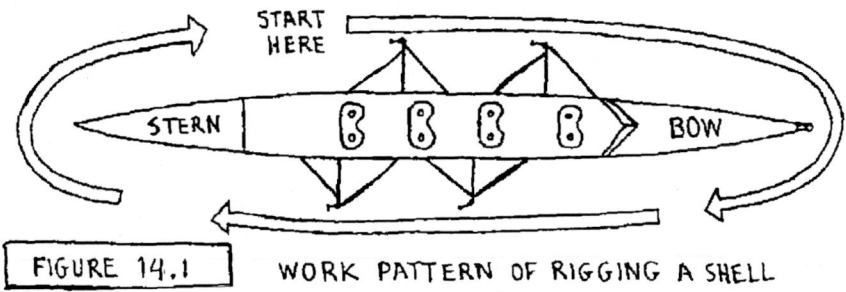

FIGURE 14.1     WORK PATTERN OF RIGGING A SHELL

**Step 4. First Things First:** Go through and tighten all the rigger nuts snugly. If you know you'll be making adjustments to all the riggers, such as changing all the spreads, go through and loosen all the major fasteners and clamps on the riggers before you begin making the actual adjustments. Make sure the seats are in their proper places and undo any retaining straps. See JOBs 7.5 and 7.6.

**Step 5. Leverage: Spread (Span), Inboard, Blade Surface Area:** You're going to determine the length of both arcs and also their location in respect to the shell's centerline—all this by adjusting the spread and inboard. Usually when you move the spread you'll need to move the inboard. The blade surface area is nonadjustable but important to know for your leverage. See JOBs 9.1–9.5.

> If adjustments are needed to sculling riggers, use the spread method to move them. After you adjust the span, measure the overlap of oar handles at the mid-drive to verify your inside arcs are correct (see Chapter Twenty-One).

**Step 6. Pitch:** One of the key adjustments determining the efficiency of the stroke is the pitch. Accuracy counts (just like in pitching horseshoes), so take your time. See Chapter Ten, JOBs 10.1–10.5.

**Step 7. Height:** Now it's on to adjust the height, which determines the distance of the horizontal flat off the water's surface. Changes in height may affect your pitch—when you're done with your height, double-check your pitch. See Chapter Eleven, JOBs 11.1–11.3.

In sculling, because of the handle overlap, the heights are different for the port and starboard riggers (see Chapter Twenty-One). To help you keep track of these height numbers, adjust both riggers of a position before you move onto the next.

**Step 8. Work-thru: Foot Stretchers, Track Adjustments, Catch Length And Angle:** These adjustments move the pin from bow to stern and locates both arcs in respect to the foot stretchers. You'll move the foot stretchers, the rigger, and/or the tracks. See JOBs 12.1–12.5.

**Step 9. Minor Adjustments: Foot Stretcher Positioning, Oar Deflection And Balance Point, And Stability:** The heavy-duty stuff is done, but there are a few key adjustments left. You've got to make sure the foot stretchers are adjusted properly, and there are a couple of things you've got to know about your oars and the shell. See JOBs 13.1–13.4.

**Step 10. Check Your Work:** When Henry Ford's assembly line was chugging along, I've heard that every so often he would wander down to the shop, pull a car off the line, rip it apart, and measure it to make sure it met his specs. His version of quality control.

You need to do the same with your rigging, and you've got to be quite critical about it. Double-check: see if the adjustments are correct, if the fasteners are tight, if all beaten-up and broken parts have been replaced, and most importantly, if the equipment is safe to row. You're doing your own version of quality control—the last thing you need is a recall, especially during a race.

**Step 11. Test It Out:** Now give your rigging the real test—row it. Have the athletes, or yourself—if that's who you're rigging for—take the boat for a spin. First do a dock check (JOB 13.1) and height check (Chapter Eleven) to make sure things are where they need to be. Have scullers come to the release and check their hand positions. If needed, adjust the foot stretchers to locate the hands correctly (see Chapter Twenty-One). Then start the boat rowing with an easy, controlled pressure. Then put the boat through the paces. Get feedback and readjust if you need to.

**Step 12. Clean Up:** Tidy up your work space and put things where they belong.

**Step 13. Keep It Working:** You want to get the biggest and longest bang for your buck. You need to maintain your stuff with a little tender loving care and a couple JOBs. See Chapter Eighteen, *Keeping Your Equipment Alive*, JOBs 18.1–18.3.

# SECTION THREE
# RIGGING EXTRAS

# Chapter Fifteen: Your Rigging Numbers

O f all the things that have changed in the rowing/rigging world since I wrote the first edition of this book, this chapter is one that has changed the most, and at the same time has changed the least. Here is what I mean.

Rigging has gone through a great revolution the past ten years, due to the advent of new oar designs, the acceptance of the Euro-style rigger in the U.S., and production of new electronics (e.g., SpeedCoach™ Rowing Computer, GPS, stroke watches). The change in oars has meant significant changes in the numbers used for the leverage measurements. While the Euro-style rigger has significantly impacted how people adjust a rigger. And the electronics are tools/toys that help Riggers figure things out.

Yet, despite all of those changes the dependence that rowers, coaches, and Riggers have on rigging numbers and how they use and locate those numbers has not changed at all. So, many aspects of rigging numbers are really no different than from I described them ten years ago, but the numbers you find and use will be different.

Things are different, but they are still the same.

## 15.1 What Are Rigging Numbers?

A rigging number is in essence two things. First, it can be a number representing a distance of adjustment that can be made to a piece of rowing equipment. This is also known as a **rigging-measurement**. Rigging-measurements are those numbers you use for the various parts of your rowing equipment that are adjustable.

Second, it can be a number that describes a specific characteristic of a piece of rowing equipment that is nonadjustable—a.k.a. **equipment-measurement**. Equipment-measurements are those numbers concerning your equipment and are part of the equipment's design—for example, the length of the shell. For the most part, these measurements are nonadjustable. (However, more than one a coach or boatman has adjusted what didn't come as adjustable—usually with a big hammer or a sharp saw.)

## 15.2 When Do You Need Rigging Numbers?

There are basically six different types of rigging that you might be involved with and each requires that you have rigging numbers—and not just any old numbers, the correct numbers. I listed the types of rigging in Chapter Two, but they are worth repeating here.

1. **Purchasing-rigging** is planning and buying the equipment you'll be using for practices and racing.

2. **Practice-rigging** is preparing and adjusting your equipment for practices. This includes rigging to help correct technique problems and also those instances when you might have to adjust or repair riggers or equipment on the water.

3. **Race-rigging** is more involved because you are dealing with traveling, race-day preparations, and those nervous butterflies that make everything seem like a major undertaking. Specifically, race-rigging involves the fine-tuning adjustments you make to squeeze the last ounce of speed from your team.

4. **Peace-of-mind-rigging** is simply adjusting your riggers because you think or feel something may be off.

5. **Maintenance-rigging** is a routine you perform to help your equipment survive longer. For more info on maintenance, see the

Special Report *Six Steps to Get the Most from Your Rowing Equipment* at my Web site, <http://www.helpingcoaches.com>.

6. **Individual-rigging** is setting up the equipment for an individual. This differs from practice-rigging in that it is more specific to finding the proper rigging for a specific person.

## 15.3 Why Do You Need Rigging Numbers?

You need rigging numbers—the correct rigging numbers—to make sure that you are properly doing the six types of rigging just listed. And just what are the benefits of doing those six types of rigging right? I'm glad you asked:

**Benefit #1: Comfort.** Ever take a long drive while sitting in a car seat that just didn't fit very well? How about writing a term paper with a pen that is too big? Or talking on a phone where the cord is way too short? (Remember those days when phones had cords?)

If you've ever endured any of these things, or have done anything else with a piece of equipment or with a tool that didn't fit right, then you have a pretty darn good idea of what it's like to row with equipment that is not adjusted correctly.

When you chose rigging numbers, comfort of the rower has to be of prime concern. Okay, I know that rowing is a *tough* sport and we like that image, and Martha Stewart has no real place in our sport. However, when people row, especially long distances, the equipment has got to be as comfortable as possible for the rowers. Because if it's not, then only the truly masochistic rowers will survive.

Simply put, correct rigging numbers can help rowing be more comfortable.

**Benefit #2: Speed.** For rowing coaches, speed is our Holy Grail. It is that elusive item we seem to spend hours, days, weeks, months, and years chasing. Rigging numbers are critical to generating maximum hull speed. If it is speed you're after, then you need the right numbers, for without them you may find max hull speed to be very elusive.

**Benefit #3: Safety.** Rowing is about as equipment-intensive a sport as there is. That means that a rower's body is going to be in contact with the equipment. To be specific, there are four places where the body touches: the butt, the back of the calves, the hands, and the feet. These areas make up only about ten percent of a body's surface, but boy, that ten percent is important. I call these places the **hot spots**, and if there is a problem in one of these areas, that can really mess up your rowing.

For example, little nasties like blisters have been known to stop armies dead in their tracks, and they certainly can make your rowing uncomfortable and inefficient. So can a smashed knuckle. Or even worse, an incredible case of *screaming boat-butt.*

In my clinics I often relate the story of seeing eight stud-type rowers get off the water after a spin in one of the first boats in the country with adjustable tracks. The boat was new and no one was quite sure how to adjust the tracks—in this case, they were adjusted about five inches too far toward the stern. With each new stroke, the end of the tracks jabbed into their calves, and the end product was eight bleeding, limping, and grumbling rowers

Using the correct rigging numbers won't totally eliminate these types of injuries, but they sure can help reduce them.

**Benefit #4: Smart Money:** There is another benefit of rigging numbers of which you may not have thought: helping you make a wise purchase of equipment (see Chapter Nineteen for more info on buying equipment). Knowing exactly what you need when you buy something, whether new or old, is critical to a good purchase. And knowing your rigging numbers can help you know what you need to buy.

**Benefit #5: Helping the Equipment Last Longer:** How do rigging numbers make a difference in how long your equipment lasts? It's similar to the air pressure in your tires. When properly inflated, tires will last a lot longer. When over- or under-inflated, the tires wear incredibly fast. And the same goes for rowing equipment. For instance, significant, incorrect pitch settings on a rigger can cause premature wear of an oarlock or of a collar. Proper rigging numbers can make the difference in rowing equipment's lasting two years or twenty years, and who can afford to replace oars, riggers, and shells every two years?

**Benefit #6: Less Torture.** I have one last benefit I want to throw out: more than once I've had unpleasant rigging experiences when I didn't have the correct rigging numbers. When you need to rig, especially when it's important to get it right, not having those numbers around can be like torture. In other words, rig a boat poorly and lose a race by .5 seconds—don't expect a good night's sleep.

## 15.4 Danger! Danger! Danger!

I have to throw out two big words of caution here.

First, be very, Very, VERY careful of WHERE *you get your rigging numbers*. For example, a rigging chart produced from the rigging of the men's eights rowed at the 1999 World Championships gives the numbers that those folks rowed at that regatta. But "those folks" are well-trained, high-performance athletes, of very homogeneous traits, who execute at the upper end of human abilities. You are not likely to find many, if any, similar people in your programs/boats. And the rigging numbers that push one of these athletes to the brink of his endurance when racing a 2000-meter race will absolutely crush lesser rowers very early on in the race (that is, if they make it to the race at all).

Second, *know how measurements were taken*!

There's not much controversy in rigging, but if you're going to see an argument, it's probably going to be over the topic of measuring things. Many times different folks will make the same measurement differently.

That means that what may turn out to be a spread measurement of 85 cm for you might be 86 cm for me—that is, if we measure things differently. That's a big difference. This is an extremely important thing to keep in mind when looking at rigging numbers from charts and other folks. Always ask, "How did you measure that?"

At the end of this chapter, you will find my rigging charts. You'll notice two things. First they come in ranges. Second, accompanying those charts is a table that explains how they were measured. Both of these steps are taken to help make your selection of rigging numbers safer.

## JOB 15.1: DETERMINING RIGGING NUMBERS FOR FIRST-DIMENSIONAL RIGGERS.

**Problem:** You need to determine your rigging numbers, and you are just starting out in the wild and wacky world of rigging and/or rowing.

**Needed:** Patience, willingness to learn, supportive learning environment.

**Step 1. Keep It Simple:** I'm here to tell you that as a First-Dimensional Rigger you need to know very little—except for one specific thing. And that specific is that you need to know *very little*.

There are so many other things that you need to know about in the world of rowing if you're just getting into it. Items like safety and injury prevention are so much more critical than rigging and rigging numbers. Don't let anyone tell you differently.

So, at this stage, put knowledge about rigging numbers way the heck toward the bottom of your list of things to do!

However, if you're like most stubborn rowing-coach types, you won't feel productive unless you are knowing/learning something about them. With that in mind, here is what I suggest. . . .

Forget about what I call **rigging-measurements** (adjustable measurements), and just try to absorb any basic **equipment-measurements** (non-adjustable measurements) you see. For example, focus on simple things, such as the size of the boat. Three of the best ways to learn at this stage learn are: (a) observe, (b) ask questions, and (c) read.

**Step 2. Observe:** Watch your rowers, look at other rowers, check out other Riggers, watch the oars move through the water. Look, stare, gaze, scrutinize, give the once-over, reconnoiter, and survey whatever you can.

Observation is an important part of the learning process that many ignore, and it is absolutely critical for First-Dimensional folks. You need to get a mental picture of what good rowing and good rigging look like. Look for problems with the rowing; watch how different body sizes adapt to different rigging; see how other people rig. Remember, as a "firstie" you're trying to learn; observing is a great way to do it.

**Step 3. Ask Questions—Many!** How does a three-year-old learn? She asks questions, hundreds . . . thousands . . . millions of them. And that is what I prompt you to do. Be inquisitive. Stay curious. Ask questions—thoughtful questions, tough questions. This is a great way to learn. Kids do it, and so should we.

Oh yeah, you know that saying, "There are no stupid questions . . ."? As someone who teaches for a living, I want to tell you, "Oh yes, there are!" So when you're asking questions, think about the question first. And if it is a reasonable and appropriate one, ask away. And if it's not, store it for a later date.

**Step 4. Read:** An excellent way to learn is to read. I suggest that you read everything about rowing and rigging and rigging numbers that you can get your hands on. Get it from the Web, or books, or magazines, or bathroom walls. Get it, read it, and digest it.

But notice, I am not saying *believe* it all. That would be a mistake. There is so much silly, lame, and downright wrong stuff out there that you need to be careful about what you believe. Be picky.

## JOB 15.2: DETERMINING RIGGING NUMBERS FOR SECOND-DIMENSIONAL RIGGERS.

**Problem:** You need your numbers, and you are a second-dimensional Rigger.

**Needed:** What you'll need to be successful here are the rigging charts at the end of this report, a quiet place, a few deep breaths, and possibly a phone.

**Step 1. Read:** Before you begin your numbers hunt, take five minutes and go back and get familiar with Chapter Four, *The Equipment,* and Chapter Seven, *The First Steps of Rigging.*

**Step 2. Relax:** Too often—way too often—I've seen people get to this stage of the game and freak out over rigging and rigging numbers. Don't place undo importance upon rigging numbers—it's a dark and evil place to go.

Instead, realize that rigging numbers can help you do a better job, but they are not the end-all. If you feel that you don't quite have the right ones, no worries, we'll get them. Locating them is not too hard, especially if you take it one step at a time.

**Step 3. To The Charts With You:** At this stage in your learning, rigging charts are one of the best sources of information available. That is, if the numbers come from a credible source. (The ones in the back of this chapter do come from a credible source—me). One thing about the charts I've included: you'll notice that they give ranges instead of specific numbers. These ranges have been determined by the rowing world through many years of trials and experimentation. Stop here a second, flip to the charts at the end of this chapter, and look at the chart to see what I mean.

Why ranges? Ranges are given because there are so many variables (e.g., rower's size, race length, conditions, technique, etc.) that will impact the numbers you use to rig. So ranges are not a cop-out; they are exactly what you need to start the process of maximizing your numbers. Once you've found ranges for your numbers you need to narrow the ranges down.

**Step 4. Fine Tune.** You'll need help for this step. For help, call someone whose rigging opinion you respect to see what he or she suggests. Ask around and see what other folks are using for their numbers. Maybe you'll get some good ideas. Maybe you'll get reinforcement that the numbers you've picked are the best. Maybe you'll get the cold shoulder.

At race courses, ask coaches what they are using for their numbers (but make sure it's not five minutes before a big race). After regattas, find out what the winning crews used for their measurements, and find out what the slower crews used. There's probably not too much of a difference. Record all of this groundwork so you can narrow your ranges down to a specific number. (If you can't find help with narrowing your ranges, play it conservative and just go for the middle of the range.)

**Step 5. Danger! Danger! Danger!** Be very, Very, VERY wary of the numbers in rigging tables and charts, and numbers that you might get at regattas. The reason, as we discussed before, is that those numbers may be totally useless for you and your rigging, and, in fact, might be down right dangerous. So be cautious, be careful, be wary.

**Step 6. Use Them:** Once you've got your numbers, and a range that you think is right, it's time to do something with them. You may need to get someone to assist you with the rigging, or even have them do it for you while you observe. If you work slowly, rig the best you can, and things look good, then you're done with the hands-on part of rigging for now. Here comes the hard part—**leave your rigging alone!** It's fine; don't touch it (except to check if something may have slipped!).

**Step 7. Write Them Down:** Once you've got the numbers and done your rigging, record everything for future reference. Don't skip this step! ! ! For suggestions and guidance on how to record your rigging numbers, see my Special Report, *How to Maximize Your Rigging Numbers*, at my Web site <http://www.MaxRigging.com>.

# JOB 15.3: DETERMINING RIGGING NUMBERS FOR THIRD-DIMENSIONAL RIGGERS.

**Problem:** You're in the Third Dimension and you need numbers to rig with.

**Needed:** What you'll need to be successful are the rigging charts at the end of this chapter (or similar ones), your own rigging numbers if you have them, and some testing equipment (e.g., SpeedCoach™).

**Step 1. Get The Numbers:** Finding your numbers is not all that much different from the method First- and Second-Dimensional Riggers use (look it up, ask people, etc.) except for one thing: You should have your own.

By now, you should have a store of different rigging numbers you have used in the past. From these numbers, you should have a good idea about what you want to use, and what works and what doesn't. These numbers are a resource you need to put to good use.

**Step 2. Testing:** Not to sound offensive, but when you're at this stage of the game, the numbers you get from books, charts, friends, or your own rigging should not be good enough for you at face value. You should feel a need to prove that these numbers will work for you and for your crew. To do this, you need to do a few tests, record the results, make some comparisons, and determine what will work best. Following are two suggested ways to do such tests. For more information and more suggestions of other tests to perform, see my Special Report, *How to Absolutely Maximize Your Rigging Numbers* which can be found at my Web site <http://www.MaxRigging.com>.

## Method #1: Measured Course.

Find a protected area of water, a nice spot where you can reduce the effects of boat traffic, wind, and current as much as possible. Set yourself up a distance and mark it well. If you're interested in boat speed, or efficiency, you should have your crew row this distance and time the results.

It doesn't matter how long the distance is, as long as it is a consistent distance that is well marked. The important element is the markers must be easily seen and set up in such a way to form two imaginary planes that extend out into the water. When the bow ball of the boat breaks the first plane, start the watch, and stop it when the second plane is broken.

For this test to work you need to be accurate. Start and stop the watch at the exact same place and have the crew at a consistent pressure. Do several pieces in both directions (to account for wind or for current) and determine an average time, making sure the rowers have plenty of time to recover. Then make your rigging change. For example, lighten the inboards a full centimeter.

Now do the pieces again and record the results. Do several. Compare the times. If the crew is faster after the changes, you may be on to something. If the crew is slower then go back to the original numbers (which you wrote down) and try again.

This method will let you test any rigging-measurement (even sneaker size!), different equipment, different rowers, ratings, coxswains, and different race strategies. Try to set yourself up a permanent course you can use over many seasons to compare results year to year.

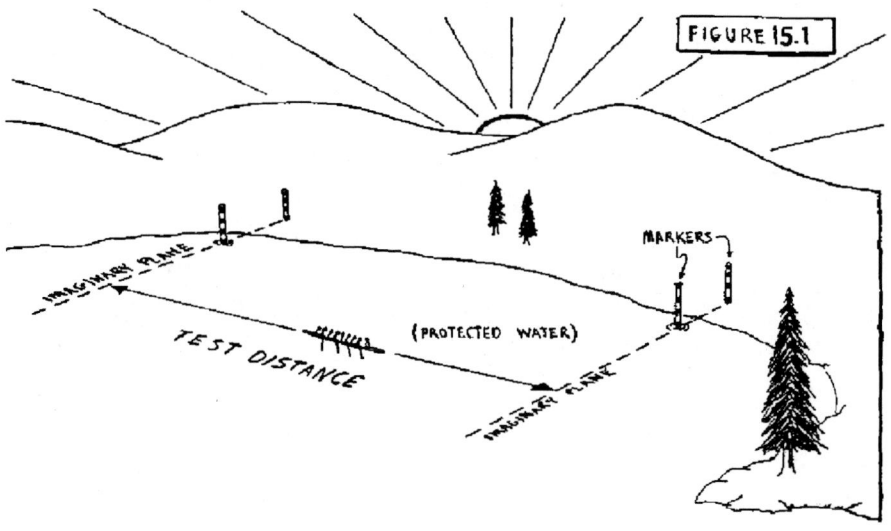

FIGURE 15.1

TEST DISTANCE (PROTECTED WATER) IMAGINARY PLANE MARKERS

If you're using a course with marked intervals, for example a 2000-meter course with every 500 meters marked, you can learn about your rigging and rower(s) by comparing the interval times (called "splits"). Normally, the first 500-meter split will be several seconds faster than the other three 500-meter splits, which usually will be within one to two seconds of each other. Noticeably slower times in the second half of the course, specifically in the fourth 500 meters, might indicate that your leverage is too heavy.

A variation on this format is to do the test pieces in only one direction. An advantage is that the effect of the conditions should be consistent for each piece. Make a rigging change after a piece and use the time to row back to the starting position for the rowers to get accustomed to the change.

You can (and should) double-check your testing. On the last test piece, return your rigging to the way it was on the first test piece. Row the piece and check the results (time) with the first test piece. The results should be very close if you're doing things right, if the rowers are getting enough rest time, and if the conditions haven't changed greatly.

### Method #2: High Tech.

Another testing method is to use some of the electronic devices that are now popular on the market. If you're one of those high-tech folks, there are some neat toys for you. One such item that I'm talking about is the SpeedCoach™ by Nielsen-Kellerman <http://www.nkhome.com>.

The SpeedCoach™ is in essence a speedometer for your boat, giving you a read-out of the speed of a shell, among other things. From this info, you can run tests that tell you the impact of your rigging numbers on the hull speed of your boat.

The nice thing is that you don't need to rely on a marked course on shore when using a SpeedCoach™. You can do experimental pieces just about anywhere, and of just about any length or duration. (I'm a big fan of 30-stroke pieces.) The SpeedCoach™ offers a lot of other information you can use (maybe too much). On the down side, it is something else for the coxswain to carry, and a pricey item for you to worry about; but on the up side, it can yield invaluable data that can help you greatly in your rigging. If you have the bucks, and the time to get comfortable with all the bells and whistles, give it a spin.

Before you get into testing, a must-read can be found on Concept II's Web site at:

<http://rowing.concept2.com/concept2/v02/products/oars/oartesting2.asp>

They advocate, and so do I, 30-stroke pieces as being a good number of strokes to take when testing.

**Step 3. Record.** For any of these tests to be meaningful, you need to record results, measurements, and conditions in a manner so that you will be able to understand. Confusing little scribbles on scraps of paper probably won't mean anything to you two days after the test. Try to neatly file your results so you can find them easily and in such a manner that a year from now you'll be able to understand what the heck went on.

For suggestions and help on recording your numbers and testing, see my Special Report, *How to Absolutely Maximize Your Rigging Numbers*, at my Web site <http://www.MaxRigging.com>.

**Step 4. A Word Of Caution:** Don't jump up and down over your first results without further testing, especially if you get some bizarre results. To be accurate, do your test more than once just on the outside chance something screwball might have happened (like one of your rowers turned into the Incredible Hulk during one of the pieces).

## Method #3: Leverage Formula.

There is a formula, called the Leverage Formula, which I think you will find truly powerful. It allows you to figure out how changes in one leverage measurement will effect other leverage measurements. Let me give you an example of how it works.

Let's say you've been invited to the Head of the Piranha on the Amazon. Brazil is a long, long way and it's too expensive to take your own equipment, so you've made arrangements to borrow a shell and oars when you get there. When you arrive, the first thing you want to do is rig the equipment. Well, what numbers do you use?

If the equipment you're borrowing is exactly the same as what you were training in at home, it's no big deal. Pull out your rigging records and just rig it. But what if the equipment is not the same? What if the oars are 371 cm instead of 375 cm and the riggers are nonadjustable at 84 cm and you want 83.5 cm? And you don't have time for doing extensive speed testing. Have any ideas?

Use the all-purpose Leverage Formula to save the day. Here is the formula:

$$\text{LEVERAGE} = \frac{(L - I) - B/M}{S}$$

$L$ is the total length of the oar, $I$ is the inboard, $B$ is the length of the blade, and $S$ is the spread. $M$ is a variable. If you have Big Blade oars and variations of it, $M$ is equal to 2. The distance of $B/M$ is subtracted because that is approximately where the blade's center of pressure is located. All distances need to be in the same units.

So to be helpful on your trip to Brazil, you pull out your rigging records and figure out the leverage you were rowing with at home. Next, plug into the formula any limiting numbers from your borrowed equipment, those that can't be adjusted (in this example, it's the oar length and the spread).

Now solve the formula for the remaining unknowns (in this case the inboard) while trying to get the answer to be as close as possible to your leverage at home.

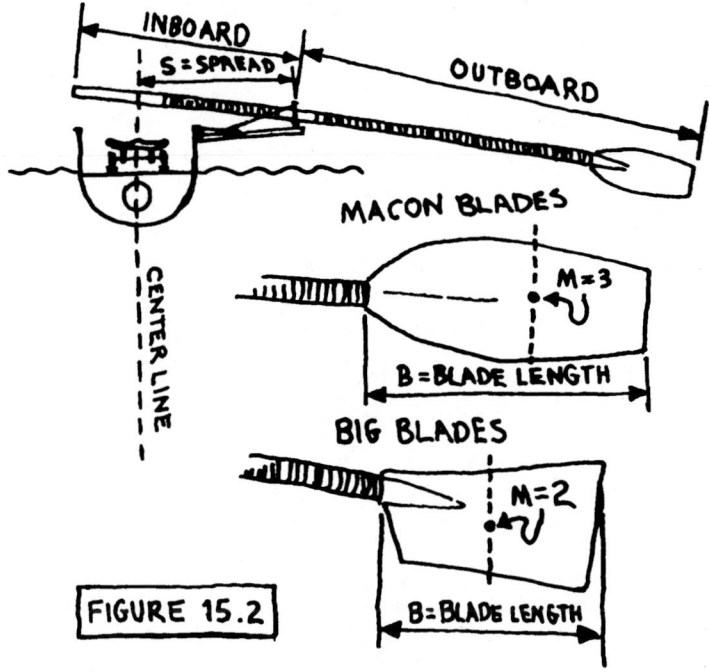

FIGURE 15.2

Use a calculator because you want to get your answer to two decimal points. This will give you the inboard you need to rig the borrowed stuff so the rowers will have a "feel" and "efficiency " just like home.

Use this formula only as a guideline, nothing more. One reason why is that this formula assumes a lot. It assumes that both the blade surface area and the curvature of the blade remain the same. Because of these assumptions you can't use this formula when changing blade surface area, like switching from a Big Blade to a Vortex to an Apex (although, you can use it for any type of blade, as long as the blade type remains the same). You also should not use it if you make adaptations to an oar, like if you retrofit a Big Blade to a Vortex.

You'll find the Leverage Formula is handy for a lot of things, such as figuring out rigging numbers when you have: (a) small changes in equipment (a new set of oars that are slightly longer than the older set), (b) changes in the size of a crew, (c) changes in race course length (less leverage for longer races), (d) changes in strength of crew (stronger crews can handle more leverage), and (e) changes in weather (less leverage for rowing into a head wind, more with a tail wind).

The formula is also a great way to keep track of your rigging from year to year. Figure out the leverage of your rig. If it worked well for you then next year use the same leverage as a base for your rigging numbers and a point from which you can experiment. But just keep this in mind: the formula will not work when the blade surface area changes.

## JOB 15.4 DETERMINING RIGGING NUMBERS FOR FOURTH-DIMENSIONAL RIGGERS.

**Problem**: At this stage of the game, you are a person in the know. Some-one who should be very comfortable with all aspects of rigging numbers. A Czar or Czarina of rigging. That means it's time to push the envelope.

**Needed:** A willingness to experiment and draw outside of the lines.

A Rigger in the Third Dimension needs to test-drive his or her rigging numbers to try to establish objectively if the adjustment made to the equipment will give the outcome desired. When you are in the Fourth Dimension, things are different.

It is time be innovative, to be creative. It's time to experiment. It's time to push the envelope. We experiment with rigging numbers to try to learn something new, to see what will happen when we say, "Gee . . . I wonder what would happen if . . . ?"

If you're going to experiment (and at this stage, you should), I would like to make a few suggestions.

**Step 1. Start Simple:** When experimenting, you're trying to learn some-thing, and that almost requires you to break things down into their basic ingredients and to pick them apart. For instance, if you want to know what pitch of rigger is best for your crew, simple works best.

In this instance, removing as many variables as possible from the equation is important. So I would have the crew row, and then when a rigging change was made, I would make sure that as many of the variables as possible remained the same: same coxswain, same weather, same type of day . . . etc.

By breaking it down into parts and by keeping it simple, you are more likely to find out what you are after. If there are a multitude of variables, well . . . the feedback you get might be almost useless. So keep it simple, and try to isolate what you want to examine.

**Step 2. Start Small:** When experimenting, be cautious and change only one adjustment at a time. There are two reasons for this. First, if you make several changes at once, you won't know what was a good change and what was a bad change. Second, large changes—especially to the leverage (oar length, inboard, spread)—could cause injury to an athlete. So, do changes gradually to avoid injuries.

**Step 3. Record Everything:** I experiment quite a lot. And one thing that I learned early on in the process is to record, record, record everything I can. I look at the time I invest in recording my results as time wisely invested in my sanity. More than once I have seen coaches experiment, and at the end of the experiment, not be pleased with the results. And so they want to go back to where they started. Those coaches who did not write down their rigging numbers of the equipment before the experiment are basically lost.

**Step 4. Be!:** As you experiment, there are a few things you should *be*.

> *Be* **precise** detailed and specific. Why? Because the proof is in the pudding, and the pudding is made up of details, and that is what can make or break an experiment.

> *Be* **accurate** as free from errors as possible.

> *Be* **aware** of any applicable rigging guidelines or rules. In sweep rowing, you need to keep in mind the *Thirty-Centimeter Rule* (where it is recommended that the inboard be about thirty centimeters more than the spread). Sculling has a similar rule called the

*Overlap Rule* (where the crossover/overlap of the handles should be about 18–22 cm at the mid-drive).

*Be* **careful** of your reaction to your findings. If you get results that are out of the ordinary or to an extreme, be cautious about what you do with those results. Don't go overboard. Don't make wholesale changes based on initial results. They might be faulty. . . . Retest, several times if need be.

**Step 5. Evaluate Carefully:** I am always skeptical of the results I get from my experiments. I have to be—there is a lot at stake. If you are going to live by the experiment, be careful, because you may also die by it.

**Step 6. More Information:** There are two sources you might want to refer to for more information on experimenting. One, of course, is my Special Report, *How to Maximize Your Rigging Numbers,* at my Web site <http://www.MaxRigging.com>. Another is Concept II's Web site <www.Concept2.com>.

# JOB 15.5: WHAT TO DO WHEN THE BLADE SURFACE AREA CHANGES.

**Problem:** The blade surface area of your oar is changing for one of many reasons (new oars, retrofits, crazy person with a saw). What do you do?

**Needed:** Patience, telephone.

**A Little Background.** For about thirty years, Macon blades were the most commonly used blades, and during that time the blade surface remained standard. Then around the early 1990s came the introduction of blades with larger surface areas, such as the Big Blades, and variations of that design. Those new designs caused (and still do cause) many Riggers to question what numbers to use to rig their boats. And that is exactly when the first edition of this book came out, and it was a rather turbulent time—in terms of determining your rigging numbers, that is.

You see, back then the rowing world was in the midst of some major growing pains. Blade shapes were changing, and it looked like that was going to be a painful process—exciting, but nonetheless painful. One reason that it was painful was that changes in blade shape usually meant changes in many of the leverage measurements—specifically oar length, spread, and inboard.

That wasn't the first time that an "oar revolution" had occurred. Back in the late 1960s there was a flurry of hectic activity as the shape of the standard blade went through changes. That process took several years for things to sort out, and the end result was the acceptance of the Macon blade as the new standard shape for rowing, and a better rowing world.

What I find interesting is that the growing pains that started in the early 1990s are still with us today and blade shapes and oar designs continue to change and be refined. But that's the way it is in rowing; it takes quite a while to figure things out. Look at it this way—it took the sliding seat a good fifty years to actually catch on!

**And today?** If you find confusing the prospect of some of the new blade shapes and the corresponding changes in oar length, you're in good company. The dynamics of blades are very, very complex. The whole reason the rowing community is willing to go through this continual process is to get a more efficient blade, and in turn, faster hull speed.

Blade and oar design have been the subject of many scientific papers, discussions, and research groups. Doug Martin, from Martin Marine, who has spent a lot of time and effort on blade design, told me ten years ago, "The Big Blades are a giant step in finding a more effective blade shape and area, and the process has a long way to go." And he certainly was correct, for the process is still ongoing.

So the original question behind this JOB is still floating out here, and it is, "What the heck are you supposed to do if you change your oars to a different shape or design?"

The answer depends on your dimension of rigging.

**Step 1. First- and Second-Dimensional:** If you are a First- or Second-Dimensional Rigger, and you have an opportunity to try a new/different set of oars, such as the *Vortex* oars from CII or *Apex* oars from Durham

Boat Company, call up the manufacturer. Get on the phone, tell them what type of oar you *were using*, what type you *are thinking of using*, and ask them what changes they recommend you make to the leverage when changing to their oars. They'll know.

**Step 2. Third-Dimensional:** Do the previous step, turn to JOB 15.3, and get ready to do the following: (a) test, (b) listen to your athletes, and (c) listen to your gut instinct. All three of those items are really important.

**Step 3. Fourth-Dimensional:** Do steps 1 and 2. Then take those numbers, put on your thinking cap and experiment away. Remember, at this level, you should be pushing the envelope. These new oars designs are radical and new, and they are pushing the boundaries of what we know. Your job here should be to experiment wisely with them to see if they work well for you.

## JOB 15.6: USING THE RIGGING CHARTS.

**Problem:** Time to find your numbers.

**Needed:** The charts that follow.

The following charts contain ranges of rigging numbers for you to consider for your equipment.

Ah . . . ranges, you say, but you want specific numbers. Well, I've put ranges in these charts because the rowing world is full of way too many different size people, of different ages, who race different distances, in too many different conditions, in different times of seasons, with different styles. It is impossible to do justice to all these variables in a few simple charts. For the small amount of extra time you need to narrow down your range, I think you'll be much happier with the results.

You'll notice there are two charts for sweep rowing and two for sculling. To find your ranges:

**Step 1.** Determine the type of rowing and the skill level of the person(s) you are rigging for. Then . . .

**Step 2.** For the type of rowing you're doing, locate the range for oar length, pitch, height, and foot stretcher adjustments under the column for the correct skill level. Then . . .

**Step 3.** Determine the class of boat you need to rig. Then . . .

**Step 4.** Find the proper shell class and locate ranges for work-thru, leverage, and arc location measurements.

**Step 5.** When you've done these four steps you should have all the ranges you need. Now just narrow them down. A few thoughts to keep in mind:

> 1. The faster the hull speed of a shell the greater the catch length, catch angle, and work-thru you need. (If you feel you need a review of hull speed, see Chapter Twelve). So in a pair. these three dimensions will be less than those in an eight, and at the same time, a slow pair will have less catch length, catch angle, and work-thru than a fast pair.

> 2. The faster the hull speed of a shell, the smaller the inboard and spread you need. So in an eight, these two dimensions will be less than those in a pair, and a fast eight should have smaller inboard measurements and spread, than a slow eight.

> 3. For sweep rowing, remember the Thirty-Centimeter Rule—the inboard should always be about 30 cm ($\pm$ 2 cm) greater than the spread. For sculling, the oars should overlap 18–22 cm.

> 4. For oar and oarlock numbers, favor the right side of ranges for younger or less experienced rower(s), favor the left side of ranges for older or more experienced rower(s). Be consistent with your selection—if you favor the left side of a range for one dimension, favor the left side for all the dimensions. Not to sound sexist, but do the same for female rowers (favor the right side of the ranges), and for male rowers favor the left side of the ranges.

5. If in doubt as to what part of a range to use, be conservative; start in the middle of a range.

6. Numbers in parentheses are possible numbers to consider in exceptional circumstances, like a very small or a very large rower(s).

**Step 6.** For these numbers to really mean anything, you must know where they are measured from. The chart on the following page should help.

**Step 7.** Once you've got your numbers and rigged the equipment, don't be afraid to look, listen, and experiment. Look at the rowing and at the rowers to see how the rigging is working. Listen to the rowers for their feedback ("Oh . . . my height is just too low . . ."). And experiment to see if the numbers you've chosen work for you, and them.

As I mentioned before, you need to know how measurements are taken and from where they are measured for them to be any use to you at all. The following chart shows how I take the measurements and how I recommend that you take them.

| Measurement | Where Measured From |
|---|---|
| Oar Length | From butt of oar handle to blade tip |
| Stern Pitch | With the oarlock at the catch, mid-drive, and release |
| Outward (Lateral) Pitch | With the oarlock at mid-drive |
| Height: Oarlock | From top of seat to middle of horizontal flat (oarlock sill) |
| Height: Heel Cup | From top of seat to inside of heel cup (vertically) |
| Work-Thru | Distance along centerline from oarlock pin perpendicular to perpendicular across front stops |
| Inboard | From blade side of button to butt of oar handle |
| Spread (sweep + sculling) | From middle of oarlock pin to centerline of shell |
| Span (sculling) | From middle of one oarlock pin to middle of opposite side oarlock pin |
| Catch Angle | From oarlock pin perpendicular to oar shaft at stern end of inside arc |
| Catch Length | From oarlock perpendicular to butt of oar handle at stern end of inside arc |

# RIG CHART
## SUGGESTED *SWEEP* RIGGING NUMBERS
## BY <u>SKILL LEVEL</u>

| Skill Level → | Youth < 14 yrs. | Junior 14–18 yrs. | Senior 19–27 yrs. | Master > 27 yrs. |
|---|---|---|---|---|
| Oar Length | 363–368 cm | 371–376 cm | 372–380 cm | 370–380 cm |
| Blade Size* | 52–55.5 cm | | | |
| Pitch: Stern (At Mid–Drive) | 5–7 degrees | 4–6 degrees | 3–5 degrees | 4–6 degrees |
| Pitch: Lateral (At Mid–Drive) | 0–1 degrees | | | |
| Height: Oarlock | 11–15 cm | 13–17 cm | 15–17 cm | 15–18 cm |
| Height: Heel Cup | 12–16 cm | 14–18 cm | 16–20 cm | 16–20 cm |
| Foot Stretcher Angle | 38–42 degrees | | | |
| Opening Angle | 23–27 degrees | | | |

*Note: These blade sizes are for Concept II Big Blades only, and do not include Macon blades or other manufacturer's oars. See page 194 for reference chart of other sizes, or contact the manufacturer directly.

# RIG CHART
## SUGGESTED *SWEEP* RIGGING NUMBERS
## BY <u>BOAT CLASS</u>

| Boat Class → | 2+ | 2– | 4+ | 4– | 8+ |
|---|---|---|---|---|---|
| **Work-Thru** | (–2)–2 cm | 0–2 cm | 2–4 cm | 4–8 cm | 8–12 cm |
| **Inboard** | 114–118 cm | 114–118 cm | 111–117 cm | 111–116 cm | 111–115 cm |
| **Spread** | 86–88 cm | 85–88 cm | 84–87 cm | 83–86 cm | 81–84 cm |
| **Catch Angle** | 43–50 degrees | 43–50 degrees | 43.5–52.5 degrees | 46–54 degrees | 45.5–55 degrees |
| **Catch Length** | 71–95 cm | 71–95 cm | 79–96 cm | 81–97 cm | 81–97 cm |
| **Finish Length** | 66–68 cm | 66–68 cm | 63–67 cm | 64.5–66 cm | 61.5–66 cm |
| **Leverage Ratio** | 2.59–2.66 | 2.62–2.66 | 2.69–2.71 | 2.72–2.75 | 2.79–2.82 |

# RIG CHART
## SUGGESTED *SCULLING* RIGGING NUMBERS
## BY <u>SKILL LEVEL</u>

| Skill Level → | Youth < 14 yrs. | Juniors 14–18 yrs. | Senior 19–27 yrs. | Master > 27 yrs. |
|---|---|---|---|---|
| Oar Length | 279–284 cm | 288–294 cm | 290–296 cm | 290–296 cm |
| Blade Size* | 43.5–46.5 cm | | | |
| Pitch: Stern (At Mid–Drive) | 5–7 degrees | 5–7 degrees | 3–5 degrees | 4–6 degrees |
| Pitch: Lateral (At Mid–Drive) | 0–1 degrees | | | |
| Height: Oarlock | 11–15 cm | 12–17 cm | 15–17 cm | 16–18 cm |
| Height: Heel Cup | 12–16 cm | 14–18 cm | 16–20 cm | 16–20 cm |
| Foot Stretcher Angle | 38–42 degrees | | | |
| Opening Angle | 23–27 degrees | | | |

*Note: These blade sizes are for Concept II Big Blades only, and do not include Macon blades or other manufacturer's oars. See page 194 for reference chart of other sizes, or contact the manufacturer directly.

# RIG CHART
## SUGGESTED *SCULLING* RIGGING NUMBERS
## BY BOAT CLASS

| Boat Class → | 1X | 2X | 4X |
|---|---|---|---|
| **Work-Thru** | (–2)–2 cm | 0–4 cm | 2–6 cm |
| **Inboard** | 86–90 cm | 86–89 cm | 85–89 cm |
| **Span** | 158–160 cm | 157–159 cm | 156–158 cm |
| **Handle Overlap** | 18–22 cm | | |
| **Leverage Ratio** | 2.16–2.22 | 2.12–2.25 | 2.14–2.26 |

# JOB 15.7: RECORDING YOUR RIGGING NUMBERS.

**Problem:** You've gotten all this important information about your rigging. It's going to get lost (I speak from experience). What should you do with it?

**Needed:** The charts that follow.

**Step 1. Why Record?:** Recording your rigging numbers will make your rigging life so much better. It will save you time. It will save you effort. It will make you better looking (okay . . . two out of three isn't bad).

Seriously, the benefits of recording your numbers are significant, while the downside of not having the numbers when you need them can be a major hassle. You'll be pleasantly surprised at how much time and effort you can save yourself by having, right at you fingertips, the length of every oar, the spread of any rigger, and all your other rigging numbers. This information can come in handy, for example, after transporting a boat to a race when you're short on time and you're under pressure to do your rigging.

**Step 2. Get Organized:** One of the keys to being a good Rigger is to be organized. To help you get organized, you need to do something constructive with all the numbers and information you are gathering. I suggest you write them down.

Well, actually, I don't mean just write them down anywhere, I mean write them down on cards so you file them away neatly and pull them out every time you rig. I call them **rigging records,** and they are very important if you want to maximize your rigging numbers!

**Step 3. Use The Cards:** On the next pages you'll find a few charts. They include spaces for all the rigging-measurements and equipment-measurements that you probably will ever use. (There are actually more rigging numbers than there are spaces on the charts.)

I use these charts. I've made the charts fairly large so I can copy them and store them easily in a notebook. I have also copied them and shrunk them down to the size of an index card and put them in a small notebook that fits into my toolbox or pocket.

## DATE:

### SHELL

Name:

Make:

Serial Number:

Weight Class:

### CREW

Average Weight:

Gender:

Skill Level:

Race Length:

### OARS

Marking:

Type:

Make:

Deflection:

Handle Size:

Blade Size:

Pitch:

Serial Number:

### COMMENTS

| Leverage | 8 | 7 | 6 | 5 | 4 | 3 | 2 | 1 |
|---|---|---|---|---|---|---|---|---|
| Spread/Span | | | | | | | | |
| Inboard/Length | | | | | | | | |
| Blade Size | | | | | | | | |
| Blade Type | | | | | | | | |
| Leverage | | | | | | | | |
| **Oarlock** | 8 | 7 | 6 | 5 | 4 | 3 | 2 | 1 |
| Pitch (Stern) | | | | | | | | |
| Pitch (Lateral) | | | | | | | | |
| Height | | | | | | | | |
| **Arc Location** | 8 | 7 | 6 | 5 | 4 | 3 | 2 | 1 |
| Work-Thru | | | | | | | | |
| Catch Angle | | | | | | | | |
| Catch Length | | | | | | | | |
| **Foot Stretcher** | 8 | 7 | 6 | 5 | 4 | 3 | 2 | 1 |
| Angle | | | | | | | | |
| Heel Cup Height | | | | | | | | |
| Opening Angle | | | | | | | | |
| Location | | | | | | | | |

# Chapter Sixteen: This, That, and Tricks

Following are a variety of JOBS that you might find helpful at some time or another. If you have a JOB that you would like to share with readers, you can submit them at my Web site, <http://www.MaxRigging.com>, and I will try to get it into the next edition.

## JOB 16.1: WHAT TO DO WHEN YOU'RE STUCK.

**Problem:** You're stuck, hit a mental road block, at an impasse, lost, without a clue . . . get my drift?

It happens. Everyone gets stuck. I call it **Rigger's block**. It'll creep up on you sooner or later, usually when everything is going along smoothly, whamo . . . something goes wrong, and you don't know what to do. Rigger's block is a frame of mind. If you're rigging and Rigger's block hits you try one of these steps . . .

**Step 1. Check Your Previous Work:** If you're doing a JOB you've done before, stop whatever you are doing and backtrack. Sometimes we do a JOB so often it becomes automatic, like tying shoelaces. If we get interrupted or stop to think about this automatic task the brain goes blank. Going back and looking at the task can help get your mind back on track. Check out a previous JOB—does it help? If not, then . . .

**Step 2. S.O.S.:** If you're stuck on a JOB and you truly don't know how to do it—ask! Find someone you can ask for help. Ask a friend, a fellow coach, or call the builder. Hey, if your pride is in the way, swallow it and get the info to do the JOB right! Never, ever be embarrassed to say you don't know how to do something. It's part of the growing and learning process. If your S.O.S. fails, try . . .

**Step 3. Take Chances, Make Mistakes, Get Messy:** Ever watch *The Magic School Bus*? It is a great kids cartoon-show that adults (especially Riggers and rowers) could greatly benefit from. Why? A constant theme appears in the show followed with the saying,

"Take chances! Make mistakes! Get messy!"

It encourages people to experiment, and to not be afraid of the consequences.

If you're an independent thinker and think you've got a solution, go for it. Don't be afraid to experiment (especially when rigging for sculling). I hope you realize rigging is not a static, stagnant science (or is it an art?) that is written in stone. You're not a bad person if you don't rig the way others rig—just the opposite. We need to have experimentation; that's how the sport grows.

Ever read Tom Peters? Try him. He encourages the exploration, the experimentation, the pursuit of what he calls *Wow*! How do you find *Wow*!? Easy—*take chances, make mistakes, get messy!*

What about the first folks who came up with the swivel lock or the sliding seat? Were they cheaters or disrespectful to the sport of rowing? Not to me, they just had an idea that turned out to make a difference.

What I'm getting at, the long way, is don't be afraid to experiment with your rigging any way you want to. Just don't be afraid to make mistakes because you will make them. And don't be static. Be safe, but not static.

If nothing seems to work and you're getting overwhelmed, try . . .

**Step 4. Take a Breather:** Give your mind a rest. Attacking the problem with a fresh mind and a better mental attitude might get you unstuck.

A pal of mine goes "metal fishing" whenever he gets stuck. He ties a large magnet to a string and trolls around the dock looking for tools, parts, and whatever else that has fallen into the water. In one year, he found three seats, four wrenches, an outboard propeller, and a megaphone that sunk when a coach fell in. He says the thrill of the hunt helps him relax. Guess he likes to Mullet over. Thought I throw that in for the Halibut.

---

I had a major dose of Rigger's block one day. I was in a big hurry to get an older boat rigged with a set of new oars. I finished, and the rowers took it to the dock to row. Everything was fine—except they couldn't get the oars into the oarlocks. We tried, and tried, and tried, but the oars just wouldn't fit. I spent all afternoon trying to figure out what the problem was. The next morning, as soon as I woke, the solution dawned on me. The oarlocks were sculling oarlocks and there was no way the oars were going to fit. I had to get away from the problem, and clear my mind, before I could figure it out.

---

**FIGURE 16.1**

## JOB 16.2: THE HUMAN TORQUE WRENCH.

**Problem:** How do you tighten all those fasteners enough, but not too much?

**Needed:** Wrenches that fit fasteners, brain (yours preferably), and a pair of hands.

Most fasteners (nuts, bolts, screws) are tightened or loosened with a twisting motion called **torque**. You can measure torque with a nifty little tool called a **torque wrench**. It's a wrench with a gauge that tells you how hard something is being twisted. This is handy when doing work on things like motors and fine machinery, which require precision in how tight the fasteners are turned.

Proper amounts of torque keep a car's engine from falling apart on the freeway or the bolts holding the seat on your carnival ride from bouncing loose in mid-spin. In rowing, we don't require such precision, but we do want to make sure the fasteners are turned to a certain degree of torque for two reasons. First, if too little torque is used, the fastener will loosen, and second, if too much torque is used, things are going to get broken.

The purpose of fasteners in rowing (rigger nuts, rigger clamps, oarlock pin fasteners, foot stretcher fasteners) is to compress several things together so they stay put. If any of these fasteners are overtightened, there is a darn good chance something is going to suffer. I've seen guerrilla-rowers crush, splinter, and implode the knees of a boat by overtightening rigger nuts—making the boat unrowable until the knees were replaced or repaired. I've witnessed nervous coaches crank down on top nuts so hard that the oarlock pin snaps in two. A wrench is a dangerous tool in a mindless body.

In our boathouse we give the coxswains and coaches their own torque wrenches. Actually, those folks come equipped with them—they just don't know it. What I'm talking about is their hands.

We use a method called the "**finger system**." If someone is tightening a nut, we first have them finger-tighten it (twisting the nut with the fingers only—no wrench). Then we have them hold the wrench like figure 16.2 with their first two fingers and thumb. They put the wrench on the Work and begin turning. When they start meeting resistance, their fingers will begin to bend. When the fingers bend as far as they will go, the Work is about as tight as you want it. What you've got to remember, if you use this system, is that people come in different sizes and strengths—this has made me hesitant about giving different folks tools. But this system hasn't failed us yet, and it sure has saved a lot of damage.

For rigger nuts, we use *two-finger tight*. For the top nut on riggers, and most fasteners squeezing metal, we also use *three-finger tight*.

There may be a couple of fasteners you need to tighten that don't quite fall into the finger system. For example, the bottom rigger nut on some older riggers and on the new Euro-style riggers. Here, we use something I call a *palm-and-hip tight*.

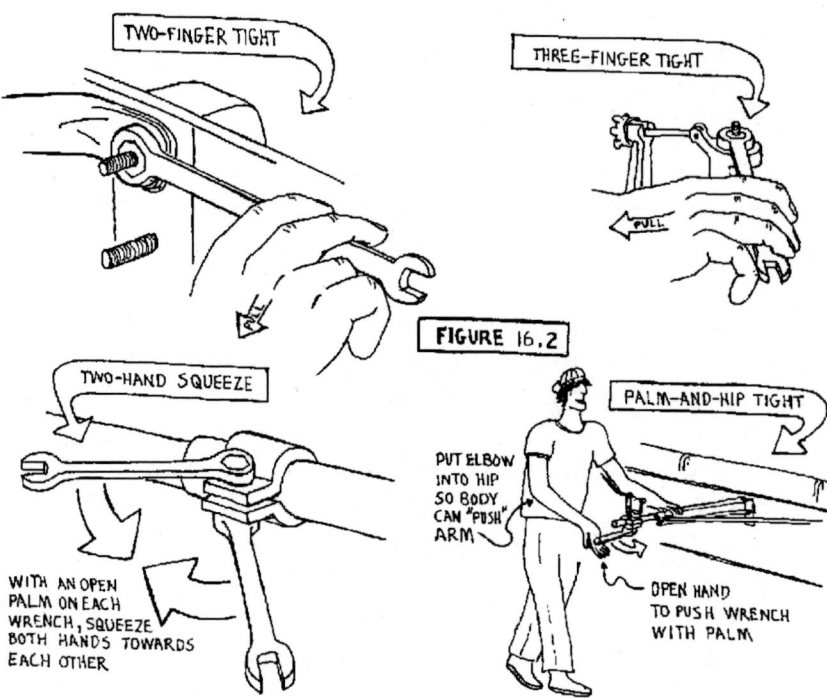

**FIGURE 16.2**

If these nuts slip, the whole adjustment of the rigger is shot. You've really got to crank them down and sometimes that's tough to do without bashing a knuckle or straining a muscle. With the wrench in the palm of the hand, set it on the nut, place the hip on the elbow of the wrench hand, and gradually, but firmly, lean into the wrench with your body weight to tighten the nut (at the same time holding the rigger top stay for stability). Keep leaning until you meet solid resistance—it should be tight enough.

The clamps on rigger stays are a bother because both the nut and bolt turn. Tightening or loosening these requires two wrenches and a push-pull motion that can result in slipping wrenches, flying hands, and rounded fasteners. To make things easier we use a **two-hand squeeze**. Put a wrench on both nut and bolt head—hold the bolt head steady while tightening down the nut until firm resistance is felt. Now offset the wrenches just enough so when your fingers are locked together the wrenches will fit in the palm of your hands (see figure 16.2). Now squeeze your hands together and push. Reset wrenches and push again until the resistance is solid. You'll find that you can generate some great torque and reduce damage to the Work and to yourself.

## JOB 16.3: STUCK FASTENERS.

**Problem:** You're here because something that's supposed to move is stuck, frozen, bunged up, or busted.

**Needed:** Travel tool kit, even temper, flexibility between the ears.

Something has gone wrong with a fastener. It's not working like you need it to. Time's short; you've got to row the boat in a couple of minutes, and your in-laws are coming. Don't freak; there may be hope. With the fastener, that is—you're on your own with the in-laws.

**Get your head on right!** First thing's first: breaking the head off a bolt or stripping a thread can be a hassle, but it shouldn't give you a bad attitude.

Take a few minutes and clear the frustration out of your head. The world hasn't ended. Go for a walk, count to ten in German, eat an apple, watch some clouds. Do whatever you need to do to get a good dose of positive mental attitude. To solve the problem, you're going to need some finesse, and you can't have finesse in a foul mood. Turn to JOB 6.1 for some help if needed.

**Problem 1. Stuck Rigger Bolt:** Rigger bolts, which connect the rigger to the hull, sometimes need to be replaced or removed. They usually slide right out with gentle pressure, but not always. You may need to use some gentle persuasion. The trick is to do it with out destroying the threads on the bolt.

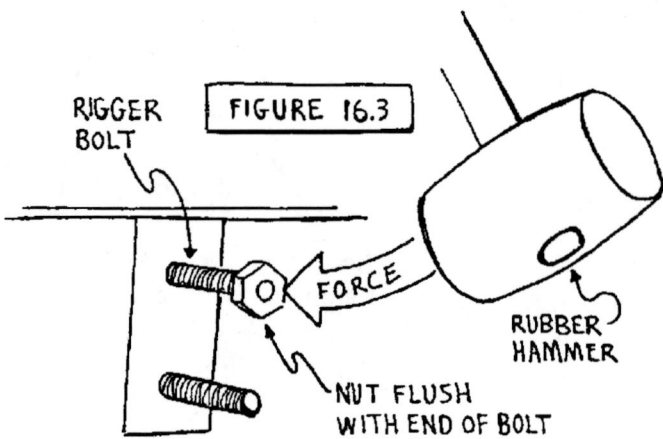

Figure 16.3: RIGGER BOLT — FORCE — RUBBER HAMMER — NUT FLUSH WITH END OF BOLT

When the rigger is off, take the rigger nut and thread it back onto the rigger bolt. Have the nut flush with the bolt so no threads are showing past the nut (figure 16.3). Now with your trusty rubber mallet, tap the nut and bolt towards the hull. If you're using a metal hammer, place a small block of scrap wood over the nut for protection, and then tap the nut and bolt. Once the nut is flush with the gunwale, take it off the bolt and remove the bolt from the knee.

**Problem 2. Rounded Nut Or Bolt Head:** This happens often to rigger clamps because both the bolt and nut turn and wrenches tend to slip easily. If signs of rounding are just beginning to show (the edges of the Work are wearing), I suggest you replace the fastener a.s.a.p., before major hassles appear. Go get your locking pliers if the problem is to the point of making the fastener non-moveable.

Get a grip on the rounded part with the pliers. Get a good purchase, set the pliers, and hold them tight. Put a wrench on the other end and turn it (do not turn the pliers—remember, they are a holding tool) being careful not to cause more damage. If this works, loosen the problem and replace it. If the pliers won't work, try this . . .

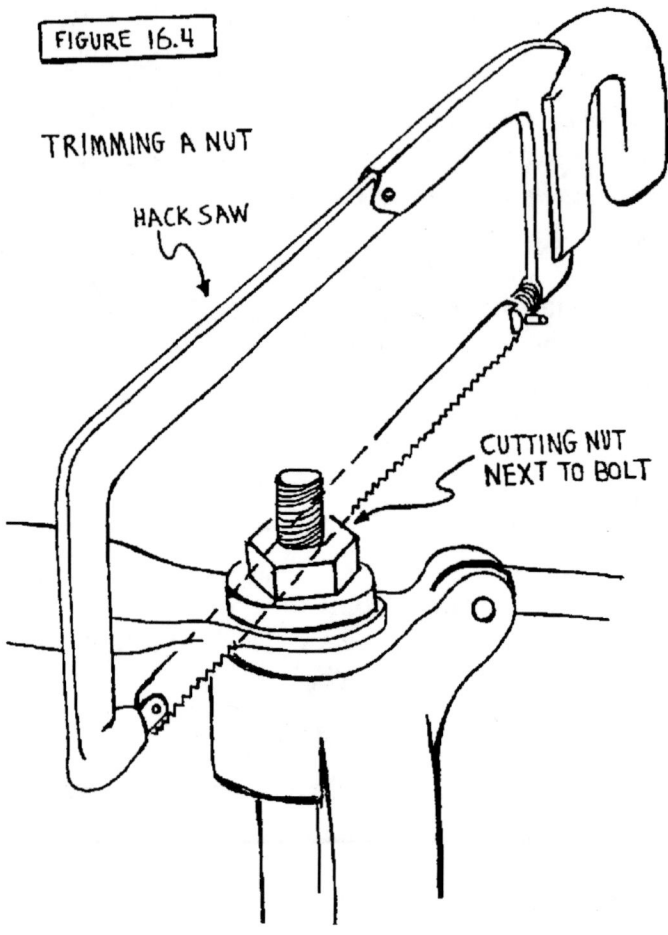

FIGURE 16.4

TRIMMING A NUT

HACK SAW

CUTTING NUT
NEXT TO BOLT

In some places that have two rigger bolts (mid-drive knee) the top and bottom ones may be connected. If so, you'll have to remove both at the same time.

Grab a hacksaw and cut the problem as in figure 16.4. Most likely, the fastener is still attached to the equipment, so take your time and be careful with your cuts—don't cut your rigger in two!

Remember that most fasteners will, or should, be made of stainless steel, which is slow cutting. Once the cuts are made, get an adjustable wrench,

socket, or locking pliers on the Work and loosen the fastener. Once it's free, replace both the nut and bolt and wipe up all the cuttings.

**Problem 3. Frozen Nut Or Bolt:** Fasteners can be a stubborn lot. Sometimes they just won't move . . . you know they want to . . . everything looks fine, but they just won't turn. The trick here is to persuade the stuck villain to see things your way without causing any destruction.

Are you turning the right way? Rightee-tightee, leftee-loosey. No go? Grab a hammer and a can of penetrating oil. Squirt the oil liberally around the fastener and wipe off any drips. Now with your hammer gently, **GENTLY**, tap the Work several times.

You're not trying to knock the silly thing free, just trying to set up vibrations that will help the penetrating oil seep into the threads and slipperize things. This method is going to work almost every time. Tap again and let it sit for a moment. Now try to turn. Hopefully you're successful. If not, try a little more muscle and maybe a slightly longer wrench for more leverage. If all attempts fail, you may have to cut the nut similar to figure 16.5, but only as a last resort.

**Problem 4. Stripped Screw Head Or Rotating Rigger Bolt:** Ouch. Every once in a while the slot in a screw head will strip, or a rigger bolt will come free of the **knee cap** and rotate so you can't free it. Either of these problems can be a drag because wood is usually involved and you want to make sure you don't mess it up. Here we have two different problems with the same solution. With your hacksaw, carefully cut a small slot in the head. Make it deep enough to get a screwdriver into it. When this is done, gently turn the screw or bolt, and presto—your problem is solved.

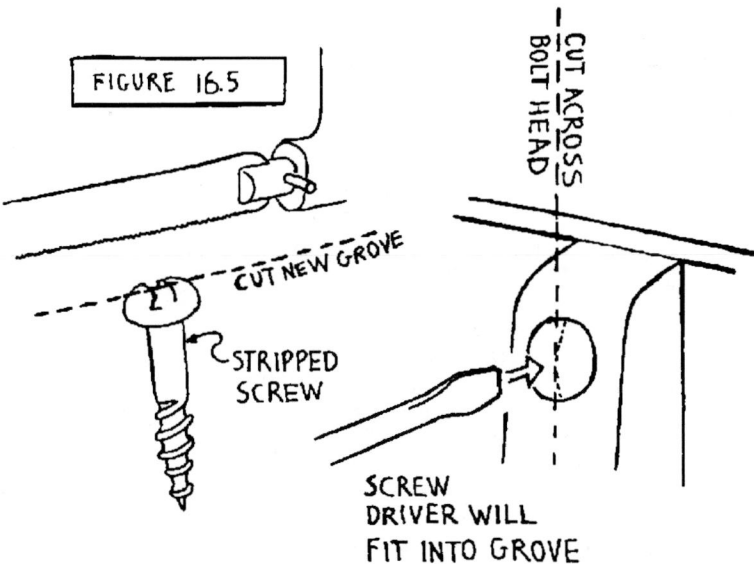

**Problem 5. Stuck screw:** There aren't more than a few screws involved in rigging nowadays. If you happen upon one that's in wood and won't turn, try this trick: hold a hot soldering iron on the screw head for about 30 seconds. This will cause the screw to expand. Then let it cool for a few minutes, and try to turn it. The expanding and cooling should cause the surrounding wood to compress and let the screw turn more easily.

## JOB 16.4: CONVERTING METRIC TO U.S. CUSTOMARY.

**Problem:** For whatever reason, you need to switch between the two systems.

Metric is the wave of the future. To ride the wave you don't necessarily need to go out and spend a whole lot of money. You might be lucky enough to have tools that fit both metric and U.S. fasteners already. I strongly suggest that you start stockpiling metric tools as your wallet allows, but in the meantime, the following chart will help you out with sizes that fit both systems.

### Conversion Chart

These sizes are "switch-hitters," meaning the metric size will fit the U.S. size and vice versa. The fit might be tight, but they should work well in a pinch

| |
|---|
| 11 mm will fit/take a 7/16 inch |
| 13 mm will fit/take a 1/2 inch |
| 14 mm will fit/take a 9/16 inch |
| 16 mm will fit/take a 5/8 inch |
| 19 mm will fit/take a 3/4 inch |

**Right Fit?** If the wrench you're using doesn't fit snugly on the fastener, don't use it. Find the proper size wrench or carefully use an adjustable. A sloppy fit will damage the Work.

## JOB 16.5: DESIGNS: TWO HELPFUL ITEMS FOR YOUR RIGGING.

**Design 1: Splashguards.** Frequently crews have to row when the water is not perfect, or not even near perfect. On those days, water has a habit of flying around and going places where you don't necessarily want it: like in your boat, on your rowers, or into your coxswain's face—which on a cold day is an eye closer.

There's a handy little item that can help reduce water-attacks; it's called a **splashguard**. And you may want to consider using it, especially if your shell has a low freeboard.

Splashguards go at the junction where the rigger meets the hull. They cut down on the spray and keep things a little dryer. That's all they do; they don't make rough water easier to row in; they just keep things a little dryer. I've used two types of splashguards, tape and pre-cut plastic.

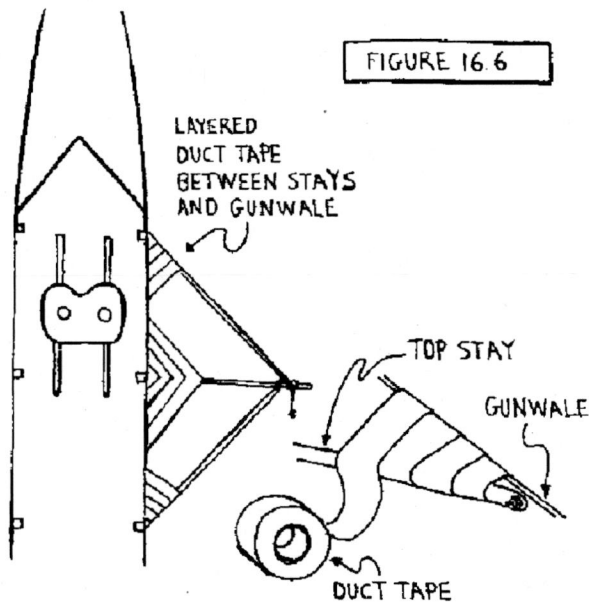

The easy, but messy, way to use splashguards is duct tape. I usually bring several rolls any time we race. If the water starts to get wavy, I put it on. You don't need much, just a couple of pieces here and there, but it can make a difference (figure 16.6). A little more involved method is to use pre-cut plastic triangles that also fit at the junctions. They may look better, but they're usually held on with tape anyway and the tape works just as well.

Don't get carried away with the tape; a little goes a long way. Once, I made the mistake of putting too much tape on the riggers of a pair. I used so much tape that, when a wave crashed over the rigger, landing on the tape, the force was enough to almost flip the boat. Don't overdo it; you're trying to cut down splashes—not tidal waves.

**Design 2: Tool Tray.** A tool tray is one of those things that you don't really notice how handy it is until you start using one. It's a great organizer and time saver and easy to make.

Get yourself something about the size and shape of a cafeteria tray. A few charming words at the local eating establishment may land you one of these trays easier than you think. Cut two supports about thirty inches long and attach them underneath the tray. Put a little padding on the supports to protect any innocent gunwales, and cut slots in them. The slots will sit on the gunwales, keeping the tray steady if the boat tilts—hopefully keeping all your tools from clanging onto the ground. Now all you have to do is use it. Move it from position to position as you rig. You should find you spend less time looking for that lost wrench and more time rigging.

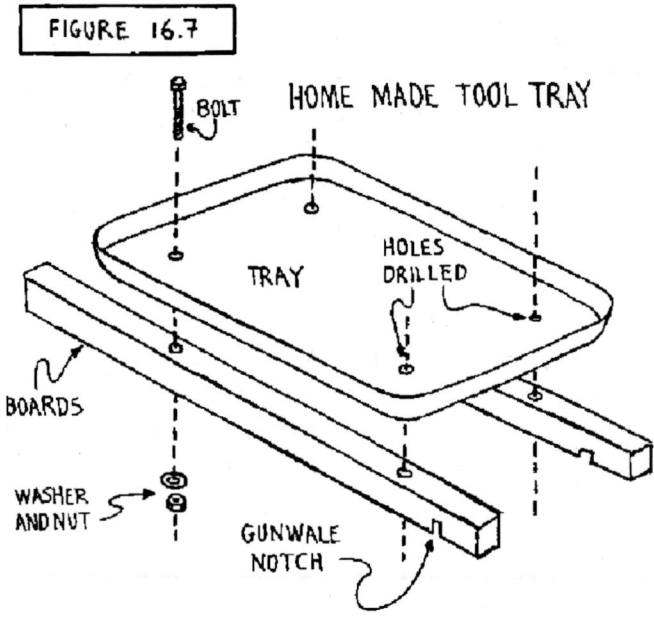

FIGURE 16.7

HOME MADE TOOL TRAY

## JOB 16.6: GETTING A LITTLE MORE SPREAD.

**Problem:** You need more spread than your rigger can give you—might be due to too small a rigger or older, nonadjustable rigger.

**Needed:** Set of eyes, blocks of hardwood, drill and bits, longer rigger bolts (carriage), time.

### Adjustable Riggers
If you're using adjustable riggers (most new riggers, Euro-style riggers) and switching things around a bit (like making a port-stroke boat into a starboard-stroke boat), chances are you are going to run into a problem

with one or two riggers being too long/too short. This usually happens in eights because they get quite narrow towards the stern and bow, and in those seats the rigger frames need to be wider to get the pin out to where it should be. When you try to change a "two" rigger's length into a "one" rigger's length, problems usually pop up.

So what do you do if your rigger is too long/too short? Exchange it.

Most new boats now come with what is known as "mirror riggers." These are riggers designed for just such a problem. For example, Vespoli USA ships their eights with 10 riggers, eight for the shell rigged as purchased (port or starboard stroke) and two mirror rigger frames in case you decide to change the stroke side. Those riggers are usually stamped with an "M" on the rigger plate, so instead of reading "1" the mirror rigger might read "M1." Therefore, if you're switching things around, and need a longer/shorter rigger frame, look for the *mirror*.

---

Right frame?—make sure that the rigger frame has been made for the same size boat you are rigging. A rigger frame for a four is not a good rigger frame for an eight.

---

## Nonadjustable Riggers

A long time ago, riggers were not made to be adjusted; the man was made to adjust to the rigger. If you've got one of these nonadjustable riggers and you need to increase the spread (or you want to squeeze more spread from other riggers), you've got only one choice, and that is to **block** the riggers out.

Blocking will only work for riggers that need more spread, not less. If you're handy with tools, you can also use blocks to increase/decrease the outward pitch. I've had to use blocks several times. They're a hassle to make, and if I had the money I'd buy a better rigger, but in times of need you do what you've got to do.

**Step 1. Numbers:** Figure out how much you need to increase your spread. The limiting factor here is the size of the rigger bolts.

**Step 2. Cut Your Block:** Go to the scrap wood box, or lumber store, and get a couple of pieces of hardwood. Don't use softwood because it will split easily. Trace the connecting plate for the rigger on the wood and cut out your block. You're going to need a block for each stay of your rigger.

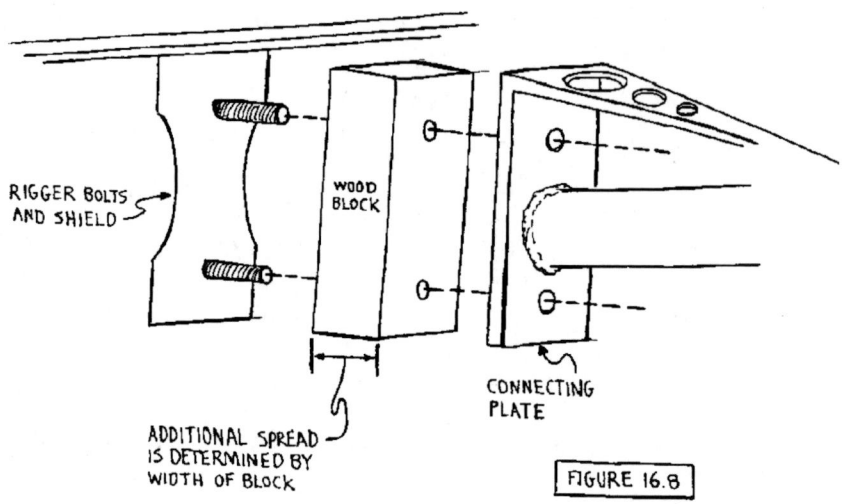

RIGGER BOLTS AND SHIELD

WOOD BLOCK

CONNECTING PLATE

ADDITIONAL SPREAD IS DETERMINED BY WIDTH OF BLOCK

FIGURE 16.8

**Step 3. Drill The Holes:** Here's the fun part. Put the connecting plate again on top of the block and mark where the rigger bolt holes are. With the wood secured, drill the holes using a drill bit larger than the diameter of the rigger bolt. When both holes are drilled, try to slide the block into position over the rigger bolts. You may need longer rigger bolts and you might find you have to drill the holes larger for the block to fit. Keep playing with it until you get a good fit.

**Step 4. Rigger On:** When you're happy with the fit, put the blocks on and attach the rigger. Now to check your work. Measure your new spread. If you designed correctly, you've got what you need. Measure the pitch, both stern and outward, and height. Hopefully they're right. If not, adjust the rigger if you can, shim it, or take the mid-drive block off and shape it to get the outward pitch and height right.

## JOB 16.7: FIXING A BENT RIGGER STAY.

**Problem:** You've got a bent stay.

**Needed:** Rubber mallet, vise, willingness to bash something, gentle touch.

A bent stay is a sign that something exciting, forceful, and not necessarily pleasant has happened to a rigger: such as a crab, bashing into a buoy, or whacking the boathouse door.

A bent stay will never be the same. You may get it back to its original shape and be able to use it again, but when the material bends, it is weakened. Moving it back just weakens it more; it does not repair it. It may work fine for many years, but a straightened stay is substandard.

With that in mind, do you use a straightened rigger stay? Depends on how bad the bend was, how good the fix is, and how you're set for spare parts. If the bend is more than 45 degrees don't even try to straighten it—it's done for. If it's less than 45 degrees try these steps:

**Step 1. Hammer It:** Take a large rubber mallet, not your metal hammer, place the stay on a solid surface, hold it carefully, and forcefully pound the bend down towards the surface. Once you get most of the bend out finish off with . . .

**Step 2. Vice Squad:** Sandwich the stay between two pieces of wood like figure 16.9 and slowly tighten the vice. You may have to rotate the stay and re-tighten it several times, but this should take most of the kinks out.

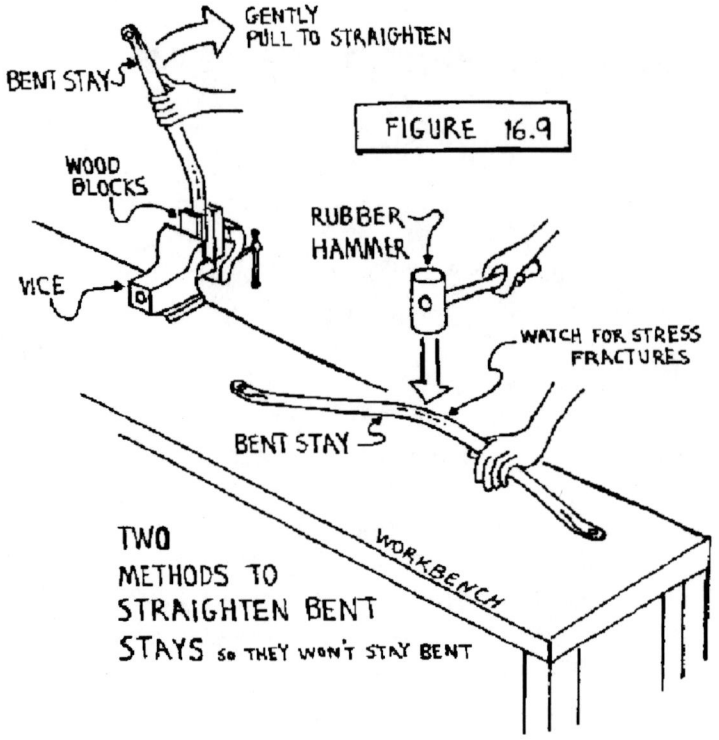

GENTLY PULL TO STRAIGHTEN

BENT STAY

FIGURE 16.9

WOOD BLOCKS

RUBBER HAMMER

VICE

WATCH FOR STRESS FRACTURES

BENT STAY

TWO METHODS TO STRAIGHTEN BENT STAYS SO THEY WON'T STAY BENT

WORKBENCH

---

Row/no row? If there are stress fractures on the stay, it is no longer safe to use. Give it a decent burial and replace it.

# Chapter Seventeen: Taking Your Equipment for a Trip

Rowers are a different breed. Nowhere does that become more apparent than when we travel. We're on the move constantly, probably more so than the average person. When we travel, we are usually in a hurry, hungry, and tired. We make bizarre, almost-impossible-to-keep plans. We're certainly not built for traveling. And somewhere we've brought all our stuff with us . . . carloads of it . . . trailers full of it . . . planes full of stuff.

Traveling is tough, and because of the equipment we take with us and the way we travel with it, it can be one of the most hazard-filled parts of our sport. The other day, a good friend was telling me how he was returning from a regatta on a bus full of rowers. He was caught in this lengthy traffic jam. When the bus finally approached what seemed to be the cause of the traffic jam, he saw, to his horror, his team's trailer overturned in the middle of the interstate. Boats, equipment, and trailer were destroyed, and two assistant coaches were in shock . . . lucky to be alive. Unfortunately, traveling accidents like this are more common than you might think.

## 17.1 Why Focus on Safe Traveling?

Two main benefits should immediately pop to mind when the topic of safe traveling comes up. One is getting the equipment there in one piece, and another is getting it there on time. Both are important, especially on race day.

But those are the self-centered benefits; there are other benefits, such as not hurting other people on the highway (which has happened) and not giving members of the local law enforcement more things to do (which has certainly happened).

However, I see the biggest benefit of safe traveling to be this—if you're responsible for moving rowing equipment, whether that be simply from the boathouse to the dock to launch for practice or across the country to attend the Great Bow Ball Regatta, you have an obligation to move the equipment safely. And if you move the equipment safely, you're doing what you are supposed to do.

## 17.2 How to Travel Safely

A lot of rowers expect their equipment to magically appear at a regatta, just waiting to be unloaded. They hardly give it much thought. Unfortunately, neither do some people in charge of moving the equipment. Accidents that happen while transporting equipment account for thirty percent of all damage done to it.

Although transporting equipment is not simple, a few simple steps can certainly help make the process go smoother.

> Warning: Be advised that these are not inclusive of all the steps that you should take for safe equipment transportation. I advise you to check with local experts about your individual needs and requirements for safe transport.

## JOB 17.1 TRANSPORTING EQUIPMENT ON A CAR TOP.

**Problem:** The equipment has got to get there, and it's going on top of a car.

**Needed:** Reliable vehicle, bomb-proof racks, excellent straps, flag(s).

If you're car-topping, you're going to have your hands full, mostly because driving a car with a shell on top is a lot different from just driving the car. So here we go with some very critical steps . . .

**Step 1. Plan It:** I'm not going to go into a lot of detail here, but let me say that one of the foundations for a safe and smooth rowing trip is planning. Time and energy invested in planning is often the deciding difference between being safe or having an accident, between having hassles or having fun, between getting there on time or missing your race. I can almost guarantee that the level of success of a trip is in direct proportion to the quality of effort involved in planning it. For more information on planning a trip, see my Special Report *Get It There in One Piece: Safe Traveling With Your Rowing Equipment* at <http://www.MaxRigging.com>.

**Step 2. Regulations:** A trip with rowing equipment on top of a car is not the same as a quick jaunt to the Stop and Shop. One of the reasons why is that there very well might be regulations (local, state, federal) that may affect your trip. Mostly, with car-topping, those regulations involve the overhang of the shell past the length of the car.

Usually four feet is the acceptable amount of overhang, but as I have mentioned before, that varies from locale to locale. I would recommend calling the state police for each state you would be driving in. In the past, they have been a good source of information. (Make sure that you use a non-emergency number.) Basically, any shell larger than a pair or double belongs on a trailer.

**Step 3. Insurance:** I'm going to be pretty straightforward about this . . . you've got to have insurance if you're going to be involved in the equipment transport process. Both the car and the equipment should be insured, along with yourself. If you skip on this step, chances are great that sooner or later (probably sooner), you're going to deeply regret not having the proper coverage.

I don't have the space or the expertise to go into detail here, but proper insurance is critical. Call your own insurance agent, tell him or her what you are planning on doing, and ask what the recommendation for coverage is. Then contact the Leonard Insurance Group,

<http://emporium.turnpike.net/~coxing/insurance.html>,

and get a quote. Over the years, Fred Leonard has been insuring a large part of the rowing community and has been very helpful. Compare the quotes and the coverage, and go from there.

**Step 4. Vehicle Preparation**: Regardless of whether your boat is sitting on the roof of your car or sitting on a shell trailer, you need to know if your vehicle can handle what you are going to dish out. If your car is in good running condition, it is most likely fine for car-topping. However, before you go, check the little things, which really aren't that little.

Check all the fluids, the tires, the spare tire, racks, blinkers, etc. Breaking down on the highway is a hassle enough in a plain old car. Breaking down with rowing equipment on your roof, especially with a starting time staring you right in the face, is enough to make a sculler switch to sweep rowing.

> Warning: Do not, I repeat Do NOT! use a 15-passenger van for car-topping equipment. You are putting your life, the life of anyone in the vehicle, and the life of others on the highway in danger.

**Step 5. Rack, Straps, and Flags:** When it comes time to load that equipment, you need to make sure that your rack and your straps are bomb-proof. They should be of the best quality, especially the tie-downs. I suggest double-strapping the boat at both ends, just to make sure—the price of the extra pair of straps is minimal, compared to the extra amount of protection that you get. I also recommend that both the bow and the stern be tied to the bumpers with strong safety lines. (See my article *Tie-Downs* in the article archive at <http://www.MaxRigging.com> for more information.)

**Step 6. Drive It:** If you're driving a car with a shell strapped to the roof, the only change you need to make to your driving is to be a little more careful than normal. Watch the overhangs and the stopping distance. Also, stop and check the boat quite often, since straps can loosen. I stop and check every 100 miles, which is also a good time to take a safety break.

**Step 7. Review Trip:** After all is done, and everyone is home safe and sound, dedicate a few minutes to reviewing your trip. What worked? What didn't? A simple review can help make your traveling safer in the future.

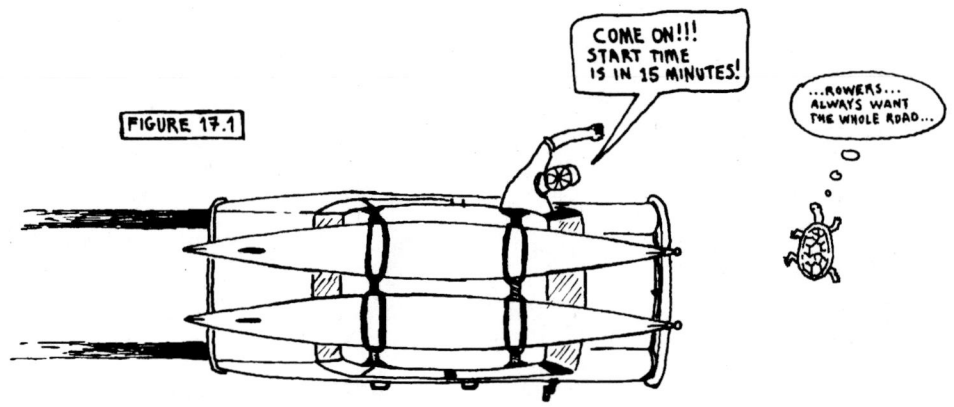

FIGURE 17.1

COME ON!!! START TIME IS IN 15 MINUTES!

...ROWERS... ALWAYS WANT THE WHOLE ROAD...

## JOB 17.2 TRANSPORTING EQUIPMENT ON A SHELL TRAILER.

**Problem:** The equipment has got to get there, and it's going on a shell trailer.

**Needed:** Reliable tow vehicle, bomb-proof trailer, excellent straps, flag(s), a very good driver(s), and an extra set of eyes.

Let me say this here: if you are going to be driving a shell trailer, then you need to be darn serious about what you are doing. Driving a shell trailer is dangerous stuff, and you, your equipment, and innocent people can get hurt, seriously hurt, if you don't do it right.

I've driven trailers in dozens of countries and over hundreds of thousands of miles, and it never ceases to amaze me how many folks I see that mindlessly hop behind the wheel of a vehicle towing a shell trailer with little or no experience or preparation. You have to know what you are doing when driving a shell trailer—plain and simple.

The three most common causes of accidents involving shell trailers are poor driving skills, lack of good visibility, and improper tying of shells. These three items will constantly need your attention.

**Step 1. Plan It:** As I noted in the previous JOB, the time and energy invested in planning is often the deciding difference between being safe or having an accident, between having hassles or having fun, between getting there in time or missing your race. This is even more critical when driving a trailer, especially since the length of a loaded shell trailer and tow vehicle can be longer than the average tractor-trailer you find on the highway.

**Step 2. Regulations:** There are a ton of regulations pertaining to traveling on highways. Most of the rules are geared toward commercial vehicles, but nonetheless, there are rules that affect transporting rowing shells, especially those that are being trailered. Before you even consider leaving your boathouse, check with all states you will be traveling through. Here are some of the items that you need to be concerned with:

- **Overhang of the shells.** This is the distance a shell extends past the end of a trailer or tow vehicle. The allowable legal length of overhang varies greatly from state to state. In some states, if you exceed their limit, you might need to purchase a permit to travel on specific roads. In other states, you may not be allowed on the highways at all. For most states, four feet of overhang is the maximum allowed.

- **Class of drivers license.** A basic license is fine for cartopping, but some states may require the driver of a shell-trailer to have more than the basic driver's license. They may require a chauffeur's license or a higher class.

- **Dimensions of shell trailer.** This is usually not a concern with most shell trailers since they probably don't exceed the maximum measurements for width, length, or height, but the total combined length of truck and trailer might. Something to keep in mind, and to check on.

- **Capacity information.** You are required to have information regarding certain specifics of a trailer's capacity, such as the *Gross Vehicle Weight Rating*. Depending on the state, this information may need to be displayed on the trailer itself or may only be required on the registration card. Be sure to carry the registration card with the trailer at all times.

- **Special equipment on trailer.** There may be requirements for some types of special equipment on the trailer. This might include the braking system, lights, safety chains, flags, and/or mirrors.

- **Restrictions.** Some states have special speed limits for trailers. Others may require a special permit or charge fees for using their highways. Some may require you to stop at weigh stations. Don't assume that the regulations for automobiles are the same for shell trailers.

So what do you do about these regulations? You call all the different states you are going to be traveling through and check, and then follow the regulation! It may be a hassle, but a few minutes on a phone and doing what needs to be done is nothing compared to the hassle of being stuck on the side of the road with the state police getting ready to confiscate your trailer and tow it away.

**Step 3. Insurance:** No need to mince words here—you've got to have insurance. You, your equipment, and your vehicle should all be insured. And with insurance there usually follows requirements, such as: minimum age of drivers, storage security, and certain safety equipment. Check with your insurance company to make sure that you are following their guidelines and not voiding your insurance. Also, if trailering, make darn sure that the trailer itself is insured.

**Step 4. Driver Preparation:** Let me throw out one word here that can make all the difference between successful trailering and disaster . . . that one word is "practice." As rowers, we happily commit hours upon hours to learning the skills of our sport. Why not give the same attention to detail for driving a trailer? To become a safe and efficient trailer driver, you need to practice.

Hook up the truck and trailer (an empty trailer is best), and go drive. Go to a shopping mall (when the stores are closed and the lot empty) or a large open area and drive, drive, drive. Practice backing, practice parking, practice driving, practice blowing the horn. When you feel comfortable with all that, crank it up a notch and do the same with a loaded trailer. Then, when ready for the highway, find an experience trailer driver (bribe him or her with whatever they want) and head out for a road trip.

Look, you wouldn't expect to row well or to be competitive in a shell with no practice, would you? The same holds for trailering. Want to be safe and efficient? Then practice.

Lecture over.

**Step 5. Vehicle Preparation:** In the world of shell trailering, the towing vehicle often consists of anything handy with a hitch, and this can cause problems—big ones. The tow vehicle is critical to a safe trip. It has to have enough horsepower to pull the trailer on normal roads, to climb hills, and to keep control in winds that can greatly affect shell trailers. It also has to have a brake system that will stop the monster when you need it to stop. Other items to be concerned about are the cooling system, suspension system, lights, and the transmission. If in doubt about your vehicle, seek out an expert for their advice.

**Trailers.** A shell trailer is one of the most used and abused pieces of equipment a team owns. Often, they are parked outdoors for months on end, usually in areas subject to terrible weather. When they are needed, they are dragged out, loaded to capacity (if not more), driven like crazy to a race, unloaded, reloaded, driven home, unloaded once more, and then left again outside—ignored. A very tough life. Because of this abuse, a trailer should be constantly checked to ensure everything is working properly. Nothing can be quite as disappointing as training for a race all year only to miss your chance to compete because your shell trailer never arrived.

**Step 6. Equipment Preparation:** Getting the stuff, all the stuff, that we take to regattas takes time—often more time than people leave to do the job right. Your concern is that the equipment (shell, riggers, oars, tools, slings, etc.) get there without damage. Following are just a few of the steps that I take to prepare our stuff for travel:

1. Check labeling on all riggers and oars (see JOB 18.2 for tips on labeling your equipment).

2. Wrap all riggers in protective blankets or padding.

3. Strap in all seats.

4. Tighten all nuts and bolts.

5. Tie a rope in the stern of all boats, run it through all the foot stretchers, and then tie it in the bow. (This has saved at least a dozen foot stretchers from death on the highway.)

6. Place tape over the impeller on all SpeedCoaches.

7. Layer padding between oars to protect the spoons.

**Step 7. Loading:** The key to safe trailering is how you load your shells and tie your boats. This depends mostly on your type of equipment and the method you are used to. Regardless of your system, here are some dos and don'ts that might make things go a little smoother for you:

*Before loading:*

- **Plan it.** It's usually a very wild and crazy time when loading a trailer. A what-goes-where sketch (loading diagram) is a great help and makes things a lot less confusing. I've enclosed one that you can copy and use.

- **Block it.** Before loading or unloading a trailer, place blocks around the wheels. This will stop the trailer from rolling, especially when it is unhitched.

- **Check it.** It's a lot easier to work on a trailer or tow vehicle when it is unloaded, so check for problems beforehand. Inspect the hitch and tire air pressure (including the spare's) before loading. Also, periodically check to see that the wheel bearings are in good shape and properly greased—this will usually have to be done by a mechanic.

*While loading:*

- **Point it.** Fifty-five miles per hour of wind can do a lot of damage. I've found less damage happens to the rudders, skegs, and interior of shells when the bows are pointed towards the tow vehicle.

- **Secure it.** All equipment should be safely tied down. Seats should be immobilized in the shells or put in crates, and foot stretchers should be tightened. Tuck sound system wires up into boats to protect them. Oars and riggers should be lashed down so they don't bounce out. You are legally responsible for anything that falls of your trailer! (See my free article *Tie-Downs* for more information on straps at <http://www.MaxRigging.com>.)

- **Chain it.** There must be safety chains attaching the trailer to the vehicle. These should crisscross under the tongue of the trailer. In case the trailer comes off the hitch, the chains will keep the tongue off the ground and prevent the trailer from flipping end over end.

- **Don't overload it.** Know your capacity. A basic rule of thumb is that you should not tow a loaded trailer that outweighs the towing vehicle.

- **Balance it.** An unbalanced load can cause the trailer to fishtail and make braking and turning extremely difficult. Try to center the load on the axles. The weight on the trailer tongue should be somewhere between five and seven percent of the total weight of the trailer.

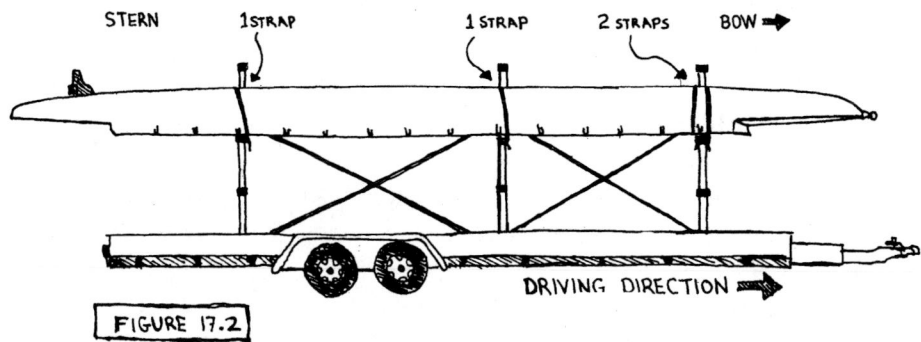

FIGURE 17.2

- **Flag it**. Make your overhangs as visible as possible. Get in the habit of putting a red flag on both the bow and sterns. Overhangs of four feet or more should be flagged, and in many states must be. For night travel, a set of lights at the stern of the boats will increase your visibility.

*After loading:*
- **Recheck it.** When all is loaded and things have mellowed out, recheck how well the equipment is tied down. If you are driving it, you are responsible for it.

- **Park it.** Place the trailer somewhere out of the way and safe so you won't get blocked in or the shells damaged.

## DRIVER'S CHECK LIST

| Check Trailer's | Check Tow Vehicle's | Check Driver's |
|---|---|---|
| ❏ tie downs | ❏ oil, water, gas | ❏ license |
| ❏ lights | ❏ lights | ❏ directions |
| ❏ flags | ❏ hitch | ❏ insurance |
| ❏ tires | ❏ registration | ❏ money |
| ❏ safety chains | ❏ fire extinguisher | |
| ❏ insurance | ❏ litter bag | |
| ❏ registration | ❏ first aid kit | |

**Step 8. Drive It:** At their best, shell trailers—and shell trucks—are difficult to drive. At their worst, they can be a hazard on the highway to yourself and others. A trailer loaded with un-sectioned eights is as long as, if not longer than, most tractor trailers.

It's crucial when driving a shell trailer that you plan your route ahead before beginning your journey. Rush hour and construction traffic can add time to your trip, but they are not your real worries. Dangerous turns and especially low overheads are where you really need to be concerned because that is where you can damage your shells and cause accidents.

To help avoid problems with low overheads, measure the total height of the trailer after the shells are loaded. Make your measurements from the ground to the tip of the rudder or skeg—most trailers with shells on the top rack will be around ten feet high. I usually add four inches to the number as a safety margin. Then write this information down and tape it to the dashboard. This could save you a lot of embarrassment at such places as low bridges, gas stations, and drive-throughs.

When choosing who drives, don't put inexperienced people behind the wheel. In fact, most insurance companies demand that the driver of the vehicle be experienced and at least twenty-one years of age, which prohibits many students from driving. Drivers should carry their licenses, registration(s), and insurance information with them. And I strongly suggest a minimum of two drivers in the vehicle. An extra set of eyes will make driving the shells safer, especially on long trips when one driver gets tired.

When you finally hit the road, constantly look, listen, and feel for anything unusual with the vehicle or load. If you notice anything, pull over as soon as it is safe and check for the cause. And speaking of checking, get in the habit of checking the trailer and load every time you stop—on long trips, I suggest you stop every 100 miles. Check the tie downs, flags, equipment, lights, hitch, and tires for any problems.

> Every time you stop to get gas or eat, walk around the truck and trailer before you get in and leave. I did this once and found that the stern of one of my boats has been ripped off by a bus. The end of the boat was actually imbedded into the windshield of the bus. If I had just hopped in and took off I would have never known what had happened.

Many trailering accidents happen because people try to drive a shell trailer like a car. The acceleration of a trailer is much slower than a car, and the stopping distance is much greater. You must allow more time for simple automobile tasks like pulling out into traffic, changing lanes, and passing. Extra caution will especially be needed for backing up, cornering, and pulling into service areas. Make absolutely sure that a lane is clear before changing, and use your turn signals.

The two most difficult parts of driving a shell trailer are cornering and handling the overhang of the shells. Trailers turn inside the track of the tow vehicle, meaning you need to take corners wider than normal. But the overhang is what gives most trailer drivers problems. Remember—you may be driving one of the longest vehicles on the highway, with thousands of dollars of shells just hanging out.

If you're not comfortable with this thought—or with your driving skills—go practice. Load up the trailer one Sunday and go to a parking lot and improve your skills. It's a good investment of your time, especially considering that the alternative may be waiting three months for a boat that's in the repair shop.

When you finally arrive where you are going, plan...Plan...PLAN...ahead where you will park. There's nothing more annoying then getting blocked in at a regatta and having to wait hours to leave because you're stuck.

As I mentioned before, the three most common causes of accidents involving shell trailers are poor driving skills, lack of good visibility, and improper tying of shells. If, after all your best preparations, you are unfortunate enough to have an accident, there are several things you should do.

First, activate the emergency flashers and place emergency signals to warn approaching traffic. Next, give appropriate first aid if needed and make sure that everyone is in a safe place. Notify law enforcement and your supervisor promptly. When things get under control, record as much information as possible: names, address, phone numbers, and driver's license numbers. Also get information from witnesses. Try to document the scene as well as possible, and if you have your camera with you, take pictures.

**Step 9. Review of Trip:** After all is done, and everyone is home safe and sound, dedicate a few minutes to review your trip. What worked? What didn't? A simple review can help make your traveling safer in the future.

# Chapter Eighteen: Keeping Your Equipment Alive

Your rowing equipment represents a big chunk of money. Like most folks, you want to get as much from this investment as possible. Rowing stuff is designed to survive the hardships of daily use; however, even the toughest stuff isn't ready to withstand the hardest challenges of its life, like transits, storage, pinhead coaches, and novice rowers. How you take care of your equipment will make the difference in its lasting two years or twenty, and who can afford to replace oars, riggers, and shells every other year?

Following are several JOBs to help your equipment last longer.

## JOB 18.1: TUNE-UPS.

**Problem:** You want to keep your rowing stuff working as long as possible.

At one of your practices, a crew will hop into the boat, take a couple of strokes, and there will be something wrong. It may be something broken, out of place, or badly adjusted. The older your equipment, the more often this will happen, although age isn't the prime factor. You want to avoid these glitches because sooner or later the problems will start taking away from your water time.

In our boat-shack, we have a procedure we do periodically to prevent problems; we call it a *tune-up*. It requires the basic level tool kit, waterproof marker, colored tape, and a share of common sense. We still have a few problems, but by faithful practice of tune-ups, we've cut down drastically on repair time, and that gives us more time for rowing.

## JOB 18.1A: DAILY TUNE-UP.

**Problem:** The equipment has just been used. What should you do?

**Needed:** Garden hose, rags to clean hull and tracks, solvent (mineral spirits), pencil and paper to record problems.

Giving your boat a daily look-over to catch trouble will take about five minutes of the coxswain's and your time.

**Step 1. Report:** We have a place identified in the boathouse in which coxswains can write down any problems they or the rowers have with the equipment. The athletes often have a different point of view than you, so in this case, value their feedback. Things such as worn sneakers, bad seats, broken braces should be noted and paid attention to as quick as you can.

**Step 2. Cleaning:** After each row, the boats should be rinsed off or wiped down with a towel to remove grime and river sludge; and if a hose is handy, the inside of the boats should be sprayed. Each track should be wiped down to get the grease and dirt off. A clean rag or one with mineral spirits on it will clean the track. Also, each inspection port should be left open for drying the compartments.

**Step 3. Glance:** When the boat is racked, give the hull a once-over to see if the skeg and rudder are okay. Coxswains can run over stuff and not even know it. Also, look to see if there are any dings or dents that might need attention. Give the riggers and oars a quick look to see if anything is out of place, like slipped inboards or oarlock pins off their spread marks.

**Step 4. Fix It:** Look at your notes and plan when you can fix the problems. Spending twenty minutes repairing a little problem as soon as it appears often will save you many hours of hassles down the road.

## JOB 18.1B: BI-WEEKLY TUNE-UP.

**Problem:** Your equipment has been used for about fourteen practices, or it has just been trailered.

**Needed:** Slings, paper and pencil, basic rigging kit, cleaning supplies, a few moments of peace and quiet.

**Step 1. Walk-Around:** With the boat seats-up and a note pad in hand, take a brief stroll around the boat. You're looking for anything that jumps out for your attention. Start at the stern, walk around one side, around the bow, and back up the other side.

---

**Focus!** When doing a walk-around, you're looking for problems big and small. Don't get distracted. If the phone rings, let it ring. If someone has a question, ask them to wait. This is your time to get a feel for the boat. You're giving it a physical, Dr. Rigger, so take your time.

---

If you see a problem, write it down and keep moving. Check the rigger labeling (see JOB 18.2 for labeling suggestions) to make sure that the riggers are in the right places. Look at the spread markers to see if any of the pins have slipped. Are the seats facing the right direction? Is the decking okay? Is the wash-box still solid? Is the skeg straight and rudder working? Tracks equal? Give the bow ball a feel; is it on tight? Bare spots in the varnish or chips in the paint? See anything broken, bent, worn, torn, or out of line? Look for old war injuries (old and worn out that is). If you see any, write them down, but don't stop.

**Step 2. Rigger Tighten:** Once you've got a feel for what's going on, it's time for some action. Before you do anything, grab a rigger tool, start at the stroke seat and go through and tighten all the rigger nuts. You're looking for two-finger tight (see JOB 16.2). Check to see if any washers have been put between the hull and the rigger connecting plate—a fairly common mistake.

**Step 3. Rigger Check:** When the riggers are tight, go through and tighten all the rigger fasteners, especially the top nut/bolt. Again, start at the stroke's seat. I say start there because it's a good landmark. Go back once more to the stroke seat and do a work-thru check. Look to make sure both

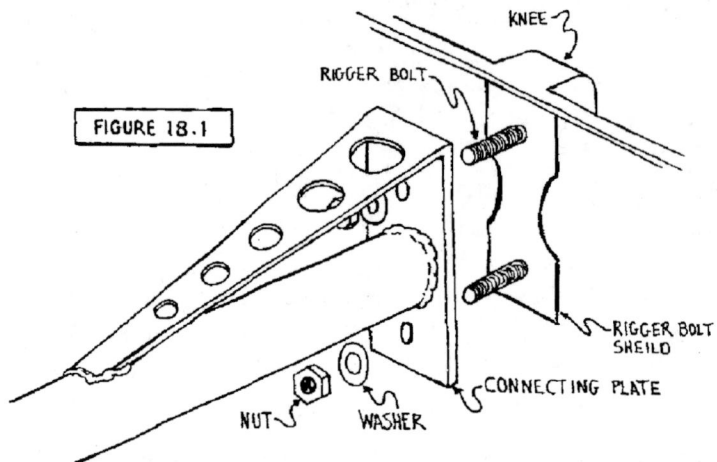

FIGURE 18.1

tracks are even, and with your tape and rigging stick check the measurement.

Now check the pitch. Pull out your rigging cards and find your dimensions and stabilize the boat. The pitch is a great tip-off for major problems, and if it is off you could have other problems, like the spread's slipping. If the pitch is not correct, you should check all the other dimensions of the rigger.

At the same time, look for anything that needs replacing. Any signs of old age (oarlocks, tracks, sneakers)? If so, replace them. When you're done checking the pitch, give all the faces of the oarlock and the pins a good cleaning. Now take a break for a few, go get some fresh air, and get ready for one last walk-around.

**Step 4. Hands-on Check:** Time for a little hands-on with the foot stretchers. You're interested in two things: Is everything tight, and is everything in good shape? In time, foot stretchers can loosen—not only the tracks (a.k.a. **adjustment channels**) but also the fasteners that hold them together. With both hands, grab the stretchers and give a good, solid shake. If there's movement, you've got to spend some attention here. The adjustment channels should be rock solid ,as with the **cross tubes**. Note loose fasteners, demolished sneakers, or frayed laces.

> **Tie It!** Sneakers now come with heel strings to tie the heel to the foot stretcher. This makes it a lot easier for the rower to pull their feet out of the sneakers in an emergency, like an overturned shell. Make sure all the heel strings are tied and broken ones repaired.

While you've got your hands inside the boat, inspect the seats. Give them a roll. They should move smoothly with no bumps or grinds. Are the wheels in good shape? Take a rag and run it along the track. It should be nice and clean. If not, clean the tracks and make this part of your daily tune-up.

**Step 5. Oar Check:** Unless you've planned differently, all the inboards should be the same. Survey the oar handles. Look at and feel the blades for damage.

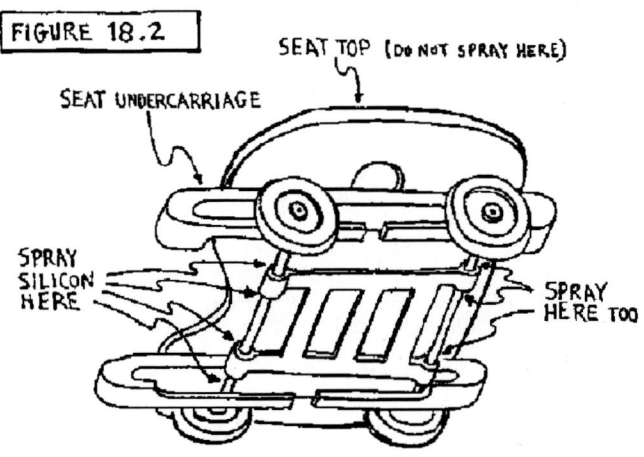

WHERE TO SPRAY SILICON ON SEAT UNDERCARRIAGE

**Step 6. Coxswain Seat Check:** If you've ever sat in a coxswain's seat for a period of time, then you know they're not built for comfort, but instead for function. A coxswain's position needs as much attention as any other spot in the boat.

First check the seat itself. Are the seat and the back brace in good shape? Does the rudder move smoothly and freely? When it's straight. are the holders even on the cable? Inspect the sound system. Grab a buddy and find out if all of the speakers work. If the boat has got a stroke meter/SpeedCoach™, does it work accurately?

**Step 7. A Few More Things:** If you've got a sectional shell, give the section a quick check (to identify if your boat has a section, see this chapter, JOB 18.3, Step 1). The bolts should be three-finger tight. Inspect the compartment covers; they make the compartments watertight in order to keep the boat from sinking if it swamps. If the covers are missing or broken, you could be in for big trouble.

Go over the hull. Run your hands along the surface, feeling for dents or bruises. Look for paint chips or breaks in the varnish. Give the skeg a gentle wiggle; if there is play in it, it needs repair. Inspect your slings, looking for rotting materials or weakening supports. Write down the problems you find.

**Step 8. JOBs to Do:** Pull up a chair and look over the note pad and/or blackboard. Rewrite your complete list of JOBs to do and prioritize them. Then start at the top of the list and get done what you can.

**Step 9. Spic and Span:** I suggest you try to have the shells and oars washed thoroughly every one or two weeks during heavy use. Besides everything looking cleaner, there are actually two good reasons for this.

One is speed. If the hull is dirty, then there will be more friction as it moves through the water, which will slow you down. The other reason to clean stuff is health. Oar handles can be a grubby place. Wash the oars and make sure the handles get washed with a disinfectant. This will help keep the germoids from getting into rowers' blisters.

## JOB 18.1C: SEASONAL TUNE-UP.

**Problem:** It has been a while since the equipment has been used.

The off-season is a great time for boat work because everything should be dry. This is the time to do major maintenance you didn't have the time or energy to do before.

Focus on major JOBs such as gluing, painting, and structure repairing. I can't get into the nitty-gritty of repairs; that would be a whole book in itself. I suggest you go through the equipment like your *Bi-Weekly Tune Up,* with paper in hand. When you've got your list of repairs, mark off what you have the skills to do. If there are repairs that are beyond your talents, then look for a resource who can do the work for you. If you're not finding any help, then try contacting the builder. Some builders do refurbishing work, or they may be able to suggest a direction to turn to.

---

**Is old slow?** In 1962, a Russian crew came to Philadelphia to race in the People's Regatta. Not having their own boat, their American guests arranged for them to pick any boat out of all the boathouses along Boathouse Row. They picked one, raced, and won, beating Vesper, several college crews, and the Canadian National Team. What makes this interesting is that the Vesper boat they beat was the fore-runner of the American eight that won the Olympic gold in 1964. What makes this even more interesting is that the boat they selected and rowed was built in 1947, making it fifteen years old, and it had spent almost all of those fifteen years on the racks, being rowed very seldom. Allen Rosenberg, who was involved in the coaching of the Vesper eight at the time says, "The Russians proved that day that old boats can win races."

---

Following is a checklist to help make your equipment last as long as possible:

## <u>Daily</u>

### Before Rowing

- ✓ Check rigger fasteners
- ✓ Keep shoes (and dirt) out of boat
- ✓ Keep boat off of dock

### After Rowing

- ✓ Clean tracks
- ✓ Clean hull
- ✓ Clean oar locks and oar sleeves
- ✓ Do a quick check for any problems
- ✓ Open ports to promote drying

## <u>Bi-Weekly</u>

- ✓ Walk around boat looking for problems; record and fix them
- ✓ Tighten all rigger fasteners
- ✓ Check rigger adjustments

## <u>Bi-Annually</u>

- ✓ Treat hull with rubbing compound
- ✓ Wax hull
- ✓ Pay insurance premium
- ✓ Lubricate ball bearing seats and touching unlike metals

## JOB 18.2: LABELING YOUR EQUIPMENT.

**Problem:** You need to mark things so you and everyone else knows what goes where.

Before you label your equipment, you've got to figure out how it's going to be used. A friend of mine has his equipment organized so that the first time the rowers walk into the boathouse they are assigned an oar. For as long as they row, that is their oar. No matter in what seat or in what shell they sit, they use the same oar. This means a lot of inboard adjusting, but my friend swears by this system.

I, on the other hand, have oars assigned to a position in a specific boat. No matter who rows in that seat, they will use that oar. Both ways require a different labeling method.

There are a zillion different ways you can label your stuff. To keep our equipment straight and to avoid mass chaos, we use colored tape and a waterproof marker. We assign each shell a specific color tape. For example, one of our eights, the *Clo Truslow*, is assigned the color red. We put a little piece of red tape on the gunwale, near the bow, so every one can see it.

For sectional shells, we put tape on the bow and stern to make sure the right pieces get put together. We put a piece of red tape on the bottom of each seat, and write the seat position on the tape. On each rigger, we put a wrap of red tape and write the rigger number on it (depending on the type or rigger, we might also use this tape as the spread markers). Then we put a wrap of red tape around each oar and use the manufacturer's numbers supplied to mark the positions. We also have colored tape on the boat rack so coxswains will know where the boat goes, and tape on the oar rack to direct the oars into the right spots.

As you can see, we like colored tape.

What happens when you run out of tape choices, which can happen in large boathouses? Use two wraps of tape to give you more options. So with a couple rolls of colored tape and a waterproof marker, you can have things pretty well organized, and bring some color into your boathouse.

Tape is only one of a zillion ways to label. I've seen paint and engraving used in other boathouses, but both are a little too permanent for me. If you do plan on using paint, then consider paint pens made by Testors Paint Company (called *Gloss Paint Marker*). They are very handy, non-messy, and inexpensive.

## JOB 18.3: SECTIONING A SHELL.

**Problem:** You've got to put together or take apart a sectional shell.

**Needed:** Basic rigging kit, petroleum jelly, solvent, blanket or large towel, a couple of rags, two slings, a couple of reliable bodies.

Sometimes, shells, mostly eights, can be broken down into two or three pieces. Each of these pieces is called a **section**. Usually you will find the divider placed smack dab in the middle of the shell between the four's and five's stateroom.

A sectional boat makes transportation easier, but it also adds weight (about ten pounds), cost (a couple of hundred dollars), and hassles. Sectioning a boat several times a season ages a boat quickly. If not done carefully, every season a boat is sectioned takes an extra season of use off of the boat. There are a bunch of different ways to section a boat; here are my suggestions . . .

**Step 1. Is It Or Isn't It?** Telling if you've got a sectional shell is a snap. The easiest way is to look at the outside of the hull for a seam that runs from gunwale to gunwale perpendicular to the centerline, a sign the boat is sectional. You will usually find it amidships. If the boat is seats-up, look for a large brace running along the inner contour of the hull, loaded with fasteners, again usually amidships. Monocoque decks tend to hide the section, so you may have to look closely.

**Step 2. Setup:** Roll the boat seats-up into slings. Try to locate the slings a little closer amidships than normal: if you're splitting an eight, put them around the two's foot stretcher and under the seven's seat.

**Step 3. Prepare to Section:** Take the riggers off and do what other preparations you need to do to get the boat ready to travel. If you've got a sound system/speed-measuring system make sure you disconnect the bow part from the stern part. There should be a connector located somewhere around the section. If not, you'll either need to pull the system out of one section or cut the wires and put a connector in yourself. If you are cutting, make sure the connector is waterproof.

Sectioning should be done with two to four people. More than four people is a party, and only one person is pretty tough—although it has been done. I'll assume you've got three, yourself and two handy helpers. Send one helper to the bow ball and the other to the stern. Get your wrenches ready and go to the section.

**Step 4. Section:** Have each helper hold the boat. Their JOB is to balance their section—you'll see why in a second. Take a towel, old rag, or blanket and lay it over the gunwale where you're going to work. This JOB can be gggrreasssy so watch your clothes. Take a peek inside the shell. The section is a wide band, usually of wood, that runs along the inside profile of the hull. It's made of two parts; one goes with each part of the shell. Your JOB is to locate and loosen the nuts and bolts that hold the two parts together.

Look at the section carefully and locate the fasteners; there will be a bunch. They may be different sizes, so try to get a mental picture of which fastener goes where. Both the nut and bolt head will turn, so you'll need two wrenches; sockets come in handy here. Start at one side of the hull and begin loosening. Don't loosen any one fastener all the way. Instead, loosen one a couple of turns, then loosen another a couple, and so on. This will keep you from damaging the section.

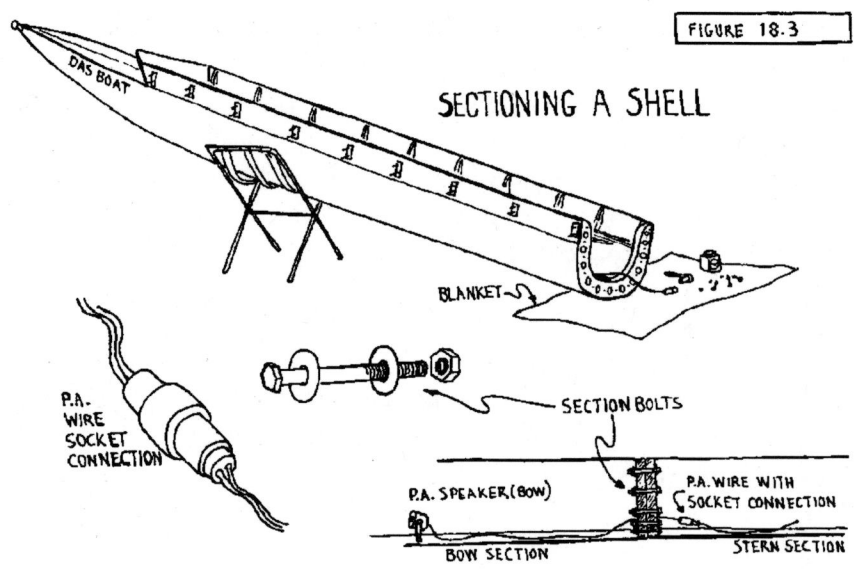

FIGURE 18.3

SECTIONING A SHELL

As you get the fasteners loose, talk to your helpers and get them to keep their section level. This is where you can really hurt the boat, when the fasteners are loose but still connected—so be careful. You're trying to keep both parts level to prevent damaging the wood or bolts.

As your helpers hold the boat level, you will have to talk to them; they won't be able to tell if it's level from where they are. As they work to level it, remove the fasteners and any washers. I usually keep a coffee can handy and put all metal goodies inside, then splash a little solvent in to get the grunge off.

You've got all the fasteners free, right? Have each helper gently pull and separate the sections by about two feet. They should come easily apart. If it's a battle to split the boat, you've probably forgotten a fastener or the sound system/speed system wiring. When the sections are free, have the helpers steady their pieces and place something soft, like a towel or blanket, on the ground. Now place the sections down on the blanket and stabilize the pieces by moving each sling about a stateroom closer to the ends of the boat. See figure 18.3.

Clean the faces of each section well. What should you do with all the nuts, bolts, and washers? After cleaning, put the bolts back through one section and put the washers and nuts back on them. Give them a couple of finger turns and you are ready to transport. Your other option is to carry the nuts, bolts, and washers separately. In many years of doing it my way I've only lost one bolt, yet I know of several people who have left all their section bolts at home because they did not put them back in when transporting the boat.

**Step 5. Together Again:** To resection, just work backwards. Before you begin, you'll need to put sealant between the sections to help make the seal water-tight. I suggest petroleum jelly. It's inexpensive and works well; however, it's a little bothersome when it's cold. Wipe the section faces clean and smear a thin layer of fresh jelly on both sections and you're ready to resection.

> Petroleum jelly will dry out in time, and if your boat has been in the racks for a long spell, your watertight seal may begin to leak. If that's the case, section your boat and reapply the jelly.

Be careful not to overtighten the section fasteners. Get them finger-tight, then tighten each one down 1/4 to 1/2 a turn until they are all three-fingers tight (see JOB 16.2). One good turn deserves another, until they're all tight. Hook up the sound system/speed system, slap on the riggers, and you're ready to row.

# Chapter Nineteen: Storing Your Equipment

If you are one of the lucky sorts who can keep rowing all year long, then read no further and just keep rowing—this chapter is not for you. But if you are like many of us, then winter's approach means its time for your rowing equipment to hibernate inside while things get nasty outside.

Now keep in mind that rowing equipment is designed to survive the traumas of daily use. Yet when we store rowing gear, some very bad things can happen. Many folks store their stuff well, taking into account a lot of the problems that can pop up. However, there are a few concerns that people usually don't think about when they plan their storage.

Rowing equipment usually spends much more time in storage than in active use. Sometimes the way it is stored is a lot harder on the equipment than rowing itself. A lot of equipment is damaged or destroyed while it's not being rowed. When considering storage there are several prime "equipment-killing" villains, and a few evils, you need to know about and to try to avoid.

I'll discuss the villains and evils first, then get to some specifics about your equipment.

## 19.1 The Villains

**Sunlight** is one of the worst villains. The rays that bake you to a brown and beautiful crisp at the beach can send your equipment to an early grave. Ultraviolet rays from the sun bathe the earth whenever it is daylight—cloudy or not. The shorter rays, which are dangerous to plants and animals, are blocked by the ozone (at least they used to be), but the longer rays aren't blocked and these can destroy your equipment by a process called **photodegration**.

As ultraviolets bombard the surface of a material, they're absorbed. This revs up the electrons of the material to a higher state of activity, causing breakdown. This breakdown can range from discoloration to loss of strength. Some builders now add ultraviolet absorbers to their products to help defeat photodegration. Although normal daily exposure to ultraviolets, like while you're rowing, will not affect your gear, long-term exposure will, so store all of your equipment out of direct sunlight.

Most boathouses are uninsulated, so **temperature** extremes (the second villain) can dip to 10 degrees or lower in winter and soar to 140 degrees and above in the summer. These temperature ranges will cause little long term problems with most gear, but short-term ones can show up. Several types of plastics and as well as fiberglass will begin to soften and bend at temperatures over 100 degrees. Around 150 degrees plastics may deform. This may sound like a high temperature to find around a boathouse, but remember, most are closed up tightly, and in the summer, uninsulated buildings can get super hot.

If you store oars in the attic or rafters of a boathouse, the heat may cause permanent deformation. To avoid these extremes, store your equipment in areas that keep normal house temperatures. Make sure your boathouse has vents to avoid overheating. Be careful where you store your boat and think about heat, especially when traveling to summer races. I once witnessed a fiberglass shell get so hot that the hull actually collapsed around the slings it was sitting in. A very ugly sight.

If you've got hard-decked boats, make sure inspection-port covers for bow and stern compartments are left open when the boat is not being rowed. These covers are water- and air-tight, and if they're closed, a drastic temperature change could cause severe damage to the compartment.

The third villain of storage is the **position** in which you store your stuff. Your shells should be stored seats-down, on their gunwales, on a solid set of racks. A good rule of thumb is to have one rack for approximately every twenty feet of shell (three racks for an eight, two racks for a four). Make sure the racks are level and padded to reduce gunwale damage. Some people store their boats long-term in slings—a bad idea. This can cause hull problems, especially if it gets hot.

Because of a lack of space, shells may get shuffled outside. If this is the case, try to find a protected area. A seats-up boat could easily hold a couple thousand pounds of water, which would collapse any slings, so store boats seats-down! Also, make sure they're strapped down. Falling off of racks is one of the leading causes of damage to boats. If you're storing a fiberglass hull long-term outside, it might help to cover the outer hull with a good wax (like car wax) that has ultraviolet inhibitors. This will help the glass survive longer, especially those non-white colors.

---

**On or off?** Should you leave the riggers on a boat during the off-season? I've had people tell me to leave them on, and others tell me to take them off. I'm not sure if leaving riggers on the boat long-term will cause damage, but I often take them off and stash them in a nice protected place because I don't want anyone rowing the shell while I'm not around.

---

You also need to think about oar storage. There are two major types of oars: wooden and synthetic. About the only care necessary for the latter is to store them out of the sun, standing vertical—so the water can drain away from the handles. A wooden oar, on the other hand, can absorb tons of tender loving care. A good rule of thumb with wooden oars is to never let anything sharper than water touch them. If they do get scraped or dinged, you'll need to give first aid in order to avoid dry rot, which I'll discuss in the next section.

## 19.2 The Evils

**Mildew** is a whitish or brown growth produced on many surfaces by molds, and they are notorious for attacking stored objects. Specifically, mildew is a fungus that flourishes wherever it is damp, warm, and poorly ventilated, which are the conditions you tend to see in most boathouses.

The stuff will grow on practically anything, but it thrives on natural fibers such as cotton, silk, wool, and wood.

Besides its unpleasant smell, mildew causes discoloring, and if left long enough, it will eat into natural fibers so severely things will fall to pieces. The best way to avoid mildew is to wash everything clean. Dirt on shells can supply enough food for mildew to grow. Oily films such as those from perspiration on sneakers can also contain food for mildew. It's moisture mildew loves, so try to make sure your storage area is as dry as you can get it.

Not to sound paranoid, but **insects** are another evil just waiting for you to store your equipment. They will eat it, live in it, and pop out at the worst time to scare the shorts off some unsuspecting rower. Although most man-made materials (plastics, nylon) are not on the menu of insects, the natural materials, like wood, are open to insect abuse. Several insects such as the furniture beetle and powder post beetle actually love to eat wood.

Besides chewing up things, insects can do damage by nesting. Carpenter ants tunnel through wood to build elaborate nests, and there is nothing quite as shocking as laying hands on a shell and having a nest of cockroaches land on your feet. Bees and wasps seek shelter when they nest, and the insides of shells seem ideal for them. This should be of major concern if any rowers are allergic to their stings.

When storing wooden equipment, make sure the wood is well varnished, and try to cover over inspection-port openings if you're worried about insects (normally you should leave them open), preferably with a breathable material that will keep bugs out. If you're really worried about insects, you might try an insecticide, but check the label thoroughly because some will damage synthetics and are downright toxic.

**Dry rot** is neither dry, nor a rot, but a deterioration of wood caused by fungus. It can devastate wooden boats and oars so thoroughly people believed it was invented by a boat maker as a form of job security. Like most fungi, dry rot thrives in moist, warm areas. Spores attach to the wood and produce a powdery mess, spreading if not stopped.

One of the favorite spots for dry rot is the areas of wood whose surfaces have been bruised, allowing moisture to enter through the protective coating (varnish). These places will soon form dry rot, and if the rot is not removed, it will cause soft spots in the wood that are prone to breakage. The best prevention against dry rot is to varnish your wooden equipment and store the stuff in dry areas that have plenty of ventilation. Be careful of your oar handles; don't varnish them but keep them dry!

While using your wooden equipment, be sure you have several good coats of varnish applied, preferably the type with ultraviolet inhibitors. If cracks or bruises in the surface happen, apply new coats as soon as possible. If you wait, dry rot might form and then it must be removed and treated.

And finally, the nastiest of storage evils, **rust**, which never truly sleeps. A brownish substance that appears on the surface of iron and steel, rust is formed by oxidation—the mixing of oxygen from the air with iron. Luckily, we don't have to worry about rust because most metal parts are either anodized (a protective coating), have been replaced with plastic, or made of stainless steel—which resists rust.

Now for the steps you can take:

## JOB 19.1: STORING YOUR EQUIPMENT.

**Problem:** What the heck do you do with your rowing stuff when it's not being used?

**Step 1. Store The Shells:** When placed in the water with their seats up, rowing shells make pretty good boats. When placed in the boathouse with their seats down, rowing shells make much better homes. Homes, specifically to critters, big and small, who are looking to get out of winter's chill.

You may be an environmental type who is sighing, "Oh, now what's the harm if a few little bugs and such find shelter inside my shell?" Not much, I would say, but I'm not talking about a few bugs. I am talking about some big things, like a six-foot black snake. Or a nest of bats. Or a raccoon who thinks the bow compartment makes a wonderful winter hide-out.

What's the harm? Well, getting in a shell and having a sleepy, and probably grumpy, big snake slither out from under the decking may send more than a few rowers (or coaches) scurrying for a different sport. And bats, which are quickly becoming welcomed in many yards because of their beneficial nature, have a habit of leaving deposits of . . . well . . . bat stuff, which is a real pain to clean up. And we won't even get into what damage a raccoon can do to a shell with those sharp claws when it is having a restless winter's sleep.

How do you keep the critters out? I have found two successful ways.

One, of course, is to make sure that your boathouse is closed up tight, reducing the access points that animals can use. The second method involves taking a leap into the kingdom of technology. Wheel in a VCR and begin playing that world-famous rowing movie *Oxford Blues*. All of the critters in your boathouse will go into such a sound, coma-like sleep from the movie that you will be able to come in, swoop them up, and deposit them in a much better home without them ever arousing.

**Step 2. Store The Oars:** You may not have given this much thought, but when you store oars, you really need to ask yourself this question, "Exactly where are the bathrooms located?" How come, you ask? Well, let me tell you why.

A few years ago in a certain boathouse whose name I have committed to secrecy, a team stored their oars like all good teams do, standing straight up with their handles on the ground. Sometime during one of those winter nights a drain pipe that serviced the bathroom sprung a leak (an appropriate choice of words, I think). A lot of raw sewage was freed and does what most liquids tend to do—flow to the lowest point they can find. In this case that low point happened to be the exact spot where the oar handles were resting. Then those wooden oar handles, which were very dry, did what most dry oar handles do; they absorbed the moisture.

When it came time to row, the oars were grabbed, shells launched, and rowing began. It wasn't until the crew was several miles away from the dock that someone noticed the rather strong odors the handles were emitting. What to do? Well, they notified their coach, who promptly fell to the bottom of his launch laughing, then they turned around, rowed home, and spent quite a bit of time in the bathroom washing their hands.

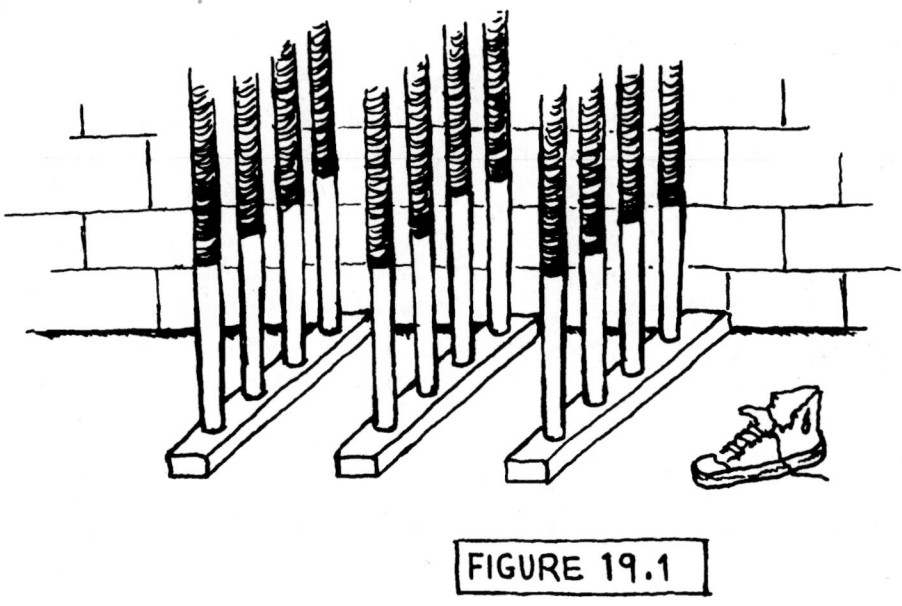

**FIGURE 19.1**

So, when storing your oars, be aware of the surroundings. And usually, if you keep them in their racks, they will be fine.

**Step 3. Store The Electronics:** I have found over the years that there is not to much to worry about when you store your electronic stuff (megaphones, stroke watches, amplifier systems). As long as you unplug them, keep them warm and dry, and don't stick them underneath the bottom of a woodpile, then I've found they survive storage pretty well.

Actually, though, there is one problem that I have found. Mice, and their ratty big cousins, seem to have a fondness for chewing on electronic things. In particular, they are attracted to the wires and headbands. The current theory (oh, yes, pun intended) is that they are drawn to salt that may be on the wires—put there either from the water you row in or from perspiration.

The solution here would be to wash the items off before you store them, and try to store the stuff out of Mickey's reach (which might be nearly impossible).

**Step 4. Store The Motors:** Finally, this brings us to the workhorse of most rowing programs across the country—outboard motors. A lot of people think winter storage of motors is a cinch. You just shut them off, take them off the launch, toss them in the boathouse, and *ta da*, you're done. Not quite!

There are two things to consider here. First, most boathouses are not insulated. That means when it gets cold outside, it gets cold inside. Consequently, liquids, like water and gas inside the motor, could freeze. When liquids freeze, they expand, and this expansion can cause damage to your motor's tender parts. It is best to drain the motor of both water and gas before you tuck it away.

Next, I suggest you do you a yearly motor maintenance before you store it. That way, you beat the spring rush to the motor-shop to get your motor ready. In addition, if the weather suddenly turns nice before you expect it to, then your horsepower is ready to go.

# Chapter Twenty: Buying Rowing Equipment

Your stars are aligned, your karma is hot, and it's time to buy a new piece of equipment. If you know what you want, I mean you really, absolutely, fur shur know what you want, then read no further. Your mind is made up, so go bolster that economy.

But if you have doubts, read on.

From an equipment standpoint, there are two ways to look at the future of your rowing: either you are happy with the state of your rowing equipment and you don't plan on buying any soon, or you are getting ready to make some equipment-maker smile because you are about to shell out some of your hard-earned money.

If it looks like your future has a few purchases upcoming, then let's discuss how both you and the equipment-maker can end up smiling after you have spent your money. Specifically, let's talk about how to make a successful purchase.

## 20.1 A Successful Purchase

My definition of a successful purchase is getting exactly what you need, for the price you can afford, exactly when you need it. Does that sound a little difficult? It shouldn't.

Making a successful purchase is not that hard; you just need to organize your thoughts. With that said, the following seven steps can help you make a successful purchase, and they should only take about sixty minutes of your time.

## JOB 20.1: SEVEN STEPS TO A SUCCESFUL PURCHASE.

**Problem:** You've got the urge/need to buy a piece of new equipment.

**Needed:** Pencil and paper, builder's info, smart friends.

**Step 1. Establish What Your Needs Are:** Before you go digging for your checkbook, the very first thing to do is to figure out exactly what rowing equipment you need, and in fact, if you really need it. Now don't panic, this is a lot easier than it sounds—especially because you know most of the answers already. For instance, even with a minimum amount of rowing experience, you know: what type of rowing you are going to do, what doesn't feel right to you, and what your limitations are (space, money, etc.).

There are two very important things to keep in mind. First, let the emotions go and try to be as objective as possible. In an activity like rowing, where we invest so much of our time, effort, and energy, it is often very difficult to be objective. But we need to be, because if we are not, we can end up doing some pretty silly stuff—like a fellow I rowed with.

One day, he went out and bought a new boat. What is silly is that he had just bought a new boat the month before. He bought the second boat because he could never feel quite comfortable in the first one. He never spent the time to adjust the first boat properly, so of course it didn't row right. If he had just been objective and adjusted his boat correctly, he could have had a boat that rowed well and saved himself a big dent in his checkbook—and I'm sure some nasty conversations on the home front.

Second, look at the big picture—try a little long-range planning. If you are coaching a team, can you make projections about the team's size or skill level? Those projections may impact your equipment needs. In addition to this planning, do an inventory of all your equipment. Somewhere in the deepest, darkest recesses of your boathouse, you may already have what you need.

Ah . . . but what if you are new to rowing, and you have just started sculling? You need to keep this in mind: your rowing equipment needs will change as you become a more skilled rower. There is a progression that you should follow in equipment; the more skilled you become, the more precise your equipment should be. This is a very important part of the big picture.

**Step 2. Prioritize Your Needs:** How are you going to prioritize this information, you ask? Good question. First, take the information you now have and make like Santa Claus—make a list and check it twice. List all the items you came up with, and then double-check them to make sure that you in fact really need them.

Second, and this is the fun part, be judgmental. Just like Ms. Thornbush did to your tests in elementary school, grade your list. Look at each item and assign it a grade.

If you're having a difficult time grading, here are the criteria I use:

> - Items that are safety related get an "A"
> - Items that will have an impact on boat speed get a "B"
> - Items that affect enjoyment (rowers or coaches) get a "C"

The As are something to be purchased immediately, the Bs are scheduled to be bought after the As, and the Cs after the Bs. I know it sounds very simplistic, but I've found it to work for me.

**Step 3. Determine The Amount Of Money You Can Spend:** Ah-hah . . . time for a dose of reality. Grab a pencil, make sure it has got a good point to it, and figure out exactly how much money you can spend. Take a second and read those last words again— "how much money you *can* spend" is what you want to know, not "how much you *want* to spend." Those are little words that make a big difference.

Many people have bought rowing equipment and have gotten themselves into hot water (actually boiling water) because they didn't know the bottom line. The bottom line is how much money can you spend without sending yourself into a stressful financial state that has a negative impact—especially on the home front. Yes, it might make you a little faster to get that spiffy looking, state-of-the-art, whiz-bang boat (might, but probably not). However, if you don't have time to row it because you had to get a second job to pay for it, what good does it do for you?

**Step 4. Determine What Make Of Equipment To Buy:** At this point, you know what you need to buy, and you also know how much you can afford to spend. Now whose stuff do you purchase? Keeping with the theme of being objective, there are three important items you need to look at: quality, service, and price.

Many consumers think that price is the most important reason to buy an item. Those are the same folks that own an Edsel and have a chunk of swampland in Florida. **Quality** is what counts. Get the best quality that you can within your price range. Quality lasts, sub-quality annoys—and breaks. How do you determine quality? A few tips are included in JOB 20.2.

The second item to consider is **service**. Are you buying just an item, or are you buying a company?

Try this: if you have some time before you make your purchase, call up the manufacturer, or dealer, at their place of business. Ask some questions about their product. How are you treated on the phone? What type of responses do you get to the questions? Then talk to some of their customers and ask them how pleased or displeased they are with their purchase and with the dealer.

Some dealers will have test equipment they lend out. This is a great service that can really help you decide what to purchase. It is refreshing to know that the dealer believes in the equipment enough that it will sell itself. If you do take advantage of test equipment make sure that the equipment is insured, because as we all know, mistakes happen.

Lastly, go ahead and look at the **price tag**. If the first two things are equal (quality and service), then price is probably your determining factor on what to buy.

What tends to make this whole process somewhat easier to swallow is that dealers usually have their wares set up at major regattas. This gives you an opportunity to look at the equipment without the high pressure of a salesroom. In addition, most manufacturers and dealers have a background in rowing. They have either rowed, coached, or coxswained, or they have some connection with the sport of rowing. This means they are usually very understanding about the needs and wants of rowers.

**Step 5. Pick Your Options:** One thing you will notice is that most rowing equipment comes with options. The days of "making the man fit the boat," as George Pocock used to say, are long gone. Now the boat and most other equipment is made to fit the person rowing it, which means plenty of choices.

When you start looking at the options available, you may get overwhelmed. Where do you put the coxswain, in the bow or in the stern? What pitch do you want on the oars? What height range do you want on your riggers? What shoe sizes? What color? The list goes on and on.

There is no way I could possibly go through the vast amount of options available in this short space. However, I'll tell you how I handle choosing options—I get a complete list of all the choices available. Then I go through each one, choosing what is best for me. If I get stumped with a choice, I ask for advice from other coaches, or from the equipment builders themselves. When you are picking options, be aware that different options will most likely affect the price of the equipment.

**Step 6. How Much Is It Going To Cost You?:** By now you are probably getting the urge to write that check, but hold off one more moment. Look at *all* the costs involved with your purchase. How about insurance, shipping, taxes? These all need to be added into the total cost. Are there any other parts that you need? Do you need slings for your boat? An amplifier system? If the purchase is coming from overseas, do you have to pay import fees or a duty?

Review and research all these questions to make sure there isn't some hidden charge that is going to bust your budget.

**Step 7. Buy It:** Finally, the time is here to grab your wallet and go out and give the economy a big boost. Just remember what you are after: a successful purchase. If at any time you get the feeling that you are making a mistake with the purchase, even though you've thought it out well, put it off until you can determine why you're getting the internal warnings. It will be darn hard for you to smile in your new boat if you've got a great big dose of buyer's remorse.

Of course, all of these recommendations are just my own opinion. You are perfectly welcome to do it your own way. But if you do, and you end up rowing a pink shell with purple polka dots, when you really wanted a purple boat with pink polka dots, don't yell at me.

## JOB 20.2: WHAT'S QUALITY, WHAT'S NOT?

**Problem:** You are thinking of buying something (new or used). Is it quality or not?

All rowing equipment is not created the same. Unfortunately for us consumers, rowing equipment is not an area that any of the consumer magazines have turned their attention towards. That means when we are deciding what to buy, you and I are pretty much on our own. Here are a few suggestions that might help you in your quest for a quality piece of equipment.

**Step 1. Back to the Past:** An excellent way to determine the quality of a piece of rowing equipment is to look at an older version. What you are looking for is how well it has held up to the years of use and abuse. A boat that has been rowed hard for five years and is still in good working condition is a boat that was well made. This is a sign that the builder makes quality products.

**Step 2. Snoop:** Another way to check on quality is to be snoopy. According to Dickie Pereli, owner of Stillwater Designs, "Look in areas that the builder would not expect you to look in, like the bow or stern compartment. There you can find signs of quality, or lack of it." And while you are looking around, here are a few things to check on:

| Shell | Look at the seems where the material is joined together—they should be finished well (clean and sanded). |
|-------|--------------------------------------------------------------------------------------------------------|
|       | Check the welds on the rigger—they should be solid and not show any signs of cracking. |
|       | The ribs of the boat should be solid and form a solid joint with the gunwale. |
|       | The paint should be first rate in application and quality. |
|       | All fasteners should be noncorrosive (e.g., stainless steel, plastic). |

| Oars | Look at the seems where the material is joined together—they should be finished well (clean and sanded). |
|------|--------------------------------------------------------------------------------------------------------|
|      | Attachment of blade to shaft should be solid and watertight. |
|      | Look at the sculling grips or the wood used in a sweep handle. They both should be of the best materials. |
|      | Adjustable handles should be attached solidly—yet be easy to adjust when needed. |

**Step 3. Warranty:** And one final place to check on quality—the warranty. What type of warranty does the builder offer? Often a longer warrantee period is a sign that the builder has confidence in the equipment, and that it is a quality product.

## JOB 20.3: HOW TO BUY A USED SHELL.

**Problem:** A new shell is out of the question. What about a used one?

**Needed:** A lot of *Ps*—Paper and pencil, patience, persistence, phone.

If your funds or time frame won't accommodate buying a new boat, you may want to consider a **used shell**. The used shell market is a funky place; it's like buying a used car, except there isn't a used boat lot. There's no *Blue Book* to help you on prices, and sometimes a decent used boat is very tricky to locate.

If you're in the market, you'll find some good deals and some truly horrendous ones. Be cautious. It amazes me the lack of effort some people put into buying a used shell. Here's a couple of things I've learned from the *School of Hard Knocks*.

**Step 1. Locate It:** Once you get an idea of what boat you're after, call the builder to see if they have any refurbished ones for sale. It's usually a good place to find a good used shell. If they don't have one, ask if they know of any used ones for sale. If you strike out here, you'll need to make some phone calls and check the Web. For leads, try some of the major rowing programs in your locale, and call USRowing— they often have used equipment information—or call a few friends.

**Step 2. Eyeball It:** When you've finally found a potential boat, it's time to check it out. You need to give it a thorough visual inspection. Start with the area it's stored in; this should give you some idea of how it has been treated. Now look at the boat: watch for signs of accidents, wear and tear, torture, and abuse. Are the bow and stern original, or have they been replaced? Write down anything of note on your paper.

Put the boat in slings and go through it. Turn it seats-down and run your hands along the hull. All hulls get dings and dents, but you're looking for signs of major repair work. If you find some, that should be a warning sign to be cautious. Look at the paint: is it chipped, peeling, or good as new? How well has the boat been cared for? Boats in programs with full time Riggers will be in better shape than those with no Riggers.

To get a quick idea how well a shell has been maintained, I look at two places; the sneakers and the oarlocks. If either is beaten up or worn, it's a sign of poor maintenance. Look at the fasteners. Have the bolt heads and nuts been rounded? A small sign of possible bigger problems. How often has it been rowed? Twice a day for the whole year, or saved just for those Sunday morning rows. It makes a difference. How old is it?

While on your visual search, look for the boat's serial number. It could be about anywhere so you might have to dig, but the number will give you some valuable info. At my Web site, <http://www.MaxRigging.com>, I have a short worksheet on how to find a serial number.

**Step 3. Hands On:** Do a quick vibe check. How do you feel about things so far? Is the boat something you'd like to have at home, or do you have a feeling you're wasting your time? Be honest with yourself. If things are groovy, let's keep checking.

Put the boat seats-up and do a stiffness check (see JOB 13.4, *Measuring Shell Stiffness*). This is important feedback, so make sure you do it. Write down the quality of the stiffness. Start at one end and look at the nitty gritty: check out the decking, the tracks, seat assemblies, foot stretchers and their tracks, the bracing, and anything else you can. Grab hold of things and give a good wiggle. Write down any parts that will need repair or replacement.

See if you can rig the boat and have your crew row it—would you buy a car without driving it? When rowing the shell, try different pressures and different ratings. Give it a good test. Apply the brakes—have the rowers stop the boat suddenly and watch what happens. Any signs of weakness? How does it steer? Listen for any funky noises. What feedback does the crew have? How about from the coxswain?

An important part of this whole process is what sort of karma does the boat have? Does it call out to you and say, "Hey, I'm a winner; take me home with you"? Or does it say, "I'm really tired; leave me alone." Has it won any races? Does it look cool? All things for you to consider.

**Step 4. How Much?** If you're still high on the boat, now is the time to talk price. Tell the seller you need a couple of minutes, then head to a phone.

Call the maker of the boat and see if you can get a suggested price. If that's a no-go, at least get an estimate for the parts you noted that need repair or replacement. For a ballpark idea on the price of the boat, take about five to ten percent off of the new purchase price for each year the boat has been rowed. So a five-year-old boat that originally sold for $20,000 may be worth $17,500 to $15,000, depending on its condition. From there I subtract the price of parts and any labor to get the boat in good, safe condition.

Now you have a number to work from. Remember, leave your emotions out of the process. You know how much you have to spend and what the boat is worth. If you don't know yet, you need to see what the price tag is. Go up to the owner, look right in his/her eyes, and get the price. Get any feeling that there's room to haggle, or is the price firm? Can you make your budget and the sellers price meet? If so, shake hands and you've got a deal. If not, keep looking; the right boat is out there.

# Chapter Twenty-One: Rigging For Sculling

T en years ago, in the first edition of this book on rigging I placed a chapter way in the back of the book about rigging for sculling. And because of that (placing the chapter in the back) I was taken to task by several scullers.

> "How dare you put us in the back of the book? What do you have against us . . .?"

And we talked, and I listened. And after those discussions where I explained that the nature of this book is all about rigging (for both sweep and sculling) those folks informed me that it was okay to have specific sculling stuff in the back of the book . . .

> "But for crying out loud at least make it a *chapter*, and just not an *appendix*."

So done.

And apologies to any scullers who feel that I have demeaned the sport (especially to my wife, who is an avid sculler).

## 21.1 Karma of Rigging for Sculling

To be straightforward, I feel there is little difference between rigging for sculling and rigging for sweep. Yeah, yeah, yeah . . . I know there are some differences—a few—and those differences are important, and I'm going to discuss those in a moment. But I realistically think a comfortable knowledge about sweep rigging will allow you to do a very good job in sculling rigging (and those folks comfortable rigging sculling stuff should be able to do a good job rigging sweep stuff).

If you can rig sweep, you can rig sculls, and vice versa.

But . . . (yup, there is always a *but*) . . . the level of skills for one type of rigging is usually not the same as the level of skills for another.

My skills for rigging sculling equipment are not nearly as good as my sweep skills—the main reason is practice time. I rig sweep stuff all year long, but rig sculling stuff only three or four months a year. Practice makes perfect, and I don't practice enough. So don't be upset if you find your abilities are not the same in both types of rigging.

I spent my younger days rowing with a sweep oar. Back then, I had this stereotypical vision of sculling as an activity that attracted two types of people: those folks who weren't good enough to row sweep and those with whom no one else would row. One summer day, I was lounging on the dock at our boathouse when I struck up a conversation with a sculler.

After a few minutes of chatting, he asked (or was it "challenged?") me if I would like to try his boat. Being the self-assured individual I am, I accepted his offer, hopped in his boat and got ready to show off my rowing skills. I learned several things in that next hour.

First, my stereotype of scullers lacking rowing skills was wrong. and it quickly disappeared as my world literally turned upside-down. Second, sculling is definitely more difficult than it seems. And third, some scullers are sadistic people with whom no one else will row.

Now there are some very strong similarities between rowing and sculling and in the Karma of how you rig for them. I approach sculling rigging with the same mental and physical attitude as I would sweep rigging. The thoughts whirling through my mind and the end goal of my rigging are the same—rig for comfort and efficiency, and do a good job.

However there are some distinct differences in the karma of the rigging we need to discuss.

## 21.2 Difference #1: Inside a Skull (with a *k*, not a *c*)

A little evolution music please . . .

Way, way back when rowing was just becoming the "in" thing with human beings, sweep rowers were nothing more than slaves stuck in a seat and literally rowing for their lives. One day, a Roman named Ull was standing on the shore watching one of the Caesars water ski behind a galley. Ull thought to himself, "Wow, that's for me! I want to try this rowing thing. But I'd rather do it by myself, without all those other guys, especially that one big dude with the whip."

So old Ull went home, built himself a boat, put his one oar in, and tried to row. He spent the next hour going around and around in circles. His buddy, Scu, watched all this, and noticed a problem—mainly Ull was making himself dizzy. So he hollered, "Hey, Ull, something's wrong. Why don't you and I put our heads together and fix your problem?"

That they did, and after many long hours of trial and error, our friends finally came upon a workable solution: to try two oars instead of one. You know the rest of the story. Their experiment worked, they went on to become famous boat makers, and had a boat named after them, the Scu-Ull—which, of course, is nowadays known as the Scull.

Since those early days, the mental difference between sweeping and sculling hasn't changed much. Sweepers tend to row in groups under the guidance of someone (the guy with the whip has been replaced by a coach—told you things hadn't changed much). Whereas scullers tend to putter around on their own, asserting their independence.

And there lies one important reason rigging sculling equipment is different from sweep stuff. A vast majority of scullers, because of their independence, receive very little coaching, and very little rigging help. Scullers usually take responsibility for their own rigging, which can make the task harder and sometimes less productive.

## 21.3 Difference #2: Inside a Scull (with a *c*, not *k*)

Years ago, we started a program at our boathouse in which we train our sweep rowers to scull during the fall season. We learned two things from our experiences. One is that *sculling teaches better rowing skills than sweep rowing.*

In an eight or a four, bad technique can be absorbed by the crowd and may be very hard to identify. The problems one rower generates (like balance troubles) may be negated by the actions of another rower. But in sculling boats, especially in singles, that won't happen. Every time something is done in a scull, whether it's right or wrong, the equipment talks back. If the technique is good, the boat responds well. If the rowing is incorrect, you'll know it; every stroke, since the boat will react in a not-so-positive manner.

This reaction is called **biofeedback**. And the biofeedback from sculling is loud and clear—unlike sweep rowing where it can be muffled. Biofeedback is a great teaching device, and we've found the threat of capsizing a great enhancer of good rowing technique.

Second, *I spend more time rigging the sculling equipment than rigging the sweep equipment.* Actually, I guess I should say I spend more time fine-tuning the rigging. I tend to think of rigging like a piece of clothing. The rigging in an eight should fit someone like an old, comfortable pair of pants, with room to move around in. But the rig in a scull needs to fit better, more like a pair of expensive skintight gloves. To get this fit, I find I need to fine-tune quite often and double-check my work carefully. So be prepared to be very picky with your sculling rigging.

Also, be aware that novice rowers tend to be very hard on the equipment, and sculling equipment is somewhat more fragile than sweep stuff. If you have novice scullers, get ready to put more time into your maintenance rigging than you would with experienced people.

## 21.4 Sculling Equipment

If you've read Chapter Four, then you have a pretty good knowledge of the equipment. But there are a few sculling items we need to discuss in particular.

In sculling, there are two oars per rower, unlike in sweep rowing. Sculling oars, or **sculls** as they are called, are smaller than sweep oars—both in blade surface area and total oar length. Their oar handles are small and they are usually covered by a rubber tube, called a **grip**. Since there is only one hand per oar, this grip helps the rower hold onto the handle and greatly assists in the feather and squaring motion.

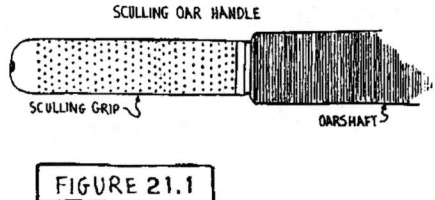

FIGURE 21.1

Like the oars, sculling riggers are smaller in dimensions than their sweep counterpart, and again, there are two per person. The forces generated in a sculling rigger are not as great as those in a sweep; therefore they do not need to be as sturdy as their counterparts.

The steering of a sculling boat is another critical item. You will find a skeg sticking out from the hull of all sculling boats (unless it's been bopped off on the dock or while rowing), but you may or may not find a rudder.

Singles are steered by the oarsman varying the pressure during the stroke, primarily at the catch, where one leg will attack the drive just a whisker sooner, moving the shell to one side or the other. Therefore, there is no need for a rudder. Doubles may also use this system, or they may, like most quads, have a rudder. Without a coxswain, like 99.9% of all sculling boats, the steering is left up to one of the rowers. The rudder is attached to one of the foot stretchers and is activated when the rower moves their foot to one side or the other. This is called **toe-steering**, **toe-ruddering**, or just a **toe** for short.

With all that said and out of the way, here's how to use this book for sculling rigging . . .

## JOB 21.1: HOW TO USE THIS BOOK TO RIG FOR SCULLING.

**Problem:** You need to rig for sculling and not sweep rowing.

**Needed:** A few minutes to read this section.

If you've just flipped to this section as you were reading Chapter One make sure you return there after you read this or you'll be getting ahead of the game. It is very important you read Chapters One through Five. In Chapter Two you will find a short quiz that's critical. This book is arranged for different levels of knowledge (which I call Dimensions), and how comfortable you are with your knowledge will affect the way you rig. The quiz tells you what Dimension you are in, so make sure you take it.

Then I suggest you read through the introductory information in every chapter. You need to become familiar with this information regardless of whether you feel it is sweep-related or not. Turn back here after each topic and read this chapter to see if there are differences or suggestions you need to be aware of for sculling.

Once you have that knowledge, you're ready to begin, so turn to JOB 2, this chapter. When you're ready to start a JOB, allow yourself extra time, about twice as much as you think you'll need. Read the JOB all the way through once, go back to the beginning, and start the task, going step by step. You may find you'll have to read between the lines and experiment a little because of the format (for reasons I explained above I didn't outline all the steps for sculling equipment). If you get stuck, turn to Chapter Sixteen, JOB 16.1, for help. When your work is done, double-check it, put away your tools, clean up, and head on to other things like that big slice of cheesecake in the fridge.

## JOB 21.2: RIGGING FOR SCULLING.

**Problem:** It's time to do some sculling rigging.

**Step 1. Read:** Before you start, read all of Chapter Six to get acquainted with the rigging basics and procedures. Then . . .

**Step 2. What's Wrong?** Identify the problem with your rigging. If you see poor rowing and think the cause is a rigging problem, turn to the index and look up technique problems. Then turn to those pages and see if that info helps you pin down the troubles. Once you know what's wrong, turn to the list of all JOBs in the front of the book. Then . . .

**Step 3. Read Again:** Read the appropriate chapter for your troubles and read this chapter to see if there is anything here you need to know. You're armed with the info, so now for the nitty-gritty . . .

**Step 4. Rig Away:** Follow the steps in Chapter Six and the ones outlined in each JOB. I've mentioned you may need to read between the lines and experiment when rigging for sculling. If you find yourself stuck, JOB 16.1 is there to help. You may also want to check my Web site for any Special Reports or articles that might help. When you're done . . .

**Step 5. Finish Up:** Finish off by cleaning up, recording your information, double-checking your work, and watching the rowers to see if you've solved the problem.

## JOB 21.3. LOCATING THE ARCS IN SCULLING.

**Problem:** You need to locate your arcs (inside and outside) for your single/double/quad.

**Needed:** Chapter Seven.

Everything you read in Chapter Seven holds true for both sweep rowing and sculling, but there are two notable differences you'll face with sculling rigging. First, the arcs (inside and outside) are larger for scullers. A sweep rower is limited in the extension of the outside arc by their outside shoulder. This is not so in sculling and the outside arc can be significantly larger. In fact, a problem with some novice scullers is extending their outside arc too far.

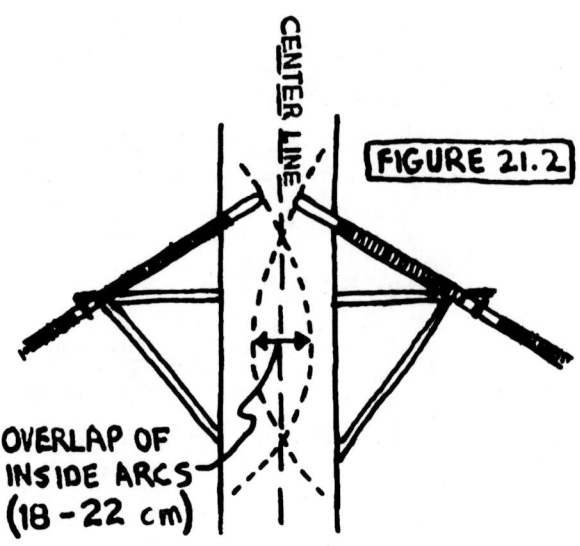

**FIGURE 21.2**

CENTER LINE

OVERLAP OF INSIDE ARCS (18 - 22 cm)

Second, there are two inside arcs per person instead of just one as in sweep. The reason this is a concern is that there is not much room between gunwales in sculling boats, therefore, these two inside arcs tend to bump into each other. Actually, they cross over. This cross over means the oar handles will overlap both during the drive and the recovery parts of the stroke. It's critical this overlap of the inside arcs is set just right so the rower can find the proper body positions at the catch and at the release. The normal range for the overlap, when the oars are at the mid-drive position, is 18 cm–22 cm.

In sweep rigging, we use the work-thru the pin as the major adjustment for locating the arc with fine-tuned adjustments done by moving the foot stretcher, the catch length, or the catch angle. Well, in sculling, work-thru is not nearly as critical to the arc location, so we locate the arcs a little differently, but we can still get good results. There are three simple steps:

**Step 1. Check The style:** Before we do any rigging, the rower(s) should have a comfortable and efficient style, regardless of experience level. If you're dealing with a beginner, don't worry about the arcs yet. Instead, focus on teaching good rowing and instilling good habits. Once the basic technique is down you can start fine-tuning the rigging by . . .

**Step 2. Average Numbers:** Set the work-thru, span, inboard, and oar length at reasonable lengths. Check the rigging charts in Chapter Fifteen and make sure that you're using numbers within the acceptable ranges. Remember, *the faster the shell, the greater work-thru.* So a quad will have a larger work-thru than a double, which will be greater than a single. Then . . .

**Step 3. Locate The Release Position:** This is where you need to be picky. At the release in a single, you want the handles at the fore-most part of the inside arc so the thumbs are just touching the side of the ribs. Or, in other words, the hands should be just on top of the hip bones when the oars are extracted. (This is in a single; in a double and in a quad, the hands should finish slightly more in front of the body.)

FIGURE 21.3

HANDS FINISH OVER HIPS CLOSE TO RIBS

FINISH POSITION IN SCULL

You can accomplish this by moving the foot stretchers so the hands are in the right spot. It may take several attempts to get the hands right, but once they're in the correct spot, all your angles (catch angle, finish angle) should be properly located for the person rowing that shell.

For more information on sculling technique, refer to *Sculler at Ease*, by Frank Cunningham.

## JOB 21.4: FINDING THE LEVERAGE FOR YOUR SINGLE/DOUBLE/QUAD.

**Problem:** You need the leverage numbers (blade surface area, span, inboard, oar length) for a single, double, or quad. These dimensions are measured exactly the same as sweep equipment, so follow the info in Chapter Nine. For span read on.

**Needed:** Tape measure, rigging cards.

Span, like spread, is one of the critical ingredients of the gearing, and we must know the exact size of it to row well. Measuring span is easier than spread.

**Step 1. Tighten Riggers: All types:** Be positive all the riggers are tightened down and that there are no washers in the wrong place (see JOBs 7.5 and 16.2 for help on tightening).

**Step 2. Measure:** We don't need to use the centerline; instead, take your tape measure and, at the seat position where you need to know the span, measure directly across from the center of one oarlock pin to the center of the other. That's your span.

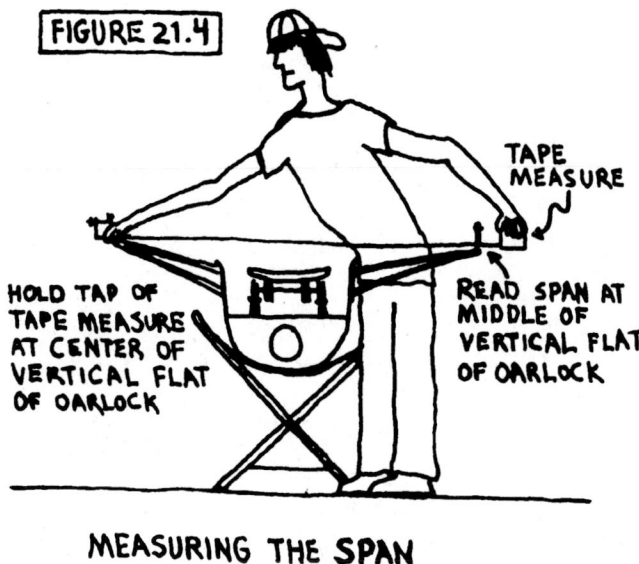

FIGURE 21.4

TAPE MEASURE

HOLD TAP OF TAPE MEASURE AT CENTER OF VERTICAL FLAT OF OARLOCK

READ SPAN AT MIDDLE OF VERTICAL FLAT OF OARLOCK

MEASURING THE SPAN

**Step 3. Enter The Data:** Record the spans even if you're going to change them. If the new dimensions don't work, you'll have the numbers to come back to. If it's time to change, then . . .

## JOB 21.5: ADJUSTING THE SPAN.

**Problem:** The span is not where you want it.

**Needed:** Chapter Fifteen, basic rigging kit, rigging cards.

So the span is off and you want to adjust it. Remember, the span is the distance from the center of one sculling pin to the center of the other. When it's time to adjust a sculling rigger, span isn't much of a help since there's no reference point to tell how far you've moved the pin from the middle of the boat. So how do you make sure the riggers are adjusted equally on both sides? You use spread.

But you thought spread was just for those silly sweepers? Not so, not so! For your spread number, just divide the span number in two. Then for adjustments, follow the steps in JOB 9.4.

**Step 1. What Numbers:** To find your rigging numbers, follow the steps in Chapter Fifteen.

**Step 2. Make The Changes:** Adjusting the span is just like adjusting the spread, so follow the steps in JOB 9.4. Use the centerline; you need it as a reference point. If your oarlock is a pinless type, check my Web site for a resource to help.

**Step 3. Open Your Eyes And Ears:** Once you've made the changes, follow the advice in Chapter Fifteen. First- and Second-Dimensionals, leave your rigging alone and watch what the effect is of what you've done.

If you're in the Third-Dimension, listen to the rower's feedback, possibly more than you would in sweep rowing. Also, keep an eye on the speed of the oar handle at the catch and the very beginning of the drive. If you've rigged the leverage too heavy, you may notice the rower has problems accelerating the oar just after the catch (use slow-mo video if you need too). Make sure the position of the hands at the finish is correct. If they are not, adjust the foot stretchers to fine-tune things.

## JOB 21.6: MEASURING THE HEIGHT IN A SCULL.

**Problem:** You need to know what your height is on your sculling rigger.

**Needed:** Some biofeedback. Basic rigging kit, boat in slings.

**Step 1. A Difference In Sides:** Do you remember the overlap of the inside arcs we discussed? Well, something must be done so these two arcs don't collide.

Scullers basically handle (pun intended) the overlap in one of two ways. One solution is that they avoid the situation altogether by rowing a style where one hand leads the other on the drive and recovery. This means both hands are in the same vertical plane with one slightly in front of the other. This usually causes no problems with the height, if the riggers are set okay.

The other solution is rowing in a style where both the hands pull equally. This means one hand will need to be right on top of the other during the drive and the recovery. I call this the **scratch method** because of the abuse the lower hand usually takes. In the U.S., where this style is popular, the left hand is usually the upper hand, and we say "left-over-right."

If your solution to the overlap problem is "left-over-right," or even "right-over-left," you will have to rig the heights of your two oarlocks differently. The upper hand's oarlock should have about 1.3 cm (1/2 inch) more height than the lower hand's.

LEFT OVER RIGHT (HANDS)

FIGURE 21.5

**Step 2. The Best Method:** In sculling, sensing what is going on is critical to rowing well and also to determining if the boat is rigged correctly. So use your senses to tell if the height is correct.

<u>Feel</u>: When you row, where do the handles come at the release? Are they at your mid-rib area? They should be. Does the height feel okay?

<u>Look</u>: Check out at your knuckles after a practice. Are they bloodied and banged up? They shouldn't be. Also, look at your oars as you drive. Are they going deep in the water, or washing out? Again, they shouldn't be.

<u>Listen</u>: Is your body giving you warning signals (loud and clear) about incorrect height? Are your shoulders or your lower back hurting?

If you sense something is off, then try the next method to double-check. I would also have someone either videotape or observe you row (someone who knows sculling) to see if they sense something that you might be missing.

**Step 3. The Next Best Method:** The next best method to determine your sculling height is to measure it. Turn to JOB 11.1, and use the steps there to measure your rigger heights. Just do the exact same steps for each rigger.

Why is this not the *best* method? Those steps can be difficult to do, since they require being comfortable with a rigging stick and having a secure boat, and because the freeboard in a scull is usually so small that it may be awkward, or even impossible, to work your rigging stick around so you can get it where you need it.

In response to that issue, one solution I have used is to tape small blocks of wood to the base of my rigging stick at the spots where it sits on the gunwales. These allow us to extend the stick up high enough so we can measure the seat top, yet not so high that we can't measure the rigger. It may be a solution to your problem.

If you cannot get this method to work for you, and some scullers/Riggers cannot, just go back to Step 2, and trust your senses.

# JOB 21.7: ADJUSTING YOUR SCULLING HEIGHTS.

**Problem:** You're here because your heights are not where you want them.

**Needed**: Basic rigging kit, height numbers, clean rag, shell seats-up (this can be done upside-down, but why kill yourself?), access to the Web.

At this point, things are not right with your height. It is time for some serious surgery on your rigger.

**Step 1. Change the Spacers:** A great many sculling riggers today use spacers to change the rigging height. Look at your rigger. Are there spacers? Are they easy to get too? If you have a Euro-style rigger, you're golden with this step. (If not, off to Step 3.)

If so, then remove the top nut/bolt and shift your spacers around. Then put things back together correctly, with a three-finger-tightened top nut/bolt.

**Step 2. Re-measure:** After things are back together, double-check the rigger height. Then go row to see how it feels.

**Step 3. More Difficult:** If it looks like your height is going to be more difficult to change due to rigger design (and many riggers are), I'm going to suggest two things. First, experiment. Go ahead, give it a shot, but only if you think that your chance of success is pretty darn good.

If experimenting isn't meant for you today, then go to my Web site, <http://www.MaxRigging.com>, and see if there are any resources there for you. If so, download the specific information for your boat, and get ready to operate.

**Step 4. No Luck:** If experimenting isn't for you and you cannot find a resource on my Web site, pick up the old telly-phone and give your mentor or the builder a call. Ask for help, adjust the rigger, and you're off to bigger and better things.

# A PARTING THOUGHT

Thousands of pages and ten years ago, I started an effort to make the part of rowing known as *rigging* a little less mysterious, a little more comfortable, and little more doable for the average coach/rower. It seems like it is working. I certainly hope so. Please let me know if it is, or isn't, working for you.

And that brings me to a point that I would like to leave you with—there are many other parts of our sport where similar efforts need to be made.

One part is the environment. Rowers as a group should be some of the leading activists for a cleaner environment. Face it, we do what we do outside and we need clean air and clean water to do it. Where are the efforts from us to keep it clean and clean it up?

One answer to that question is that the efforts are happening at the grassroots and boathouse level. But what about at a national level? Where is the league of concerned rowers fighting hard for the environment? A handful of rowers cannot do it all.

Another part is safety . . . what about making rowing safer? Okay, rowing is not classified as a *hazardous sport*; however, there certainly are dangers inherent in our sport. And sometimes people are severely injured and even killed while involved in rowing. Where are the efforts to make it safer?

Well, one answer to that specific question is the Kippy Little Foundation. Here are folks who are putting their own time, money, and energy into making rowing safer for all involved. Bravo to them. We need more people and more efforts like them.

And a final part—who is striving to make rowing more fun?

Listen, over the years of my involvement with competitive rowing I have seen rowers, coxswain, coaches, administrators, officials, and everyone under the sun take on Herculean efforts to make a boat go fast. And you know what I have also seen along those same lines? A multitude of people crushed, left by the wayside.

Time and time again, I see athletes (at all levels) throw down their oars in disgust after the very last stroke of the season, vowing never to row another stroke for the rest of their life. And coaches are not immune either—a multitude of good coaches leave rowing, burned out.

Good people leaving a good sport.

Lots of pressure. Where is the fun? One answer to that question is my book *Finding Happiness Sitting on Your Butt Going Backwards*. But that is just one book. We need more people to focus on the fun of rowing, to make it more fun for all involved.

If there is a twentieth-anniversary edition of this book (in 2012), it will be interesting to see if there is change/improvement in any of those three parts I just mentioned (environment, safety, fun).

I really hope that there is.

All the best for your rowing and rigging.

Peace!

Church Hill, MD
September, 2002

# Appendix One: Rigger Talk

**F**ollowing are terms you may happen upon in your rigging:

Adjustment: moving the dimensions on rowing equipment to best suit the needs of the rower(s)

Aft: towards the stern or the back of a boat

Back stop: small blocks on the fore part of the slide that prevent seat assembly from rolling off the slide

Beam: width at the widest part of a boat, usually measured from inside of gunwales

Blade: end of an oar that is placed in the water

Bow: front end of a boat

Button: a ring around the shaft of an oar; when the oar is in the oarlock, the button sits flush against the oarlock and keeps the oar from sliding outward

Carbon fiber: whiz-bang space-age material used in shells, a lot like fiberglass except it's made with carbon pieces

Catch: part of the rowing stroke where blade is placed into water

Catch angle: angle between oar handle and oarlock perpendicular when the oar is at the catch

Catch length: distance along centerline between the oarlock perpendicular and farthest extent of oar handle when the oar is at the catch

Centerline: a very important yet imaginary line that bisects a shell from the bow to stern

Check: (a) ding or dent in the hull of a boat; (b) backwards motion of shell caused by rowers transferring their body mass aft to fore

Collar: see *button*

Degree: an angular measurement used to determine the pitch

Designed water line: depth of the hull to which the builder designed the boat to sit in the water when the proper weight is in the boat

Dimension: (a) number used for rigging adjustments; (b) a label for your level of knowledge

Drive: part of rowing stroke from catch to release when oar is in water

Eight: shell with eight rowers and one coxswain

Fastener: nuts, bolts, and all the other little goodies that hold the rowing equipment together

Fin: piece that extends from hull, below water line, used for longitudinal stability, usually located near rudder

Foot stretcher: part of shell that accommodates rower's feet

Fore: towards the bow or front of a boat

Four: shell with four rowers and a coxswain (called four with) or shell with four rowers and no coxswain (called four without or straight four)

Front stops: small blocks on aft part of slide, keep seat from derailing and protect rowers' legs from sharp end of slide

Gunwale: top part of hull (when boat is seats-up) where the riggers attach; may or may not be made of same material as rest of hull

Height: distance from the oarlock sill (horizontal flat) to the water's surface, usually measured from sill to top of seat

Horizontal flat: one of the flat parts of the oarlock that supports the oar, important for oarlock height

Hull: part of the boat that keeps the inside in and the outside out

Inboard: distance from butt of oar handle to the blade side of the button

Inter-axle distance: see *spread*

Keel: one of the main parts of the shell structure, runs from bow to stern along inside of bottom of the boat following the centerline

Knee: bracing that runs vertically from the keel to the gunwale

Knuckle: joint of a rigger where pieces meet

Lateral pitch: see *outward pitch*

Leverage: the mechanical advantage of a lever—in our case, the oar and rigger

Loom: part of oar from the oar handle to the beginning of the blade

Metric System: measuring system based on quadrants of earth used by most of the world

Monocoque: type of bracing system inside a shell that uses a flat deck that runs the length of the shell

Oar handle: part of oar rower holds during stroke

Oar: long, skinny thing used to propel boats; different from a paddle because oars are attached to the boat and paddles are not

Oops, mistake, error, goof-up, uh oh: part of the learning process

Outboard: distance from the blade side of button to tip of the blade

Outward pitch: slight slant on oarlock pin away from centerline of shell

Pair: shell with two rowers and a coxswain (called a pair with) or shell with two rowers and no coxswain (called a pair without or straight pair)

Perpendicular: another very important, and imaginary, line that extends 90 degrees from the centerline

Pin: part of rigger on which oarlock rotates

Port: left side of boat when looking towards the bow

Puddle: depression in the water left after blade is removed; the harder the oar is pulled, the bigger the puddle, assuming good rowing is happening

Rack: support used to store boat in a seats-down position

Recovery: part of rowing stroke from the release to the catch, blade is out of water

Release: part of stroke where blade is removed from the water

Rib: see *knee*

Rig: the arrangements of riggers on the boat, a *German*-rigged eight has 2 rowers (at 4 and 5) on the same side, an *Italian*-rigged eight has all the rowers on the same side in pairs, except the bow and stroke

Rigger: (with capital *r*) person who adjusts the mechanics of the boats to suit the needs of the rowers

rigger: (with small *r*) funky metal thing hanging off of the shell, officially called an outrigger, but that has been shortened to rigger

Rigging: the science/art of adjusting rowing equipment in such a manner that an oarsman will be in a comfortable and effective position to apply power

Rudder: part of hull extending below water line and used to steer boat

Seat assembly: all the seat parts

Seat: part of seat assembly rower sits on

Shaft: see *loom*

Shell category: the size of shell determined by number of people it holds

Shell weight classification: average of crew's weight the shell is designed to hold, usually divided into three categories: heavyweight, midweight and lightweight; now classifications for women-specific sizes are being made

Shell: name used for racing boats powered by rowers, came about because early shells were made with thin hulls and were literally as fragile as an egg shell

Silicon: waterproof lubricant

Sill: platform that gives support

Skeg: see *fin*

Sleeve flat: the flat part of the sleeve, critical to the pitch

Sleeve: tube of material that surrounds oar, under the button, that protects the loom from damage

Slide: piece of shell on which seat assembly rolls

Sling: support used to store boat in a seats-up position

Slippage: amount of motion of blade in the water from a "locked" position

Span: distance from the center of one sculling oarlock pin to the center of another at the same position

Spread: shortest distance from the centerline of the shell to the center of the oarlock pin

Starboard: the right side of a boat when facing the bow

Stateroom: distance inside of hull from one foot stretcher to another

Stay: part of rigger used for support and strength

Stern pitch: aft slant on blade when oar is square in the water

Stringer: a horizontal brace

Stroke: one complete cycle of the oar from the catch to the release and back to the catch again

Thwartship distance: see *spread*

Track: see *slide*

U.S. Customary System: measurement system based on parts of human body, used by only a few countries in the world

Undercarriage: the lower part of a seat that allows it to move, includes the wheels, axles, etc.

Vertical flat: vertical part of the oarlock that is flat and about parallel to the oarlock pin, critical to the pitch

Washout: problem with rowing stroke where the blade slips too much through water and causes an inefficient stroke

Work-thru: distance from perpendicular through the oarlock pin to a perpendicular across the front-stops of the slide

# Appendix Two: Web Documents

Following is a list of documents available for download at my Web site <http://www.MaxRigging.com>. Delivered right to your computer, these downloads are designed to help you make the most of your rigging and your rowing. Please note, this list may frequently change.

## Special Reports

Special Reports, are in essence, short e-books. Each covers a broad area of rigging. Here are some of the current titles:

*Absolutely Maximize Your Rigging Numbers: Getting The Most From The Numbers You Use For Rigging Your Rowing Equipment*

*Get It There In One Piece: Safe Traveling With Your Rowing Team And Rowing Equipment*

*Seven Steps To A Smart Rowing Purchase: How To Make Wise Purchases Of Rowing Equipment, New And Used*

*Eight Weeks To Great Rigging: How To Improve Your Rigging Dramatically Over The Course Of One Season*

*Six Steps To Help Your Rowing Equipment Last Almost Forever*

*How To Maximize Your Euro-Style Rigger*

## Worksheets

Worksheets are documents that describe in detail a specific area of rigging. Plans are to have many titles up by late 2002. Please check the site for updates.

# Appendix Three: Resources

## BOOKS

Here are a few other books to go along with the ones already mentioned. All of these books have been helpful to me—in one way or another.

*A Textbook of Oarsmanship*, by Gilbert C. Bourne (Sports Books Publisher, 1987). Mr. Bourne passed away in 1933 after many years as a rower, coach, and energy source for the sport. First published in 1925 and reprinted in 1987, this book has a lot, a whole lot, of information on the sport—from history to theory. It is at times hard to read, but not nearly as dated as I thought it would be. Without an index, it's a tough book to use for reference, but if you've got the time, it has got the info.

*Basic Rigging*, by Thor Nilsen and Volker Nolte (F.I.S.A. Development Commission, 1987) and *Intermediate Rigging*, by the same folks. These are handouts put together by F.I.S.A., the international organization for rowing. They give some good information, although it doesn't flow that well. Can be ordered from USRowing or from F.I.S.A.

*Candidate Manuals (Levels 1 to 3)*, published by US-Rowing. Each manual details specifics about rigging that are helpful. Well-written and informative, each manual is full of helpful stuff. Instead of just getting the manual, sign up for their courses.

*Long Strokes: A Handbook for Expanding the Rowing Experience,* by Bruce Brown (International Marine Publishing, 1988). I liked this book a lot more than I thought I would. Very friendly and informative. It is written mostly about recreational rowing, with not too much about rigging. Nonetheless, it has opened my eyes to the fact there is more to rowing than racing.

*Rigging*, by Michael Purcer (Regatta Sport, 1987). The first book I know of devoted just to rigging. It assumes a basic understanding of rigging, but it is by no means overwhelming to those just learning how to rig. If you can afford it, get two copies, one for home and the other for the boathouse. It has a glossary/index—yeah!

*Rowing Fundamentals: A Manual for Coaches*, edited by John A. Ferriss (USRowing, 1987). This is a mishmash of articles on many different aspects of rowing. Only four cover rigging, but they are informative, and the other information will help broaden your view of the sport as a whole.

*Rowing: Level 1* and *Level 2*, by Peter Klavora (Canadian Amateur Rowing Association, 1980 and 1982). These are the manuals C.A.R.A. uses for their National Coaching Certification Program. Well-thought-out and well-written, while not overpowering, and fun to read. Good information on the whole picture of rowing with good stuff on rigging. They have a humorous aspect, which is nice to see.

*Rowing for the Hell of It: A Manual for Recreational Rowers*, by Peter Raymond (Charles River Books, 1982). Great title, good book.

*Rudern (Rowing)*: *The G.D.R. Text of Oarsmanship*, by Dr. Ernst Herberger, et al. (Sports Books Publisher, 1983). A translation from the original German text, this book is a good resource. Great info on rigging and theory. Another no-index book, but it's laid out plain enough to make it a must. Get the latest edition that you can and keep it hidden because everyone wants/needs a copy.

***Sculler at Ease,*** by Frank Cunningham (Grandview Street Press, 1999). If you row (sweep or sculling), get this book. Never mind why, just get it.

***The Complete Steve Fairbairn on Rowing***, edited by Ian Fairbairn (The Kingswood Press, 1990). A compiling of five books written by Steve Fairbairn, who is considered one of the mega-fossils of rowing. A good read, with pictures no less. The best part is the 366 points on rowing in the back of the book, one for each day of the year. It's almost an early rowing version of the *Far Side* calendar.

***The Book of Rowing,*** by D. C. Churbuck (The Overlook Press, 1988). When I first flipped through this book, I thought it was outdated, mostly because of the wealth of old pictures. But just the opposite; it's current with some interesting sections—such as "Women in Rowing" and "The Olympics." It covers a lot, maybe too much, but it's still very interesting.

***The Complete Sculler***, by Richard Burnell (originally printed in 1973, reprinted by Sports Book Publishers, 1987). A great book on sculling, he talks in length. comparing sculling and sweep rowing. Actually, it seems to be a combination of the best of several of Burnell's books. It has lots of info and gives a good view (not overwhelmingly technical) of how those folks on the other side of the puddle look at rowing/sculling.

## SUPPLIERS

Following are many of the suppliers/makers of equipment that I use for my rigging and for this book. These folks are the ones I mostly deal with, but there are many, many others in the world of rowing.

**Alden Rowing Shells**
POB 368, Eliot, ME 03903
(800) 477–1507 (phone), (207) 439–0762 (fax)
<http://www.rowalden.com>

**Bill Leavitt Rigging Tools**
20 Brookwood Court, Princeton, NJ 08540
(908) 274–2628 (phone)

**Canadian Amateur Rowing Association** (C.A.RA.)
333 River Road, Ottawa, Ontario, Canada K1L 8B9
<http://www.rowingcanada.org>

**Concept II, Inc.**
RR1, Box 1100, Morrisville, VT 05661–9727
(800) 245–5676 (phone) 7:30 am to 5:00 pm, (802) 888–4791 (fax)
<http://www.concept2.com>

**Dirigo USA**
596 Elm Street, Biddeford, ME 04005
(207) 283–3026 (phone), (207) 985–6814 (fax)
<http://www.dirigousa.com>

**Durham Boat Company**
264 Newmarket, Durham, NH 03824
(603) 659–2548 (phone)
<http://www.durhamboat.com>

**Empacher Bootswerft**
6930 Eberach A. N., Germany
(011) 49–6271–80000 (phone), (011) 49–6271–800099 (fax)
<http://www.empacher.com>

**Federation Internationale des Societes D'Aviron** (F.I.S.A.)
3653 Oberhofen am Thunersee, Switzerland
(41) 33–435053 (phone)
<http://www.fisa.org>

**Kaschper Racing Shells Ltd.**
Box 40, Lucan, Ontario, Canada
(519) 227–4652 (phone), (519) 227–4247 (fax)
<http://www.kaschper.com>

**Nielsen–Kellerman**
201 East 10th Street, Marcus Hook, PA 19061
(800) 462–7731 (phone), (215) 494–9537 (fax)
<http://www.nkhome.com>

**Pocock Racing Shells**
2212 Pacific Avenue, Everett, WA 98201
(206) 252–6658 (phone), (206) 259–3583 (fax)
<http://www.pocock.com>

**Potomac Company**
29908 S. Stockton, Farmington Hills, MI 48336
(800) 477–0440 (phone)
<http://www.potomacrowing.com>

**Resolute Racing Shells**
PO Box 1109, Bristol, RI 02809
(401) 253–7384
<http://www.resoluteracing.com>

**SportWork**
Main Street, P.O. Box 192, Church Hill, MD 21623
(410) 556–6030 (phone/fax)
<http://www.MaxRigging.com>

**Tapco, Inc.**
225 Rock Industrial Park Drive, Bridgeton, MO 63044
(Elevator bolts, great for sneaker attachment. I use their number 1
flat counter shank head bolts, 1/4 –20 x 1 1/2 inch)

**USRowing**
201 S. Capitol Avenue, Suite #400, Indianapolis, IN  46225
(317) 237–5656 (phone)
<http://www.usrowing.org>

**Vespoli USA** (rowing shells)
385 Clinton Avenue, New Haven, CT  06513
(203) 773–0311 (phone), (203) 562–1891 (fax)
<http://www.vespoli.com>

# Appendix Four: Travel List Check-Off

**DID YOU?**

❏ check all fluids in vehicle(s)
❏ check all lights
❏ check all tire pressures
❏ check hitch for trailer
❏ clean all equipment
❏ close bow and stern hatches
❏ gas vehicle before loading
❏ label all equipment
❏ load and secure shells
❏ put covers on boats
❏ put flags on boats
❏ secure foot stretchers
❏ secure seats
❏ tie down loose equipment

**HAVE YOU PACKED?**

❏ all oars
❏ all riggers
❏ all seats
❏ assorted rigger parts
❏ bailer cups for shells
❏ bicycle/lock
❏ bow ball
❏ chairs for coaches to sit on
❏ cleaning supplies
❏ cox boxes and chargers
❏ cups for water
❏ extra tie downs

- ❏ fin (skeg)
- ❏ fire extinguisher
- ❏ first aid kit
- ❏ food for athletes
- ❏ ice and cooler
- ❏ insurance card for vehicle(s)
- ❏ keys for truck
- ❏ microphone
- ❏ nuts and bolts
- ❏ oar locks
- ❏ oarlock pins
- ❏ rags
- ❏ registration for trailer
- ❏ registration for vehicle(s)
- ❏ rudder
- ❏ rudder cable
- ❏ seats and parts
- ❏ slings
- ❏ sneaker bin for launching at course
- ❏ spare oars (2)
- ❏ spare rigger(s) for each shell
- ❏ splash guards
- ❏ supports to rest boats on
- ❏ supports to rest oars on
- ❏ tarpaulin/tent
- ❏ trash bags
- ❏ water for athletes
- ❏ weight for boat/coxswain weigh-in

**Tools:**
- ❏ tool box(es)
- ❏ basic rigging kit
- ❏ travel tool kit
- ❏ tape
  - ❏ duct
  - ❏ adhesive
  - ❏ electrical
  - ❏ packing
  - ❏ masking
- ❏ height stick
- ❏ pitch meter
- ❏ wire brush for oar handles

☐ shims
☐ petroleum jelly
☐ silicon
☐ rubbing compound for hulls
☐ buffing rags
☐ cordless drill with bits

## DO YOU HAVE?

☐ directions
☐ money for gas and tolls
☐ waivers for regatta
☐ hotel information
☐ extra set of vehicle keys
☐ tax exempt form
☐ U.S.R.A. numbers for regatta
☐ bow number(s) for shells
☐ video:
    ☐ camera
    ☐ battery(s)
    ☐ recharger
    ☐ tape
☐ binoculars
☐ stroke watch
☐ walkie-talkie
☐ rain gear

## IMPORTANT EXTRAS:

☐ did you **really** check flags on boats?
☐ did you **really** check the lights on the trailer?
☐ did you **really** check the tie downs on the trailer?
☐ do you **really** have a spare set of vehicle keys?
☐ emergency kit
☐ flashlight
☐ spare tire(s) and changing tools
☐ water bottles for athletes

# TOTAL HEIGHT OF THE TRAILER IS :

_____ ' _____ "

## Gas Tank is on which side

(tape to dash board)

# CREDITS

Whenever I write a book, I always find the hardest section to write is this one, the credits. It causes fear in me. One reasons why is that I'm always afraid that I will forget to mention someone. And then there is the whole issue of misspelling someone's name . . . arggh . . . it's enough to keep you up at night.

Regardless, here I go. . . .

Right up front, I need to thank my family, for all their support and for putting up with all my writing at 4 AM—and all the other weirdness that goes with being an obsessed writer—especially one writing about rowing and rigging . . .

Thanks to my editor, Robyn Alvarez, for reading, reading, reading, and having the patience to guide me to the world of correct comma usage. . . .

Thanks to every darn person in the rowing community, who for the past ten years has put up with my questions, theories, and thoughts; lent me equipment; and helped me when so often it would be easy to tell me to take a long hike on a short dock. And this goes especially for all the equipment manufacturers . . .

Thanks to all the folks who have been selling this book for the past ten years . . . especially to Potomac Rowing and to Alden for their input and assistance. . . .

Thanks to every assistant coach I've had for the past ten years, for being cool when asked to read the tenth version of the fifth draft of the eighth account of how to adjust the pitch in an oarlock. I know it was sooooo exciting. . . .

Thanks to Peter Martin for being educational and patient, and for helping put fun into our sport through his great drawings. . . .

Thanks to Cathi Stevenson, <http://www.bookcoverexpress.com>, and Heather Coleman, <http://ebooksearchengine.com/covers.html>, for all their help with the covers. . . .

A special thanks to the Washington College community, especially to John Wagner for making my life so much easier and to Bryan Matthews, the Athletic Director, for caring what the heck is going on in the world of rowing and for trying to make it better. . . .

Thanks to my Web czars, Kari Hughes and Shane Brill, for keeping the Web site going and for making sure that I don't bring down the entire World Wide Web with one key stroke. . . .

Thanks to Nicky Williams, Glenn Merry, Liza Dickson, Caren Saunders, Chris Torney, and Brianna Beacom for reading, reading, and reading and correcting, correcting, correcting.

I want to thank all the instructors at my alma mater where I learned most of my rigging—the *School of Hard Knocks*. It's a great school, they accept students all year round, tuition is free, and it's located at the boathouse nearest you. . . .

Finally, I want to again thank my folks, Dot and George, for never asking that one question . . . "When are you going to get a real job?"

# INDEX

## S

# WHO MADE THIS BOOK?

### Mike Davenport, Author

Mike has been involved in the sport of rowing since 1975. He started rowing at Florida Institute of Technology as a novice, where he didn't know a port from a starboard. Now he is the head rowing coach at Washington College, in Chestertown, MD.

For several years Mike was lucky enough to be involved with the U.S. National Team, as their Boatman. And in 1996 he was the Boatman for the U.S. Olympic Rowing Team. Currently, his company, SportWork, is the leading educational consultancy for USRowing and their Coaching Education Program.

This is Mike's tenth book, seven of which are about rowing. His Web site <http://maxrigging.com> and his monthly e-zine *MaxRigging* strive to supply the latest and greatest information about the rigging of rowing equipment.

Mike currently lives in Maryland with his wife and two sons.

### Peter Martin, Illustrator

Peter's life has been one full of strokes. He started stroking at Cornell University. Then he started to build wooden boats in Albany, New York. By some stroke of luck, he met Mike and began to try a little coaching.

After two years behind the megaphone his true love led him to the stroke of the pen, and he began to illustrate illustrious rowing books. Then he became an art director for an ad agency in the big city. When he had enough of stroking other people's backs in the corporate world he decided it was time for graduate school. After grad school, Peter and his wife moved to Qatar, where he is currently teaching.

# FINDING HAPPINESS SITTING ON YOUR BUTT GOING BACKWARDS

## A Step-by-Step Guide to Finding Fun and Enjoyment While Rowing

When was the last time you had fun rowing?

Come on now—when was the last time you enjoyed, really enjoyed, your rowing?

Fun and enjoyment don't just appear—you must work to find them. This book assists you in doing just that by providing tips, insights, tasks, and paths to help you get to the place where fun, enjoyment, and happiness exist in the world of rowing.

It is the first and only book written on how to get the most fun and enjoyment out of your rowing

*Finding Happiness While Sitting On Your Butt Going Backwards* is available online <http://www.MaxRowing.com >and at book dealers nationwide.

*Finding Happiness While Sitting On Your Butt Going Backwards,* **First Edition, by Mike Davenport.**

ISBN 0-963900-2-8

## <u>Whaddaya Think?</u>

How did you like this book? Was it helpful? Want to tell others about it? We're look for endorsements. If you have any you would like to share, let me know. Loud and clear.

Just fill out the info below, and send off to:

>SportWork
>Main Street
>PO Box 102
>Church Hill, MD 21623
>(410) 556-6030 (p/f)
>mike@helpingcoaches.com

Your help is greatly appreciated. Endorsements usually appear in the following year's edition.

Name : _____

Address: _____

City: _____ State: _____ Zip: _____

E-mail: _____

Comments: _____

_____

_____

_____

_____

_____

# Information Update Form

Your feedback is very important to help make this book a better product. If you have information you would like to share, or notice areas of this book that can be improved, let me know. Loud and clear.

Just fill out the info below, and send off to:

> SportWork
> PO Box 102
> Main Street
> Church Hill, MD  21623
> (410) 556-6030 (p/f)
> mike@helpingcoaches.com

Your help is greatly appreciated. Corrections to the text usually appear in the following year's edition.

Name :_____

Address:_____

City:_____ State: _____ Zip: _____

E-mail: _____

Comments: _____

_____

_____

_____

_____

_____

## Quick Order Form

**STEP 1:** Grab a Pen/Pencil
**STEP 2:** Complete All Information Below
**STEP 3:** Mail This Form and Payment (Check / Purchase Order) To:

SportWork, Main Street, PO Box 192, Church Hill, MD 21623.

# Shipping Information

| | | |
|---|---|---|
| Name: | | |
| Organization: | | |
| Address: | | |
| Address: | | |
| City: | State: | Zip: |
| Phone: | E-mail: | |

# Ordering Information

| *Nuts and Bolts Guide To Rigging* | Quantity | Price | Total |
|---|---|---|---|
| | _____ | @ $34.95 | _____ |
| | | Quantity Discount [1] | _____ |
| | | Shipping [2] | _____ |
| | | Tax [3] | _____ |
| | | Total enclosed [4] | _____ |

[1] **Discounts:**
    3–11 books: 20% off retail price
    12–36 books: 40% off retail price
    37 books and up: 55% off retail price

[2] **Shipping:** Books are shipped via UPS ground unless other arrangements are made. Price is $6.50 within continental U.S. If shipment is required to other areas than continental U.S, please call SportWork at 410-556-6030.

[3] **Tax:** Maryland residents are required to add 5% sales tax per book ordered.

[4] **Payment:** Prepayment is required on all orders prior to shipping. Checks and institutional purchase orders are accepted. To pay by credit card, please use our Web site, <http://www.MaxRigging.com>.

## Quick Order Form

**STEP 1:** Grab a Pen/Pencil
**STEP 2:** Complete All Information Below
**STEP 3:** Mail This Form and Payment (Check / Purchase Order) to:

SportWork, Main Street, PO Box 192, Church Hill, MD 21623.

# Shipping Information

| Name: | | |
|---|---|---|
| Organization: | | |
| Address: | | |
| Address: | | |
| City: | State: | Zip: |
| Phone: | E-mail: | |

# Ordering Information

| | Quantity | Price | Total |
|---|---|---|---|
| *Nuts and Bolts Guide To Rigging* | | @ \$34.95 | |
| | | Quantity Discount [1] | |
| | | Shipping [2] | |
| | | Tax [3] | |
| | | Total enclosed [4] | |

[1] **Discounts:**
> 3–11 books: 20% off retail price
> 12–36 books: 40% off retail price
> 37 books and up: 55% off retail price

[2] **Shipping:** Books are shipped via UPS ground unless other arrangements are made. Price is \$6.50 within continental U.S. If shipment is required to other areas than continental U.S., please call SportWork at 410-556-6030.

[3] **Tax:** Maryland residents are required to add 5% sales tax per book ordered.

[4] **Payment:** Prepayment is required on all orders prior to shipping. Checks and institutional purchase orders are accepted. To pay by credit card please use our Web site <http://www.MaxRigging.com>.

*(continued from the back cover)* . . .

*Nuts and Bolts Guide to Rigging* contains a wealth of information to help you with the mechanics, theories, and realities of the rigging of rowing equipment. This book is divided into three sections. Each section covers specific aspects of rigging and is the most comprehensive resource for rigging on the market.

*Nuts and Bolts* explains the technology of rigging, along with the basics. Perhaps you've heard that rigging is hard? Many coaches and rowers are told that, but they are never told what they can do to make it easier for themselves. That is, until now.

This book contains many useful tips and tricks, and is full of common-sense advice. Between these pages, you will discover:

*   The best ways to buy and use rigging tools
*   Methods to rig almost any type of rowing equipment
*   How to identify rigging problems
*   Methods to solve rigging problems
*   How to find answers to your tough equipment questions
*   Ways to ensure your rigging solutions will work
*   How to buy, store, and maintain your rowing equipment

**"A book that meets a long-standing need in American rowing: a clear, detailed treatment of rigging for relatively inexperienced coaches and rowers."**

— Bill Leavitt, owner, Leavitt Rigging Tools

Mike Davenport has helped thousands of coaches overcome the mysteries, hassles, and difficulties of using rowing equipment. He has written dozens of articles and given a multitude of clinics about rigging. Coaches connect with Mike because he is one of the leading authority on learning how to use and how to rig rowing equipment.